QuarkXPress 3.3 For Dumm...

S0-DVD-614

Cheat Sheet

A Selection of QuarkXPress Palettes

The Measurement palette comes in three flavors (text, picture, and line) depending on what item is active.

Measurement palette — text

Location of active text box.

Rotation and number of columns of active text box.

Width and height of active text box.

Leading arrows

Font

Type size

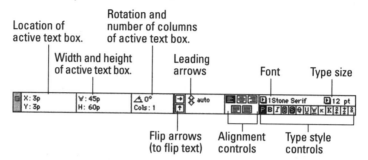

Flip arrows (to flip text)

Alignment controls

Type style controls

Measurement palette — picture

Rotation of box and box contents.

Move picture in active picture box

Location of active picture box.

Flip arrows (to flip picture)

Rotate contents of box

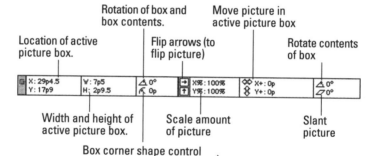

Width and height of active picture box.

Scale amount of picture

Slant picture

Box corner shape control

Measurement palette — line

Width and height of active line

Location of active line

Weight (thickness) of active line.

Endcap style

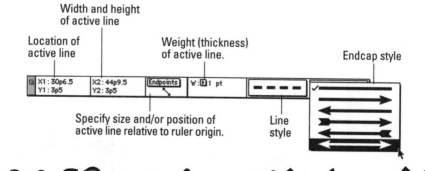

Specify size and/or position of active line relative to ruler origin.

Line style

FOR DUMMIES™

COMPUTER
BOOK SERIES
FROM IDG

QuarkXPress 3.3 For Dummies

Cheat Sheet

Tool palette

Click on a tool to select it. The tool you select determines what you can do with the keyboard and mouse as well as which menu entries are available.

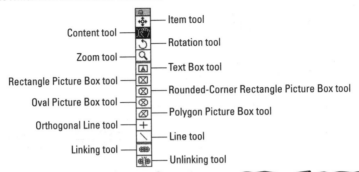

- Content tool — Item tool
- Zoom tool — Rotation tool
- Rectangle Picture Box tool — Text Box tool
- Oval Picture Box tool — Rounded-Corner Rectangle Picture Box tool
- Orthogonal Line tool — Polygon Picture Box tool
- Linking tool — Line tool
  — Unlinking tool

Style Sheet palette

This palette lists style sheets currently defined for the document.

- Style names
- Keyboard equivalents for styles

Document Layout palette

Use this palette for creating, deleting, duplicating, naming, and arranging master pages.

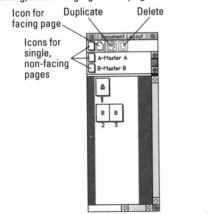

- Icon for facing page
- Duplicate
- Delete
- Icons for single, non-facing pages

Colors palette

Use this palette to control the color of items.

- Apply color to background
- Apply color to selected text
- Shade pop-up menu
- Apply color to frame of active picture box or text box
- Linear blend designator
- #1 is first color in linear blend; #2 is second color.
- List of available colors
- The angle at which the two colors blend

. . . For Dummies: #1 Computer Book Series for Beginners

QUARKXPRESS 3.3 FOR DUMMIES™

by **Barbara Assadi and Galen Gruman**

Foreword by Monica A. L. Vella

IDG BOOKS

IDG Books Worldwide, Inc.
An International Data Group Company

Foster City, CA ♦ Chicago, IL ♦ Indianapolis, IN ♦ Braintree, MA ♦ Dallas, TX

QuarkXPress 3.3 For Dummies

Published by
IDG Books Worldwide, Inc.
An International Data Group Company
919 E. Hillsdale Blvd.
Suite 400
Foster City, CA 94404

Library of Congress Catalog Card No.: 94-79840

ISBN: 1-56884-217-1

Printed in the United States of America

10 9 8 7 6 5 4 3 2 1

1B/SS/RS/ZU

Distributed in the United States by IDG Books Worldwide, Inc.

Distributed in the United States by IDG Books Worldwide, Inc. Distributed by Macmillan Canada for Canada; by Computer and Technical Books for the Caribbean Basin; by Contemporanea de Ediciones for Venezuela; by Distribuidora Cuspide for Argentina; by CITEC for Brazil; by Ediciones ZETA S.C.R. Ltda. for Peru; by Editorial Limusa SA for Mexico; by Transworld Publishers Limited in the United Kingdom and Europe; by Al-Maiman Publishers & Distributors for Saudi Arabia; by Simron Pty. Ltd. for South Africa; by IDG Communications (HK) Ltd. for Hong Kong; by Toppan Company Ltd. for Japan; by Addison Wesley Publishing Company for Korea; by Longman Singapore Publishers Ltd. for Singapore, Malaysia, Thailand and Indonesia; by Unalis Corporation for Taiwan; by WS Computer Publishing Company, Inc. for the Philippines; by WoodsLane Pty. Ltd. for Australia; by WoodsLane Enterprises Ltd. for New Zealand.

For general information on IDG Books in the U.S., including information on discounts and premiums, contact IDG Books at 800-434-3422 or 415-655-3000.

For information on where to purchase IDG Books outside the U.S., contact IDG Books International at 415-655-3021 or fax 415-655-3295.

For information on translations, contact Marc Jeffrey Mikulich, Director, Foreign & Subsidiary Rights, at IDG Books Worldwide, 415-655-3018 or fax 415-655-3295.

For sales inquiries and special prices for bulk quantities, write to the address above or call IDG Books Worldwide at 415-655-3000.

For information on using IDG Books in the classroom, or ordering examination copies, contact Jim Kelly at 800-434-2086.

is a registered trademark of
IDG Books Worldwide, Inc.

About the Authors

Galen Gruman is the executive editor for features and news at IDG's *Macworld* magazine and the desktop-publishing reviewer at IDG's *InfoWorld*. Barbara Assadi is editorial services manager at Quark, Inc., and the word-processing reviewer at *InfoWorld*. Both were pioneers in desktop publishing and have more than a decade's hands-on experience in desktop publishing. Gruman and Assadi are coauthors of IDG's highly regarded *Macworld QuarkXPress 3.2/3.3 Bible* and *QuarkXPress For Windows Designers Handbook*. Gruman has also coauthored IDG's *PageMaker 5 For Macs For Dummies* and *PageMaker 5 For Windows For Dummies*.

Welcome to the world of IDG Books Worldwide.

IDG Books Worldwide, Inc. is a subsidiary of International Data Group, the world's largest publisher of computer-related information and the leading global provider of information services on information technology. IDG was founded more than 25 years ago and now employs more than 7,000 people worldwide. IDG publishes more than 220 computer publications in 65 countries (see listing below). More than fifty million people read one or more IDG publications each month.

Launched in 1990, IDG Books Worldwide is today the #1 publisher of best-selling computer books in the United States. We are proud to have received 3 awards from the Computer Press Association in recognition of editorial excellence, and our best-selling ...For Dummies™ series has more than 12 million copies in print with translations in 25 languages. IDG Books, through a recent joint venture with IDG's Hi-Tech Beijing, became the first U.S. publisher to publish a computer book in the People's Republic of China. In record time, IDG Books has become the first choice for millions of readers around the world who want to learn how to better manage their businesses.

Our mission is simple: Every IDG book is designed to bring extra value and skill-building instructions to the reader. Our books are written by experts who understand and care about our readers. The knowledge base of our editorial staff comes from years of experience in publishing, education, and journalism — experience which we use to produce books for the '90s. In short, we care about books, so we attract the best people. We devote special attention to details such as audience, interior design, use of icons, and illustrations. And because we use an efficient process of authoring, editing, and desktop publishing our books electronically, we can spend more time ensuring superior content and spend less time on the technicalities of making books.

You can count on our commitment to deliver high-quality books at competitive prices on topics consumers want to read about. At IDG, we value quality, and we have been delivering quality for more than 25 years. You'll find no better book on a subject than an IDG book.

John J. Kilcullen

John Kilcullen
President and CEO
IDG Books Worldwide, Inc.

IDG Books Worldwide, Inc. is a subsidiary of International Data Group, the world's largest publisher of computer-related information and the leading global provider of information services on information technology. International Data Group publishes over 220 computer publications in 65 countries. More than fifty million people read one or more International Data Group publications each month. The officers are Patrick J. McGovern, Founder and Board Chairman; Kelly Conlin, President; Jim Casella, Chief Operating Officer. International Data Group's publications include: **ARGENTINA'S** Computerworld Argentina, Infoworld Argentina; **AUSTRALIA'S** Computerworld Australia, Computer Living, Australian PC World, Australian Macworld, Network World, Mobile Business Australia, Publish!, Reseller, IDG Sources; **AUSTRIA'S** Computerwelt Oesterreich, PC Test; **BELGIUM'S** Data News (CW); **BOLIVIA'S** Computerworld; **BRAZIL'S** Computerworld, Connections, Game Power, Mundo Unix, PC World, Publish, Super Game; **BULGARIA'S** Computerworld Bulgaria, PC & Mac World Bulgaria, Network World Bulgaria; **CANADA'S** CIO Canada, Computerworld Canada, InfoCanada, Network World Canada, Reseller; **CHILE'S** Computerworld Chile, Informatica; **COLOMBIA'S** Computerworld Colombia, PC World; **COSTA RICA'S** PC World; **CZECH REPUBLIC'S** Computerworld, Elektronika, PC World; **DENMARK'S** Communications World, Computerworld Danmark, Computerworld Focus, Macintosh Produktkatalog, Macworld Danmark, PC World Danmark, PC Produktguide, Tech World, Windows World; **ECUADOR'S** PC World Ecuador; **EGYPT'S** Computerworld (CW) Middle East, PC World Middle East; **FINLAND'S** MikroPC, Tietoviikko, Tietoverkko; **FRANCE'S** Distributique, GOLDEN MAC, InfoPC, Le Guide du Monde Informatique, Le Monde Informatique, Telecoms & Reseaux; **GERMANY'S** Computerwoche, Computerwoche Focus, Computerwoche Extra, Electronic Entertainment, Gamepro, Information Management, Macwelt, Netzwelt, PC Welt, Publish, Publish; **GREECE'S** Publish & Macworld; **HONG KONG'S** Computerworld Hong Kong, PC World Hong Kong; **HUNGARY'S** Computerworld SZT, PC World; **INDIA'S** Computers & Communications; **INDONESIA'S** Info Komputer; **IRELAND'S** ComputerScope; **ISRAEL'S** Beyond Windows, Computerworld Israel, Multimedia, PC World Israel; **ITALY'S** Computerworld Italia, Lotus Magazine, Macworld Italia, Networking Italia, PC Shopping Italy, PC World Italia; **JAPAN'S** Computerworld Today, Information Systems World, Macworld Japan, Nikkei Personal Computing, SunWorld Japan, Windows World; **KENYA'S** East African Computer News; **KOREA'S** Computerworld Korea, Macworld Korea, PC World Korea; **LATIN AMERICA'S** GamePro; **MALAYSIA'S** Computerworld Malaysia, PC World Malaysia; **MEXICO'S** Compu Edicion, Compu Manufactura, Computacion/Punto de Venta, Computerworld Mexico, MacWorld, Mundo Unix, PC World, Windows; **THE NETHERLANDS'** Computer! Totaal, Computable (CW), LAN Magazine, Lotus Magazine, MacWorld; **NEW ZEALAND'S** Computer Buyer, Computerworld New Zealand, Network World, New Zealand PC World; **NIGERIA'S** PC World Africa; **NORWAY'S** Computerworld Norge, Lotusworld Norge, Macworld Norge, Maxi Data, Networld, PC World Ekspress, PC World Nettverk, PC World Norge, PC World's Produktguide, Publish& Multimedia World, Student Data, Unix World, Windowsworld; **PAKISTAN'S** PC World Pakistan; **PANAMA'S** PC World Panama; **PERU'S** Computerworld Peru, PC World; **PEOPLE'S REPUBLIC OF CHINA'S** China Computerworld, China Infoworld, China PC Info Magazine, Computer Fan, PC World China, Electronics International, Electronics Today/Multimedia World, Electronic Product World, China Network World, Software World Magazine, Telecom Product World, **PHILIPPINES'** Computerworld Philippines, PC Digest (PCW); **POLAND'S** Computerworld Poland, Computerworld Special Report, Networld, PC World/Komputer, Sunworld; **PORTUGAL'S** Cerebro/PC World, Correio Informatico/Computerworld, MacIn; **ROMANIA'S** Computerworld, PC World, Telecom Romania; **RUSSIA'S** Computerworld-Moscow, Mir - PK (PCW), Sety (Networks); **SINGAPORE'S** Computerworld Southeast Asia, PC World Singapore; **SLOVENIA'S** Monitor Magazine; **SOUTH AFRICA'S** Computer Mail (CIO),Computing S.A.,Network World S.A., Software World; **SPAIN'S** Advanced Systems, Amiga World, Computerworld Espana, Communicaciones World, Macworld Espana, NeXTWORLD, Super Juegos Magazine (GamePro), PC World Espana, Publish; **SWEDEN'S** Attack, ComputerSweden, Corporate Computing, Macworld, Mikrodatorn, Natverk & Kommunikation, PC World, CAP & Design, Datalngenjoren, Maxi Data,Windows World; **SWITZERLAND'S** Computerworld Schweiz, Macworld Schweiz, PC Tip; **TAIWAN'S** Computerworld Taiwan, PC World Taiwan; **THAILAND'S** Thai Computerworld; **TURKEY'S** Computerworld Monitor, Macworld Turkiye, PC World Turkiye; **UKRAINE'S** Computerworld, Computers+Software Magazine; **UNITED KINGDOM'S** Computing / Computerworld, Connexion/Network World, Lotus Magazine, Macworld, Open Computing/Sunworld; **URAGUAY'S** PC World Uraguay; **UNITED STATES'** Advanced Systems, AmigaWorld, Cable in the Classroom, CD Review, CIO, Computerworld, Computerworld Client/Server Journal, Digital Video, DOS World, Electronic Entertainment Magazine (E2), Federal Computer Week, Game Hits, GamePro, IDG Books, Inforworld, Laser Event, Macworld, Maximize, Multimedia World, Network World, PC Letter, PC World, Publish, SWATPro, Video Event; **VENEZUELA'S** Computerworld Venezuela, PC World; **VIETNAM'S** PC World Vietnam.
11/16/94

Acknowledgments

The authors are grateful to the many people who helped us with this book, particularly Fred Ebrahimi, Tim Gill, Patti Cahill, Kevin Dormeyer, Kelly Kordes, Don Lohse, Kim Sayers, and Monica Vella of Quark, Inc.; Rob Francisco, our technical reader; and Tim Gallan and Megg Bonar from IDG Books. Special thanks to Charlotte Isoline and Kathie Longenecker for their encouragement and support.

(The publisher would like to give special thanks to Patrick J. McGovern, without whom this book would not have been possible.)

Dedication

To Camron, Lisa, and Jordan for being the reasons why. —Barbara Assadi

Credits

**Executive Vice President,
Strategic Product Planning
and Research**
David Solomon

Editorial Director
Diane Graves Steele

Acquisitions Editor
Megg Bonar

Brand Manager
Judith A. Taylor

Editorial Managers
Tracy L. Barr
Sandra Blackthorn

Editorial Assistants
Tamara S. Castleman
Stacey Holden Prince
Kevin Spencer

Acquisitions Assistant
Suki Gear

Production Director
Beth Jenkins

**Associate
Project Coordinator**
Valery Bourke

Pre-Press Coordinator
Steve Peake

Associate Project Editor
A. Timothy Gallan

Editors
Jeffrey Waggoner
Michael Simsic
Julie King

Technical Reviewer
Rob Francisco

Production Staff
Tony Augsburger
Paul Belcastro
Cameron Booker
Chris Collins
Tyler Connor
Sherry Dickinson Gomoll
Drew R. Moore
Carla Radzikinas
Dwight Ramsey
Patricia R. Reynolds
Kathie Schnorr
Gina Scott

Proofreader
Kathleen Prata

Indexer
Nancy Anderman Guenther

Cover Design
Kavish + Kavish

Contents at a Glance

Cartoons at a Glance

By Rich Tennant

page 1

page 7

page 284

page 63

page 245

page 125

page 349

page 297

page 366

page 197

Table of Contents

Foreword

Like most of you, I have experienced the frustration of learning a new software package. Once I have managed to master the basics, I am usually pretty excited about what I can do. Given their respective positions in the high-tech industry, both Barbara and Galen have an unusually keen understanding of that initial frustration with new software. More importantly, their combined knowledge of desktop publishing shines through each and every page of this book.

I receive a lot of samples and input from customers who are constantly challenging the feature set of QuarkXPress. Of all the comments I receive, the one that is most common among new and experienced users is that QuarkXPress has helped them to better communicate their information. After you read this book, I am positive that you too will be well on your way to challenging the capabilities of QuarkXPress.

Monica A.L. Vella
Product Manager, QuarkXPress

Introduction

Isn't <u>Q</u>uarkXPress Too High-End for Me?

There's a story you may have already heard. A man is walking down the street when he comes upon a construction site where a group of three brick masons are busily at work. He stops to talk to the first brick mason and asks, "What are you doing?" The brick mason answers, "I'm putting bricks on top of other bricks."

The man continues down the sidewalk until he comes to the second brick mason. Again he asks the same question, "What are you doing?" The second brick mason answers, "I'm putting some bricks together to make a wall."

The man then walks on until he comes face-to-face with the third brick mason. The man poses the same question to the third brick mason: "What are you doing?" The third brick mason answers, "I'm building a beautiful cathedral."

The 5th Wave   By Rich Tennant

"WE FIGURE THE EQUIPMENT MUST HAVE SCARED HER AWAY. A FEW DAYS AFTER SETTING UP, LITTLE 'SNOWBALL' JUST DISAPPEARED."

Right now, you are probably wondering why on earth we are telling this story as part of the introduction to a book on QuarkXPress. Good question. But, when you think about it, the people who use QuarkXPress are a lot like those brick masons, and QuarkXPress is a lot like the mortars and lathes used by those brick masons to do their work.

What we are saying is this: there are all kinds of users of QuarkXPress. Some do very simple, one-color documents. Some do moderately challenging documents, which include photos, illustrations, and complex charts. Still others — like the third brick mason who was building a cathedral — use QuarkXPress to create high-end, highly designed and illustrated works of art.

QuarkXPress — like the mortar and lathe used by the brick masons in our story — is a *tool*. Nothing more, nothing less. It works for the world's most-celebrated designers. It also works for people who create simpler documents, such as school newsletters.

The point is, QuarkXPress is never too high-end for you, or for anyone else, because you pick and choose which parts of this tool you need to use. Also, keep in mind that if you create *any* type of document, you can benefit from the program's features. Sure, it's true that if your documents are simple, you won't need to use all the sophisticated features in QuarkXPress. But, when you think about it, isn't it nice to know that these features are available when and if you ever need them? And that you won't outgrow the program as you become more proficient with document design? We think so.

How to Use This Book

Although this book has information that any level of desktop publisher needs to know to use QuarkXPress, this book is also for those of you who are fairly new to the field, or who are just becoming familiar with the program. What we try to do is to take the mystery out of QuarkXPress and give you some guidance on how to create a bunch of different types of documents. Here are some conventions used in this book.

Menu commands are listed like this:

   Style⇨Type Style⇨Bold

This means that you pull-down the Style menu (using the mouse), choose the Type Style command, and then choose the Bold option.

Keyboard shortcuts are listed like this:

   ⌘-Option-Shift-M

This means that you should press and hold the ⌘ (Command) and Option and Shift keys while you press the M key. (This keyboard shortcut accesses the font field in the Measurements palette.)

One last thing: If you need help setting up your computer, getting acquainted with its operating system, managing files, and doing other, so-called basics, you may want to take a look at *Macs For Dummies* and *Macintosh System 7.5 For Dummies* if you're a Mac user, or *PCs For Dummies* and *Windows For Dummies* if you're a Windows users. All of these references are published by IDG Books.

How This Book Is Organized

We've divided *QuarkXPress 3.3 For Dummies* into seven parts, not counting this introduction. Each part has anywhere from two to four chapters, so you don't have to wade through too much explanation to get to the information you need. Note that the book covers QuarkXPress on three platforms: Macintosh, Power Macintosh, and Windows. Because the application is almost identical on all three, we only point out platform-specific information when we need to, or when we remember to, or both.

Part I: Page Layout 101: Good Design

Trying to perform page layout on a page when you don't know anything about page design is like trying to drive a car blindfolded. You might be able to use your feet to accelerate or stop, but you won't know where you're going and will likely end up a mangled mess.

In this part, we show you some examples of good design. We also show you some bad design, and we give you hints about how to tell the difference. But before we even get to those issues, we define some words that you need to know if you are going to be a desktop publisher worth his or her salt. And we also explain the basics about how to get QuarkXPress to do what you want it to.

Part II: Setting Up Your Document

Designing a document is a combination of science and art. The science is in setting up the structure of the page: How many places will hold text, and how many will hold graphics? How wide will the margins be? Where will the page numbers appear? And so on. The art is in coming up with creative ways of filling the structure to please your eyes and the eyes of the people who will be looking at your document.

This part of the book shows you how to set up the basic structure of a document and then how to begin filling the structure with words and pictures. It also tells you how to bring in text and graphics created in separate word processing and graphics applications.

Part III: Fine-Tuned Text

Good publishing technique is about more than just getting the words down on paper. It's also about tweaking the letters and lines — and the space between them — to make your pages shine. This part of the book shows you how to do all that and a lot more.

Part IV: The Picasso Factor

Let's be honest. Pablo Picasso didn't become famous for realistically portraying people. His claim to fame is based on how he took facial features and then skewed, slanted, stretched, and shrunk them into new forms. Some folks loved his work; others found it hard to figure. But you had to admire the fact that it was unique.

We named this part of the book after the famous artist because it tells how to take normal-looking text and graphics and distort them. Why would you want to do this? Good question. The answer could be that, like Picasso, you want to present ideas in a visually interesting way. Either that, or you want to see how your relatives might look with their faces rearranged. QuarkXPress enables you to manipulate text and art in interesting ways, and we show you how.

Part V: The Big, Bad World Out There

If you've followed along throughout the book to this point and have figured out how to create a document, this part will give you some tips on how to get it out of your computer and onto some other medium, such as film or paper. We give you some solid suggestions on how to print and how to work with all those other people in the world who know how to help you get the job done.

Part VI: Guru in Training

After you master the basics, why not pick up some of the tricks the pros use? This part gives you some power-user tips and shortcuts and also explains how QuarkXPress works on Windows machines and Power Macs.

Part VII: The Part of Tens

This part of the book is like the chips in the chocolate chip cookies; you could eat the cookies without them, but you'd be missing a really good part. It's a part of extremes, of bests and worsts. It's like a mystery novel that's hard to put down until you read the very last word. In fact, you might even be tempted to start reading here and then go back to Chapter 1, but don't. The concepts in this book will make more sense to you if you read the other six parts of the book first.

Icons Used in This Book

So that you can pick out parts that you really need to pay attention to (or, depending on your taste, to avoid), we've used some symbols, or *icons* in this book.

This icon tells you that we are about to pontificate on some remote technical bit of information that might help explain a feature in QuarkXPress. The technical info will definitely make you sound impressive if you memorize it and recite it to your friends.

If you see this icon, it means that we're mentioning some really nifty point or idea that you might want to keep in mind as you use the program.

If you skip all the other icons, pay attention to this one. Why? Because ignoring it could cause something really, really bad or embarrassing to happen, like when you were sitting in your second-grade classroom waiting for the teacher to call on you to answer a question, and you noticed that you still had your pajama shirt on — backwards. We don't want that to happen to you!

Sometimes things work a certain way for no apparent reason. When you see this icon, it means you are about to read about some QuarkXPress mystery. But don't worry: we tell you how to solve it.

This icon points out specific information for those Windows users out there.

Once in awhile, we give you some step-by-step instructions to follow. We don't do it all the time, though, because we don't want you to confuse this book with the documentation that came with your package of QuarkXPress. And just to make the difference between the two books really clear, we did a couple of things:

- ✔ We made the cover of this book bright yellow; your QuarkXPress documentation is white, orange, and purple.

- ✔ We took a lighter approach in explaining things to you in this book (in fact, we even attempt some jokes now and then); your QuarkXPress documentation is serious, boring, grown-up stuff.

Part I
Page Layout 101: Good Design

"YOU MEAN TO TELL ME YOU KNEW THIS WAS SACRED INDIAN BURIAL GROUND, AND YOU BUILT THE COMPUTER ROOM HERE ANYWAY?! YOU FOOL! YOU FOOL!"

In this part ...

The whole point of desktop publishing is to do layouts, but there's no sense in doing desktop publishing — or traditional publishing, for that matter — until you know how to do layout. It's like deciding to hire someone without knowing what the job is. Page layout is not something we learned to do in school or from our parents. It's a skill that is passed on from one professional to another. It's not a science, so there are no magic formulas, although there are some guiding principles. The three chapters in this part will show you those principles and pass on some of the basic skills and knowledge to get you started. Think of this part as your survivor's kit as you enter the exotic world of publishing.

Chapter 1

Terminology Tutor: Breaking the Code

- -

In This Chapter

▶ Words you should know

▶ How the QuarkXPress interface works

▶ The various pointer icons you'll see while working in XPress

- -

*"P*sst . . . Buddy! Wanna buy a word? Better yet, how about a few hundred of 'em?"

It's true: If you like learning new words, you'll like producing documents with QuarkXPress. Like many specialties, desktop publishing has its own jargon of intricate-sounding words, with a good sprinkling of acronyms thrown in for good measure. Just think — within a short time you'll be impressing your friends with terms such as *serif, pica, kerning,* and *crop.*

Beyond the thrill of impressing your friends, it's also a good idea to learn the lingo. Knowing the correct buzzwords will not only make you sound impressive, but also may keep you from making mistakes by confusing the professional printer who prints your documents, or someone who works in a service bureau to output your documents. Here are definitions of some of the basics terms you need to know, grouped by publishing task.

Design Terminology 101

Typography terms

Typography terms describe the appearance of text in a document. These terms refer to things like the amount of space between lines, characters, and paragraphs, and the size and style of the typeface used.

Measurement units

A *pica* is a measurement unit used to specify the width and depth of columns and pages. A pica is just a little less than $1/6$ of an inch (most people round up to an even $1/6$ inch). A *point* is a measurement used to specify type size and the space between lines. There are 12 points in a pica, so there are about 72.27 points to the inch — most people round down to 72 per inch. Another unit is the mighty cicero. Neither a self-promoting Roman orator nor a congested suburb of Chicago, no, the cicero is a unit of measure used in many parts of Europe. One inch equals about 5.62 ciceros.

The terms *em*, *en*, and *punctuation space* (also called a *thin space*) are units of measurement that reflect, respectively, the horizontal space taken up by a capital *M*, capital *N,* and lowercase *t.* Typically, an em space is the same width as the current point size; an en space is $1/2$ of the current point size; and a punctuation (thin) space is $1/4$ of the current point size. In other words, for 12-point type, an em is 12 points wide, an en space is 6 points, and a punctuation or thin space is 3 points. A *figure space* refers to the width of a numeral, which usually is the same as an en. (In most typefaces, all numerals are the same width so that tables align naturally.)

Spacing

Leading, also called *line spacing,* refers to the space from the base of one line (the *baseline*) to another. (Leading is named after the pieces of lead once used to space out lines.) Figure 1-1 shows the effects of two different leading settings.

Tracking determines the overall space between letters within a word. *Word spacing* defines the preferred, minimum, and maximum spacing between words. *Letter spacing* (sometimes called *character spacing*) defines the preferred, minimum, and maximum spacing between letters. QuarkXPress uses your preferred spacing specifications unless you justify the text; if you justify text, the program spaces letters and words within the limits you set for maximum and minimum spacing.

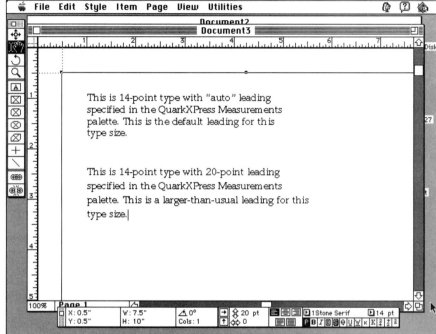

Figure 1-1:
Tight leading, like the sample on top, looks a bit more forbidding than the more loosely leaded sample on the bottom.

Kerning is the adjustment of the space between two letters. You kern letters to accommodate their specific shapes. For example, you probably would use tighter kerning in the letter pair *to* than in *oo* because *to* looks better if the *o* fits partly under the *t*. *Pair kerning* is a table, called the *kerning table* in QuarkXPress, that indicates the letter pairs you want the publishing program to kern automatically. Figure 1-2 shows the difference between kerned and unkerned character pairs.

Justification (or just *justified*) adds space between words (and sometimes between letters) so that each line of text aligns at both the left and right margins of a column or page. *Ragged right* and *flush left* both refer to text that aligns against a column's left margin but not its right margin; *ragged left* and *flush right* text means that the text is aligned against the right margin but not against the left margin. *Centered* text is aligned so that there is equal space on both margins. *Justification* also can refer to the type of spacing used: justified, ragged right, centered, or ragged left.

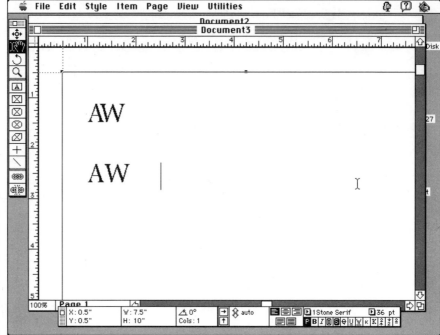

Figure 1-2:
The
character
pair on the
top is
kerned; the
bottom pair
is unkerned.

Vertical justification adds space between paragraphs (and sometimes between lines) so that the tops and bottoms of each column on a page align. (This term often gets confused with *column balancing,* which ensures that each column has the same number of lines.)

Characters

A *font* is a set of characters at a certain size, weight, and style (for example, 10-point Palatino Bold). This term now is used often as a synonym for *typeface,* which is a set of characters at a certain style in *all* sizes, weights, and stylings (for example, Palatino). A *face* is a combination of a weight and styling at all sizes (for example, Palatino Bold Italic). A *font family* is a group of related typefaces (for example, the Franklin family includes Franklin Gothic, Franklin Heavy, and Franklin Compressed).

Weight describes typeface thickness. Typical weights, from thinnest to thickest, are *ultralight, light, book, medium, demibold, bold, heavy, ultrabold,* and *ultraheavy.* Figure 1-3 shows an example of how weight affects the appearance of type.

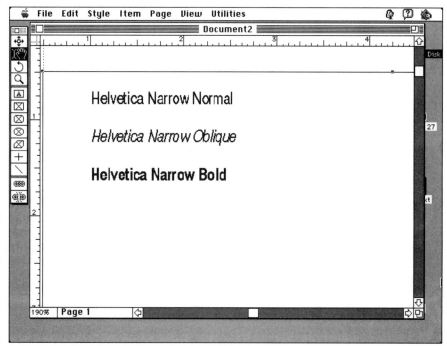

Figure 1-3:
A sample
sans serif
typeface
with
different
stylings.

Type can have one of three basic *stylings*: *Roman* type is upright type; *oblique* type is slanted type; and *italic* type is both slanted and curved (to appear more like calligraphy than roman type). Type also may be *expanded* (widened), *condensed* (narrowed), or *compressed* (severely narrowed).

The *x height* refers to the height of the average lowercase letter, usually the letter *x*. The greater the height, the bigger the letter looks when compared to letters in other typefaces that are the same point size but have a smaller x height. *Cap height* is similar; it refers to the size of the average uppercase letter (based on the letter *C*).

In a letter such as *q,* the part of the letter that goes below the baseline is called a *descender.* The part of a letter that extends above the x height (as in the letter *b*) is called an *ascender.*

A *serif* is a horizontal stroke used to give letters visual character. The strokes on the upper-left and bottom of the letter *p* in a typeface such as Times are serifs. *Sans serif* means that a typeface does not use these embellishments; Helvetica is an example of a sans serif typeface. Figure 1-4 shows the ascender, descender, and serifs in a serif font.

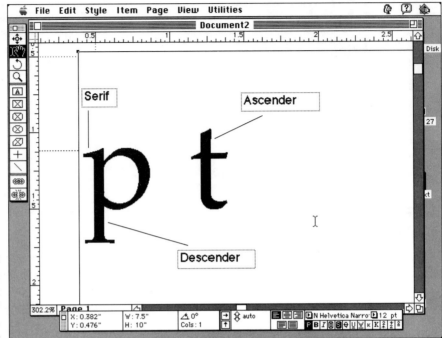

Figure 1-4:
Different
elements of
a typeface.

Paragraphs

Often, printers indicate each new paragraph with an *indent*, which inserts a fixed space in front of the paragraph's first letter. An *outdent* (also called an *exdent*) shifts the first character past the left margin and places the other lines at the left margin; this paragraph alignment typically is used in lists. A *block indent* moves an entire paragraph in from the left margin, a style often used for long quotes. A *hanging indent* is like an outdent, except that the first line begins at the left margin and all subsequent lines are indented.

A *bullet* is a character (often a filled circle) used to indicate that a paragraph is one element in a list of elements. Bullets can be indented, outdented, or kept at the left margin. Figure 1-5 shows a typical bullet.

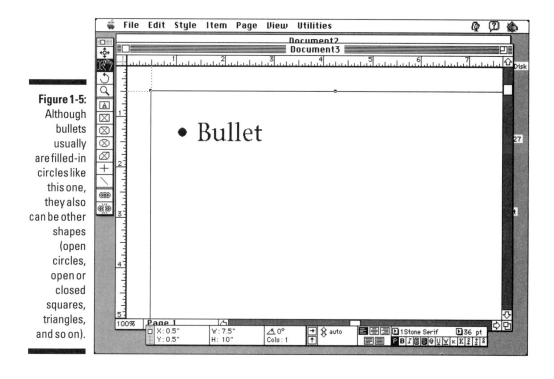

Figure 1-5:
Although bullets usually are filled-in circles like this one, they also can be other shapes (open circles, open or closed squares, triangles, and so on).

A *drop cap* is a large capital letter that extends down several lines into the surrounding text (the rest of the text wraps around it). Drop caps are used at the beginning of a section or story. A *raised cap* is the same as a drop cap except that it does not extend down into the text; instead, it rests on the baseline of the first line and extends several lines above the baseline.

Style sheets contain named sets of such attributes as spacing, typeface, indent, leading, and justification. A set of attributes is known as a *style* or *style tag*. Essentially, styles are formatting *macros*, or mini-programs. You *tag* each paragraph with the name of the style you want to apply. Any formatting changes made to one paragraph are automatically reflected in all other paragraphs tagged with the same style.

Hyphenation

A *hyphen* indicates the division of a word at the end of a line and joins words that combine in order to modify another word. *Hyphenation* is determining where to place the hyphen in split words. *Consecutive hyphenation* determines how many lines in a row can end with a hyphen (more than three hyphens in a row is considered bad typographic practice). The *hyphenation zone* determines how far from the right margin a hyphen can be inserted to split a word.

An *exception dictionary* lists words with nonstandard hyphenations. You can add words that the publishing program's default dictionary does not know and override the default hyphenations for words such as *desert* that are hyphenated differently as a noun (*des-ert*) than as a verb (*de-sert*). Placing a *discretionary hyphen* (also called a *soft hyphen*) in a word tells the program to hyphenate the word at that place if the word absolutely must be split. A discretionary hyphen affects only the word in which it is placed.

Layout terms

Document layout is the placing of text, pictures, and other items on a page. In desktop publishing, document layout involves using a computer and page-layout software to place the elements of a page — text, headlines, pictures, and so on — into position.

Layout tools

A *grid* is the basic layout design of a publication. It includes standard positions of folios (page numbers), text, graphics, bylines, and headlines. A layout artist modifies the grid when necessary. Grids also are called *templates.* A *dummy* is a rough sketch of the layout of a particular story. *Guidelines* show the usual placement of columns and margins in the grid. In some programs, guidelines are nonprinting lines you can use to ensure that elements align.

An *overlay* is a piece of transparent paper or film laid over a layout board. On the overlay, the artist can indicate screens in a different color or overprinted material such as text or graphics. Some illustration and paint programs have electronic equivalents of overlays, called *layers.*

Design elements

A *column* is a block of text. When you place two or more columns side by side, the space between columns is called the *gutter.*

The *margin* is the space between the edge of a page and the nearest standard block of text. Some designers allow text or graphics to intrude into the margin for visual effect.

A *bleed* is a graphic element or block of color that extends to the trimmed edge of the page.

A *wrap* refers to a textual cutout that occurs when graphics or other text intrude upon a column. The column margins are altered so that the column text goes around — or wraps around — the intruding graphic or text instead of being overprinted by the intruding element. A wrap can be rectangular, polygonal, or curved, depending on what the text wraps around and the capabilities of the layout program; QuarkXPress supports all three shapes.

A *folio* is the page number and identifying material (such as the publication name or month) that appears at the bottom or top of every page.

White space is the part of the page left empty to create contrast to the text and graphics. White space provides visual relief and emphasizes the text and graphics.

Most desktop publishing programs use *frames* to hold layout elements (text and graphics) on a page; QuarkXPress refers to these frames as *boxes*. Using a mouse, you can delete, copy, resize, or otherwise manipulate boxes in your layout. The boxes that hold layout elements can have ruling lines around them; Quark calls these lines *frames*. You can create a *template* by filling a document with empty boxes and defining style tags in advance; you then can use the template repeatedly to create documents that use the same boxes and styles.

Image manipulation

Cropping an image means to select a part of it for use on the page. *Sizing* an image means to determine how much to reduce or enlarge the image (or part of the image). Sizing also is called *scaling*. With layout programs, you often can *distort* an image to size it differently, either horizontally or vertically, which creates special effects such as *compressing* or *stretching* an image.

Reversing (also called *inverting* in some programs) exchanges the black and white portions of an image, which is like creating a photographic negative.

Color terms

Spot color is a single color applied at one or more places on a page, such as for a screen or as part of an illustration. You can use more than one spot color per page. Spot colors can be process or Pantone colors.

A *process color* refers to any of the four primary colors in publishing: cyan, magenta, yellow, and black (known as a group as *CMYK*). A *Pantone Matching System color* (called *Pantone* or *PMS* for short) is an industry standard for specifying a color. The printer uses a premixed ink based on the Pantone number you specify; you look up these numbers in a table of colors. *Four-color printing* is the use of the four process colors in combination to produce most other colors. A *color separation* is a set of four photographic negatives — one filtered for each process color — shot from a color photograph or image. When overprinted, the four negatives reproduce that image. A *build* attempts to simulate a Pantone color by overprinting the appropriate percentages of the four process colors.

Color space is a method of representing color in terms of measurable values, such as the amount of red, yellow, and blue in a color image. The EfiColor XTension, included with QuarkXPress, works with three color spaces: *RGB* (which represents the red, green, and blue colors on video screens), *CIELAB* (which specifies colors by one lightness coordinate and two color coordinates — green-red and blue-yellow), and *CMYK* (which specifies colors as combinations of cyan, magenta, yellow, and black). *Color gamut* is the range of colors that a device, such as a monitor or a color printer, can produce.

Production terms

Registration marks tell a printer where to position each negative relative to other negatives (the registration marks must line up when the negatives are superimposed). *Crop marks* tell a printer where to cut the negatives; anything outside the crop marks is not printed. Crop marks are used both to define page size and to indicate which part of an image is to be used.

A *screen* is an area printed at a particular percentage of a color (including black). For example, the border of a page may have a 20-percent black screen.

Trapping refers to the technique of extending one color so that it slightly overlaps an adjoining color. Trapping prevents gaps between two abutting colors; such gaps sometimes result from the misalignment of color plates on a printing press.

Introducing QuarkXPress

If you're like most of us, the first time you tried to record a program on your VCR you fumbled with the buttons and switches, and maybe — after an hour or so — resorted to reading the instructions. (Okay, admit it: you maybe even mumbled an expletive or two.) See, when you use *anything* for the first time, it's bothersome. It takes time to learn how to deal with the way things work, or the *user interface*.

What lessens the new-user pain with QuarkXPress is the user interface's strong similarity to that used by other Macintosh programs. If you use other Macintosh programs, you already know how to use such QuarkXPress interface components as file folders, document icons, and the set of menus at the top of the document window. Because so many Windows programs came from the Mac, Windows users will probably find QuarkXPress to be familiar, too.

When you open a document in QuarkXPress, the program displays a document window similar to the one shown in Figure 1-6.

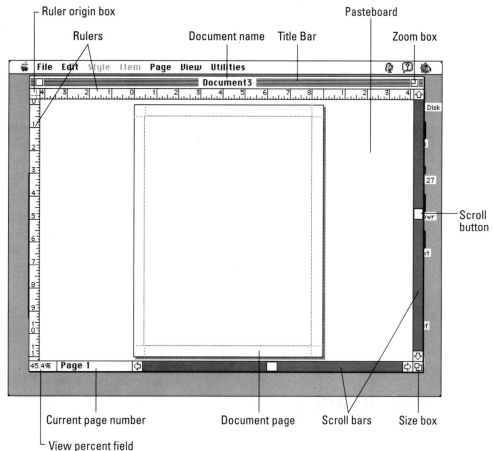

Figure 1-6:
The QuarkXPress document window.

- ✔ The *ruler origin box* lets you reset and reposition the ruler origin, which is the point at which the side and top rulers are 0 (zero).

- ✔ The name of the open document appears on the *title bar*, located beneath the menu bar. You can move the document window around in the screen display area by clicking and dragging the title bar.

- ✔ If you have reduced or enlarged a document, clicking the *zoom box* at the top right corner of the document window returns it to its previous size.

- ✔ The *vertical* and *horizontal rulers* on the left and top of the window reflect the measurement system currently in use.

- ✔ The *pasteboard* is a work area around the document page. You can temporarily store text boxes, picture boxes, or lines on the pasteboard. Items on the pasteboard do not print.

- ✔ QuarkXPress displays a shadow effect around the document page. The shadow indicates the edges of the document.

- ✔ If you select Automatic text box in the New dialog box (which you access by selecting New➪Document from the File menu), a text box appears on the first page of the new document.

- ✔ Clicking and dragging the *size box* resizes the document window as you move the mouse.

- ✔ The *View Percent* field shows the magnification level of the page that's currently displayed. To change the magnification level, enter a value between 10 and 400 percent in the field; then press the Return key or click elsewhere on the screen.

- ✔ Use the *scroll bars, boxes,* and *arrows* to shift the document page around within the document window. If you hold down the Option key while you drag the scroll box, the view of the document is refreshed as it "moves."

Active and selected items

Throughout this book, you'll see instructions such as *select the text box* or *apply the change to the active line. Selecting* an item is the same as *activating* it — which you simply must do before you modify an item in QuarkXPress. If you want to make a change to an entire item, just select or activate the item by clicking on it with the Item tool. If you want to make a change to the item's contents, click the Content tool on the item. When an item is selected or active, you see small black boxes, or sizing handles, on its sides and corners.

QuarkXPress menus

The menu bar appears across the top of the document window. To display, or "pull down," a menu, click the menu title and hold down the mouse button. (On Windows, just click the menu title; there's no need to hold the mouse button down.)

From the menu, you can select any of the active menu commands. QuarkXPress displays inactive menu commands with dimmed (grayed-out) letters. When a command is dimmed, it means that these commands are not currently available to you.

To select one of the active menu commands, hold down the mouse button as you slide through the menu selections. (As you get more used to the program, you can avoid using menus by using the keyboard equivalents for menu selections instead. Keyboard equivalents are displayed to the right of the command name in the menu.)

If an arrow appears to the right of a menu command, QuarkXPress displays a second, associated menu when you choose that command. Sometimes this secondary menu appears automatically when you highlight the first menu command; other times, you must continue to hold down the mouse and slide it to the submenu name in order to activate the menu. Figure 1-7 shows the Style menu and the secondary menu that appears when you select the Font menu command.

Dialog boxes

Some menu commands are followed by a series of dots called an ellipsis (. . .). If you choose a menu command whose name is followed by an ellipsis, a *dialog box* will appear. Figure 1-8 shows an example of a dialog box. Dialog boxes give you a great deal of control over how QuarkXPress applies specific features or functions to your document.

Some dialog boxes also contain *submenus*. If a menu has a submenu associated with it, an arrowhead appears to the right of the menu entry. In addition to submenus, QuarkXPress includes several *pop-up menus,* which appear when you make certain selections in a dialog box. Figure 1-8 shows a pop-up menu for text justification.

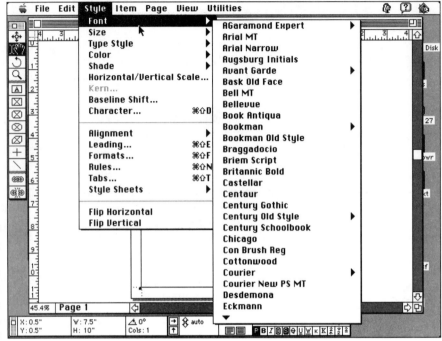

Keyboard shortcuts

You can select some QuarkXPress functions through pull-down menus, some through palettes, some through keyboard shortcuts — and some through all three options. Most new users begin by using menus because menus are so readily available. But, as you become more comfortable with using the program, you will be able to save time by using keyboard shortcuts.

Suppose that you want to move from page one of a document to page three. You can change pages by choosing Go To from the Page menu, or you can use the keyboard shortcut: press and hold the Command key (⌘) while you press the J key. In this book, we write this key combination as follows: ⌘-J. We use the same format for all keyboard shortcuts.

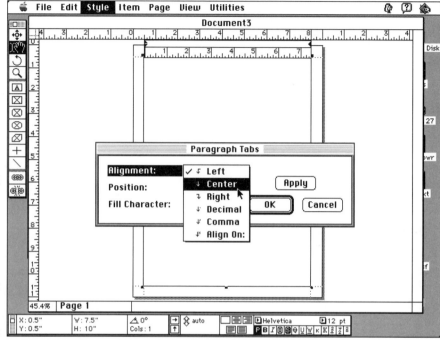

Figure 1-8:
The
Paragraph
Tabs dialog
box,
showing the
Alignment
pop-up
menu.

Palettes

One of the coolest features of the QuarkXPress interface is its *palettes*, which let you perform a wide range of functions on an open document without having to access pull-down menus. Palettes are the biggest time-saving feature of the QuarkXPress interface, and undoubtedly you will find yourself using a couple of the palettes — the Tool palette and the Measurements palette — all the time.

The Tool palette

The Tool palette, shown in Figure 1-9, is one you will use any time you are fiddling with a document in QuarkXPress. When you first open the program, the Tool palette appears along the left edge of your computer's monitor; if it's not there, you can get it to appear by selecting Show Tools from the View menu. This palette contains tools you use to create, change, link, view, and rotate text boxes, picture boxes, and lines.

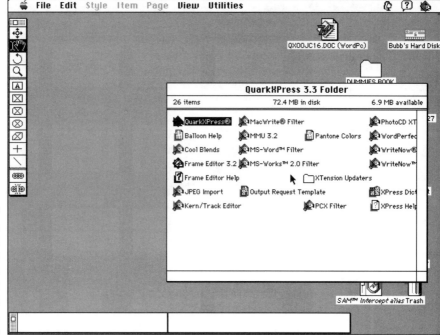

Figure 1-9:
The
QuarkXPress
Tool palette
(on the left
side of the
screen).

To use a tool on the palette, you first need to activate it. To activate a tool, use the mouse to place the cursor on the tool icon you want to use and then click the mouse button. Depending on which tool you select, the cursor takes on a different look to reflect the function the tool performs. When you click the Linking tool, for example, the cursor changes to look like links in a chain.

In the chapters that follow, we explain in greater detail many of the functions you can perform with the Tool palette. But, for now, here are brief descriptions of each tool.

Item tool

The Item tool takes care of the *external* aspects of an item on a page. The Item tool controls the size and positioning of items. When you want to change the shape, location, or presence of a text box, picture box, or line, use the Item tool. The Item tool enables you to select, move, group, ungroup, cut, copy, and paste text boxes, picture boxes, lines, and groups. When you click the Item tool on a box, the box becomes *active,* which means that you can change or move the box. Sizing handles appear on the sides of the active box; you can click and drag these handles to make the box a different size.

Content tool

The Content tool controls the *internal* aspects of items on a page. Functions you can perform with the Content tool include importing (putting text into a text box or putting a picture into a picture box), cutting, copying, pasting, and editing text.

To edit text in a text box, first select the Content tool. Then select the areas of text you want to edit by clicking and dragging the Content tool to highlight the text or by using different numbers of mouse button clicks, as follows:

- **To position the cursor:** Use the mouse to move the I-beam pointer (it looks like a large capital *I*) to the desired location and click the mouse button once.

- **To select a single word:** Use the mouse to move the pointer within the word and click the mouse button twice.

- **To select a line of text:** Use the mouse to move the pointer within the line and click the mouse button three times.

- **To select an entire paragraph:** Use the mouse to move the pointer within the paragraph and click the mouse button four times.

- **To select the entire document:** Use the mouse to move the cursor anywhere within the document and click the mouse button five times.

In a picture box, the Content tool cursor changes to a hand shape. You can use this tool in a picture box to move the contents of the box. You also can use it when manipulating the picture's contents, such as applying shades, colors, or printing effects.

Rotation tool

Use the Rotation tool to rotate items on a page. Using the Rotation tool, you can click a text box, picture box, or line and rotate it by dragging it to the angle you want. You also can rotate items on a page in other ways, which include using the Measurements palette and the Modify command in the Item menu.

Zoom tool

You may want to change the magnification of a page on-screen. For example, you may be making copy edits on text that is set in 8-point type; increasing the displayed size of the text makes it easier to see what you are doing as you edit. The Zoom tool lets you reduce or enlarge the view you see in the document window. When you select the Zoom tool, the cursor looks like a small magnifying glass; when you hold the cursor over the document window and click the mouse button, QuarkXPress changes the magnification of that section of the screen up or down in increments of 25 percent.

Another way of changing the magnification of the page is to enter a percentage value in the bottom left corner of the document window; when a page is displayed at actual size, that percentage is 100%. QuarkXPress lets you select any viewing amount, including those in fractions of a percent (such as 49.5%), within the range of 10% and 400%.

Text Box tool

QuarkXPress needs to have a text box on the page before it can let you import text from a word processor file or before it will let you enter text directly onto a document page using the word processing features built into QuarkXPress. You can instruct QuarkXPress to create text boxes on each page of the document automatically. Or you can create a text box manually — which you do using the Text Box tool.

To create a text box, select the Text Box tool and place the cursor at the approximate location where you want the box to appear. Click the mouse button and hold it down as you drag the box to size.

Picture Box tools

Picture boxes hold graphics that you import from graphics programs. QuarkXPress offers four Picture Box tools. Using these tools, you can draw four different box shapes:

- ✔ **Rectangle Picture Box tool:** For rectangular or square picture boxes.

- ✔ **Rounded Rectangle Picture Box tool:** For picture boxes that are rectangular but have rounded corners. You can change the curve of the corners by using the Modify command in the Item menu.

- ✔ **Oval Picture Box tool:** For oval or circular picture boxes.

- ✔ **Polygon Picture Box tool:** For creating any shape of picture box you want. The only restriction is that the box must have at least three sides.

You create the first three styles of picture boxes (rectangle, rounded rectangle, and oval) in the same manner as text boxes: Place the cursor at the approximate spot you want the box to appear on the page, click the mouse button, and hold it down as you drag the box to size.

To create a polygon picture box, draw the first line in the box and click the mouse button once to end the line. Continue drawing the lines of the box, clicking the mouse button once to end each line. Close the box by connecting the final line to the originating point of the polygon.

Line tools

The two Line tools let you draw lines, or *rules*. After you draw a line, you can change its thickness (*weight*) or line style (dotted line, double line, and so on). The Orthogonal Line tool (top) draws horizontal and vertical lines. The Diagonal Line tool (bottom) draws lines at any angle.

To use either of the line tools, click the tool to select it and position the cursor at the point where you want the line to begin. Click the mouse button and hold it as you draw the line. When the line is approximately the length you want, release the mouse button. After you draw a line, use the Measurements palette to select the line weight and line style.

Linking and Unlinking tools

The bottom two tools in the Tool palette are the Linking tool (top) and the Unlinking tool (bottom). The Linking tool lets you link text boxes together so that overflow text flows from one text box into another. Use the Unlinking tool to break the link between text boxes. Linking is particularly useful when you want to *jump* text — for example, when a story starts on page one and jumps to (continues on) page four.

The Measurements palette

The Measurements palette was first developed by Quark and is now being widely imitated by other software developers. This palette is one of the most significant innovations to take place in the evolution of desktop publishing, and (honest!) you will use it all the time. The Measurements palette gives you precise information about the position and attributes of any selected page element, and it lets you enter values to change those specifications. If you want to see the Measurements palette, you need to have a document open as you choose View⇨Show Measurements.

The information displayed in the Measurements palette depends on the element currently selected. When you select a text box, the Measurements palette displays the text box position coordinates (X: and Y:), size (W: and H:), amount of rotation, and number of columns (Cols:), as shown in Figure 1-10. Using the up- and down-pointing arrows on the palette, you can modify the leading of the text box (or you can simply type in a value in the space next to the arrows); use the right- and left-pointing arrows to adjust kerning or tracking for selected text.

Specify text alignment — left, center, right, or justified — by using the alignment icons. In the type section of the palette, you can control the font, size, and type style of selected text.

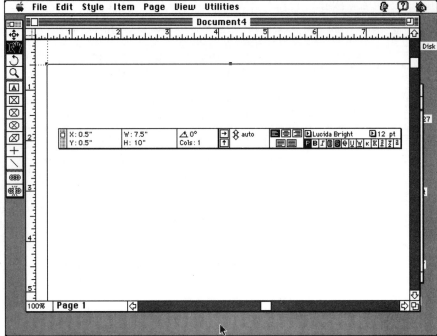

Figure 1-10:
The
Measurements
palette
when a text
box is
selected.

For a picture box, the Measurements palette displays a different set of information. It shows the position of the box (X: and Y:), its size (W: and H:), the amount it is rotated, its corner radius, its reduction or enlargement percentage (X%: and Y%:), its repositioning coordinates (X+: and Y+:), the amount of picture rotation within the box, and the amount of slant. Figure 1-11 shows the Measurements palette for a picture box.

For a line, the Measurements palette displays the location coordinates (X: and Y:), line width, line style, and endcap (line ending) style. The line style list box lets you select the style for the line. Figure 1-12 shows the Measurements palette for a line.

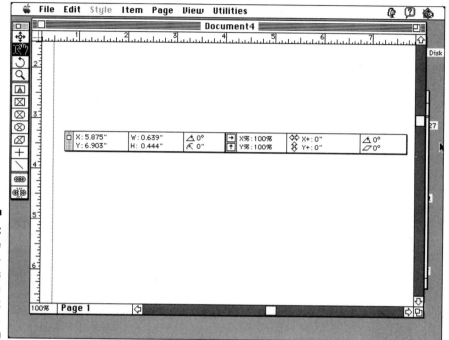

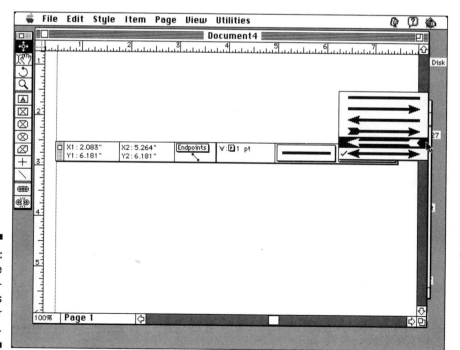

The Document Layout palette

With the Document Layout palette, shown in Figure 1-13, you can create, name, delete, move, and apply master pages. You also can add, delete, and move document pages. To display the Document Layout palette, choose Show Document Layout from the View menu.

The Colors palette

Figure 1-14 shows the Colors palette. This palette lets you designate the color and shade (percentage of color) you want to apply to text, pictures, and backgrounds of text and picture boxes. You also can produce color blends, using one or two colors, to apply to box backgrounds. To display the Colors palette, choose Show Colors from the View menu.

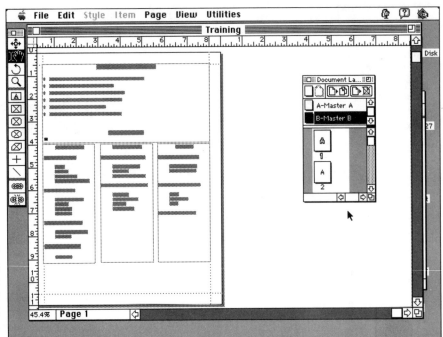

Figure 1-13:
The
Document
Layout
palette.

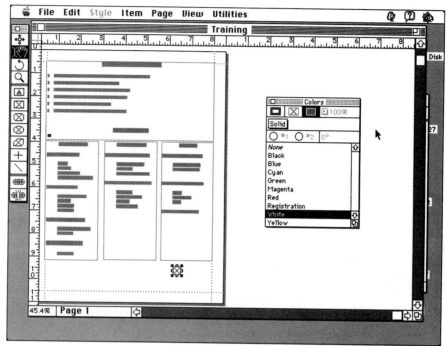

Figure 1-14:
The Colors
palette.

The Style Sheets palette

The Style Sheets palette lists the names of the style tags attached to selected paragraphs and also lets you apply style sheets to paragraphs. To display the Style Sheets palette, shown in Figure 1-15, choose Show Style Sheets from the View menu.

The Trap Information palette

Trapping controls how one color in a document prints next to another color. In the Trap Information palette, shown in Figure 1-16, you can set or change trapping specifications for selected items.

A word of warning: don't use this palette unless you know what you are doing. It is considered an expert feature, and using it without knowing what you are doing can produce uneven results when you print your document.

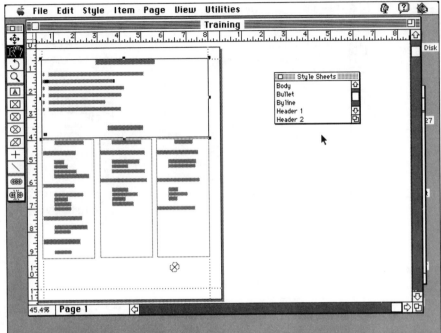

Figure 1-15:
The Style
Sheets
palette.

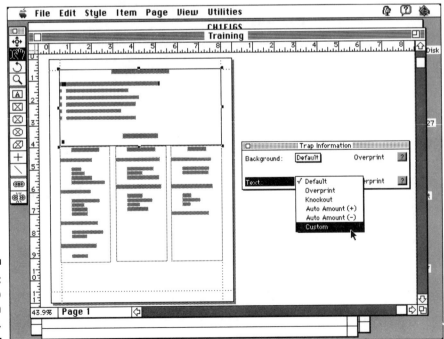

Figure 1-16:
The Trap
Information
palette.

Library palettes

QuarkXPress lets you store layout elements (text or picture boxes, lines, or groups) in one or more Library palettes. To use this feature, you select the element from the document or the pasteboard and drag it into an open library palette. You then can use items stored in the library in other documents. To create a library palette, choose File⇨New⇨Library.

Mouse Pointers

When you use the Macintosh or Windows, you use the mouse. It's the same with QuarkXPress. What you notice after a while is that the program gives you a visual hint about what tool you are currently using. It does this by changing the mouse pointer (also called *cursor*) so that it looks different. Here are the various renditions of the mouse pointer you can expect to see in QuarkXPress:

Standard pointer: The most common pointer. It appears as you move through dialog boxes, menus, and windows. It also appears as you move over non-selected elements.

Creation pointer: Appears if you have selected a box or line tool. Use it to draw boxes and lines.

Sizing pointer: Appears if you select one of the handles on a text or picture box (with either the Item or Content tool selected) or on a line. You can resize the item by holding down the mouse button and dragging the handle.

Item pointer: Appears if the Item tool is selected and you have selected a box or line. You can move the selected item by holding down the mouse button and dragging the item.

Lock pointer: Appears if the Item tool is selected and you have selected a locked text box, picture box, or line. The lock pointer indicates that the box will not move if you try to drag it (you can move it, however, by changing the coordinates in the Measurements palettes or via Item⇨Modify).

I-beam (text) pointer: Appears if the Content tool is selected and you select a text box. If the cursor is blinking, any text you type inserts where the cursor appears. If the cursor is not blinking, you must click at the location in the text box where you want to edit text.

Grabber pointer (a.k.a. page-grabber hand): Appears if the Content tool is selected and you have selected a picture box containing a graphic. You can move the graphic within the box by holding down the mouse button and dragging the item.

Zoom-in pointer: Appears if you select the Zoom tool and click the mouse button (clicking the mouse button zooms in on the image by the pre-defined amount, which by default is 25 percent). You can also select an area to zoom into by clicking the mouse at one corner of the area of interest, holding the mouse button down, dragging the mouse to the opposite corner, and then releasing the button.

 Zoom-out pointer: Appears if you select the Zoom tool and hold the Option key down while clicking the mouse button (clicking the mouse button zooms out by the predefined amount, which by default is 25 percent).

 Link pointer: Appears if you select the Link tool. Click the pointer on the first text box and then on the second text box in the chain of boxes you want text to flow through. If there are more boxes, select them in the flow order as well. You can switch pages while this tool is active to flow text across pages.

 Unlink pointer: Appears if you select the Unlink tool. Click the pointer on the first text box and then on the second text box in the chain of boxes that have the link that you want to break. If there are more boxes to unlink, repeat this process. You can switch pages while this tool is active to unlink text flow across pages.

Chapter 2
What Makes Good Design

*1*ntimidating.

That's what design is to many people. We grow up hearing stories about anguished artists who cut off their ears in rapid descents into madness. An Artist? Why, a *real* Artist is a genius, a prima donna, an unruly bohemian smug in his or her bizarre neo-modern abstract tastes, an unappreciated martyr who sacrifices all for the sake of Art.

With that kind of build-up, it's no wonder that the rest of us are intimidated! We just don't have what it takes. We're not pure enough. We don't suffer enough. Our living rooms will never make it into *Architectural Digest.* Poor us: we're just not true, free-spirited artists.

But guess what? Design doesn't have to be that way. Oh, you'll find a few folks who never get it. But usually they're the same people who don't enjoy any music, never get any jokes, and never get out of their caves in the Idaho wilderness. Chances are, that description doesn't describe you, so you can relax. In fact, you should even get excited, not scared, because good, basic design is not difficult. Good design requires you to master only one basic principle: simplicity combined with interest. Sounds like one of those ultrathin artists who paints big yellow squares and walks around in all-black? Maybe, but it's true. Read on and find out the basics you need to know to create good designs. And don't worry: you won't need to buy a beret or sound like a snob.

As you read, remember the two parts of the basic principle of good design: keep it simple, and add visual interest. *Visual interest* means many things to many people. When we say visual interest in this book, we mean the use of typography, graphics, and placement of elements that both attracts and pleases the reader's eye. Visual interest can come from an unusual font, a pleasing symbol, or staggered columns — anything that keeps an otherwise simple design from getting deadly dull.

Seeing visually arresting design is like entering a simple, well-lit living room whose natural wood or off-white colors are dominated by vivid stone pottery. The room's simplicity does not distract you; it only accents the vividness of the pottery. Yet the wood and light furniture have different textures, too; when you do stop looking at the pottery, you have pleasant furnishings to look at. In fact, they're arranged to draw you from one furnishing to another. And the longer your gaze lingers, the more subtleties you notice. That's good design — exactly what you want to give your readers. First, you want them to notice the important elements — like the top news story in a newsletter — and then see the other stories or illustrations, all the while enjoying the overall look and not having difficulty finding the content.

Alas, bad design is also easy. You can always just cram stuff onto a page or mix things that simply don't mesh, like green silk and orange spandex. It's only too easy for your layout to look like a garage-sale home: you can pack your layouts with interesting elements. But, as interesting as each part is on its own, they just aren't compatible when they occupy the same space.

The Good, the Bad, and the Ugly

But enough of theory. It's time to get into the practice of design before we start sounding like beret-toting artists. We'll start by looking at some examples of what works and what doesn't. We've picked a simple newsletter design as an example. Figures 2-1 through 2-4 show four *bad* examples. Here's what's wrong with each one of them.

Why the bad designs are bad

The layout in Figure 2-1 is too cramped. The body text is small — only 8 points — and the margins are narrow — just a half pica (a twelfth of an inch) — for the main text. The headlines are small, too. Everything is small. This layout makes you want to turn the page and look at something else. No one likes to read the fine print, which is why lawyers always make it so small. The lesson here: *don't scrunch up your layouts.* Granted, with larger text you'll have to take more pages to show off your work effectively — but, hey, having more pages looks like you did more work!

Future Thinker   Vol 12, No. 3

The Shape of Interfaces to Come

Do you know what your operating system will look like in two years?

BY GALEN GRUMAN

Don't get too comfortable. Just as we've settled into the latest graphical interfaces, the world is about to change. Again. We've become more sophisticated, more demanding. We expect our computers to be simpler to use, easier to master, more flexible, and more functional. And software companies are responding: Microsoft is readying Windows 4.0; Apple is preparing Copland, a major upgrade to its System 7 operating system; and IBM continues to retool OS/2 while developing the Workplace OS and collaborating with Apple and Hewlett-Packard on Taligent. And from developers large and small, we'll get metaphors, guides, animated agents, feedback, and environments as likely to overwhelm as to enchant.

What will these options mean for you? Change, to be sure. But also more freedom of choice. Within the next few years, you may find yourself playing the operating system market.

Should you continue to buy the software you've already invested your energy and money in, or is it time to consider something new and different? How will you keep from buying into a dead-end technology? Advance knowledge is the best defense.

Interfaces Get Real

The DOS command-line interface may seem primitive today, but the idea of issuing direct, English-like commands was originally a powerful way of making computing more accessible to professionals. Unfortunately, it was neither intuitive nor flexible, and it eventually gave way to graphical user interfaces (GUIs) like in the Mac OS and Windows. GUIs use representations of real objects—an icon of, say, a trash can to represent a place to discard files—to help users perform tasks. Windows or the Mac OS use "reaching in" interfaces: They require you to use a device like a mouse or keyboard to manipulate the objects that represent your data and tasks. This type of interface has

continued to evolve, first to make the representations more intuitive, and second to make the interactions with them more fluid, through methods like drag and drop.

The newcomer is the "real world" interface, where you are "inside" a highly realistic, often 3-D setting, and the mouse represents you, not just your fingers. This style, popularized by games like Broderbund's Myst, is now entering the mainstream. For instance, the interface in MECA's Managing Your Money is a cartoonish desk, while the initial screens of two on-line services—Sierra Online's ImagiNation and Apple's e-World—are stylized "towns"; you click the Newsstand to enter a news section or the Learning Center to get educational programs. General Magic's Magic Cap interface, developed for a series of forthcoming personal information devices, employs a city-and-buildings metaphor. Personal information manager Lotus Organizer takes realism even further, with an interface that deftly mimics a paper-based Day-Timer.

So will developers abandon the "reaching in" interface of today's real world? Don't count on it. Interface developers agree that the reaching-in metaphor needs refinement but is nowhere near the end of its life. For one thing, a well-implemented GUI *can* make computing easy to comprehend. Besides, the real-world interfaces to date "have barely scratched the surface," says Scott Converse, group manager of research and development for e-World.

Nolan Larsen, WordPerfect's director of human factors development, agrees. "These real-world approaches need to be compelling enough so people will abandon the desktop metaphor to use them," he says. Larsen instead expects real-world interfaces to augment today's GUIs. The richer approach of the real world style will get a foothold in the consumer product market before creeping into the business world. "Real-world *continues on p.*

Figure 2-1.
An example of a bad layout: the sardine-can look.

Interface Tour

The first Mac interface, which debuted in 1984, popularized graphical interfaces on the desktop. Since then, the interface's evolution has been subtler than Windows' (except for color, which was introduced in 1987), although it too has added live links, shortcut icons, and 1994's System 7.5, guided help.

Released just after Windows 1.0, Digital Research's GEM was so Mac-like that Apple sued. A retooled version languished, with only then-preeminent desktop publisher Ventura Publisher adopting it.

Originally codeveloped by Microsoft and IBM in 1987, IBM's OS/2 Presentation Manager looks and acts a lot like Windows (the current version, 2.1, is shown here). A notable difference: It uses context-sensitive palettes, which provide current options for and information about files and programs. The forthcoming Chicago interface applies the same concept.

Lotus 1-2-3 for Windows Release 4 popularized several by-now-familiar trends in today's interfaces, including button bars and tabbed windows.

Chicago uses context-sensitive pop-up menus to provide shortcuts to available options.

Chicago uses guided help to ease driver installation. Such active help is increasingly common in both operating systems and applications. WordPerfect, for example, uses the approach in its Coach system, Microsoft offers Wizards, and Lotus's *continues on p. 5*

A Brief History of the Desktop Interface

Computer interface design has come a long way since the Altair excited the oscilloscope-and-ham-radio set in the late Seventies. Back then, you programmed your computer by switching levers up and down. Soon, Apple, IBM, and others—borrowing an idea from the mainframes of the day—adopted the command-line interface still on display in DOS. It was a huge advance because it allowed users to interact with their PCs via typed-in words rather than dip switches.

A few years later, Apple tapped ideas coming out of Xerox's Palo Alto Research Center, a pinnacle of advanced computer science thinking, to introduce 1984's Macintosh. Because it used a familiar metaphor (the desktop) and a human approach to interacting (pointing, grabbing, and moving), it was embraced as easy to use. Today, the original Mac interface looks cute but woefully limited. Back then, it tantalized and seduced people from all walks of life.

Other companies were exploring similar concepts: Digital Research had GEM (Graphics Environment Manager), VisiCorp offered VisiOn, and Microsoft was

brainstorming on Windows. Xerox itself came out with Star, but couldn't translate its brilliant research into a practical, affordable product. VisiOn soon fell by the wayside, but GEM hung on for several years, mainly because Ventura Publisher, then the top PC publishing program, adopted it. The Geoworks interface of 1990 promised a GUI that would work on low-power system like a 286-based PC AT, but users made the switch to 386s and 486s, and Geoworks soon disappeared as a viable operating environment, although it's still used in some DOS programs like America Online to provide a graphical interface.

Windows, when it was released in 1985, was a poor imitation of the Mac. Slow and bloated, it made little headway with users until version 3.0 came out in 1990. Still a sluggish performer, at least it finally offered a workable interface. And it ran on DOS machines, which were populating desks everywhere.

Suddenly the Mac, with its much-touted System 6, had real competition in its own area of strength. In 1992, Windows took the lead for good with version 3.1, which fine-tuned performance and added drag and drop, OLE 1.0, scaleable

type, and greater stability. Apple countered with System 7, but too late to slow Microsoft's momentum.

The Windows-Mac competition was the prime focus of the era, though other wannabes—Amiga, NeXt's NeXTSTEP, and IBM's OS/2 among them—won praise for innovation. All had superior capabilities in one or more areas. In fact, multitasking, 32-bit apps, objects—all trendy ideas today—derive much from Amiga, NeXTSTEP, and OS/2. But these operating systems couldn't attract substantial customer bases because they couldn't address a key interface issue: compatibility. People were clearly willing to compromise on features for the promise that all their software would run on their machine.

If anyone changes the game from just a Microsoft-Apple contest, it will be IBM's OS/2. Originally developed in 1987 by Microsoft and IBM, it quickly foundered when the two companies went separate ways in 1989 (Microsoft's version became Windows NT, IBM's kept the OS/2 name). But with 1993's version 2.1, OS/2 has reemerged with about 4 million users, compared to about 35 million for Windows and 10 million for the Mac. *continues on p. 5*

At first glance, the layout in Figure 2-2 is not bad. But, as you look more closely, you'll notice that each block of text is in a different font. While the individual blocks look good, there's really no rhyme or reason — what a designer would call a visual theme — to the text selections. The lesson here: *make sure things look good together for the whole document, not just in pieces.* Make sure you see the forest for the trees.

Future Thinker Vol 12, No. 3

The Shape of Interfaces to Come

Do you know what your operating system will look like in two years?

BY GALEN GRUMAN

Don't get too comfortable. Just as we've settled into the latest graphical interfaces, the world is about to change. Again. We've become more sophisticated, more demanding. We expect our computers to be simpler to use, easier to master, more flexible, and more functional. And software companies are responding: Microsoft is readying Windows 4.0; Apple is preparing Copland, a major upgrade to its System 7 operating system; and IBM continues to retool OS/2 while developing the Workplace OS and collaborating with Apple and Hewlett-Packard on Taligent. And from developers large and small, we'll get metaphors, guides, animated agents, feedback, and environments as likely to overwhelm as to enchant.

What will these options mean for you?

Change, to be sure. But also more freedom of choice. Within the next few years, you may find yourself playing the operating system market. Should you continue to buy the software you've already invested your energy and money in, or is it time to consider something new and different? How will you keep from buying into a dead-end technology? Advance knowledge is the best defense.

Interfaces Get Real

The DOS command-line interface may seem primitive today, but the idea of issuing direct, English-like commands was originally a powerful way of making computing more accessible to professionals. Unfortunately, it was neither intuitive nor flexible, and it eventually gave way to graphical user interfaces (GUIs) like the Mac OS and Windows. GUIs use representations of real objects—an icon of, say, a trash can to repre-

sent a place to discard files—to help users perform tasks. Windows or the Mac OS use "reaching in" interfaces: They require you to use a device like a mouse or keyboard to manipulate the objects that represent your data and tasks. This type of interface has continued to evolve, first to make the representations more intuitive, and second to make the interactions with them more fluid, through methods like drag and drop.

The newcomer is the "real world" interface, where you are "inside" a highly realistic, often 3-D setting, and the mouse represents you, not just your fingers. This style, popularized by games like Broderbund's Myst, is now entering the mainstream. For instance, the interface in MECA's Managing Your Money is a cartoonish desk, while the initial screens of two on-line services—Sierra Online's ImagiNation and Apple's

continues on p. 5

Interface Tour

The first Mac interface, which debuted in 1984, popularized graphical interfaces on the desktop. Since then, the interface's evolution has been subtler than Windows' (except for color, which was introduced in 1987), although it too has added live links, shortcut icons, and with 1994's System 7.5, guided help.

Released just after Windows 1.0, Digital Research's GEM was so Mac-like that Apple sued. A retooled version languished, with only then-preeminent desktop publisher Ventura Publisher adopting it.

Originally codeveloped by Microsoft and IBM in 1987, IBM's OS/2 Presentation Manager looks and acts a lot like Windows (the current version, 2.1, is shown here). A notable difference: It uses context-sensitive palettes, which provide current options for and information about files and programs. The forthcoming Chicago interface applies the same concept.

Lotus 1-2-3 for Windows Release 4 popularized several by-now-familiar trends in today's interfaces, including button bars and tabbed windows.

Chicago uses context-sensitive pop-up menus to provide shortcuts to available options. Chicago uses guided

continues on p. 5

A Brief History of the Desktop Interface

Computer interface design has come a long way since the Altair excited the oscilloscope-and-ham-radio set in the late Seventies. Back then, you programmed your computer by switching levers up and down. Soon, Apple, IBM, and others—borrowing an idea from the mainframes of the day—adopted the command-line interface still on display in DOS. It was a huge advance because it allowed users to interact with their PCs via typed-in words rather than dip switches.

A few years later, Apple tapped ideas coming out of Xerox's Palo Alto Research Center, a pinnacle of advanced computer science thinking, to introduce 1984's Macintosh. Because it used a familiar metaphor (the desktop) and a human approach to interacting (pointing, grabbing, and moving), it was embraced as easy to use. Today, the original Mac interface looks cute but woefully limited. Back then, it tantalized and seduced people from all walks of life.

Other companies were exploring similar concepts: Digital Research had GEM (Graphics Environment Manager), VisiCorp offered VisiOn, and Microsoft was brainstorming on Windows. Xerox itself came out with Star, but couldn't translate its brilliant research into a practical, affordable product. VisiOn soon fell by the wayside, but GEM hung on for several years, mainly because Ventura Publisher, then the top PC publishing program, adopted it. The Geoworks interface of 1990 promised a GUI that would work on low-power system like a 286-based PC AT, but users made the switch to 386s and 486s, and Geoworks soon disappeared as a viable operating environment, although it's still used in some DOS programs like America Online to provide a graphical interface.

Windows, when it was released in 1985, was a poor imitation of the Mac. Slow and **continues on p. 5**

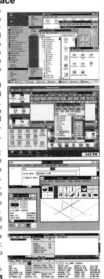

continues on p. 5

Figure 2-2: Another example of a bad layout: the garage-sale look.

The layout in Figure 2-3 is straightforward. In fact, it's too straightforward — so straightforward it's boring. This layout uses the two most boring typefaces on the planet: Helvetica (in the headlines) and Times (in the text). But there's no life here. No fun. No razzmatazz. No nothing. Not good.

Future Thinker   *Vol 12, No. 3*

The Shape of Interfaces to Come

Do you know what your operating system will look like in two years?

by Galen Gruman

Don't get too comfortable. Just as we've settled into the latest graphical interfaces, the world is about to change. Again. We've become more sophisticated, more demanding. We expect our computers to be simpler to use, easier to master, more flexible, and more functional. And software companies are responding: Microsoft is readying Windows 4.0; Apple is preparing Copland, a major upgrade to its System 7 operating system; and IBM continues to retool OS/2 while developing the Workplace OS and collaborating with Apple and Hewlett-Packard on Taligent. And from developers large and small, we'll get metaphors, guides, animated agents, feedback, and environments as likely to overwhelm as to enchant.

What will these options mean for you? Change, to be sure. But also more freedom of choice. Within the next few years, you may find yourself playing the operating system market. Should you continue to buy the software you've already invested your energy and money in, or is it time to consider something new and different? How will you keep from buying into a dead-end technology? Advance knowledge is the best defense.

Interfaces Get Real

The DOS command-line interface may seem primitive today, but the idea of issuing direct, English-like commands was originally a powerful way of making computing more accessible to professionals. Unfortunately, it was neither intuitive nor flexible, and it eventually gave way to graphical user interfaces (GUIs) like in the Mac OS and Windows. GUIs use representations of real objects—an icon of, say, a trash can to represent a place to discard files—to help users perform tasks. Windows or the Mac OS use "reaching in" interfaces: They require you to use a device like a mouse or keyboard to manipulate the objects that represent your data and tasks. This type of interface has continued to evolve, first to make the representations more intuitive, and second to make the interactions with them more fluid, through methods like drag and drop.

The newcomer is the "real world" interface, where you are "inside" a highly realistic, often 3-D setting, and the mouse represents you, not just your fingers. This style, popularized by games like Broderbund's Myst, is now entering the mainstream. For instance, the interface in MECA's Managing Your Money is a cartoonish desk, while the initial screens of two on-line services—Sierra Online's ImagiNation and Apple's e-World—are stylized "towns"; you click the Newsstand to enter a news section or the Learning Center to get educational programs. General Magic's Magic Cap interface, developed for a series of forthcoming personal information devices, employs a city-and-buildings metaphor. Personal information manager Lotus Organizer *continues on p. 5*

Interface Tour

The first Mac interface, which debuted in 1984, popularized graphical interfaces on the desktop. Since then, the interface's evolution has been subtler than Windows' (except for color, which was introduced in 1987), although it too has added live links, shortcut icons, and with 1994's System 7.5, guided help.

Released just after Windows 1.0, Digital Research's GEM was so Mac-like that Apple sued. A retooled version languished, with only then-preeminent desktop publisher Ventura Publisher adopting it.

Originally codeveloped by Microsoft and IBM in 1987, IBM's OS/2 Presentation Manager looks and acts a lot like Windows (the current version, 2.1, is shown here). A notable difference: It uses context-sensitive palettes, which provide current options for and information about files and programs. The forthcoming Chicago interface applies the same concept.

Lotus 1-2-3 for Windows Release 4 popularized several by-now-familiar trends in today's interfaces, including button bars and tabbed windows.

Chicago uses context- *continues on p. 5*

A Brief History of the Desktop Interface

Computer interface design has come a long way since the Altair excited the oscilloscope-and-ham-radio set in the late Seventies. Back then, you programmed your computer by switching levers up and down. Soon, Apple, IBM, and others—borrowing an idea from the mainframes of the day—adopted the command-line interface still on display in DOS. It was a huge advance because it allowed users to interact with their PCs via typed-in words rather than dip switches.

A few years later, Apple tapped ideas coming out of Xerox's Palo Alto Research Center, a pinnacle of advanced computer science thinking, to introduce 1984's Macintosh. Because it used a familiar metaphor (the desktop) and a human approach to interacting (pointing, grabbing, and moving), it was embraced as easy to use. Today, the original Mac interface looks cute but woefully limited. Back then, it tantalized and seduced people from all walks of life.

Other companies were exploring similar concepts: Digital Research had GEM (Graphics Environment Manager), VisiCorp offered VisiOn, and Microsoft was brainstorming on Windows. Xerox itself came out with Star, but couldn't translate its brilliant research into a practical, affordable product. VisiOn soon fell by the wayside, but GEM hung on for several years, mainly because Ventura Publisher, then the top PC publishing program, adopted it. The Geoworks interface of 1990 promised a GUI that would work on low-power system like a 286-based PC AT, but users made the switch to 386s and 486s, and Geoworks soon disappeared as a viable operating environment, although it's still used in some DOS programs like America Online to provide a graphical interface.

Windows, when it was released in 1985, was a poor imitation of the Mac. Slow and bloated, it made little headway with users until version 3.0 came out in 1990. Still a sluggish performer, at least it finally offered a workable interface. And it ran on DOS machines, which were populating desks everywhere.

Suddenly the Mac, with its much-touted System 6, had real competition in its own area of strength. In 1992, Windows took the lead for good with version 3.1, which fine-tuned performance and added drag and drop, OLE 1.0, scaleable type, and greater stability. Apple countered with System 7, but too late to slow Microsoft's momentum.

The Windows-Mac competition was the prime focus of the era, though other wannabes—Amiga, NeXt's NeXTSTEP, and IBM's OS/2 among them—won praise for innovation. All had superior capabilities in one or more areas. In fact, multitasking, 32-bit apps, objects—all trendy ideas today—derive much from Amiga, NeXTSTEP, and OS/2. But *continues on p. 5*

Figure 2-3:
Yet another example of a bad layout: the boring look.

Not enough razzmatazz in Figure 2-3? No problem. The layout in Figure 2-4 has enough razzmatazz for at least two layouts. For one layout, though, Figure 2-4 is so busy that it's overwhelming. Not only does the layout have way too many elements — pictures, fonts, lines, boxes, and just plain stuff — but the elements are way too decorated. For example, not only is there a drop cap for each story, but it's bold. And outlined. And shadowed. And italic. Look at the pull-quote: different (bold) font, boxed, and partially underlined. And what's this line through the logo? Or the different-size words in the top headline? Enough already! You've seen people who wear checkered red-and-green pants, an orange T-shirt, and a sky-blue jacket to go play golf? That's what this layout is like. Layouts should attract attention, yes, but make sure it's the right kind of attention. If Uncle Lee is known for his outrageous golf outfits, that's probably not how he wants to be known (and you certainly wouldn't want to be known as his taste-impaired relative or friend, now would you?).

Figure 2-4: Still another example of a bad layout: the my-cup-runneth-over look.

Why the good designs are good

Okay, take a second to recover from this horror show, and then look at the next set of examples. All four are *good*, as your eye will tell you when you look at Figures 2-5 through 2-8.

What makes these layouts good? Several things, but they all boil down to that basic principle we introduced at the first of this chapter: the layouts in Figures 2-5 through 2-8 combine simplicity with items of interest. There's no one absolutely right good way to design, which is why we show you four good examples of the same document, each intended to have a different feel. It's important to know what kind of feel you want your document to evoke in people *before* you design it. By knowing the feel you want in advance, you can choose the right techniques to make sure that your design achieves your goals. Let's look at the four examples to learn what the goals were and what techniques helped them succeed. This is the basic exercise of design that you'll need to perform time and time again.

We wanted the layout in Figure 2-5 to be casual, so we used slightly rounded fonts for the headlines (Poppl-Laudatio) and a simple font for the body text (Stone Serif). We also made a point of not having too many boxes or lines, though we did include one box with a line around it. By itself, the box separates the enclosed story from the other story, but it's sedate; it doesn't call much attention to itself. The staggered design of the images in the sidebar add visual movement to the page. But the movement's not random. All three images fit within the two right columns. And instead of making sidebar text go in the space at the middle right, we inserted a caption — that way, the reader doesn't have to hunt for part of the sidebar text, which could easily get lost if wedged into that nook. Notice how the continued lines are in the same font as the headlines, and so is the caption — carefully using identical fonts provides continuity and keeps the number of fonts manageable. (A good rule of thumb is to have no more than 10 faces — remember, that includes bold and italic variants of a font — on each page.) Finally, notice how we positioned the graphic at the top of the main story. By being wholly in column 2, that graphic doesn't distract you by falling between two columns. There's nothing wrong with columns wrapping around graphics, but since we already used this effect on the page, we thought it best to not add any more instances of it. The intent is to *not* go over the line in balancing simplicity with visual interest. Too much wrap would have crossed that line.

Future Thinker

Vol 12, No. 3

The Shape of Interfaces to Come

BY GALEN GRUMAN

Don't get too comfortable. Just as we've settled into the latest graphical interfaces, the world is about to change. Again. We've become more sophisticated, more demanding. We expect our computers to be simpler to use, easier to master, more flexible, and more functional. And software companies are responding: Microsoft is readying Windows 4.0; Apple is preparing Copland, a major upgrade to its System 7 operating system; and IBM continues to retool OS/2 while developing the Workplace OS and collaborating with Apple and Hewlett-Packard on Taligent. And from developers large and small, we'll get metaphors, guides, animated agents, feedback, and environments as likely to overwhelm as to enchant.

What will these options mean for you? Change, to be sure. But also more freedom of choice. Within the next few years, you may find yourself playing the operating system market. Should you continue to buy the software you've already invested your energy and money in, or is it time to consider something new and different? How will you keep from buying into a dead-end technology? Advance knowledge is the best defense.

Interfaces Get Real

The DOS command-line interface may seem primitive today, but the idea of issuing direct, English-like commands

was originally a powerful way of making computing more accessible to professionals. Unfortunately, it was neither intuitive no<None>r flexible, and it eventually gave way to graphical user interfaces (GUIs) like in the Mac OS and

W indows. GUIs use representations of real objects–an icon of, say, a trash can to represent a place to discard files–to help users perform tasks. Windows or the Mac OS use "reaching in" interfaces: They require you to use a device like a mouse or keyboard to manipulate the objects that represent your data and tasks. This type of interface has continued to evolve, first to make the represen-

Continues on p. 5

A Brief History of the Desktop Interface

Computer interface design has come a long way since the Altair excited the oscilloscope-and-ham-radio set in the late Seventies. Back then, you programmed your computer by switching levers up and down. Soon, Apple, IBM, and others–borrowing an idea from the mainframes of the day–adopted the command-line interface still on display in DOS. It was a huge advance because it allowed users to interact with their PCs via typed-in words rather than dip switches.

A few years later, Apple tapped ideas coming out of Xerox's Palo Alto Research Center, a pinnacle of advanced computer science thinking, to introduce 1984's Macintosh. Because it used a familiar metaphor (the desktop) and a

human approach to interacting (pointing, grabbing, and moving), it was embraced as easy to use. Today, the original Mac

Three Faces of Windows Microsoft Windows has undergone a major transformation over the years. Top to bottom: Windows 1.03, Windows 3.1, and the forthcoming Windows 4.0 (Chicago).

interface looks cute but woefully limited. Back then, it tantalized and seduced people from all walks of

Continues on p. 5

Figure 2-5: An example of a good layout: the casual look.

Now look at the layout in Figure 2-6. Do you see a firm, almost military look of authority in this layout? We wanted this layout suggest authoritativeness. To reach that goal, we started with a bold logo that projects authority. (Notice how the graphic gives the logo both weight and visual interest.) The headline font is American Typewriter Bold (condensed for the sidebar), which we used because the typewritten look reminds people of official reports. We also used a squared font for the body text (Melior); this font has a ramrod-straight look that reinforces a feeling of authority (or at least officialness). Finally, the arrangement of the columns and graphics is orthogonal — design speak for something that follows a grid with just horizontal and vertical alignments. Even the large-scale arrangement of this example adds to the feeling of rigid authority — this layout's as spit-and-polish as an Army drill. But despite the conservatism and sense of order, the visual elements still engage the eye. The logo certainly does. The use of bold text for the headlines and drop caps provides visual contrast to the body text. The graphics are of different sizes, which provides some visual relief from the otherwise highly ordered look.

Future Thinker

Vol 12, No. 3

The Shape of Interfaces to Come

A Brief History of the Destop Interface

Computer interface design has come a long way since the Altair excited the oscilloscope-and-ham-radio set in the late Seventies. Back then, you programmed your computer by switching levers up and down. Soon, Apple, IBM, and others—borrowing an idea from the mainframes of the day—adopted the command-line interface still on display in DOS. It was a huge advance because it allowed users to interact with their PCs via typed-in words rather than dip switches.

A few years later, Apple tapped ideas coming out of Xerox's Palo Alto Research Center, a pinnacle of advanced computer science thinking, to introduce 1984's Macintosh. Because it used a familiar metaphor (the desktop) and a human approach to

interacting (pointing, grabbing, and moving), it was embraced as easy to use. Today, the original Mac interface looks cute but woefully limited. Back then, it tantalized and seduced people from all walks of life.

Other companies were exploring similar concepts: Digital Research had GEM (Graphics Environment Manager), VisiCorp offered VisiOn, and Microsoft was brainstorming on Windows. Xerox itself came out with Star, but couldn't translate its brilliant research into a practical, affordable product. VisiOn soon fell by the wayside, but GEM hung on for several years, mainly because Ventura Publisher, then the top PC publishing program, adopted it. The Continues on p. 5

BY GALEN GRUMAN

Don't get too comfortable. Just as we've settled into the latest graphical interfaces, the world is about to change. Again. We've become more sophisticated, more demanding. We expect our computers to be simpler to use, easier to master, more flexible, and more functional. And software companies are responding: Microsoft is readying Windows 4.0; Apple is preparing Copland, a major upgrade to its System 7 operating system; and IBM continues to retool OS/2 while developing the Workplace OS and collaborating with Apple and Hewlett-Packard on Taligent. And from developers large and small, we'll get metaphors, guides, animated agents, feedback, and environments as likely to overwhelm as to enchant.

What will these options mean for you? Change, to be sure. But also more freedom of choice. Within the next few years, you may find yourself playing the operating system market. Should you continue to buy the software you've already invested your energy and money in, or is it time to consider something new and different? How will you keep from buying into a dead-end technology? Advance knowledge is the best defense.

Interfaces Get Real

The DOS command-line interface may seem primitive today, but the idea of issuing direct, English-like commands was originally a powerful way of making computing more accessible to professionals. Unfortunately, it was neither intuitive nor flexible, and it eventually gave way to graphical user interfaces (GUIs) like in the Mac OS and Windows. GUIs use representations of real objects—an icon of, say, a trash can to represent a place to discard files—to help users perform tasks.

Continues on p. 5

Three Faces of Windows Microsoft Windows has undergone a major transformation over the years. Top to bottom: Windows 1.03, Windows 3.1, and the forthcoming Windows 4.0 (Chicago).

Figure 2-6:
Another example of a good layout: the authoritative look.

Similar to the authoritative style, the stately style of the layout in Figure 2-7 projects authority, too, but here the authority is quieter, more reserved. You use the stately style when you want to convey experience and judiciousness. As you can see in the layout in Figure 2-7, the stately style shares key elements with the authoritative style: orderly arrangement and conservative fonts (Veljovic for the headlines and Janson Text for the body text). But these fonts have more character — more embellishments and angles — than those in Figure 2-6's layout, and this layout uses other subtleties to mute the authority and replace it with sophistication. One such subtlety is the use of all-capital letters for the first line after each headline. Another is the use of small caps for the byline. Note also how the word *Future* in the logo is lighter than the word *Thinker*. We designed such a logo for this layout to provide contrast in a place where you expect some visual distinction. After all, a logo is essentially a graphic composed at least partly of text, so you'd expect the text to be treated visually. Here we do treat the logo visually — but we do so *quietly*.

Future
Thinker   Vol 12, No. 3

The Shape of Interfaces to Come

BY GALEN GRUMAN

DON'T GET TOO COMFORTABLE. Just as we've settled into the latest graphical interfaces, the world is about to change. Again. We've become more sophisticated, more demanding. We expect our computers to be simpler to use, easier to master, more flexible, and more functional. And software companies are responding: Microsoft is readying Windows 4.0; Apple is preparing Copland, a major upgrade to its System 7 operating system; and IBM continues to retool OS/2 while developing the Workplace OS and collaborating with Apple and Hewlett-Packard on Taligent. And from developers large and small, we'll get metaphors, guides, animated agents, feedback, and environments as likely to overwhelm as to enchant.

What will these options mean for you? Change, to be sure. But also more freedom of choice. Within the next few years, you may find yourself playing the operating system market. Should you continue to buy the software you've already invested your energy and money in, or is it time to consider something new and different? How will you keep from buying into a dead-end technology? Advance knowledge is the best defense.

A Brief History of the Desktop Interface

COMPUTER INTERFACE design has come a long way since the Altair excited the oscilloscope-and-ham-radio set in the late Seventies. Back then, you programmed your computer by switching levers up and down. Soon, Apple, IBM, and others— borrowing an idea from the mainframes of the day— adopted the command-line interface still on display in DOS. It was a huge advance because it allowed users to interact with their PCs via typed-in words rather than dip switches.

A few years later, Apple tapped ideas coming out of Xerox's Palo Alto Research Center, a pinnacle of advanced computer science thinking, to introduce 1984's Macintosh. Because it used a familiar metaphor (the desktop) and a human approach to interacting (pointing, grabbing, and moving), it was embraced as easy to use. Today, the original Mac interface looks cute but woefully limited. Back then, it tantalized and seduced people from all walks of life.

Other companies were exploring similar concepts: Digital Research had GEM (Graphics Environment Manager), VisiCorp offered VisiOn, and Microsoft was brainstorming on Windows. Xerox itself came out with Star, but couldn't translate its brilliant research into a practical, affordable product. VisiOn soon fell by the wayside, but GEM hung on for several years, mainly because Ventura Publisher, then the top PC publishing program, adopted it. The Geoworks interface of 1990 promised a GUI that would work on low-power system *Continues on p. 5*

Interfaces Get Real

THE DOS COMMAND-LINE INTERFACE may seem primitive today, but the idea of issuing direct, English-like commands was originally a powerful way of making computing more accessible to professionals. Unfortunately, it was neither intuitive no<None>r flexible, and it eventually gave way to graphical user interfaces (GUIs) like in the Mac OS and Windows. GUIs use representations of real objects—an icon of, say, a trash can to represent a place to discard files—to help users perform tasks. Windows or the Mac OS use "reaching in" interfaces: They require you to use a device like a mouse or keyboard to manipulate the objects that represent your data and tasks. This type of interface has continued to evolve, first to make the representations more intuitive, and second to make the interactions with them more fluid, through methods like drag and drop.

The newcomer is the "real world" interface, where you are "inside" a highly realistic, often 3-D setting, and the mouse represents you, not just your fingers. This style, popularized by games like Broderbund's Myst, is now entering the mainstream. For instance, the interface in MECA's Managing Your Money is a cartoonish desk, while the initial screens of two on-line services—Sierra *Continues on p. 5*

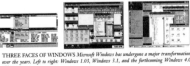

THREE FACES OF WINDOWS *Microsoft Windows has undergone a major transformation over the years. Left to right: Windows 1.03, Windows 3.1, and the forthcoming Windows 4.0 (Chicago).*

Figure 2-7: Yet another example of a good layout: the stately look.

Finally, the layout in Figure 2-8 shows a contemporary look, a jazzier feel. But it's still simple, not like that busy eyesore in Figure 2-4. The logo here has been redesigned so the graphic and text are merged. The drop shadow behind the logo makes the logo readable no matter where on the graphic it falls, and the drop shadow also lifts the logo by making it seem more three-dimensional. (We've rotated the once-plain graphic at the bottom left to strengthen the impression that this layout pops up off the page.) This layout's contemporary look extends to its other features, too. For one thing, its fonts are more modern (Myriad for the headlines and Stone Serif for the body text). We've also jazzed up this layout through its graphics: they have the same stagger that Figure 2-5's layout has — to get the same effect of movement we wanted in Figure 2-5 — and in this layout one graphic has been used instead of a drop cap. Another way we made the layout in Figure 2-8 more contemporary was to use solid black squares in several places as decorations embedded with text — in a byline, as a drop cap, and in a caption). These little blocks add tiny details that stop the eye without drawing too much attention. Finally, the simple arrangement calls greater attention to the graphics and to the headlines. It feels energetic but not busy — and that's the whole point.

Figure 2-8:
Still another
example of
a good
layout: the
contemporary
look.

Best Bets for Fonts

Fonts are in. They're as hip today as sushi was in the '80s — and fonts come in many more varieties than sushi ever did.

Everybody sells fonts. And the hundreds of choices of fonts are all the more confusing because so many fonts look the same. In fact, many fonts *are* the same, the only difference being that the names have been changed to protect the innocent. Why so much similarity between fonts with different names? The explanation is convoluted and boring. Suffice it to say that, somewhere along the way, lawyers got their hands into font distribution. To keep the lawyers away, the government decided you can sell a copy of a font as long as it has a different name and wasn't copied from a computer file (although tracing it from a printout is fine — don't worry; we don't know why, either). What does this false variety mean to you? Confusion, if you try to make sense of it. You see Helvetica and Helios and Swiss and Arial and Switzerland and Helvetia and who knows what else — and they're all the same, or close enough. The lesson: ignore the font's name. Instead, pay attention to what looks good. If you see a font you like in the list of fonts later in this chapter and then see the same font somewhere else only under a different name, go for it!

Technically, as used in desktop publishing the word *font* is incorrect. So, in case you work with an old-fashioned typographer or with a font know-it-all, here's the real definition. What you and we call a font is called a *typeface* in traditional typography: a style of text with a range of variants such as bold and italic. What a traditional typographer means by *font* is one of those variants (called a *face*) at a certain size, such as 12 points. The traditional definition is so precise because newspapers and other printed materials used to be set with pieces of lead for each character. Because each font piece was made by hand and then reproduced in a mold, only a limited selection of faces and sizes were available.

The miracle of computers has changed all that. Computers let you create endless varieties of face and size: no one today thinks of a unit as precise as a certain face at a certain size. Instead, among the computer cognoscenti the word *font* means the file that produces the desired type style. In some cases, you find a separate font file for each face, but in others (such as many TrueType fonts), there's just one font file for all the variants of a typeface. When you see ads exclaiming *100 free fonts!*, though, you can be sure they mean 100 *faces* — and, typically, that 100 faces actually means 25 typefaces because each typeface usually comes in four faces: regular (or medium), italic (or oblique), bold, and bold italic (or bold oblique). If the seller has thrown in decoratives or symbols that don't have such variants, or typefaces such as Helvetica that have hundreds of variants packaged in all sorts of combinations, the actual number of typefaces could be higher or lower than the fonts-divided-by-four calculation indicates.

We use the word *italic* throughout the book, but some fonts use *oblique* to describe almost the same thing. Oblique is the technical term for slanted sans serif text, while italic refers to the slanted *and* curved form of serif text. You could have an oblique serif by slanting it, while italicizing text actually changes the letterforms (for example, look at the roman "a" versus the italic "*a*" — see the difference?). But in these days of desktop publishing, no one (well, hardly anyone) uses the term *oblique* anymore, so we've stopped using it, too.

So what's good? Taste varies. No list of fonts appeals to everyone, just as no selection of ice cream flavors appeals to more than a roomful of people. But if you went down the hall and asked everyone you know what his or her favorite flavors are, you'd hear a lot of flavors mentioned over and over: chocolate, vanilla, cookie dough, vanilla Swiss almond, mint chip, and so on.

The same is true for fonts. Here's our list of basic, popular fonts you should collect for your design work. We've divided them into the basic classes of fonts. Don't worry about having to get all (or even most) of these fonts. We list them here to show you what makes a good collection. You'll no doubt notice, though, that some resemble others. Listing similar fonts alongside each other shows you the variety and subtlety available and helps you choose which variations you prefer.

Headlines

- ✔ Bookman Light *Italic* **Demibold** *Italic*
- ✔ Century Oldstyle *Italic* **Bold** (there is no bold italic face in the original version of this font, although some clones have one)
- ✔ Frutiger Condensed Light *Italic* Medium *Italic* **Bold** *Italic* **Black** *Italic* **Extra** *Italic*
- ✔ Gill Sans *Italic* **Bold** *Italic* Extra Ultra (there are no italic faces for the extra and ultra faces)
- ✔ **Poppl-Laudatio Regular*Italic*Medium *Italic***

Body text

- ✔ Adobe Caslon *Italic* Semibold *Italic* **Bold** *Italic*
- ✔ Caslon 224 Book *Italic* Medium *Italic* **Bold** *Italic*
- ✔ Cheltenham Light *Italic* Book Italic Bold *Italic*
- ✔ Janson Text *Italic* **Bold** *Italic*

- Melior *Italic* **Bold** ***Italic***
- New Baskerville *Italic* **Bold** ***Italic***
- Palatino *Italic* **Bold** ***Italic***

Ads, brochures, and posters

Many of these fonts — often called display fonts — don't have italic faces.

- American Typewriter Condensed Light Medium **Bold**
- Benguiat **Bold**
- **Bodoni Poster**
- COPPERPLATE 29AB
- Eras Light Book Medium **Demibold Bold Ultrabold**
- Eurostile **Bold**
- Futura Light *Italic* Book *Italic* Medium *Italic* **Bold** *Italic* Heavy *Italic* **Extra** *Italic*
- Friz Quadrata **Bold**
- **Helvetica Compressed**
- Kabel Book Medium **Demibold Bold Ultra**
- Lucida Sans *Italic* Demi *Italic*
- **MACHINE MEDIUM BOLD**

Decorative

Most decorative fonts don't have italic faces.

- American Typewriter Light Medium **Bold**
- *Brush Script*
- LITHOS EXTRA LIGHT LIGHT REGULAR **BOLD BLACK**
- *Nuptial Script*
- **STENCIL**

How to Mix and Match Fonts

Someone may have told you that you have to use a sans serif font for your headline and a plain old serif font for your body text. Nonsense! Sans serif in the headline and serif in the text is a typical combination and usually a safe choice, but it's not the only good choice. What you want are fonts that complement each other. They should either look like members of the same family, with only slight variations among them, or they should be distinct but not clashing — opposites that attract.

True Type or PostScript?

Today, most fonts come in either PostScript or TrueType format. Which should you choose? If you're like most people, it doesn't matter. Both formats have fine quality, and both work on either Macs or PCs. (You should be sure to get the Adobe Type Manager program if you use PostScript fonts, though. The Mac's new System 7.5 comes with ATM included, and many programs on PCs and Macs include a free copy of ATM. TrueType support is built into the Mac's System 7.1 and later versions and into the PC's Windows 3.1 and later versions.)

Who needs to worry about a choice between PostScript and TrueType? People who send their files to be printed by a service bureau or commercial printer. The typesetting systems these people use typically support only PostScript, so, if you use such services, you must use PostScript fonts. More and more places can print TrueType fonts, though, with both Macs and PCs capable of converting TrueType to PostScript when printing. However, you may need to send service bureaus or printers your TrueType fonts. Although most service bureaus and commercial printers have large collections of PostScript fonts, they usually have no (or only a few) TrueType fonts. Before you use a bureau or printer, check to see if they can handle TrueType. If they can't, then restrict yourself to PostScript, at least for work you send to outside printers.

Here are some guidelines you should follow to help to make sure that you put the right fonts together:

- ✔ **Don't use a lighter font for a headline than for the body text.**

- ✔ **Don't use an overpowering font for a headline** — especially not for a subhead that's inside the body text. (An exception to the not-too-heavy guideline is when you have a large headline for a major story or element; it's OK to break the rules every once in a while for impact, but don't break it so often that it just looks broken.)

TIP

> ✔ **Don't use heavily embellished fonts** — ones with curlicues and other frills — for either (or both) the body text or headlines — they look cutesy or distracting.

Now, consider some recommended mixes from the list above. Headline fonts are listed first. Suggested fonts for body text follow the word *with*.

✔ Bookman Demibold with Bookman Light, Cheltenham Light, or Palatino. All of these fonts have a rounded-square look that makes them complement each other. Note that Bookman Demibold has greater visual weight, so it's a natural headline font.

✔ Century Oldstyle Bold with Caslon, Cheltenham, Garamond Book, Goudy Oldstyle, or Janson Text. All of these are angular, but the Century Oldstyle Bold is bolder and more striking, so it can fit with the others and stands out at the same time.

✔ Frutiger Condensed Bold with Helvetica, Melior, New Baskerville, News Gothic, Palatino, or Syntax. These fonts contrast in shape but don't clash.

✔ Galliard Bold with Galliard Book, Garamond Book, Melior, Minion, New Century Schoolbook, News Gothic, Stone Serif, or Veljovic Book. These fonts are squarer serifs (or sans serifs, in the case of News Gothic) and complement each other well.

✔ Garamond Bold or Garamond Condensed Bold with Cheltenham Light, Galliard, Helvetica, Garamond Book, New Baskerville, or Syntax. All have subtle differences in their shapes that can work well together.

✔ Gill Sans Bold with Cheltenham Light, Palatino, Garamond Book, Melior, News Gothic, Optima, or Syntax. All have subtle differences in their shapes that can work well together.

✔ Goudy Oldstyle Bold with Caslon, Cheltenham Light, Galliard, Garamond Book, New Baskerville, New Century Schoolbook, Melior, Minion, Palatino, Stone Serif, or Syntax. Goudy's distinctive embellishments cry out for straightforward serifs as its complement.

✔ Helvetica Bold with Cheltenham Light, Minion, New Baskerville, New Century Schoolbook, News Gothic, Melior, Stone Serif, or Veljovic Book. The plainness of Helvetica lets you use an angular serif or slightly condensed sans serif font for the body text.

✔ Minion Semibold or Bold with Cheltenham Light, Galliard, Helvetica, Janson Text, Minion, New Baskerville, News Gothic, Palatino, or Syntax. Minion's strong corners invite a font with a softer shape as its complement. Janson Text is an exception; it is angular enough to complement the squarer Minion without being too different (as Veljovic would be).

✔ New Century Schoolbook Bold with Cheltenham Light, Galliard, Helvetica, Janson Text, New Baskerville, News Gothic, Palatino, Syntax, or Veljovic Book. Minion's strong corners invite a font with a softer or more angular shape as its complement.

✔ News Gothic Bold with Galliard, Garamond, Melior, New Baskerville, News Gothic, or Palatino. The slightly compressed sans serif News Gothic works best with a medium-weight, medium-width, simple font.

✔ Optima Bold with Garamond Book, Melior, New Baskerville, Optima, Palatino, or Stone Serif. The distinct shape of Optima cries out for a sturdy font as its complement.

✔ Poppl-Laudatio Regular or Bold with Caslon, Cheltenham Light, Garamond Book, Minion, Melior, New Century Schoolbook, News Gothic, Optima, Palatino, Stone Serif, Syntax, or Veljovic Book. Any of these fonts has individual character that makes it strong enough to stand up to Poppl-Laudatio's distinct look without clashing.

✔ Stone Serif Semibold or Bold with Galliard, Garamond Book, Goudy Oldstyle, Helvetica, Janson Text, News Gothic, Optima, Stone Serif, Syntax, or Veljovic Book. Like New Century Schoolbook or Minion, Stone Serif tends toward the squarish look, inviting the use of a sans serif or a soft or angular serif.

✔ Syntax Bold with Caslon, Cheltenham, Galliard, Garamond Book, Janson Text, Melior, Minion, New Baskerville, New Century Schoolbook, News Gothic, Optima, Palatino, Syntax, or Veljovic Book. The easy look of Syntax means that many fonts look good with it, especially those that have a squarer or angular look to complement the slight skewed curves of Syntax.

✔ Veljovic Bold with Caslon, Cheltenham, Garamond Book, Helvetica, Melior, Minion, New Baskerville, New Century Schoolbook, News Gothic, Optima, Palatino, Stone Serif, Syntax, or Veljovic Book. The font's distinctive angles make most non-angular fonts compatible with it.

You may have noticed that sometimes we recommend a bolder weight for a headline and then a lighter weight of the same font for the supporting text. That standard bold weight-lighter weight contrast may sound boring, but with some fonts the difference is enough to create visual interest while also producing an eye-pleasing continuity. One effective trick is to use the bold variants as headlines and the lighter versions as body text. You might have, say, Gill Sans Bold main headlines with New Baskerville text and New Baskerville Bold subheads, or sidebars that use Bookman Demibold for the headlines and Bookman Light for the body text. This trick works particularly well for subheads and body text, or for smaller elements like sidebars because it provides continuity (by staying in the same font family) but a sufficiently distinct difference (the difference in weight) to help the reader recognize your headlines as headlines.

The lesson: use consistency in design elements (including the fonts) to reinforce consistency in your editorial message, but also remember to use variation to help your reader navigate that message.

Chapter 3
What to Look for in Graphics

- -

- -

*I*t's easy to treat graphics as an afterthought because they're separate elements in your document that are often supplied by someone else. But you should spend as much time on selecting your graphics as you do on anything else. Good graphics are vital components of an excellent layout, and a bad graphic can make an otherwise nice design look, well, bad.

Keep in mind that taste is a personal issue, and you won't find any clear-cut standard of right or wrong that makes your graphics decisions for you. But, just as is true for layout design and typography, you should follow some basic principles to ensure that you choose good graphics.

What Makes Good Art

Art may be in the eye of beholder, but nonetheless you do have some guidelines for selecting art:

✔ **Professional art is well-composed.** The size, position, and perspective fit the image. An image should look off — such as having part of the image cropped off or being at an odd angle — only if the intent is to look different — jarring, weird, distorted, avant garde. In most cases, the subject should be the main element of attention (near the center and not dwarfed by other elements) and should be fully visible.

✔ **Professional art requires clean lines, sufficient white space (areas not filled with objects), and care to detail.** Again, if the intent is to be jarring or highly stylized (as in a cartoon), an artist breaks these rules. But even in stylized art, you can tell something that's a mishmash (random stuff everywhere) from something that is energetic (many elements to look at), that's crude (more like a kid's drawing that the parents wouldn't post on the refrigerator), or that's sloppy (pieces of elements obviously missing or awkwardly put together).

✔ **Professional art fits the overall image of the publication it's in.** *Rolling Stone* magazine uses a range of adventuresome styles that wouldn't work in *Macworld* or *Architectural Digest*. *Macworld* uses a refined, stylized, and fun look that wouldn't work in *Rolling Stone* or *Architectural Digest*. *Architectural Digest* uses classic, clean, rich styles that wouldn't work in *Rolling Stone* or *Macworld*.

✔ **Professional art conveys its message clearly.** The more messages crammed into the art, the harder it is to understand and the less it will support the text that it is paired with. Think about driving down a commercial street and looking at storefronts. If 58 signs clutter up one store window, you lose track of what kind of store it is or what's on sale, and you keep looking for a store that clearly labels what it's got or what's on sale.

No matter what style you want your publication to have, make sure you think of art in concert with the typography, layout, and words in your publication. They all should work together, reinforcing your basic image and reinforcing the basic content in the publication.

Where to Find Good Art

Good art can come from almost anywhere. If you have a staff or contract artist or photographer (or both) that's one source. But most people have to rely on supplied images, including clip art, photo houses (places that keep libraries of photographs and charge you a fee to republish them), and scanned-in images. When it's time to select art, you have to work with what's available.

The variety can be overwhelming, and the styles can range from simple sketches to elaborate full-color renderings. To give you an idea of what you might find, Figure 3-1 shows 12 different clip art images from a variety of sources. As you can see, some of the images look very rough — the chicken at upper left is a good example — and these look like something you picked up from a clip art book. (That's *not* a compliment!) Such images can look cheap, and that impression of cheapness reflects on your publication. Other clip art images look polished, though — which also reflects on your publication.

Figure 3-1:
A sampler
of clip art
shows the
variety of
styles and
subjects
available.

No matter where you get your images, look for TIFF or Photo CD formats if you're printing to an imagesetter or commercial printer. Programs like QuarkXPress will reliably print color from images in these two formats. For other formats, like PICT, there could be problems because the formats make assumptions about your computer system that may not be true, resulting in mismatched output. (Technically, the indexed color scheme used in these formats gets translated incorrectly to the static color scheme in an imagesetter or color printer. Basically, the colors don't match when translated from computer file to imagesetter or color-printer output. They do in Photo CD and TIFF, though, because these formats essentially use the imagesetter's or printer's color scheme in the first place.)

Avoiding collection overkill

You can find disks and CDs full of clip art and stock photos from many sources. (A stock photo is not a picture of a barnyard animal but an image that a photo house has on stock for rental to publications; it's the photographic version of clip art.) Just look in the back of your favorite computer magazine (like *Macworld* or *PC World*) or at your favorite software dealer. Mail-order catalogs often include them, and more and more art and publishing programs include sample images.

When you shop for clip art and photo collections, be careful. You don't have to worry about poor quality — the materials are usually fine. What you do have to worry about is buying materials you won't use. For example, Corel Corp. (613-728-3733) offers dozens of CDs with 100 photos on each in its Professional Photos series. The $50 CDs are organized thematically — such as Tigers, France, Paris, and Northern California. We've checked out a few of these CDs, and the images are nice-looking and of good quality. But who needs 100 pictures of tigers? For the collections of photos of countries or regions, just what are the chances that you'll find the picture you want of, say, Roman ruins in southern France from the France CD? Not great. Maybe there's one picture, but it doesn't quite have the look you want — that's typical. Getting 100 photos or pieces of clip art for $50 or $25 may seem to be a great deal, but chances are you won't use anywhere near 100 of them. Figure 3-2 shows some of the images available from the Tigers CD — honestly now, how many would you use?

We don't mean to pick on Corel — this problem exists with almost every clip art and stock photo collection, including the ClickArt, 3G Graphics, Metro ImageBase, PicturePak, and other clip-art collections featured in many mail-order catalogs. However, if you use, say, just five images in a 100-image, $50 CD, that's only $10 each, which is still a good deal. Just recognize that one of these CDs and disk collections with tons of images probably will just scratch the surface of your needs, and if you rely on clip art and stock photos, you can expect to pay hundreds of dollars to build a versatile collection from enough titles.

Corel does include with its CDs a nifty viewer utility called CorelMosaic, which lets you browse the contents of a CD containing Photo CD images — even those from other companies. The CDs have both Mac and Windows versions of the viewer; Windows users will also find CorelMosaic in the CorelDraw package.

But we don't want you to think that no photo collection is worth having. One worthwhile collection is the Visual Symbols Sampler from CMCD. This CD is bundled free with Apple's PhotoFlash 2.0 image management and touch-up software. (This software is for Macs only, although the symbols CD can be used by both Macs and PCs. CMCD, of course, sells CDs, too; you can reach them at 415-703-0711.) Other similar collections are available from ColorBytes (303-989-9205) and Digital Media (714-362-5103) for about $100 each.

Figure 3-2:
An oversupply of similar graphics, or a scattershot collection of images that don't give enough selection for a specific need, are the two problems most users of clip art and stock photo collections face.

Why is the CMCD Symbols Sampler different than, say, the Tigers CD? Because the photographed symbols are basic enough that you can use them as part of other artwork. That's the secret to widespread use: the use of images that can integrate with other art and thus appear fresh even when used in more than one place. It's obvious that CMCD had versatility in mind — the photos all have stark backgrounds that are easy to crop out in Photoshop or any other image-editing program (one that can handle the Photo CD format, of course). Figure 3-3 shows some sample images. For example, the Symbols Sampler CD includes an image of a No Smoking sign — you could use that in all sorts of illustrations or just as a stand-alone image. Try that with a picture of a tiger sleeping on a cliff!

If you're going to get into clip art and stock photos, you'd better invest in a CD-ROM drive, since most collections come on CD (those images take space — as much as 4MB each — and who wants to have 20 floppy disks to search through?). A double-speed (300K per second) or faster drive is fine, but don't spend a great deal of money on the newest, fastest ones. They may copy files a little faster, but they're hardly worth two to three times the price of the double-speed drives like Apple's 300i or the CD-ROM drives included in most multimedia PCs.

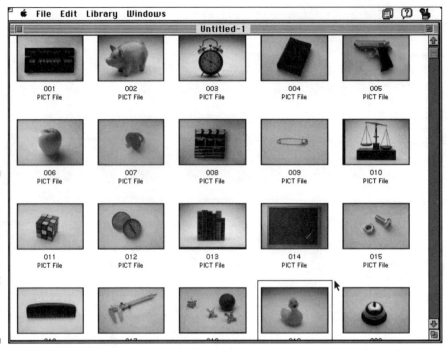

Figure 3-3:
A collection of basic symbols is more versatile than most clip art and stock photo collections.

The world is moving to faster CD-ROM drives — 4X (quadruple-speed) drives in particular. That's making double-speed (2X) drives real cheap. It's also making NEC's triple-speed drives (3X) drives cheap, as NEC tries to clear out inventory for its 4X models. (Only NEC makes a 3X drive.) The problem is, many programs have trouble reliably reading files from the 3X drives — including QuarkXPress. Typically what happens is that the drive and computer get confused about what the current status is, so the drive thinks it's waiting for the computer to ask for more (such as when you're copying a series of files or installing a program) and the computer thinks the drive is not available to give it more data. The lesson: Go really cheap and get a 2X drive, or pay the price for a 4X drive.

In addition to CD and disk collections, you can get stock photos from stock photo houses, which are companies that keep huge inventories of photos, such as the Bettman Archives. Note that these companies charge for each use of an image: if you use an image three times, you pay for it three times. That holds true even if you alter the image or combine it with other images. CD and disk collections give you unlimited use per image, but not the stock photo houses. Make sure that you know what the usage rules and costs are before you publish any images from a photo house. Also, see if the photo house offers the image in electronic format, such as TIFF, to save you the effort of scanning in the photo from a print.

Checking out on-line services

You also can find clip art and stock photos — both single images and collections — on on-line services and bulletin board services (BBSs). The quality of these photos varies widely, of course, based on the skills of their creator.

Some of the images are offered as shareware — if you like the images, you send in a fee; if you don't, you don't. Others are available as freeware — a gift from someone who needs to share their talents with the world. Whether you frequent CompuServe, America Online, or some other service, look in forums devoted to desktop publishing and art. Each service has an index of forums available.

Figures 3-4 and 3-5 show some contents of the Desktop Publishing Forum (GO DTPFORUM) on CompuServe — a great forum for all sorts of publishing utilities, fonts, and artwork. Quark even posts updates to QuarkXPress and free XTensions and scripts here (for more on Quark's updates, see Chapter 22). This forum is our favorite place to find Quark- and publishing-related files.

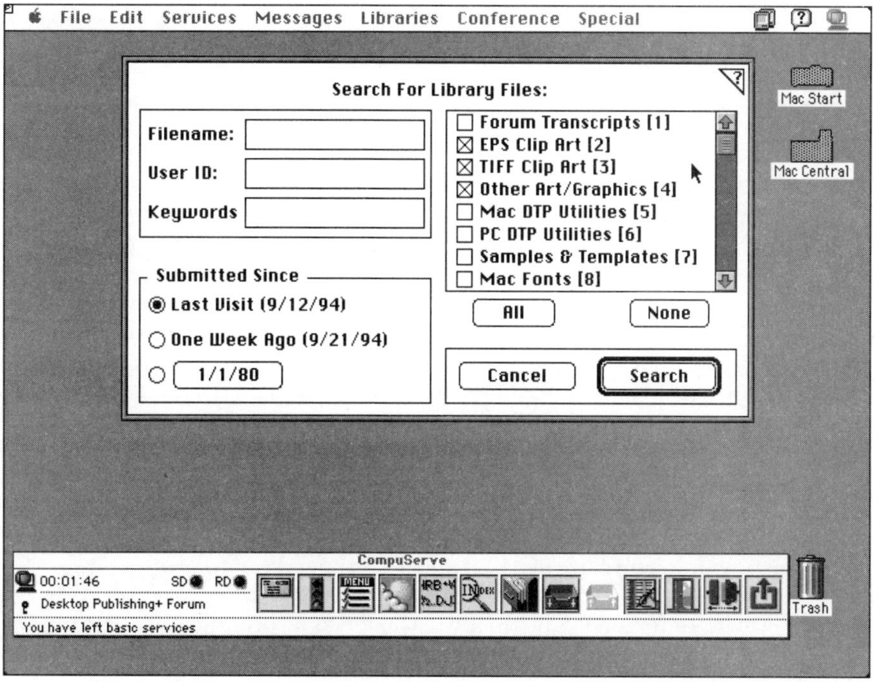

Figure 3-4:
On-line services typically have a forum dedicated to desktop publishing, such as CompuServe's Desktop Publishing Forum, that is a good place to find clip art and stock photos.

```
 File   Edit   Services   Messages   Libraries   Conference   Special

                    Search For Library Files:

    Filename: [          ]     □ Forum Transcripts [1]
                               ⊠ EPS Clip Art [2]
    User ID:  [          ]     ⊠ TIFF Clip Art [3]
                               ⊠ Other Art/Graphics [4]
    Keywords  [          ]     □ Mac DTP Utilities [5]
                               □ PC DTP Utilities [6]
                               □ Samples & Templates [7]
    ┌─ Submitted Since ─┐      □ Mac Fonts [8]
    ● Last Uisit (9/12/94)
                               [  All  ]   [  None  ]
    ○ One Week Ago (9/21/94)
    ○ [  1/1/80  ]             [ Cancel ]  [ Search ]

                          CompuServe
 00:01:46   SD● RD●
 Desktop Publishing+ Forum
 You have left basic services
```

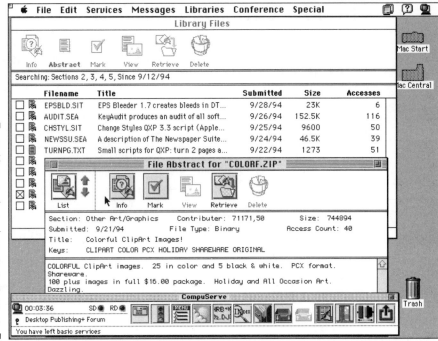

Figure 3-5:
You can get information about a specific file — before downloading it — to help you decide whether to pay for the download time.

Notice how you can get information on a file before you download it; all major on-line services and BBSs offer this capability. Knowing ahead of time what's on a file won't guarantee you'll like what you get after you download it, but it will help you narrow your choices to a reasonable set. Remember: Even if the material is free, you still pay for the download time, which can cost anywhere from a few dollars to $20 if you're downloading a few large files. Make sure you use a fast modem — at least 9600 bits per second — when downloading. Otherwise, you might as well go to the store and buy disks or CDs with the art you want; they'll often be cheaper that way compared to downloading at, say, 2400 bps. (Fast modems — those that communicate at 9600 bps or 14,400 bps — are cheap these days: just $120 or so, so don't stick with a slow modem for fear of the cost of speeding up. But don't worry yet about the more expensive 28,800 bps — also called V.34 — modems; the commercial services don't run that fast yet, so you can't use that maximum speed very often.)

It's unfortunate, but in the CD business, erotic and pornographic titles sell more than anything else. And, like it or not, these types of images are fairly popular on on-line services, too. If you're looking for these kinds images, don't expect to find them on services such as CompuServe or America Online; they remove such images. You'll have to call one of those private BBSs listed in your local computer magazine.

Of course, many of these BBSs also often have artwork that has nothing to do with sex, and they can be a great source for local artwork not widely available. Using high-quality artwork from a source not widely distributed can help ensure that the images you use in your publications aren't used by someone else. Imagine how embarrassed you would be if you and a competitor used the same image in your publications.

Scanning in photos and images

A treasure trove of images could be the photos you and your friends have taken. Vacation pictures, pictures of buildings or monuments, pictures of friends (perhaps at a picnic or at work), pictures of a job site — all may depict what you want to illustrate in your publication.

If you use a picture of a person for publication, though, make sure that you get permission first. While you don't need to do so for pictures of crowds, you should extend this courtesy when a person (or several people) are the clear focus of the image. After all, how would you feel if you were perusing a magazine and unexpectedly saw a picture of yourself?

If you have a scanner, you can convert photos to TIFF files and import them into QuarkXPress. Not everyone's photos are good enough to reproduce, but you'd be surprised how acceptable many amateurs' photos are. If you're producing mass-market magazines like *Macworld*, you should rely on professional photographers and high-end scanners. But the rest of us using laser printers or even imagesetter output for gray-scale newsletters will find that a decent flat-bed scanner and a decent 4-inch by 6-inch color print can easily fill the bill.

Of course, you also can scan in other artwork, including pencil sketches (which you or an artistically inclined colleague might produce) and images from a printed clip-art collection.

Don't scan in images or drawings published elsewhere — that's theft of copyright. To steer clear of copyright infringements, the images you print need to fall into one of three categories:

- ✔ **Original:** Created by you or someone you employ. Note that a freelancer doesn't count as an employee; the "someone you employ" has to be someone on staff (on payroll), which legally makes the art a "work for hire" — legalspeak for "I pay your salary, so I own your work."

- ✔ **Publicly available:** Old enough that the copyright has expired (usually 75 years after it was created or 50 years after the creator has died), or created by an agency of the federal government (such as NASA's space photos — we paid for them, so we can use them).

✔ **Licensed (a.k.a. commissioned):** Sold to you either for one-time use (such as from a stock photo house or freelance artist) or for unlimited use (such as from a stock photo or clip art collection). If someone offers you free use, get it in writing in case there's a dispute later.

An advantage to scanning in images, whether photos or art, is that you then can edit or modify the scanned-in images with an image-editing tool like Adobe Photoshop, Fractal Design Painter, or (on Windows only) Aldus PhotoStyler. For example, you might take a color photograph or pencil sketch, convert it to gray scale, and then use color to highlight certain elements. Or you might make a collage from several images.

Working with a professional

Whether you use a freelancer once a year or once a week, follow these guidelines to get the best results:

✔ Examine portfolios from several artists and see what styles they use. Pick an artist whose style matches the style you want for the piece of art and for your publication as a whole.

✔ Communicate clearly the idea you want the graphic or photo to convey. And don't confuse that with telling the artist what to do. Here, for example, is an appropriate comment: "The goal of the illustration is to convey the idea of limitless speed." And here is an *in*appropriate comment: "The illustration should show a racecar way ahead of the competition." Give the artist the goal of the image and let him or her suggest how that goal may be conveyed. Certainly, you should approve the concept before the artist bases an entire graphic on it, but don't take over the work yourself. That's like writing a story for the author rather than explaining what story you're seeking.

✔ Get several sketch proposals to look at before authorizing the artist or photographer to do the final work. Make sure that you and the artist are clear on the final goal. (For photography, a sketch may be difficult. In that case, in the assignment letter, clarify the tone you want in the photos, such as "close-up of person, emphasizing an angry look" or "unusual angle that makes the subject look mysterious.")

✔ For photography, review the outtakes — the entire series of images that the photographer shot — and settle on one or two for the photographer to make prints of.

Part II
Setting Up Your Document

The 5th Wave   **By Rich Tennant**

"THIS LAVA DISPLAY JERRY DEVELOPED REALLY MAKES OUR DOCUMENTS COME ALIVE."

In this part ...

To use QuarkXPress or any publishing tool, you first need to know what you want to use it for — what kind of document are you trying to create? The four chapters in this part will bring you through the basics of creating a layout, including how to prepare the text and graphics you will use in your documents. This creation work may seem tedious or overwhelming at first, but relax and bear with it. If you learn nothing more than the techniques in this part, you'll know the basics of QuarkXPress and be able to create many business documents. (Of course, we hope you'll learn the techniques in the rest of the book. If you do, you'll be a QuarkXPress dummy no more!)

Chapter 4
All about Boxes

••

In This Chapter

▶ How to create text boxes and picture boxes

▶ Why Master Pages are so helpful

▶ Linking text boxes together

▶ Special effects with boxes

••

*L*et's face it: when you think of a flat piece of paper with words and pictures on it, you don't intuitively know that those words and pictures are held in boxes, right? Not if you're like most people we know. And the boxes we're talking about now are not your typical supermarket boxes. They bear no resemblance to the corrugated cardboard containers that you pack your vintage record albums in; they would never be found in dank, dusty basements, filled to the brim with bric-a-brac or old clothes. In fact, they are unlike any three-dimensional boxes that you may be familiar with. About the only way QuarkXPress boxes are similar to those you know is that they also hold stuff — but the stuff is two-dimensional text and pictures.

Surprised? You're not alone. It never fails to amaze brand-new QuarkXPress users that just about everything on a page produced in this program fits into a box. QuarkXPress boxes may not be able to hold a great deal of memorabilia, but they are pretty powerful just the same. They serve as the placeholders for the text and pictures you use to build a page. These boxes not only define the layout of a page by controlling the size and placement of pictures, but they also delineate the white space between an illustration and its caption, and they identify the portion of a page's real estate that is covered with words.

Yes, these boxes do a lot. And if you spend any time at all working with QuarkXPress, you'll get comfortable with text and picture boxes in no time flat.

Box Basics

Composing a page in QuarkXPress involves arranging and rearranging the program's basic building blocks, which include *text boxes* that hold text and *picture boxes* that hold graphics. Once you create text and picture boxes, you can fill them with their appropriate contents. (Don't worry too much about getting the two types of boxes mixed up since QuarkXPress won't let you accidentally put text inside a picture box, or a picture inside a text box.) You also can perform an amazing number of changes on the boxes, such as moving them, changing their size, adding color, rotating them, and much more.

Tools to use

In Chapter 1, we show you the QuarkXPress Tool palette. The fact that the Tool palette contains five tools dedicated to boxes emphasizes how important boxes are to page design in QuarkXPress.

You use the Tool palette to draw text boxes. You also can have QuarkXPress create text boxes for you automatically, and we tell you how to do that a little later on in this chapter. After you have a text box, you can enter text directly into it by typing on your computer's keyboard, or you can import text from a word processor file.

Below the Text Box tool in the Tool palette, you find the remaining four box tools — all dedicated to drawing picture boxes. But you can't ask QuarkXPress to draw picture boxes for you automatically because the program isn't designed to work that way. So, if you want to have a picture on a page, you need to pick one of the picture box tools (Rectangle, Rounded Rectangle, Oval, or Polygon) to draw it.

Active and inactive boxes

Let's say you've drawn a text box or a picture box. After looking at it, you decide it's too small, and it's also too high on the page. What to do? Do you scrap the box and start over, hoping for better luck the next time you create it? No, you know that deleting the box and drawing it again takes too long, plus (to be honest about it) it would mean that you're chickening out. Be brave! You can fix that box, and we'll show you how later on in this chapter. But before you can do the first thing to the box, you have to *activate* it.

As we tell you in Chapter 1, *selecting* an item is the same as activating it. Before you can make changes to a text box or picture box in QuarkXPress, you must select it or activate it so that the program can access it to make the changes you want.

Figure 4-1 shows two boxes. The box on the left is inactive, or unselected. The box on the right is active, or selected. Activating the box means that you can modify it in many ways. As you can see, it's pretty easy to tell when a box is active because it has little black boxes, or *sizing handles* on its sides and corners.

Figure 4-1:
The sizing
handles on
the box on
the right
show that it
is active.

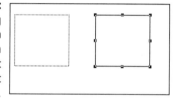

Building Text Boxes

To position text on a page with QuarkXPress, use a text box. You can create a text box by "drawing" a manual text box or by having the program make a text box for you—automatically.

Manual text boxes are nice when you want to draw a box of any size, watch the box develop on screen as you draw it, and place it in any spot on the page. Later, you can change things about the box, such as the number of columns it has and the width of its margins.

In Chapter 5, we show you how to go about filling a text box with text. But before we get there, you need to know how to create a manual text box. It's easy. Just follow these steps.

1. **Have your QuarkXPress document open to the page where you want to draw the text box.**

2. **Select the Text Box tool (in case you've forgotten it already, it's the tool in the Tool palette that looks like a little rectangle with a capital A in its center).**

   Notice that when you use the mouse to move the pointer onto the document page, the pointer changes to look like a crosshair.

3. **Press the mouse button, holding the button down as you draw the text box to the size you want it to be.**

   If you want the text box to be a perfect square, hold down the Shift key while you are drawing the box.

4. **Release the mouse button.**

Now, step back and admire your work. Is the box in the size and location you want it to be? If not, the easiest way to adjust it is to change values in the Measurements palette. (If you are looking at your screen right now and can't find the Measurements palette, try displaying it by choosing View➪Show Measurements.) The X and Y numbers in the Measurements palette show you where the box is on the page. The W and H numbers in the palette show you the width and height of the box. You can change any of these numbers by selecting the Content tool, positioning the pointer at the appropriate spot in the Measurements palette, and typing in a new number. Simple as that.

Taming the wild text box

You probably know at least one person who can be called a control freak. You know — the friend who goes berserk when he finds that a piece of paper on his desk is rotated at an angle instead of being perfectly aligned with the pencil box; the hostess who follows you around her house, carrying a towel to wipe everything you've touched; or the boss who insists on reading every word you write and knowing where you are each minute of the day.

Hey, being a control freak usually is not considered socially acceptable. But that all changes when you get into desktop publishing. The ability to make things perfect soon takes over, and you find yourself spending hours tweaking every element on the page.

Relax. When you're building a page, it's perfectly okay to be a control freak. Honestly, half the fun of using QuarkXPress is the unbelievable amount of control it gives you over everything in a page layout.

Text boxes are one of the things over which you have complete control when you use QuarkXPress. The tool you use to control a text box is the Text Box Specifications dialog box (yes, it really is as impressive as its name implies!).

You can use the Text Box Specifications dialog box any time after you've created a text box. Here's how you make this dialog box appear:

1. **Make sure that the text box is active.**

   You can activate it with either the Content tool or the Item tool.

2. **Choose Item⇨Modify to display the Text Box Specifications dialog box, shown in Figure 4-2 or use ⌘-M as a shortcut to display the dialog box.**

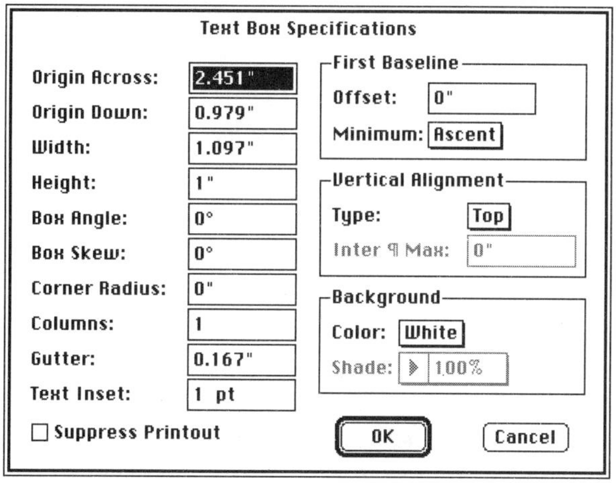

Figure 4-2:
The Text
Box Speci-
fications
dialog box.

Text Box Specifications	
Origin Across: `2.451"`	┌─ First Baseline ─
Origin Down: `0.979"`	Offset: `0"`
Width: `1.097"`	Minimum: `Ascent`
Height: `1"`	┌─ Vertical Alignment ─
Box Angle: `0°`	Type: `Top`
Box Skew: `0°`	Inter ¶ Max: `0"`
Corner Radius: `0"`	┌─ Background ─
Columns: `1`	Color: `White`
Gutter: `0.167"`	Shade: ▶ `100%`
Text Inset: `1 pt`	
☐ Suppress Printout	(OK) (Cancel)

As you can see by looking at Figure 4-2, the Text Box Specifications dialog box lets you tweak a text box to your heart's content. By entering values in the box's fields, you determine the following aspects of a text box:

- ✔ The size and position on the page
- ✔ The angle of the box's rotation
- ✔ The positioning of the text inside the text box (is it slanted? or skewed?)
- ✔ The number of columns of text that will appear within the text box, and the width of the *gutter* (the space between columns)
- ✔ The distance between the edges of the box and the text (this aspect is known as *text inset*). The program's default is one point, which works well most of the time.

  The text inset exists so that if your text box has a frame, the frame won't overprint the text — at least it won't if the inset is more than the frame width. You can get around this by having QuarkXPress put frames on the outside of the box, which you do by setting Framing to Outside in the General Preferences dialog box (Edit⇨Preferences⇨General).

- ✔ The characteristics of the first baseline

⤷ The alignment — or lack of alignment — in the text within the box

⤷ The color and shade, if any, of the text box's background

Most of the text box characteristics that you control via the Text Box Specifications dialog box also can be set by selecting or entering values in the Measurements palette. In fact, users with a bit of practice under their belts almost always prefer the convenience of the palette method.

We could give you some specific instructions on values to enter in the Text Box Specifications dialog box, but we aren't going to do it. It's not that we're being lazy; it's just that the best way to make yourself comfortable with settings for text boxes is to experiment on your own with a variety of settings. Take a few minutes to create some text boxes and then fiddle with them. Be adventuresome: try to use both the Text Box Specifications dialog box and the Measurements palette and see which one you end up liking best.

Creating irregular text boxes

Although QuarkXPress only offers one Text Box tool shape — a rectangle — you can shape a text box into an irregular shape pretty easily. Be careful, though. If you create a document full of irregularly-shaped text boxes, it can have a visual effect that can at best be described as "hodge-podge." In other words, don't make your document ugly just because you can, okay?

Here's how to create a polygon text box:

1. **Select the text box you want to change.**

2. **Choose Item⇨Box Shape to choose the new shape.**

3. **If you chose the polygon shape, use Item⇨Reshape to add or delete points.**

⤷ To move control points or line segments, hold the Shift key and — with the chevron pointer that appears — select the point or line segment that you want to move.

⤷ To add new control points, hold down the ⌘ key and select the point where you want the control point to appear.

⤷ To delete a control point, hold down the ⌘ key as you move the mouse over the control point and click the mouse button to delete it.

Making it automatic

Howie is a desktop publisher. He likes to tinker with page layout to see exactly how everything works. He has no problem spending hours in front of the computer, getting all his layout ducks in a row, luxuriating in the depth and breadth of controls offered by QuarkXPress.

Pamela, on the other hand, is always rushed. In her job, she's responsible for producing two newsletters every week. She works at speed, collecting QuarkXPress shortcuts the way some kids collect baseball cards.

Howie is perfectly comfortable with manually creating each and every text box that appears in his document. Pamela, who would be driven crazy at the thought of such a time-consuming approach, has found a way to have QuarkXPress automatically and precisely create the text boxes for her, page by page. She does this by using the program's Automatic Text Box feature each time she creates a document.

Let's say that Pamela is going to create a two-page flyer, and she wants the text to appear on each page in two columns. She starts a new document (File⇨New Document, or ⌘-N), which causes the New Document dialog box to appear (see Figure 4-3). In the Column Guides area, she specifies 2 columns. She also makes sure a check mark appears in the Automatic Text Box box. That's all she has to do; QuarkXPress takes care of the rest, drawing two columns of text boxes on each page in the document.

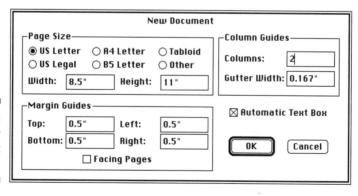

Figure 4-3:
The New
Document
dialog box.

When Automatic Text Box is checked, the text box on the beginning master page will automatically flow text to other pages as you insert them into the document. If you don't check Automatic Text Box, you will need to draw text boxes before you place text into them using the File⇨Get Text command (or by pressing ⌘-E).

One of the nifty things about choosing Automatic Text Box when you create a document is that, as text flows in from an external word processing program, QuarkXPress automatically adds as many pages as necessary to accommodate the imported text.

Learning to use Master Pages

So you're beginning to figure out that QuarkXPress gives you a great deal of flexibility as you design pages. In fact, if you want to, you can create a different-looking page each and every time. But is this always such a good idea? Simply because it's possible, should each page have an entirely different look? Or should page 3 of your document look like it may bear some resemblance to page 10?

We definitely lean toward the latter. Hey, we're all for wild and crazy page layout, but there's something to be said for consistency, too. And one of the best ways to keep your pages visually related to each other is to use Master Pages.

A Master Page holds the parts of a page that you want repeated on other pages. For example, you may want a thin rule to appear across the top of each page. Or you may want page numbers at the bottom of your center column of text. Or you may want a small graphic to appear in the top corner of each right-hand page. Accomplishing these kinds of repeating design elements is easy if you use Master Pages. What's more, QuarkXPress lets you create a whopping 127 *pairs* of Master Pages for each document. (Impressed? You should be. Aldus PageMaker, a strong competitor of QuarkXPress, lets you have only one pair of master pages.)

As soon as you've created a new document, it's a good idea to set up Master Pages for it. To set up Master Pages, you need to leave the document mode and change to the Master Page mode. To display the Master Page so that you can do things to it that will repeat on other pages, choose Page⇨Display⇨Master. Then, any change you make or item you create on the Master Page will apply to all similar pages (as in all right-hand or all left-hand pages) in the document.

Here are a couple of Master Page activities that you can practice as you become familiar with this powerful feature:

- **View a document's Master Pages** by choosing View⇨Show Document Layout. This displays the Document Layout palette, which has icons of each master page. Double-click on the icon of the Master Page you want to view.

- **Rearrange a document's Master Pages** by choosing View⇨Show Document Layout and then clicking and dragging the Master Pages into their desired position.

- **Apply a Master Page** by first selecting the page icons of the document pages to which you want to apply the master page format; then hold down the Option key as you click on the Master Page icon.

Linking and unlinking text boxes

When text boxes are drawn manually — instead of letting QuarkXPress create them automatically — you need to link the boxes together if you want to have the text from one text box "flow" into another text box.

Such a case is not the only time you might want to link two text boxes together. Another common instance when you want boxes to be connected is when, for example, you have a text box on page 2 of your document, but you want the story to continue on page 4. How do you make this "jump" (or "continued on" instance) happen? By linking the two boxes together.

An easy way to remember linking in QuarkXPress is to think of text boxes as links in a chain, just like a metal chain that has links connected to other links. The only difference is that, in QuarkXPress, you are linking boxes that hold text instead of links of metal.

When should you link text boxes together? You can link boxes any time. But we find it easier to do the linking before you fill the boxes with text. Here's how you link text boxes together:

1. **Open the document to the page that contains the first text box that you want in the linked chain of text boxes.**

2. **Click the Linking tool (it's the second tool from the bottom of the Tool palette, and it looks like a piece of chain) to select it.**

3. **Position the pointer anywhere inside the text box that you are going to have as the first box in the chain.**

   Notice that the pointer now changes to look like a chain link.

4. **Click the mouse button.**

   Notice that the text box has a moving dashed line around it, which tells you that this is the start of the link.

5. **Go to the page that contains the text box that will be the next box in the chain.**

   To get to that page, choose Page⇨Go to, or press ⌘-J.

6. **Position the pointer in the next text box that you want in the chain and click the mouse button.**

   The second text box is now linked to the first. The text will flow from the first text box in the linked chain to the second, even if the text boxes are separated by several pages. The text flow will continue on to any others in the text chain.

7. Repeat Steps 2 through 6 until all the text boxes you want in the chain are linked.

How do you know if two text boxes are linked together? It's easy. Simply select the Linking tool and look for the large, gray arrows that show you the flow of text from one text box to another. Figure 4-4 shows what this linking arrow looks like.

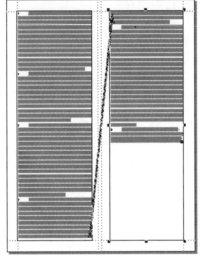

Figure 4-4:
The arrow
shows that
the two text
boxes on
the page are
linked
together.

As nice as it is to be able to link text boxes together, it's also nice to be able to change your mind about how the text does or doesn't flow. This means that you need to be able to unlink two linked text boxes. Here's how:

1. Open the document to the page that has the first text box in the chain that you want to unlink.

2. Click the Unlinking tool (it's the bottom-most tool on the Tool palette) to select it.

3. Position the pointer in the first text box in the chain and click the mouse button.

4. Go to the page that has the second box in the chain (by choosing Page⇨Go to, or by pressing ⌘-J).

5. Position the pointer inside the next text box in the chain. Then hold down the Shift key while you click the mouse button.

This step unlinks the text box from the first text box.

Holding down the Shift key helps to keep you from accidentally unlinking other text boxes that you don't want to unlink.

6. **To unlink additional text boxes, repeat Steps 2 through 5.**

As you spend more time with QuarkXPress, you'll find it very helpful to link boxes and to unlink them, depending on the circumstances.

Boxes for Pictures, Too

Now that you know how to create text boxes, you've probably already made a thousand or two of them (or maybe just five or six). But when you look at a page with nothing but text boxes on it, you start to realize that it looks, well, kind of *boring*. What you need are some pictures.

Pictures, or graphics, do more than just add visual interest to a page. A well-designed graphic actually can convey more information than a block of text can. As the old saying goes, "A picture is worth a thousand words," and a photo, drawing, or chart truly can convey some very meaningful ideas.

Okay, you're convinced. It's time to start adding some pictures to the page, and you do this by creating picture boxes and filling them with pictures.

First, you need to select one of the four picture box tools from the Tool palette. The choices for picture box tools are based on shape (your choices include a rectangle, a rounded-corner rectangle, an oval, and a polygon). Now you're ready to draw a picture box, like this:

1. **Open the document to the page on which you want to draw the picture box.**

2. **With the picture box tool of your choice, position the crosshair pointer at the location where you want one of the corners of the picture box to appear.**

3. **Press and hold down the mouse button and drag the mouse to shape the picture box.**

✔ If you are drawing a polygon picture box, press the mouse button at the starting point of the polygon and then release it. Move the mouse to the next point on the polygon and press the mouse button again. Repeat this process until you complete the polygon by ending at the same point where you began.

✔ To draw a picture box that is perfectly square, use the Rectangle Picture Box tool and hold down the Shift key as you draw the box.

Setting picture box specifications

Just as it does with text boxes, QuarkXPress lets you be pretty darned picky about every part of a picture box. To establish a bunch of parameters for your picture box, use the Picture Box Specifications dialog box, which is shown in Figure 4-5. This dialog box lets you size and position a picture box precisely, rotate it, scale it, skew (slant) it, and add color to its background. You also can use this dialog box to position or crop an image inside the picture box that holds it.

If you use the Picture Box Specifications dialog box to change a picture box before a graphic is imported into it, the settings you pick will apply to the imported graphic. But if for some reason you reimport the graphic into the picture box, the settings will be lost.

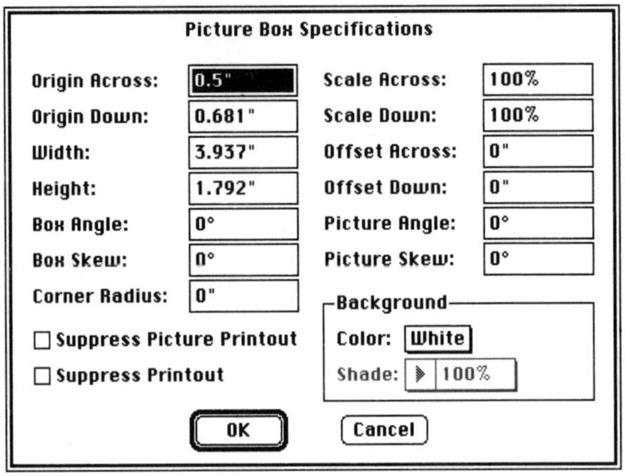

Figure 4-5:
The Picture Box Specifications dialog box.

Picture Box Specifications

Origin Across:	0.5"	Scale Across:	100%
Origin Down:	0.681"	Scale Down:	100%
Width:	3.937"	Offset Across:	0"
Height:	1.792"	Offset Down:	0"
Box Angle:	0°	Picture Angle:	0°
Box Skew:	0°	Picture Skew:	0°
Corner Radius:	0"		

☐ Suppress Picture Printout
☐ Suppress Printout

Background
Color: White
Shade: ▶ 100%

[OK]　[Cancel]

Changing the size and position of a picture box

After you've drawn a picture box, you still can tweak it in many ways. In the Measurements palette, you can change the size of the box by entering different W (width) and H (height) values, and you can change the position of the box by entering different X (vertical) and Y (horizontal) coordinates. You can make these same changes to a polygon picture box, but you can't change the individual line segments that make up the polygon picture box.

Actually, QuarkXPress gives you a rich selection of ways to make changes to a picture box. For example, you can change the size and position of a picture box in one of three ways:

- **First way:** In the Picture Box Specifications dialog box (Item⇨Modify), enter values in the Origin Across and Origin Down fields to control the position of the box, and enter values in the Width and Height fields of the dialog box to control the size of the box. Although it works fine, we aren't real crazy about this method because the dialog box blocks your view of what's happening to the picture box as a result of the new values you're entering.

- **Second way:** In the Measurements palette, enter different values into the X and Y fields to position the picture box and different values into the W and H fields to resize the box. This is our favorite method because it allows you to see the results of your work as it happens.

- **Third way:** Use the Item tool to drag the box into position. Use the same tool to grab the handles of the box to resize it.

Holding down the Option and Shift keys while you resize a box causes both the box and the graphic to resize proportionately.

Creating odd shapes

On occasion, you may want to import a graphic into a non-rectangular, or "polygon" picture box. This technique is one of many that you can use to add visual interest to a page. But, as with polygon text boxes, we recommend that you keep the use of this trick to a minimum. More than that — we recommend that you do *not* use polygon boxes unless you are using them for a well-reasoned and well-planned effect.

Okay, okay, you've heard the lecture. Now, how exactly *do* you create a polygon picture box? Here's how:

1. **Open the document to the page where you want the polygon picture box to appear and click on the Polygon Picture Box tool.**

   When you move the cursor over the page, it now looks like a crosshair.

2. **Place the crosshair pointer at the location where you want to start drawing the polygon box.**

3. **Press the mouse button and then release it.**

4. **Using the mouse, move the pointer to the next point on the polygon (you'll see a line extend from where you started to the current mouse position) and press the mouse button again.** (Note that a polygon picture box must have at least three sides.)

   Because a polygon picture box must be closed, end the drawing of the polygon at the place where you began.

5. **Click the mouse button to close the polygon.**

Figure 4-6 shows a polygon picture box on the left and, on the right, a copy of the box filled with an imported picture file.

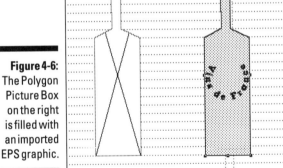

Figure 4-6:
The Polygon
Picture Box
on the right
is filled with
an imported
EPS graphic.

Pouring in the picture

After you've drawn a picture box, you're ready to fill it with a picture. Here are the steps you should follow to do this:

1. **Open the document to the page that holds the picture box that you want to fill with a picture, and click on the picture box to activate it.**

2. **Click on the Content tool.**

3. **Choose File⇨Get Picture (or press ⌘-E).**

4. **Use the controls in the dialog box to locate the graphic file you want to bring into the picture box.**

5. **After you locate the graphic file, choose OK.**

    The graphic appears in the picture box.

After the picture box is filled with the imported graphic, chances are good that you'll want to make some changes to the graphic to make it fit the picture box. Here are some pointers for how to change a graphic:

✔ **To center the graphic in the picture box,** press ⌘-Shift-M.

✔ **To fit the graphic to the box's dimensions,** press ⌘-Shift-F. (Note that this will distort the graphic, if necessary, to fit it into the shape of the picture box.)

✔ **To fit the graphic to the box while maintaining the basic essence of the width and height of the graphic, or its *aspect ratio*,** press ⌘-Shift-Option-F. When you use this command, QuarkXPress fits the graphic the best it can but leaves white space in areas of the picture box not covered by the graphic.

Tricky Effects

No self-respecting desktop publisher would be without a bag of layout tricks. You could say that they are as necessary as flies to a frog, slop to a hog, or biscuits to a dog. What we are trying to say is that it's definitely worth your while to learn how to do tricky effects with the text and picture boxes created in QuarkXPress. We should also point out that, in QuarkXPress, such tricky effects aren't just a bunch of pointless parlor tricks.

Running around

One of the features of QuarkXPress that — early on — distinguished it from its various competitors was its flexible runaround capability. A *runaround* is an area in a page's layout where you don't want text to flow. Text runaround lets you place text around an active item, fitting the text around the contours of the item.

To specify how text runaround works, you use the Runaround Specifications dialog box. To get this dialog box to display, you select the box or line that you want text to run around, and then choose Item⇨Runaround (or ⌘-T). The Runaround Specifications dialog box is shown in Figure 4-7.

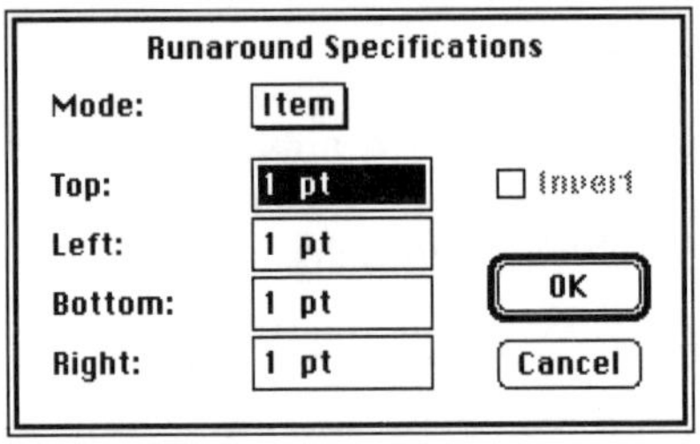

Figure 4-7:
The Runaround Speci-fications dialog box.

```
        Runaround Specifications

Mode:      │Item│

Top:      │ 1 pt │        □ Invert

Left:     │ 1 pt │
                          ┌─────────┐
Bottom:   │ 1 pt │        │   OK    │
                          └─────────┘
Right:    │ 1 pt │        ( Cancel )
```

QuarkXPress gives you four runaround options; you choose an option by selecting from the Mode list in the Runaround Specifications dialog box. Here are the choices of modes:

✔ **None:** When you select this mode, QuarkXPress causes the text behind the active item to flow normally within the text box, as if there were no runaround item there. Figure 4-8 shows the overprinting of text that happens when you choose None.

✔ **Item:** Figure 4-9 shows the effect of Item runaround. Note that you can determine how far away from the box the text will flow by entering values in the Top, Left, Bottom, and Right fields of the Runaround Specifications dialog box. In our example, we set this amount to be 6 points.

✔ **Auto Image:** When you select this mode, QuarkXPress automatically figures out the shape of the image in the picture box (note that Auto Image does not apply to text boxes), and flows text around the picture box. Enter a value in the Text Outset field of the Runaround Specifications dialog box to control the distance between the text and the item that is being run around. In our example in Figure 4-10, we set Text Outset at 6 points.

✔ **Manual Image:** Like Auto Image, this mode automatically draws a polygon around the active item. Manual Image then lets you modify the shape of the polygon by clicking and dragging the black handles on the points of the polygon. Note that this mode also only applies to picture boxes.

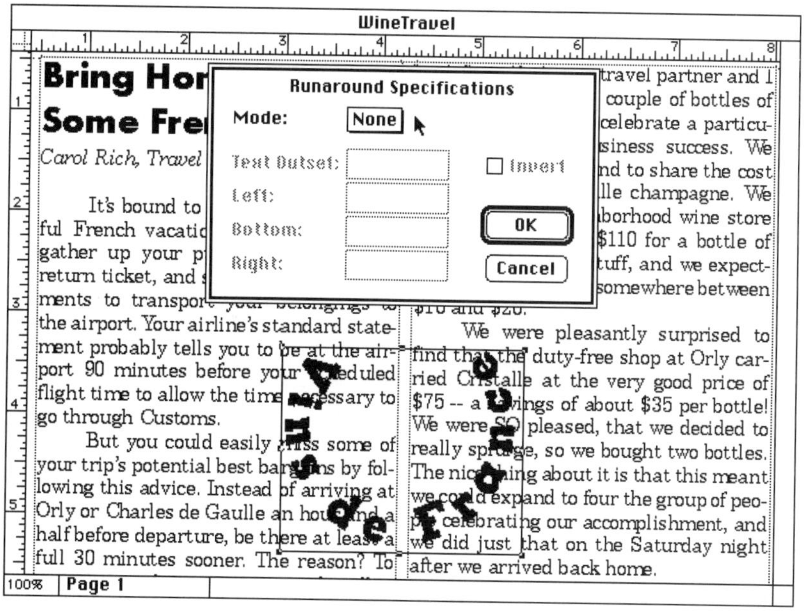

Figure 4-8:
Selecting
None as the
Mode
creates this
overprint.

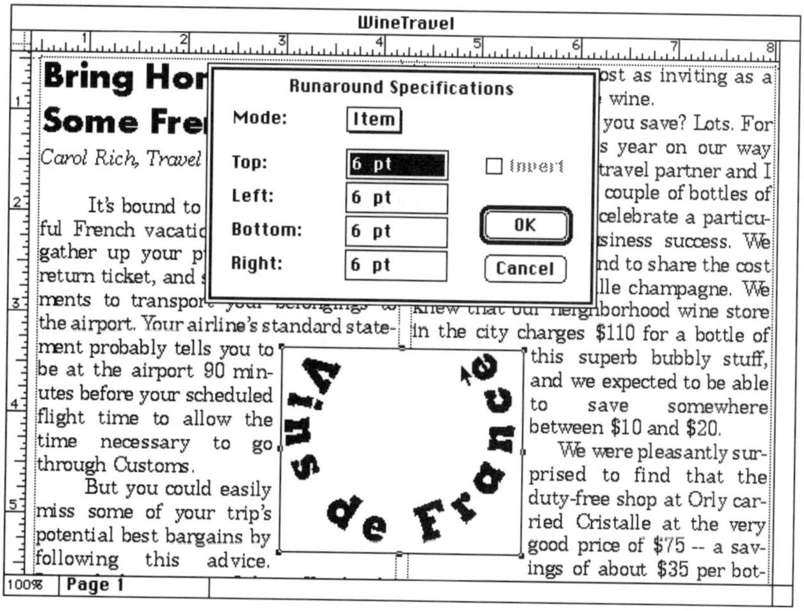

Figure 4-9:
An example
of Item
runaround.

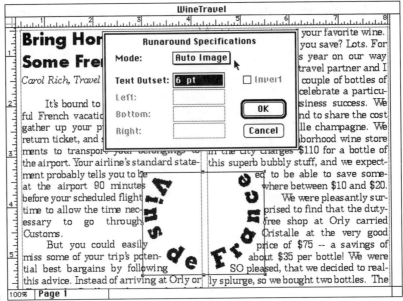

Figure 4-10:
An example
of Auto
Image
runaround.

Rotating boxes

Both text boxes and picture boxes can be rotated in QuarkXPress. If used well, rotated boxes can add additional spark to the appearance of a page. Again, as with the other tricks in your layout bag, use rotation sparingly for best results.

Figure 4-11 contains a text box that was rotated and then placed in the corner of the page. You can control the rotation of text boxes or picture boxes in three ways:

✔ **Option 1:** Select the box and choose Item⇨Modify (or press ⌘-M) to display either the Text Box Specifications dialog box or the Picture Box Specifications dialog box, depending on whether you are rotating a text or picture box. Enter a rotation amount in the Box Angle field.

To rotate the box clockwise, use a negative value in the Box Angle field; to rotate it counterclockwise, use a positive value in the Box Angle field.

✔ **Option 2:** Click the Rotation tool (located on the Tool palette). Then click and hold the mouse button as you move the mouse to rotate the box.

✔ **Option 3:** Enter a rotation degree in the rotation field of the Measurements palette.

There's no right way to rotate boxes. Experiment with all three options to see which way is most comfortable for you.

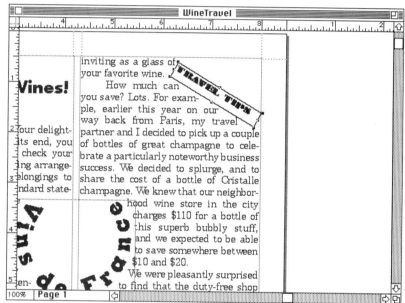

Figure 4-11:
We rotated
the Travel
Tips text
box –30°.

Slanting boxes

Here's an effect that you probably won't use too often, although it is an interesting and unique one. QuarkXPress lets you slant, or *skew* boxes. To use this feature, follow these steps:

1. **Open the document to the page that holds the text box or picture box that you want to slant.**

2. **Click on the box to make it active.**

3. **Choose Item⇨Modify (or press ⌘-M) to display the Text Box Specifications dialog box or the Picture Box Specifications dialog box, depending on whether you are working on a text box or a picture box.**

4. **In the Box Skew field, enter a value between 75 and –75.**

   A positive number slants the box to the right; a negative number slants the box to the left.

Figure 4-12 shows a slanted text box.

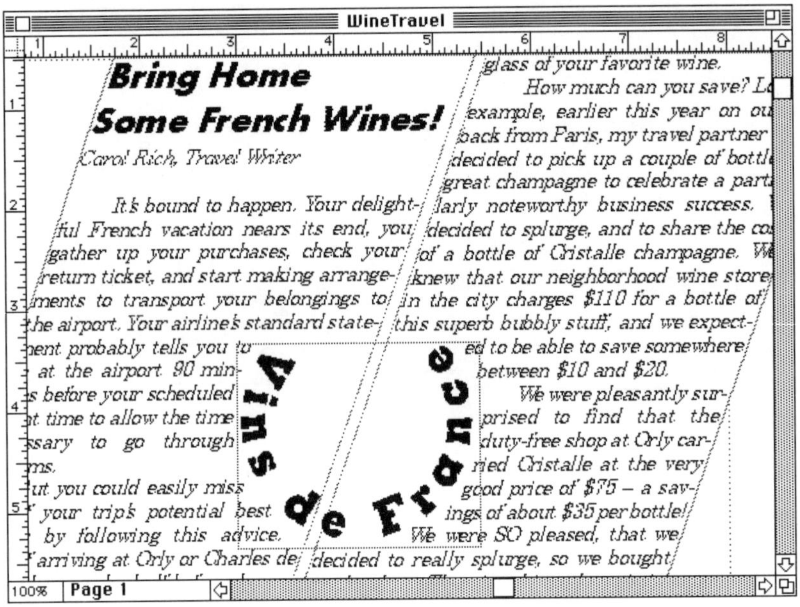

Bring Home Some French Wines!

Carol Rich, Travel Writer

It's bound to happen. Your delight-
ful French vacation nears its end, you
gather up your purchases, check your
return ticket, and start making arrangements to transport your belongings to
the airport. Your airline's standard statement probably tells you to
at the airport 90 min-
s before your scheduled
t time to allow the time
ssary to go through
ms.
ut you could easily miss
your trip's potential best
by following this advice.
arriving at Orly or Charles de

glass of your favorite wine.
How much can you save? L
example, earlier this year on ou
back from Paris, my travel partner
decided to pick up a couple of bottl
great champagne to celebrate a part
larly noteworthy business success.
decided to splurge, and to share the co
of a bottle of Cristalle champagne. We
knew that our neighborhood wine store
in the city charges $110 for a bottle of
this superb bubbly stuff, and we expected to be able to save somewhere
between $10 and $20.
We were pleasantly sur-
prised to find that the
duty-free shop at Orly car-
ried Cristalle at the very
good price of $75 – a sav-
ings of about $35 per bottle!
We were SO pleased, that we
decided to really splurge, so we bought

Vins de France

100% Page 1

Figure 4-12: The slanted text box in this example was achieved by entering a value of 20 in the Box Skew field of the Text Box Specifications dialog box.

Chapter 5

Bringing the Text In

. . . .

. . . .

*G*ive some people a computer, a word processing application, and some paper, and they think they're full-fledged publishers, ready for the big leagues.

But you aren't so easily fooled. *You* know better. That's why you're reading our book, right? You know that you can't do serious, fancy, cool-looking professional publishing with the same application that kids typically use for typing school papers. You're ready for the big leagues, or at least you're dreaming of getting there. That's why you use QuarkXPress.

Hey, don't get us wrong. We have nothing against word processing programs; in fact, we both use them all the time. It's just that we don't want you to be misled about what word processing programs can do — or do well.

The big advantage QuarkXPress has over word processing applications is that XPress gives you tremendous control over the appearance of each and every item on a page, down to the tiniest unit of spacing between characters or lines of text. Word processing programs, on the other hand, are built to make it easy to fill page after page with text; they often give you layout features — multiple columns, bold and italic characters, and so on — but they lack the precision and depth of control available in QuarkXPress.

But it's not at all uncommon for QuarkXPress users to use word processing programs. Actually, you have your choice about how to get text onto a page. Here's how it works: you can create text right within QuarkXPress text boxes — using the built-in word processor — or you can create text in separate word processing programs and then import it into QuarkXPress.

Chances are good that you'll find yourself doing both. But if you're going to use a separate word processing program to create text, check out this chapter for some tips on how to make the process go smoothly.

What Word Processing Files Work with XPress?

Whether you're deciding what's for lunch or what to wear, it's always nice to have a bunch of choices. Don't worry: you have a good range of word processing programs to pick from if you are looking for one that will import nicely into QuarkXPress. Those programs that are compatible include Microsoft Word 3.0 up to — but not yet including 6.0, WordPerfect 1.0 and later — but only up to version 3, WriteNow 3.0, Microsoft Works 2.0, and Claris MacWrite and MacWrite II.

If you want to import word processing programs that were created with a DOS or Windows version of Word, WordPerfect, or Works, be sure to save the files in the Mac format before importing them into QuarkXPress. Why? Because QuarkXPress does not support DOS or Windows versions of these programs.

Keep one important point in mind: Because word processing programs are updated according to their manufacturer's schedule — which does not necessarily coincide with Quark's — there's no guarantee that QuarkXPress will import files easily from a particular updated version of one of these packages. If your word processor is not on the list above, it's a good idea to test the "importability" of your text to see how it all works before you get into a production or deadline situation. If you run into problems, try saving the word processing file in a different file format — most word processing programs allow you to do this.

Word processing features to avoid

After you've figured out that QuarkXPress does a very good job at importing text from word processing programs, be careful not to fall victim to the temptation of using all of the word processing program's features. Here are some pointers to keep in mind:

- **Don't spend too much time doing extensive formatting in your word processor** — because a word processor's style sheets are always much less sophisticated than what you can achieve in QuarkXPress. Avoid any layout-related features in the word processor, such as page numbers and multiple columns.

- **Don't waste time formatting tables in your word processing application.** After you get the file into QuarkXPress, you will need to do extensive tab adjusting, or you will need a table XTension, such as NPath's Tableworks Plus. If you change a spreadsheet or chart into a graphic before importing it into QuarkXPress, you won't be able to edit it.

- **Don't use the word processing program as if it were a manual typewriter.** In other words, don't hit the Return key at the end of each line of text, only at the end of a paragraph. If you forget to skip this old-standby task, you will have to spend considerable time in QuarkXPress removing all the unnecessary returns, which can clutter up an otherwise tidy document. Also, don't use two spaces between sentences; professional typesetters never do that.

- **Don't try to use spaces or returns to align words or lines of text on screen** — because you will want to use QuarkXPress to tweak the spacing of words and characters.

- **Notice the version number of your word processor.** If it is a couple of versions older or newer than what your version of QuarkXPress supports, you could have trouble when you import a text file from the word processor. If in doubt, create a test file of text, using all the features you're likely to normally use, and import it into a test QuarkXPress page. You may find that you need to make adjustments to the list of word processing features that you will be able to use with QuarkXPress.

- **Don't use the fast-save option on files that you plan to import into QuarkXPress** — that is, if your word processing program *has* a fast-save option (an option that writes information about what's been changed in a text file at the end of the file, instead of rewriting the entire file each time you do a save). The fast-save option could cause problems with the imported text files. We suggest that you turn off fast save for files you will be importing into QuarkXPress. With today's super-speedy hard drives, the time you gain by using fast save is barely noticeable, anyway. In the following figure, the fast-save option is disabled.

(continued)

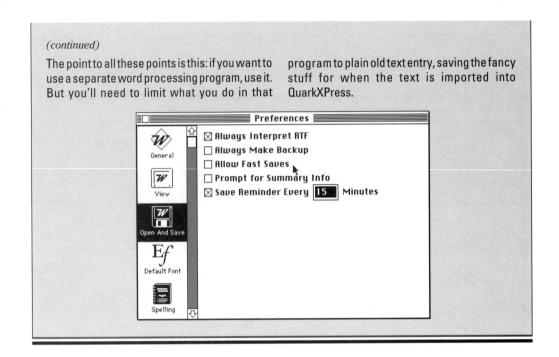

(continued)

The point to all these points is this: if you want to use a separate word processing program, use it. But you'll need to limit what you do in that program to plain old text entry, saving the fancy stuff for when the text is imported into QuarkXPress.

Getting the Text Ready to Import

Let's say you're already familiar with how to format text within the word processing program that you have on your computer. That is, you know how to create text, flow it into two columns, add a header and footer, and italicize and bold selected sections of text. It might seem like a logical thing to do as much as possible within the word processing file and then import the text into QuarkXPress.

Is this a good thing to do? No way, José. Fact is, unless you plan ahead, you risk losing some of the work you do in the word processing program after you import the text into QuarkXPress. Now why would you want to waste your valuable time?

Keep it simple

Here's a good rule of thumb: When using a word processing program to create a file that you will import into QuarkXPress, remember that you will be importing *text*, not a polished document. If you keep this simple thought in mind, you'll resist the temptation to do more formatting than necessary in the word processing program. In other words, make the most of your investment: use the power of QuarkXPress for *document* formatting.

So, knowing that you will import the text into QuarkXPress, what word processing features should you go ahead and use? There's a strong chance that any character-attribute formatting (such as italics, bold, underline) you do in the word processor will import seamlessly into QuarkXPress. Additionally, if you tell QuarkXPress to keep them when you import text into a text box, the style sheets from the main Macintosh word processing programs will come across, along with their associated text.

If you tend to use style sheets in your word processor, it's a good idea to let QuarkXPress know about it before you import the word processor file. Figure 5-1 shows the Get Text dialog box that appears when you import text from a word processor. Be sure to check Include Style Sheets to make sure that style sheets get imported along with the text. We explain more about Style Sheets in Chapter 8.

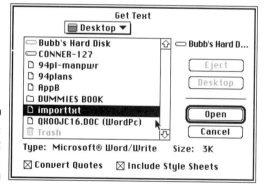

Figure 5-1:
The Get Text dialog box.

 One key to successfully importing text into QuarkXPress is to avoid using the graphics and layout features in the word processing program. Limit your word processor formatting to the kind that enhances the reader's understanding or places emphasis, such as bolding, italicizing, and varying type style.

Do sophisticated stuff in XPress

Although it's true that word processing programs often include a number of page layout capabilities — such as the ability to use built-in drawing tools and create multiple columns and footnotes — be aware that these layout effects usually do not import into QuarkXPress. In other words, just because you *can* perform some layout effects in your word processor doesn't mean that you *should*. Again, you are far better off to concentrate on making character-attribute edits in the word processor and then importing the file into QuarkXPress.

Let's illustrate this point. Figure 5-2 shows a QuarkXPress page with text imported from Microsoft Word. As you can see, simple character-based formatting imported just fine. What you can't see is that the Word document included page headers and footers — which disappeared once we had the document in QuarkXPress.

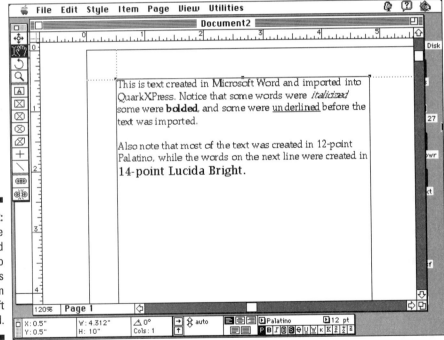

Figure 5-2:
A page imported into QuarkXPress from Microsoft Word.

Filling the Text Box with Text

Here comes the part you've been waiting for. You've created a QuarkXPress document, it has text boxes, and it's time to fill the boxes with some text.

You can fill text boxes in one of two ways: you can use the built-in QuarkXPress word processor to type in text (you simply select the text box, then select the Content tool, and start typing), or you can import text from a word processing program into the text box. Follow these steps to import the text:

1. **With the QuarkXPress document open, select the Content tool.**

2. **Use the mouse to place the I-beam pointer at the top of the text box.**

   Note that the pointer may already be at this spot.

3. **Choose File⇨Get Text (or press ⌘-E) to display the Get Text dialog box.**

4. **Use the controls in the Get Text dialog box to locate the text file that you want to place into the text box.**

5. **If you want QuarkXPress to automatically change typewriter-type dashes and quotation marks to their more sophisticated typographic equivalents, make sure to check the Convert Quotes box in the Get Text dialog box.**

   If you want to include the style sheets used in the word processor, check the Include Style Sheets box.

6. **Choose OK. The text flows into the text box or the linked chain of text boxes.**

But what happens when you want to import some text into a text box that already has some text in it? No problem. Simply place the pointer where you want the imported text to begin. Importing text does not remove the text that is already in the text box; it simply "bumps" the existing text to the end of the inserted text. If you want to replace the text, click anywhere in the text, type ⌘-A, and press Delete. Now input the new text.

Keeping Special Features of Imported Text

Okay, you already agree that today's word processors let you do a bunch of stuff beyond simply entering and editing text. Here's a list of the character formatting you can do in the two most-used word processors, Word and WordPerfect. Rest assured that these formats will import into QuarkXPress.

Character formatting features that import from Word and WordPerfect include these design nuggets:

- ✔ Boldface, outline, italicized, shadow characters
- ✔ Underline (in Word, all underlining changes to a single underline)
- ✔ Color
- ✔ Font changes
- ✔ Varied point sizes
- ✔ Small caps
- ✔ Strikethru characters
- ✔ Subscript
- ✔ Superscript
- ✔ Drop caps (in Word, these become a separate paragraph)
- ✔ Special characters

After the characters in your text are taken care of, you can deal with issues on a bigger scale: things like tables, headers and footers, and more.

Tables

If you decide to create a table in a word processing file and then import the file into QuarkXPress, be forewarned that the table will disappear. Ergo, take heed: if you like tables in your documents, wait until you are using QuarkXPress to format them. (If, on the other hand, you use the word processor's style sheets to format a table with tabs, you can import it into QuarkXPress along with the rest of the text in the file and can then modify the styles as needed in QuarkXPress.)

You can import a table created in a spreadsheet or database program (such as Lotus 1-2-3, Microsoft Excel, Claris FileMaker Pro, and so on) into QuarkXPress, but not smoothly. You need to choose between saving the files as tab-delimited ASCII text or as graphics. If you save the files as tab-delimited ASCII text, you need to do some work inside the QuarkXPress document, setting tab stops to line everything up.

Headers and footers

You probably already know what headers and footers are, but here's a quick and painless explanation just in case you don't know. *Headers* are segments of information that repeat, such as the name of the current chapter; they appear at the tops of pages in a document. *Footers* appear at the bottoms of pages and usually include information such as the current page number and the name of the document.

Now, you need to get into the habit of thinking about headers and footers as a layout issue, rather than a text issue. Because they are a layout issue, it's best to wait until you are working on your document in QuarkXPress before you worry about them. For one thing, your document no doubt will paginate differently once it's in QuarkXPress; if it does, page numbers in headers or footers will be useless, even if they did import into QuarkXPress — which they don't.

Footnotes

Several word processing programs include a footnoting feature that lets you do two things: (1) mark certain spots in text with a number and (2) have the number and some corresponding text appear at the bottom of the page containing the footnote. If you import a word processor file that contains footnotes into QuarkXPress, the footnotes no longer will appear on the same page as the text they reference. Instead, all of the footnotes for the document will appear at the end of the imported text. Also, the superscript or subscript footnote indicators in the body of the document may not import correctly.

In-line graphics

Most Macintosh and Windows word processors support *in-line graphics,* pictures that you import into your word processor and associate with certain sections of text. In most cases, QuarkXPress can import the in-line graphics with your text. Importing this way works for Microsoft Word and WordPerfect files; you might need to experiment a bit if you use another word processor that allows in-line graphics.)

One caveat: Graphics that you have embedded into your word processing document by using the Mac's Publish and Subscribe or OLE (a Mac and Windows Publish-and-Subscribe relative from Microsoft) do not import into QuarkXPress.

In-line graphics import into QuarkXPress in the form of their PICT previews, not as their original formats. Because of this quirk, the versions of the in-line graphics that end up in your QuarkXPress document probably will have a lower resolution in your QuarkXPress layout than they had in their original word processor file.

Style sheets

QuarkXPress lets you import styles created in several word processors — *if* you have checked the Include Style Sheets box in the Get Text dialog box (File⇨Get Text, or ⌘-E). Even if you don't always use style sheets in your word processor, it's a good idea to always check the Include Style Sheets box. (In version 3.3 of QuarkXPress, this box always remains checked unless you uncheck it; in earlier versions, you needed to check it each time.)

Tune in again when we tell you more about Style Sheets in Chapter 8.

XPress tags

Are you keen on secret codes? QuarkXPress has them in the form of a nifty (although tough to learn) feature that lets you insert tags into text that you're preparing for import into QuarkXPress. These secret codes are referred to as XPress tags; you can use them to give QuarkXPress instructions on how to format text being imported into an XPress document. XPress tags are actually ASCII (text-only) text that contain embedded codes that tell QuarkXPress which formatting to apply. XPress tags are similar to macros, and you embed them into the text that you create in your word processor.

XPress tags, when used correctly, are pretty powerful. But they are not widely used because of some drawbacks. The most significant shortcoming is that you can't use XPress tags in conjunction with the formatting available in your word processor. For example, if you create a file in Microsoft Word, you cannot use XPress tags to apply a style to a paragraph while using Word's ability to bold and italicize text. If you want to use XPress tags, you must use them for every formatting instruction in the file, and you must save the file as an ASCII file.

If you want to experiment with XPress tags, look in Appendix C of the QuarkXPress reference manual. We'd be surprised, though, if you ended up using them in place of the formatting available in your word processor.

Chapter 6

A Picture Is Worth…

In This Chapter

▶ What graphics formats work with QuarkXPress

▶ How to prepare graphics files for import

▶ How to import and place graphics

▶ How to crop and resize graphics

*O*kay, we admit it: many documents don't need graphics. But any document you would go to the trouble of laying out probably does. The graphic might be as simple as a logo or as complex as a series of annotated photos. When all is said and done, graphics are an instrumental part of layouts, and you'll be using them in your layouts. How do you get those graphics ready for use in QuarkXPress? And how do you fine-tune them once you've placed them in your layout? Chapter 3 describes how to find good images. In this Chapter, you learn how to use them in QuarkXPress.

Secrets to Graphics Preparation

Graphics come in two basic formats: vector and raster, better known as drawings and bitmaps. A *vector graphic* is composed of objects, like lines and circles. A *raster graphic* is composed of a series of dots, just as a photo in a newspaper is. Don't confuse the type of graphic with the kind of program that created it. For example, Adobe Photoshop saves graphics as bitmaps, even though it has tools for adding lines and circles; Photoshop converts those lines and circles to a series of dots as soon as you draw them.

To keep raster and vector straight, just remember what you use each format for. Typically, you use raster for photos, scanned images, and painted images, while vector best serves you in drawn or illustrated images. Enlarging a raster image makes each dot bigger and the overall image coarser (as when you put a magnifying glass over a newspaper photo); enlarging a drawing, though, just makes the drawing bigger (without looking grainy or coarse). Why? The answer rests entirely in the physical make-up of rasters and vectors. Remember that a raster image is composed only of those dots — that bunch of dots is *all* you have to work with. But a vector image is composed of instructions like "Okay Doc, now draw a line so thick from here to there and make it red." When you enlarge that image, the instruction just changes things like the definition of "here" and "there" and "so thick."

"But aren't all images a series of dots on a computer screen or laser printer?" you ask. "Why don't all graphics get coarser when they're enlarged?" Well, yes, all images displayed or printed on a computer *are* turned into dots — but, in a vector image, the dots are created only at the time of display or printing. (Every pixel displayed on a monitor, after all, is just a dot.) On the other hand, a raster's dots are created right when the image itself is created. For a vector graphic, the only time the dots are created is at the time of display or printing, and the creation of these dots does not replace the instructions.

Think of vector graphics as a recipe: You want a bigger apple pie; you alter the recipe to add proportionally more of each ingredient. Once you've implemented the recipe, you end up with a pie of the size you want. And once you've made the pie, you can't change your mind and make it bigger. Implementing the recipe is converting the instructions into the output — for graphics, that's the creation of the dots that make up the printed output. (In graphics, you're converting the vector to a raster — in fact, many computer artists call this process *rasterization*.) A raster image had its dots created already.

If a vector graphic is a recipe for a pie, the printer is the cook who makes the pie. A raster graphic is a pie someone else made for you; all you can do is serve it, not change its recipe. In other words, a vector image is essentially a recipe yet to be implemented, while a raster image is a recipe already implemented.

Pick a format, any format.

Preparing graphics is not hard. In many cases, you can just load them directly into your QuarkXPress document. But sometimes you need to do some prep work in advance. QuarkXPress was designed to handle a whole slew of graphics types — including some you may never have heard of. Let's go through the laundry list.

- **BMP (Windows Bitmap).** The bitmap format introduced with Windows is popular for lower-end programs. On a PC, look for the extensions .BMP and .DIB.

- **CGM (Computer Graphics Metafile).** Popularized on Unix workstations, this drawing format has become popular among technical illustrators. Only Windows QuarkXPress supports this format. Look for the extension .CGM.

- **CT (Continuous Tone).** A variant of TIFF created by high-end photo-retouching systems. On a PC, look for the extension .CT.

- **DCS (Document Color Separation).** This variant of EPS includes color-separation files, so it's actually five files, one for each of the four publishing colors plus a file that contains a preview image and the instructions on how to combine the four color files. On a PC, look for the extensions .EPS and .DCS. (The new DCS Version 2.0 format, which QuarkXPress 3.2 and later support, can have more than the four standard publishing colors, so there could be more than five component files.)

- **EPS (Encapsulated PostScript).** The publishing standard for drawings created by programs like Adobe Illustrator, Aldus/Altsys/Macromedia FreeHand (the program has changed ownership twice recently), and CorelDraw. Except for Adobe Illustrator, you'll need to export files to this format from the drawing program's native format (Illustrator's native format *is* EPS). On a PC, look for the extensions .EPS and .AI.

- **GIF (Graphics Interchange Format).** This bitmap format developed for the CompuServe on-line service can be imported only by the Windows version of QuarkXPress. Look for the extension .GIF.

- **HPGL (Hewlett-Packard Graphics Language).** This drawing format is popular on CAD programs, since it was developed for architectural plotters. Only Windows QuarkXPress can read this format. Look for the extension .PLT.

- **JPEG (Joint Photographers Expert Group).** This bitmap format uses file compression to make large photos and other scanned images into files of reasonable size. The trade-off is that the compression can make the image lose some detail. On a PC, look for the extension .JPG.

- **MacPaint.** This bitmap format supports only black-and-white — which means that it's pretty much a goner in today's color marketplace. On a PC, look for the extension .MAC.

- **Micrografx Draw.** This drawing format is used only by Micrografx Draw, a limited version of Micrografx Designer (the first drawing program under Windows), but by now long superseded by CorelDraw. Only Windows QuarkXPress can read this format. Look for the extension .DRW.

- ✔ **PCX (PC Paintbrush).** This bitmap format is the reigning bitmap format on PCs — it even predates Windows. High-end users junked it for TIFF because only recently did PCX add support for high-color (16-bit and 24-bit) images. On a PC, look for the extensions .PCX and .PCS.

- ✔ **Photo CD.** This new format was developed by Eastman Kodak for its corporate attempt to move consumers from film to CD for their picture processing. That gambit didn't work, but it did create a standard for photo libraries that is rapidly taking over the publishing industry to store stock photos. On a PC, look for the extension .PCD.

- ✔ **PICT (Picture).** This Mac format is actually two formats: a drawing format and a bitmap format. In both cases, QuarkXPress imports the format. On a PC, look for the extension .PCT.

- ✔ **RIFF (Raster Image File Format).** A not-very-popular bitmap format that you'll probably come across only if you work with Fractal Design Painter. On a PC, look for the extension .RIF.

- ✔ **RLE (Run-Length Encoded).** The bitmap format used by OS/2 is a variant of BMP. On a PC, look for the extension .RLE.

- ✔ **TIFF (Tagged Image File Format).** Probably the most popular bitmap format for designers on the Mac (and pretty popular on the PC, too), this is the standard for many scanners and photo-editing programs since it supports 24-bit images (with millions of colors). PC TIFF and Mac TIFF are slightly different, but QuarkXPress reads them both. On a PC, look for the extension .TIF.

- ✔ **Windows Metafile.** This drawing format is similar to the Mac's PICT in that it is the native format for the operating system. On a PC, look for the extension .WMF.

If you've tried to use any of the preceding formats, only to have QuarkXPress refuse to import the format you want, QuarkXPress probably thumbed its nose at you for one of two reasons. One possible explanation is embarrassingly obvious: the file may not be in the format you think it's in (or it may be corrupt). The other explanation isn't so obvious: the right filter may not be installed for QuarkXPress to import that file type. Filters for several popular file formats are installed automatically when you install QuarkXPress, but others are not. Check out Chapter 19 for details on reinstalling QuarkXPress to add filters.

If you don't use any of these formats, don't sweat it; you probably can import your graphics with the format you're using. You're doing your work in FreeHand or CorelDraw or ClarisDraw (also called MacDraw), for example. Don't worry. These programs all can save or export in one of the listed formats.

Even though QuarkXPress supports all these formats, we recommend that you stick to just two formats for your graphics because they offer the most flexibility and/or the best output: TIFF and EPS (including DCS). Runners-up are PCX, Photo CD, PICT, and Windows Metafile. Windows-only users also might pick CGM. As for the rest, use them if you have them, but ask your artists (or the person buying your clip art and stock photos) to get the images in one of the formats we recommend.

Why only these few formats? QuarkXPress offers a whole slew of controls over TIFF (see Chapter 13 for details) that it doesn't provide for other bitmap formats. EPS provides the best-quality output, lets you embed fonts, and supports color-separations better than any other drawing format; EPS's only downside is that it requires a PostScript printer, which many Windows users may not have (the PCL printer format is popular on Windows). PCX, PICT, and Windows Metafile are good second choices because they are so popular, but their formats don't offer the same capabilities that TIFF and EPS do for high-end output. Photo CD is fast becoming the standard format for stock photos — it's the photographic equivalent of clip art — so you'll likely have many images in this format to work with.

Get those files in shape.

The more complex the format, the more choices you need to make when creating images in it. If many of these options seem way over your head, stifle your impulse to panic; creating graphics isn't as complex as it seems at first. If our terms ring no bells for you, you're probably just not creating graphics yet that use features that give you all these choices. But do check these options. Even if you don't know what they mean, try to implement them, or tell the artist who provides you the graphics what we recommend.

The Many Shades of TIFF

TIFF comes in black-and-white, in gray scale, in indexed color, in RGB color, and in CMYK color. You can have LZW compression, Packbits compression, or no compression. You can save the alpha channel, or ditch it. You can save in Mac byte order or PC byte order.

Is that too many choices, or what? Here are some surefire tricks you can use to simplify TIFF:

> ✔ **If your output will be color-separated, save in CMYK color.** Many
> graphics programs don't yet support this variant of TIFF. With such
> programs, save in RGB mode and make sure that you installed

QuarkXPress's EfiColor option (see Chapter 19 for installation tips). If your output will be black-and-white, save in gray scale for photographic images and black-and-white for images that have only black or white (no shades of gray).

✔ **Use LZW compression or no compression.** Sometimes you may have an image display incorrectly in QuarkXPress if you saved it with LZW compression. An incorrect display means that there's an error in the TIFF file and that you need to regenerate the TIFF file. If regenerating the file still doesn't work, just save it uncompressed. Don't use other forms of compression that might be available in your image-editing software.

✔ **Save the alpha channel for 24-bit images**. It helps guarantee accurate color reproduction for the finer colors. Many programs won't give you the option not to save the alpha channel.

✔ **Use the byte order for the system you're using the file in** — even though QuarkXPress can handle both PC and Mac byte orders. The reason for you to pay attention is that other programs aren't as forgiving, so why create a possible problem? So what happens if a program can't handle the byte order of a different platform? The image will look like a photographic negative. If that ever happens in QuarkXPress, you can use the Style⇨Negative command on the image to make it right again.

✔ **If you use color calibration in Adobe Photoshop 2.5.1 or later, save the file with the Metric Color Tags enabled.** Enabling the Color Tags ensures the best output in QuarkXPress because QuarkXPress's EfiColor calibrator can work directly with the Metric Color Tags information.

EPS Options Galore

Encapsulated PostScript files can be complex because so many things can go into them. To keep the EPS universe simple and manageable, follow these hints for every EPS file you get:

✔ **If the file is in color, make sure that all the colors in it were defined with the same color model (CMYK or RGB).** In some cases, you'll have one of those two models plus a spot color — Pantone, Trumatch, or some other special color library. If you can, have the drawing program translate those spot colors to either CMYK or RGB; use CMYK if you will output to an imagesetter. Keep spot colors in their original format only if you plan to print those colors on their own plates. Also, if you're not using (or your drawing program doesn't support) CMYK colors, it's best to name your colors when you create them. That way, they will appear in QuarkXPress's list of colors, from which you can apply them to other objects or decide whether to color-separate them. (For details on color, see Chapter 14.)

✔ **If the file includes text, either have the program embed the fonts inside the drawing or convert the text to curves** (if the program has an option to do so; programs like FreeHand, Illustrator, and CorelDraw do). Either option ensures that the fonts will print correctly on your printer. If you can't do either option, make sure that you have the same fonts on the computer that you'll print the QuarkXPress layouts from.

✔ **If you have a choice for the EPS preview format, choose TIFF.** The preview is what you see on the screen when you import the file into QuarkXPress; it's an electronic snapshot of what the instructions in the EPS file will create during printing. Windows and Mac programs usually use different preview formats, so you may get a gray rectangle on screen in QuarkXPress when you import an EPS file created on one platform but used on the other. The image still prints okay. But if you can ensure that QuarkXPress will have the preview in a format it definitely supports — such as TIFF — then go ahead and do so.

✔ **If you use the DCS version of EPS, make sure that all five files are in the same folder or directory as the master file (the file you actually load into QuarkXPress).** Typically, these files end in .C, .M, .Y, and .K (yes, that spells CMYK!) or a similar scheme using those letters to identify the color-separated components. (Some DCS files will have more than five files if they use colors in addition to the CMYK basics.)

Photo CD Enabled

The Photo CD format uses compression to keep its file at a manageable size. That means you need decompression software (in addition to the QuarkXPress Photo CD import filter) to read those files into QuarkXPress:

✔ On a Mac, make sure that QuickTime and Apple Photo Access are installed in the Extensions folder in the System Folder. You have to get those extensions separately; they don't come with QuarkXPress for Macintosh. Fortunately, though, they do come bundled with lots of programs.

✔ On a PC, make sure that PCDLIB.DLL is installed either in the WINDOWS\SYSTEM directory or the XPRESS\XTENSION directory. QuarkXPress for Windows includes this file; so do other programs, which is why you may find the Photo CD files in several places.

On a Mac, Photo CD files often come in several resolutions. Pick the resolution you need — nothing finer. The finer the resolution (that is, the bigger the number), then the bigger the file, the slower the print time, and the slower the screen-redraw time. You can usually select the 768-by-512 or 192-by-128 resolutions unless your photos will take more than a third of a page or so.

CGM, HPGL, and Micrografx Draw Peculiarities

Three formats available only to Windows QuarkXPress have special options when you import files.

- **CGM:** For CGM, you get a dialog box with three checkboxes. Make sure that you check Force Vector Fonts; that option translates any fonts within the CGM file into curves — so you don't have to worry about the font not printing correctly from QuarkXPress. The Dot Lines option converts dotted lines to solid lines; dotted lines in CGM may not print correctly from QuarkXPress. If your CGM file came from Harvard Graphics, check the third box, Default Color Table, which ensures that QuarkXPress will convert the image's colors correctly.

- **HPGL:** For HPGL, you can assign colors to the pens used. On a plotter, each color is assigned to a specific pen on the plotter device. In this dialog box, you can change those pen assignments to use any of the many colors that QuarkXPress supports. Select the Colors and Pen Colors options.

- **Micrografx Draw:** For Micrografx Draw, you have two options. The first is Ignore Background; if you check this option, the image will have an invisible background, rather than solid white or other color. Check this option unless you want the default background color from Draw imported as part of the image. The other option is Force Vector Fonts, which translates any fonts within the CGM file into curves — so you don't have to worry about the font not printing correctly from QuarkXPress.

Bringing Graphics In

All *right* already! Enough background! It's time to get to the heart of the matter: placing graphics in your layout. In Chapter 4, you learned how to create the boxes that contain text and graphics. Now it's time to put those boxes to use.

Here are the steps you need to follow to successfully and easily bring graphics into your QuarkXPress layout:

1. **Select the Content tool.**

2. **Select the box that you want to place the graphic in.**

3. **Use File⇨Get Picture or ⌘-E to get the Get Picture dialog box, shown in Figures 6-1 (Mac) and 6-2 (Windows).**

4. **Navigate the folders and drives until you find the image you want to**

If the Picture Preview box is checked, QuarkXPress will display a thumbnail version of the image when you single-click the file name; this preview is meant to help you see whether it's the one you want. The preview may take a few moments to display after you select an image.

5. **If you're using the EfiColor option, change the EfiColor profile if needed (see Chapter 14 for details).**

6. **Click Open (for Mac) or OK (for Windows).**

The picture will appear in the box. In some cases, it may take a few moments for QuarkXPress to load the file, particularly if it is more than 200K in size, has millions of colors, or is a compressed file (such as JPEG or Photo CD).

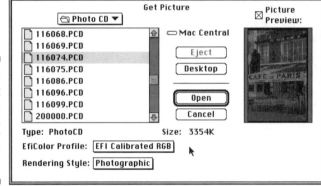

Figure 6-1:
The Get Picture dialog box for Macintosh QuarkXPress.

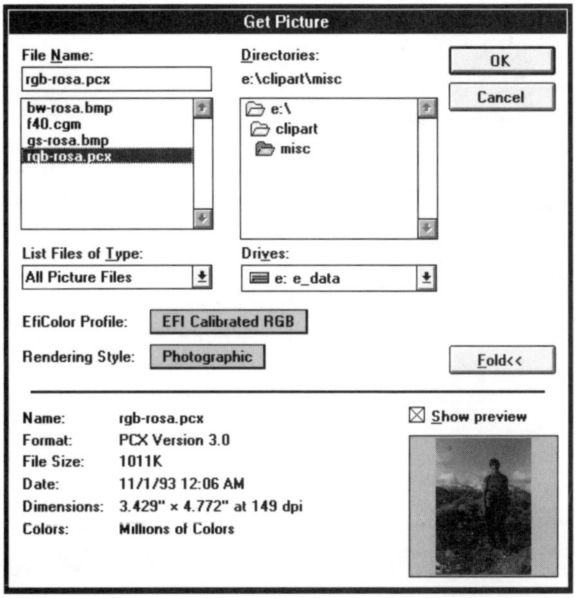

Figure 6-2:
The Get Picture dialog box for Windows QuarkXPress with the file-detail portion (at bottom) unfolded.

The Get Picture dialog box in Windows QuarkXPress has an extra button (which toggles between Fold<< and Unfold>>) that lets you preview the selected file and view details on format, size, and color depth for the selected image. On Mac QuarkXPress, the dialog box is not adjustable, and image preview is a standard component, although the file details are not.

 QuarkXPress treats objects differently depending on what tool is selected. If you select the Content Tool (shown at left), you can work with the contents of the box — the text or graphics.

 If you select the Item tool (shown at left), you can work with the box itself. Thus, to move an image within its box, select the Content tool, but to move the box and the image inside it, select the Item tool.

Making the Graphics Fit

That's not so hard, now is it?

But wait! The image doesn't fit the box! Compare the placed image in Figure 6-3 with the preview in Figure 6-1. They aren't the same: the bottom is missing in the placed image. What's going on?

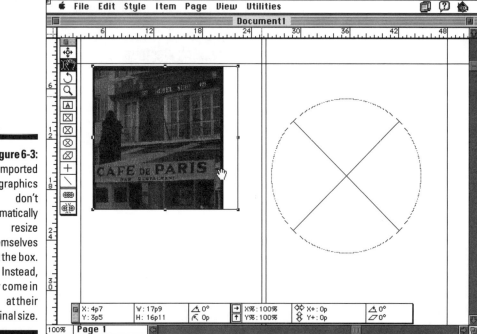

Figure 6-3:
Imported graphics don't automatically resize themselves to fit the box. Instead, they come in at their original size.

When QuarkXPress imports a graphic, it does so at the original size. If the original is 6 inches square, QuarkXPress makes it 6 inches square, no matter the size of the box it's being placed into. We think that QuarkXPress should at least have a preferences option to make imported graphics fit the boxes they're being placed into — but it doesn't, so you have to do the dirty work yourself.

In some cases, this lack of auto-fit can fool you into thinking the graphic never imported because the picture box looks to be empty. What really happened is that the graphic has a margin around it (created in your graphics program), and all you're seeing is the margin, which of course looks like nothing. When QuarkXPress places a graphic in a picture box, it puts the upper-left corner of the graphics file in the upper-left corner of the picture box. When you see nothing, that means the margin is wider and deeper than the picture box's size.

Here's how to get your graphic to fit:

✔ One method is to resize the picture box to fit the image. Just put the mouse pointer on the box handles and reposition them.

✔ If you want the graphic to fit the box's current size, make sure the Content tool is selected and press ⌘-Shift-Option-F. That finger-wrenching keyboard shortcut makes QuarkXPress resize the image so that it fits the box. Make sure that you press all four keys. If you miss the option key and press just ⌘-Shift-F, you'll get a distorted version of the image; it will be resized differently along the length than along the width. (No, we don't know why the more common option has the harder-to-use key combination.) The difference? The first shortcut keeps the image at its original proportions, while the second makes the image fit the size of the box, distorting it if necessary. Figure 6-4 shows what happens when you use each option.

There's also a keyboard shortcut to center a graphic within the box: ⌘-Shift-M. When you fit an image to a box, it also centers the graphic, so you only need to use ⌘-Shift-M when you want to keep the image at its current size but center it in the box.

 In addition to taking advantage of QuarkXPress's automatic controls, you also can manually reposition — or crop — a graphic within a box. The easiest way reposition a graphic manually is to start with the Content tool active. Then just pick up the graphic and move it. The pointer becomes a hand (called the grabber hand, which is shown in left margin next to this paragraph) when you position it over the graphic. Hold down the mouse button and move the mouse — and watch the graphic move within the box. Let go when you're done.

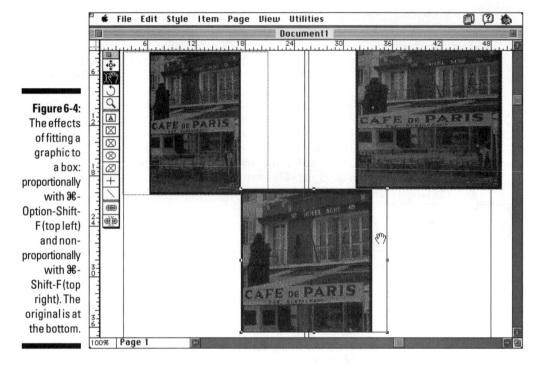

Figure 6-4:
The effects
of fitting a
graphic to
a box:
proportionally
with ⌘-
Option-Shift-
F (top left)
and non-
proportionally
with ⌘-
Shift-F (top
right). The
original is at
the bottom.

You also can specify how much you want the image to move within the box. QuarkXPress uses a floating palette — the Measurements palette — that lets you control text attributes, graphics attributes, and box attributes. Figure 6-5 shows the Measurements palette with the settings for the picture box at its upper left.

The X% and Y% values show the amount of resizing (here, 70.5%); you can change those values by typing new ones into the fields and pressing Return.

You also can change the position of the graphic by changing the X+ and Y+ values. A positive number moves the image to the right for X+ and down for Y+. Another method is to click on the arrows to the left of the X+ and Y+ fields. These arrows nudge the image up or down, or left or right, depending on which arrow you click. (Hold the Option key to nudge them in tiny steps: .001 units of the current measurement, such as inches or picas.) You can, of course, use a combination of these techniques — use the grabber hand to roughly position the graphic and then fine-tune the placement by using nudge arrows and/or changing the X+ and Y+ values manually. (A harder way to change these settings is to use Item⇨Modify, or ⌘-M, to get to the Picture Box Specifications dialog box where you can change the Scale Down, Scale Across, Offset Down, and Offset Across fields. But that's too much work.)

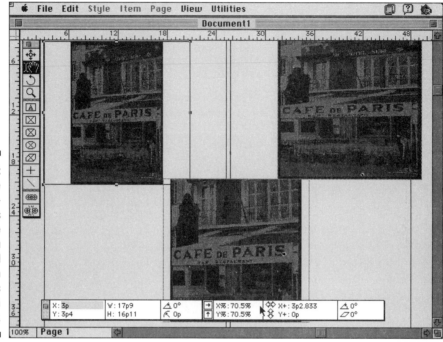

Figure 6-5:
The
Measure-
ments
palette
lets you
resize and
reposition
graphics
within a
picture box.

Chapter 7
The Final Touches

- -

In This Chapter

▶ Why you should decorate your layout

▶ How to add and create small graphics

▶ How to use lines

▶ How to create embellished folios

- -

*I*t's pretty obvious when to use a graphic, such as a photo illustration, with a story. For example, you'd expect a newspaper story on development of the space station to include a diagram showing the latest design. Or you'd expect a story about the death of actress Jessica Tandy to include a photograph of the veteran actress. Sometimes these graphics are stories all by themselves; with a caption added, they become a story that's told mainly in images rather than words. An example is a stock-market chart that shows how the Dow Jones Industrial Average has closed for the last 10 days.

But there are other uses for graphics than illustrating or telling a story — these may not be so obvious. You also can use them to decorate a story. (Never use the word *decorate* with a designer or artist — they'll freak out. In designspeak, you embellish, accent, or add a design element — you *never* decorate. You've heard of political correctness? This is artistic correctness!)

Pick up a magazine or brochure. Chances are good that lines, boxes, small shapes, and perhaps logos show up throughout the document. Together, these graphics add up to what we mean by decoration — er, design elements. These graphics provide the reader small details to look at or to attract attention as the reader flips through the document's pages. The design elements are subtle. And, if done well, they also provide continuity because the best use of such design elements is to have a consistent pattern with a little variation. (Check out Chapter 2 for more design advice.)

So let's talk turkey. Figure 7-1 shows a serviceable layout; Figure 7-2 shows the same layout modified to include some design elements. The difference is subtle but important.

Next-Generation Desktops
The Shape of Interfaces to Come

BY GALEN GRUMAN

Don't get too comfortable. Just as we've settled into the latest graphical interfaces, the world is about to change. Again. We've become more sophisticated, more demanding. We expect our computers to be simpler to use, easier to master, more flexible, and more functional. And software companies are responding: Microsoft is readying Windows 4.0; Apple is preparing Copland, a major upgrade to its System 7 operating system; and IBM continues to retool OS/2 while developing the Workplace OS and collaborating with Apple and Hewlett-Packard on Taligent. And from developers large and small, we'll get metaphors, guides, animated agents, feedback, and environments as likely to overwhelm as to enchant.

What will these options mean for you? Change, to be sure. But also more freedom of choice. Within the next few years, you may find yourself playing the operating system market. Should you continue to buy the software you've already invested your energy and money in, or is it time to consider something new and different? How will you keep from buying into a dead-end technology? Advance knowledge is the best defense.

Interfaces Get Real

The DOS command-line interface may seem primitive today, but the idea of issuing direct, English-like commands was originally a powerful way of making computing more accessible to professionals. Unfortunately, it was neither intuitive no<None>r flexible, and it eventually gave way to graphical user interfaces (GUIs) like in the Mac OS and

Windows. GUIs use representations of real objects—an icon of, say, a trash can to represent a place to discard files—to help users perform tasks. Windows or the Mac OS use "reaching in" interfaces: They require you to use a device like a mouse or keyboard to manipulate the objects that represent your data and tasks. This type of interface has contin-

Continues on p. 5

A Brief History of the Desktop Interface

Computer interface design has come a long way since the Altair excited the oscilloscope-and-ham-radio set in the late Seventies. Back then, you programmed your computer by switching levers up and down. Soon, Apple, IBM, and others—borrowing an idea from the mainframes of the day—adopted the command-line interface still on display in DOS. It was a huge advance because it allowed users to interact with their PCs via typed-in words rather than dip switches.

A few years later, Apple tapped ideas coming out of Xerox's Palo Alto Research Center, a pinnacle of advanced computer science thinking, to introduce 1984's Macintosh. Because it used a familiar metaphor (the desktop) and a human approach to interacting (pointing, grabbing, and moving), it was embraced as easy to use. Today, the original Mac interface looks cute but woefully limited. Back then, it tantalized and seduced people from all walks of life.

Other companies were exploring similar concepts: Digital Research had GEM (Graphics Environment Manager), VisiCorp offered VisiOn,

Three Faces of Windows
Microsoft Windows has undergone a major transformation over the years. Top to bottom: Windows 1.03, Windows 3.1, and the forthcoming Windows 4.0 (Chicago).

■ *Continues on p. 5*

Figure 7-1:
A serviceable layout.

Interface for all reasons Whether you use a desktop PC, Mac, portable, or PDA, your interface is likely to change.

The layout in Figure 7-2 uses black squares to draw the reader's eye to elements that might otherwise get lost, such as the byline and *continued* lines. Larger versions of the squares serve as a drop cap for the sidebar and as an embellishment to the kicker (the text above a headline). These squares provide visual resting places and serve as signposts. The layout in Figure 7-2 also uses rounded corners for the sidebar's frame, which adds a nice, modern touch to an already modern-looking layout (see Chapter 12 for details on putting frames around boxes). And there's a line beneath the kicker, which helps distinguish the kicker from the headline and presents another resting spot. If you produced the layout in Figure 7-1, people will like it. If you produced the layout in Figure 7-2, people will love it. If you have the time to spend on such embellishments, take it — it's that kind of care and attention that you yourself probably respond to when you see something well-crafted (furniture, food, sculpture, layout, whatever).

So how do you add these kinds of details? Read on.

Vol 12, No. 3

Next-Generation Desktops
The Shape of Interfaces to Come

■ *BY GALEN GRUMAN*
Don't get too comfortable. Just as we've settled into the latest graphical interfaces, the world is about to change. Again. We've become more sophisticated, more demanding. We expect our computers to be simpler to use, easier to master, more flexible, and more functional. And software companies are responding: Microsoft is readying Windows 4.0; Apple is preparing Copland, a major upgrade to its System 7 operating system; and IBM continues to retool OS/2 while developing the Workplace OS and collaborating with Apple and Hewlett-Packard on Taligent. And from developers large and small, we'll get metaphors, guides, animated agents, feedback, and environments as likely to overwhelm as to enchant.

What will these options mean for you? Change, to be sure. But also more freedom of choice. Within the next few years, you may find yourself playing the operating system market. Should you continue to buy the software you've already invested your energy and money in, or is it time to consider something new and different? How will you keep from buying into a dead-end technology? Advance knowledge is the best defense.

Interfaces Get Real

The DOS command-line interface may seem primitive today, but the idea of issuing direct, English-like commands was originally a powerful way of making computing more accessible to professionals. Unfortunately, it was neither intuitive no<None>r flexible, and it eventually gave way to graphical user interfaces (GUIs) like in the Mac OS and Windows. GUIs use representations of real objects—an icon of, say, a trash can to represent a place to discard files—to help users perform tasks. Windows or the Mac OS use "reaching in" interfaces: They require you to use a device like a mouse or keyboard to manipulate the objects that represent your data and tasks. This type of interface has contin-

■ *Continues on p. 5*

A Brief History of the Desktop Interface

Computer interface design has come a long way since the Altair excited the oscilloscope-and-ham-radio set in the late Seventies. Back then, you programmed your computer by switching levers up and down. Soon, Apple, IBM, and others—borrowing an idea from the mainframes of the day—adopted the command-line interface still on display in DOS. It was a huge advance because it allowed users to interact with their PCs via typed-in words rather than dip switches.

A few years later, Apple tapped ideas coming out of Xerox's Palo Alto Research Center, a pinnacle of advanced computer science thinking, to introduce 1984's Macintosh. Because it used a familiar metaphor (the desktop) and a human approach to interacting (pointing, grabbing, and moving), it was embraced as easy to use. Today, the original Mac interface looks cute but woefully limited. Back then, it tantalized and seduced people from all walks of life.

Other companies were exploring similar concepts: Digital Research had GEM (Graphics Environment

■ *Three Faces of Windows*
Microsoft Windows has undergone a major transformation over the years. Top to bottom: Windows 1.03, Windows 3.1, and the forthcoming Windows 4.0 (Chicago).

■ *Continues on p. 9*

Figure 7-2: The same serviceable layout from Figure 7-1 with graphical embellishments. See the difference?

■ *Interface for all reasons Whether you use a desktop PC, Mac, portable, or PDA, your interface is likely to change.*

Small Graphics

You can bring graphics into QuarkXPress in several ways. You can import a graphic created elsewhere; you can draw a graphic within QuarkXPress; or — believe it or not — you can use special symbol fonts to provide graphics. No matter what source of graphics you choose, keep a few things in mind:

- ✔ **The smaller the graphic, the simpler it should be.** Avoid very detailed graphics or graphics with lots of color or gray shades. For example, taking a photo and reducing it to an eighth of an inch by an eighth of an inch — the same size as a capital *M* at 9-point size — results in what looks like a muddy splotch. No one likes muddy splotches on their clothes — or on their documents.

- ✔ **If you use multiple graphics as embellishments, make sure that the graphics share a common thread.** Perhaps they are all solid basic shapes, like squares, circles, and triangles. Or maybe they are all different types of arrows or woodcuts or animal caricatures. The reason for having them interrelated by a theme is that you avoid the distraction of having clashing elements.

Using QuarkXPress's tools

Chapter 3 tells you where to find graphics. Clip-art libraries are good sources of images that you can use as embellishments. So we won't repeat that information here. But what we need to cover now is the use of QuarkXPress's own drawing tools.

"What drawing tools are those?" you patiently inquire. "There *are* no drawing tools in QuarkXPress — just lines," you not-so-patiently insist? Ah, but indeed there *are* drawing tools in QuarkXPress. *The secret to drawing in QuarkXPress is using the picture boxes as drawing objects* (Figure 7-3 shows the tools). With the picture boxes, you can draw rectangles, ovals, circles, polygons, even starbursts. Chapter 4 covers boxes in detail, but here's a refresher on picture box shapes for use as graphics.

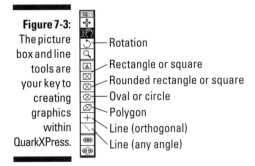

Figure 7-3:
The picture box and line tools are your key to creating graphics within QuarkXPress.

— Rotation

— Rectangle or square
— Rounded rectangle or square
— Oval or circle
— Polygon
— Line (orthogonal)
— Line (any angle)

Use the appropriate picture boxes to create the shapes you want. Overlap several shapes to create something more elaborate. Then group those boxes together — use Item⇨Group or ⌘-G — so they don't get accidentally mispositioned relative to each other later. Figure 7-4 shows some examples of several kinds of graphics you can create in QuarkXPress. Notice that many use different shades of color or gray; use the Colors palette (if it's not displayed, use the View menu to make it appear) to apply colors and shades. The three icons at top specify what part of the picture box you want to colorize: from left to right, they are the frame, contents (this will not work with several types of images placed in a picture box, including vector images and color bitmaps), and background. Note that the frame style and width must be specified via the Frame Specifications dialog box (Item⇨Frame, or ⌘-B).

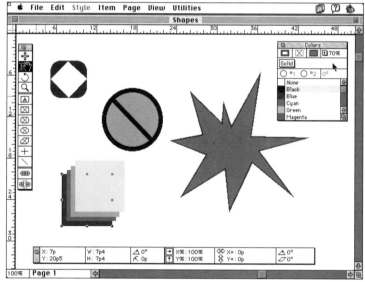

Figure 7-4:
Sample pictures created with QuarkXPress's picture-box tools.

Here are some tips for working with several of the picture box shapes:

- ✔ To get a perfect square or circle, hold the Shift key when creating a rectangle, rounded-rectangle, or oval picture box.

- ✔ To make a polygon's sides orthogonal (which means horizontal, vertical, or tilted at multiples of 45 degrees), hold the Shift key while moving the mouse to each point.

✔ To change the roundness of a rounded rectangle (or to make a regular rectangle into a rounded rectangle), change the Corner Radius setting in the Measurements palette. Change the setting at the Corner Radius icon (shown at left) or in the Picture Box Specifications dialog box (Item⇨Modify, or ⌘-M). The bigger the number, the more rounded the corners.

 ✔ To alter the appearance of an object — its shape, angle, orientation, or any or all of these — use the skewing and rotation tools. You can use the freehand rotation tool in the Tools palette, specify the rotation amount in the Measurements palette (change the setting at the Rotate icon, shown at left), or specify the rotation amount in the Picture Box Specifications dialog box. (Positive numbers rotate clockwise, while negative numbers rotate counterclockwise.) For skewing, use either the Measurements palette (change the setting at the Skew icon, shown at left below the Rotate icon) or the Picture Box Specifications dialog box. (Positive numbers skew to the right; negative numbers to the left.)

✔ To change the stacking order of items layered on top of each other, use Item⇨Send to Back and Item⇨Bring to Front. Unfortunately, you cannot move an item one layer at a time with these menu options — which means you'll have to pick an item, bring it to the front or send it to the back, pick another item, change its position, and keep repeating this process until all the elements appear in the order you want. Yes, it's as much of a pain as it sounds. There's got to be a better way, right? Right! A hidden feature in QuarkXPress is the ability to send boxes forward and backward one layer at a time. How? Hold the Option key before selecting the Item menu — Send to Back becomes Send Backward and Bring to Front becomes Bring Forward. You can also use the keyboard shortcuts Option-F5 to bring a box forward and Option-Shift-F5 to send it backward.

 (Windows QuarkXPress offers two additional stacking controls: Item⇨Bring Forward and Item⇨Send Backward, which make it easier to change the order of layers. Maybe one day the Mac version will adopt this feature in its regular menus instead of relying on a secret method.)

✔ To create new graphics, combine an imported graphic with picture boxes. For example, you would create the logo in Figure 7-5 by importing the stylized *G* graphic (created in Adobe Illustrator), placing it in a polygon picture box, putting a circular picture box behind it, applying a frame to the polygon picture box, and applying a background color to both picture boxes.

 After you create your combined graphic, you can*not* resize it with the Picture Box Specifications dialog box or the Measurements palette. Instead, you'll have to resize each element. So make sure you know what size you want the graphic to be in the first place.

But if you resize a picture or text box with an image or text inside, and you hold down the ⌘ key while resizing the box handles, QuarkXPress scales the image or text along with the box.

Figure 7-5:
A graphic created by combining picture box controls, an empty picture box, and an imported graphic.

Using typographic symbols

Hundreds of fonts are composed of nothing but symbols, and they can be *very* handy as graphics. You can either use a symbol in text — that's how we put the solid squares into the layout in Figure 7-1 — or you can create a text box, put in the special symbol, and position it as if it were a picture box containing a graphic. Which option you choose depends on how completely the symbol integrates with a particular piece of text. The more integrated symbol and text are (if the text moves, should the symbol move with it?), the better off you are using a symbol character in the same text box as the text it belongs with.

Sometimes you may want to convert a symbol character into a graphic — for example, because you want to manipulate the symbol extensively in QuarkXPress. You can pull off this trick in a program like Adobe Illustrator, Aldus FreeHand, Deneba Canvas, or CorelDraw. First, convert the symbol to an outline or to curves. Then export the graphic to EPS or some other vector format. After that, you can scale, rotate, flip, and skew the graphic in QuarkXPress to your heart's content.

Most artists have met their need to treat text as art by using that very process. But you also can convert characters to graphics if you leave symbols as text: QuarkXPress can apply all these effects to a text box, too, and whatever you do to the text box will be done to the text inside. You can even colorize text — something you can't do with all graphics formats imported into QuarkXPress.

Inserting graphics into text

QuarkXPress lets you insert graphics into text — sort of. It offers a feature called *anchoring* that lets you cut or copy a graphic or picture box (or another text box) into the Mac or Windows clipboard (via Edit⇨Copy, Edit⇨Cut, ⌘-C, or ⌘-X) and then paste it into text. What's so nice about anchoring? Instead of simply positioning a picture box next to a particular piece of text, anchoring a picture box moves the box with the text. If you add text in front of the anchored graphic, the graphic moves down accordingly. If you had simply positioned the picture box at a particular piece of text and that text moved, the picture box would not have moved with it.

The process is a little tricky:

1. Select an object (picture box) with the Item tool.

2. Copy the object to the clipboard.

3. Switch to the Content tool.

4. Click at the text location where you want to insert the graphic.

5. Then paste in the graphic (via Edit⇨Paste or ⌘-V).

Okay, that's not *too* bad — the only thing we keep forgetting when we do these steps is to switch to the Item tool.

But there's more to it than that. Specifically, two more hurdles stand in your way when you insert graphics. First, if you paste a nonrectangular object, it gets converted to a rectangle, which means that square and polygon picture boxes become rectangles — so if you want to create a triangle graphic and insert it into text, you can't do it this way. Figure 7-6 shows an example of what happens when you try. Second, if you select a grouped item, or multiple items, you will get an error message when you try to paste the graphic into the text. Basically, you can paste in only single picture boxes. These two limitations make this feature less useful than it appears to be at first glance.

Where anchoring does come in handy, though, is putting an imported graphic (a drawing or photo) inside text. That procedure will let you use complex graphics as visual elements in your text, but it means that you can't use complex objects created in QuarkXPress as those elements.

Figure 7-6:
QuarkXPress can't paste text in grouped boxes, and it converts all nonrectangular boxes into rectangles.

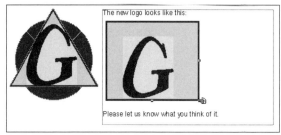

You should convert a symbol into a graphic when you want to apply special effects to the symbol and anchor it in a block of text (see the sidebar "Inserting graphics into text" for details on anchoring). You cannot select an individual character in a block of text and apply effects such as rotation to it. But unless your objective is to warp a symbol within text, don't worry about converting symbols into graphics before using them as a graphical embellishment. With the capability to anchor text boxes into text, you can apply most of QuarkXPress's design tools (like colorizing and rotating) to a symbol without needing a graphics program.

Making the Most of Lines

Lines — also called rules in the publishing world — are another great way to embellish a layout. They're great separators, putting lines between columns of text, around sidebars, or between stories. They're also great emphasizers: you underline for emphasis on a typewriter, and you underline for emphasis in desktop publishing, too. And they're great connectors, too: putting lines over several related elements makes the elements look related.

As you might expect with QuarkXPress, there's more than one way to create lines — in fact, you have your choice of three ways to create lines. One way is to draw lines with QuarkXPress's line tools. Another is to apply a frame to a text or picture box. The third way is to use underlines and ruling lines with text. Let's go through them one by one.

Drawing lines

QuarkXPress offers two line tools, the Line tool and the Orthogonal Line tool. An orthogonal line is one that is horizontal, vertical, or at a 45-degree angle. (If you use the regular Line tool, you can create orthogonal lines by holding the Shift key as you draw.) The reason for the Orthogonal Line option is to ensure that your graphics line up; no one likes lines or other elements that wander slightly out of alignment.

Drawing a line is easy. All you do is follow these steps:

1. **Select the appropriate line tool.**

2. **Move the mouse pointer to where you want to begin drawing.**

3. **Hold down the mouse button.**

4. **Move the mouse pointer to where you want the line to end.**

5. **Let go of the mouse button.**

And, just as you can with boxes, you can resize, reposition, or otherwise alter the line through the Measurements palette or through Item⇨Modify (⌘-M), which calls up the Line Specifications dialog box. An even faster way is to double-click the line. (No matter which method you use, QuarkXPress is smart enough to call the Line Specifications dialog box instead of the Picture Box Specifications dialog box — even though they share the same menu sequence and keyboard shortcut. Amazing, eh?) You also can group lines with other QuarkXPress objects.

Figure 7-7 shows a line being drawn below a newsletter's logo. You can see the Measurement palette's options for Lines; the different types of lines are displayed in a pop-up menu. Another pop-up menu lets you select different line endings, such as arrowheads. Note that all these options work whether you use the Content tool or the Item tool. A line's content is the line itself, so the distinction between the object and its content dissolves here.

Note that the line size can be anything from 0 to 864 points, in multiples of 0.1 points. You can select a size from the pop-up menu in the Measurements palette or in the Line Specifications dialog box, or you can enter in a size of your own in the size fields.

A word of advice: Use the dashed, dotted, and multiple-line lines sparingly. They can easily become distracting. A good rule of thumb on choosing line type is "If it makes sense, use it." It makes sense to use a dashed line for something you want a reader to cut out, and a dashed or dotted line can make sense when putting an annotation on a graphic. But don't get into a rut and use these special types of lines as routine replacements for solid lines. And don't make the lines too thick, either. It's pretty rare when you'll need a line thicker than 4 points; 1 to 2 points is typical.

The options in the Measurements palette for lines can change depending on which points on the line you have the palette work from. Look at Figure 7-8 to see what we mean. The same line has been rotated three ways, all at 30 degrees. The line at left is there so that you can see how each different rotation point affects the position of the rotated line. At top is the original line, unrotated. Notice how no rotation option appears for the top line's Measurements palette. That's because we've selected Endpoints, which lets us change the X and Y positions of the lines, but which also prevents us from rotating the line because you can't rotate around two points simultaneously — every circle can have only one center. In the other three lines, you see a rotation icon in the Measurements palette, but you also see X and Y coordinates only for the selected point, not for both ends. To change the active points, just select one of the four options from the pop-up list in the Measurements palette.

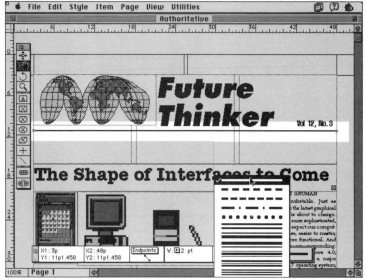

Figure 7-7:
The
Measure-
ments
palette lets
you select a
line's
thickness,
type, and
end style.

Framing boxes

Putting a line around a box is called *framing the box,* and QuarkXPress has an easy way to do the work for you.

In the bad old days of publishing, paste-up artists had to use transparent tape imprinted with lines and actually apply — by hand — four pieces of tape around each box. Then they had to cut the pieces of tape so that the corners looked right. It was easy to have crooked lines or mismatched corners. Well, the same eyesores could materialize if you use QuarkXPress to draw four lines around a text or picture box — even with QuarkXPress's ability to enter the precise coordinates for each object. And you wouldn't want unsightly boxes, now would you?

The solution is simple: Use the framing feature. Chapter 12 covers this feature in more detail, but, in a nutshell, here's how you make it work:

1. **Select a box with either the Content or Item tool.**

2. **Use Item⇨Frame, or ⌘-B, to get the dialog box shown in Figure 7-9.**

3. **Set the line thickness.**

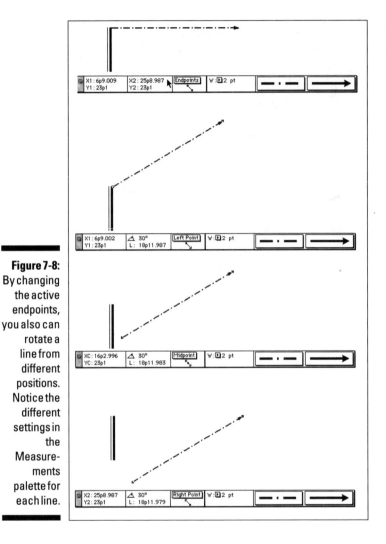

Figure 7-8:
By changing the active endpoints, you also can rotate a line from different positions. Notice the different settings in the Measurements palette for each line.

You can choose from the pop-up values or enter any value you want, in multiples of 0.1 points, from 0 to a size equal to half the thickness of the box, in any color, any shade, and any line style. Notice how the frame around the words *Frame Specification* changes to match your settings? That change lets you preview the effect.

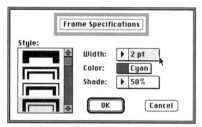

Figure 7-9:
The Frame
Specifications
dialog box.

Lines with text

Several kinds of text present opportunities for lines. Figure 7-2 shows one example, where the kicker is underlined. You also can put a line between text and, say, an author biography or contact information. Or maybe you would underline subheads in a document. Wherever or however you use them, just remember one thing: If you use lines, use them sparingly and consistently, such as only for author bios — but for all author bios. And use them for *emphasis.* Figure 7-10 shows several examples of lines that add judicious emphasis to design.

In QuarkXPress, you can apply an underline to selected text via ⌘-Shift-U or by clicking the <u>U</u> button in the Measurements palette. (The long way is via Style⇨Type Style⇨Underline, but no one should go to all this work — you're using a *computer,* for goodness' sake!) To underline an entire headline, go ahead and make the underline part of the paragraph style (see the next chapter for details on *that* process). That way, you have QuarkXPress do the underlining for you.

QuarkXPress supports two types of underlines in text: regular underline and word underline. *Regular underline* underlines all characters, including spaces. *Word underline* does not underline spaces. In most cases, you should pick regular underline. After all, underlining the spaces between words and sentences makes it clear that the text is related, as the text is joined. Another way to think of it is that you should underline spaces just as you italicize or boldface spaces (which changes their proportions to match that of the italicized or boldfaced text). Use word underline only for documents that you want to have the feel of a typed report. The shortcut for word underline is ⌘-Shift-W, or you can click the <u>W</u> button in the Measurements palette.

But underlines have a problem: you can't determine their thickness or position relative to the text. They're fine for underlining text, but not for embellishing text. Embellishing is the special province of rules. Underlines are actually a special type of rule, and a rule is the publishing word for a line. In the wonderful world of QuarkXPress, though, *rule* means a line associated with text, while *line* means a line that is its own object.

Figure 7-10:
Examples of
how lines
can dress
up a docu-
ment: to
emphasize a
label
(top), to
emphasize
a kicker and
byline
(middle),
and to
separate a
bio from a
story
(bottom).

Figure 7-10:
Examples of how lines can dress up a document: to emphasize a label (top), to emphasize a kicker and byline (middle), and to separate a bio from a story (bottom).

Board of Directors
President: Jeff Yablon
Vice President: Michael Desmond
Secretary: Diana Garelik
Treasurer: Richard Morochove

Administration
Administrator: Heidi Wagner

EUROPEAN HOLIDAYS
A Tour through France's Roman Ruins

BY INGALL BULL III

SPRING IN SOUTHERN France — the hills are redolent of fresh herbs, and the vintners are preparing the fields for new vines. In the

slightly humid, sunny air, there is quiet. And if you listen carefully, you can hear echoes of a thousand years ago, when Rome ruled the land and France was Gaul.

The legacy of that past remains through-out France today — Roman times lay on hills, while old cobble villages still house artists and laborers.

That new version, of course, will reflect the times. In the near future, interface styles will increasingly draw inspiration from central programs—suites today and perhaps OLE and OpenDoc tool sets in the future. And moving forward, those cen-

tral programs will assert their interfaces more aggressively on other applications. Farther down the road, maybe a decade from now, future technologies and ever-increasing computer processor power will likely make today's interface technologies

seem as quaint as an old DOS command.

While we're waiting, let's savor the choices coming our way. *Galen Gronson is a features editor for Macworld and the desktop-pub-lishing reviewer for PC and Mac software at InfoWorld.*

QuarkXPress lets you set up rules in the — drum roll, please — Paragraph Rules dialog box. Paragraph Rules is one of those dialog boxes that you can apply to the current text or to a style sheet (which we cover in Chapter 8). If you're working with a single paragraph, use ⌘-Shift-N or Style⇨Rules; if you're working in a style, select the Rules button in the Edit Style Sheet dialog box. (No, the shortcut makes no sense. Quark must have run out of letters when they named it!) The Paragraph Rules dialog box is weird: it has four possible appearances, as Figure 7-11 shows, depending on which boxes you've checked. You can have a rule above, below, above and below, or neither above nor below. If you set a rule above and below, you can apply separate settings to each line, as we did at the bottom of Figure 7-11.

The controls for rules are essentially the same as those for setting lines' attributes, and the basic options are shown in Figure 7-11. But do note a couple of options peculiar to rules:

✔ **In the Length pop-up menu, you have a choice of Text or Indents.** The Text option makes the rule the width of the text (if the text takes multiple lines, the rule width equals the width of the top line's text if you are putting a rule above, and the width of the bottom line if you are putting a rule below). The Indents option makes the line's width match the indenta-tion settings in the Paragraph Formats dialog box (⌘-Shift-F or Style⇨Formats, or in the Edit Style Sheet dialog box, via the Formats button). Typically, that means the width of the column. In Figure 7-10, we used Indents for the bottom example and Text for the other two.

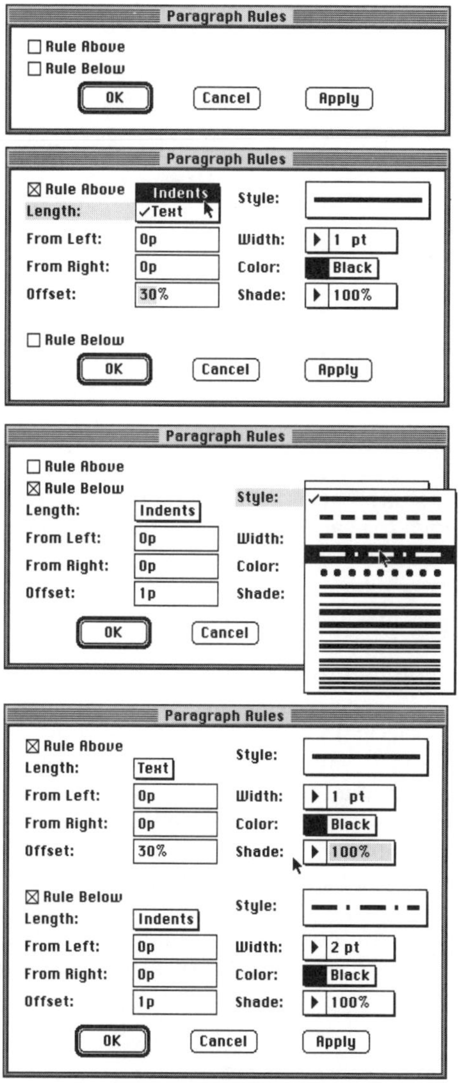

Figure 7-11:
The
Paragraph
Rules dialog
box in its
various
incarnations.

✓ **In the Offset field, you can enter either a percentage of the current leading, such as 30%, or a hard value, such as 0.5˜ or 3 pt or 0p4.** The offset amount moves the line away from the text (up if the rule is above, down if the rule is below). In Figure 7-10, you can see the effects of offset adjustment in the "A Tour Through France's Roman Ruins" example. Compare the position of the underline for the phrase "European Holidays" to the position of the rule under the byline; we moved the rule that is below the byline down more than the default of 0%.

TIP

Figuring offsets can be a royal pain, so use the Apply button to test out settings without actually leaving the dialog box. QuarkXPress is even nice enough to move the dialog box away from the rule so that you can see what the effect actually is. When you like what you see, click OK.

Fabulous Folios

What's a folio? It's the page number, publication name, issue date, and other such text that appears at the bottom or top of every text page. It's what reminds the readers of what they're reading. And it's a perfect example of something that really benefits from some decoration — er, embellishment.

Folios shouldn't be boring, but they shouldn't be loud, either, and they should look separate from the rest of the page. In this book, the folio is at the top, and (no, that's not an optical illusion) there's a line that separates the folio from the text. The page number is huge so that you can easily find it — and it prevents the folio from fading into obscurity, too. (See, form *and* function!) Figure 7-12 shows some other examples of folios. All add small graphics to make the logo classier. The graphic could be just a symbol or basic shape, or it could be your logo or a simple variant of it. As you can see, these folios are just combinations of text, lines (or rules), and graphics (or symbols).

Because a folio appears on practically every page, your best bet is to put it on a Master Page (see Chapter 4). That way, QuarkXPress will repeat it — automatically — on all pages that use the Master Page. If your document is in the form of a book or magazine — that is, a form that's bound in the middle — it's classiest to have a left-hand and right-hand version of your folio. Why's it so nice to have both versions? Because the page numbers are always on the outside of the page, where they are easy to find. When you do have both left- and right-hand folios, use ⌘-3 instead of typing an actual page number into the text box containing the folio text. This code tells QuarkXPress to fill in the page number automatically.

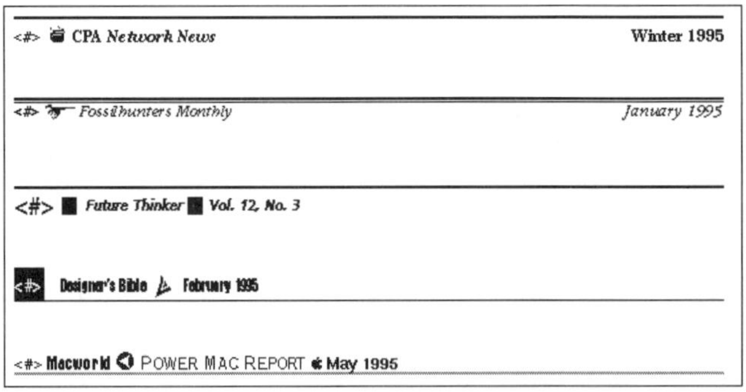

Figure 7-12:
Examples of
folios that
use graphical
embellishments.

<#> ☎ CPA *Network News*   **Winter 1995**

<#> 🐟 *Fossilhunters Monthly*   *January 1995*

<#> ■ *Future Thinker* ■ *Vol. 12, No. 3*

<#> **Designer's Bible** ✏ **February 1995**

<#> **Macworld** ◆ POWER MAC REPORT 🍎 May 1995

Part III
Fine-Tuned Text

"NOPE – I'D BETTER WAIT 'TIL ALL MY FONTS ARE WORKING. A HATE LETTER JUST DOESN'T WORK IN *Filigree Flowerbox Extended.*"

In this part ...

QuarkXPress is not a word processor, and published text is not typewritten. Seem obvious? Not to everyone. How you work with text — both editing and formatting it — plays a key role in effective layout. The four chapters in this part will show you the ins and outs of text handling, and soon you'll be amazing your friends and family with your skills. Well, maybe not, but you will be ready to produce top-notch text quality, which will make your layouts read great, not just look great.

Chapter 8

You've Got Real Style

• •

• •

*A*lthough you've heard about them, you've probably never really been into *style sheets*. Yet you know some people who use them on every single document. But something inside you says, "Style sheets? Document formatting? Whoa! Save it for the big-time publishers!" We think you should reconsider. Surely you must realize by now that half the fun of desktop publishing is being able to automate some of the tasks that used to take so long. QuarkXPress makes setting up styles for your documents easy. Best of all, using style sheets saves you tons of time.

Style sheets are just about the best invention since the snooze alarm. They define basic specifications for your text: typefaces, type sizes, justification settings, and tab settings. If you select a paragraph and apply a style sheet to it, the paragraph automatically formats itself to the font and size specified in the style sheet.

Just think of all the time this automatic styling saves you. Instead of applying each and every attribute individually to text, you can just tell QuarkXPress that you want particular swaths of text to take on all the formatting attributes established in a style tag. Then — with one click of the mouse — you send QuarkXPress on its merry way to format your document quicker than you can take a sip of coffee.

Like many publishing topics, style sheets come with their own jargon, which would be helpful for you to know:

✔ **Style sheet:** The group of styles in a document. It's called a *sheet* because, in times before electronic publishing, typesetters had typewritten sheets that listed the formatting attributes they were to apply to specific kinds of text, such as body copy and headlines. QuarkXPress treats style sheets as part of the document.

✔ **Style tag or style:** These two terms refer to a group of attributes that you apply to one or more paragraphs. You name the group, or style, so that you can apply all the attributes at once. The word *tag* is used because you "tag" selected paragraphs with the style you want to apply. Because the word *style* also sometimes refers to a character attribute, such as italics or underline, many people use *style tag* to refer to the group of attributes. This distinction helps you avoid confusing the two meanings.

The time-saving part about styles is that, when you apply them, you do so to whole paragraphs, not just to selected words or sentences. For example, first-level heads might have a header1 style, captions a caption style, bylines a byline style, body text a body text style, and so on. It's a great idea to specify a style for all paragraph types that you use often.

Styles work in two places: you can apply them on selected paragraphs in your QuarkXPress document or in the word-processing text you plan to import. Don't worry: we'll explain how to do it both ways.

Styling Your Style Sheets

We promised you it would be easy, and we were right! The keys to creating, changing, and applying styles are in one simple spot: the Style Sheets dialog box, which you access via Edit⇨Style Sheets (see Figure 8-1).

Figure 8-1:
You can do almost anything you want to style sheets from within the Style Sheets dialog box (Edit⇨Style Sheets).

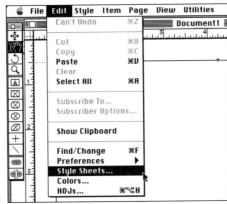

Oops! We almost forgot that there are just a couple of style-related functions that you set somewhere outside the Style Sheets dialog box. The first is hyphenation controls, which are set in the H&Js dialog box (Edit⇨H&Js). The second set of style functions that you set elsewhere are those that control character and space scaling; to set these controls, you need to access the Typographic Preferences dialog box (Edit⇨Preferences⇨Typographic).

If you are new to this style sheet business, give yourself some time to experiment. After all, you can always delete any style sheet you end up disliking by simply highlighting the style in the Style Sheets dialog box and clicking on the Delete button.

We *told* you it was easy!

What's inside the Style Sheets dialog box?

The Style Sheets dialog box, shown in Figure 8-2, gives you several choices for editing style sheets. Your choices are as follows:

Figure 8-2:
The Style
Sheets
dialog box
gives you
several
functions
from which
to choose.

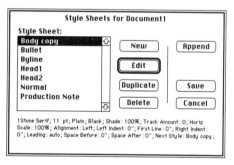

✔ **New** lets you create a new style from scratch or create a new style based on an existing style.

Let's say you just spent fifteen minutes defining text settings through the Style menu or Measurements palette. Can these settings become a style? Yes. All you need to do is position your text cursor anywhere on the text that has the desired settings. Then choose New in the Style Sheets dialog box. All settings are automatically included in the new style you create.

✔ **Edit** lets you make changes to an existing style. You also can use Edit to create a brand-new style by editing an existing style, changing the style name to a new name, and changing whichever attribute settings you want. Creating a brand-new style in this manner has the same effect as clicking the Duplicate button.

✔ **Duplicate** copies all the attributes of an existing style and gives the duplicate style the name Copy of style. You then can change any attribute settings, including the style name.

✔ **Delete** lets you delete existing styles. A dialog box asks you to confirm the deletion if you applied the style to text in the current document. Any text using a deleted style retains the style's attributes. But the Style Sheet palette and menu show these paragraphs as having No Style.

✔ **Append** lets you copy a style from another QuarkXPress document.

✔ **Save** saves all the style changes you make in the Style Sheets dialog box. Forgetting to save styles when leaving the dialog box will keep the changes from taking effect, so try to remember to save, okay?

✔ **Cancel** makes the program ignore all style changes you made in the Style Sheets dialog box.

After you make a selection in the Style Sheets dialog box, you see the Edit Style Sheet dialog box, shown in Figure 8-3. This dialog box is where most of the action takes place in setting up styles.

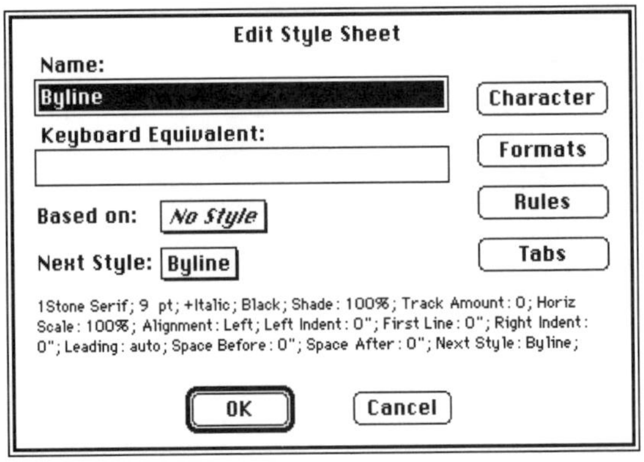

Edit Style Sheet

Name:
Byline   Character

Keyboard Equivalent:
                                          Formats

                                          Rules
Based on: No Style
                                          Tabs
Next Style: Byline

1 Stone Serif; 9 pt; +Italic; Black; Shade: 100%; Track Amount: 0; Horiz Scale: 100%; Alignment: Left; Left Indent: 0"; First Line: 0"; Right Indent: 0"; Leading: auto; Space Before: 0"; Space After: 0"; Next Style: Byline;

OK   Cancel

Figure 8-3:
The Edit Style Sheet dialog box.

Here are some of the fields in the Edit Style Sheet dialog box and explanations of what they all mean.

✔ **Name** is filled in with a name if you are editing an existing style but is empty if you are working on a new style.

✔ **Keyboard Equivalent** lets you set up keys on your computer's keyboard that make it easier to apply styles to text quickly. To enter keyboard equivalents, press the actual key or keys you want to use, including any combinations with Shift, Option, and ⌘.

QuarkXPress includes a keyboard template listing function key equivalents for often-accessed commands. You can override the original commands by assigning function keys to style sheets, but, if you do, you lose the ability to access the commands assigned to those keys. Simply add the Ctrl key as a modifier and you can assign styles to function keys, maintaining the original command equivalents. For example, assigning F2 as an equivalent keyboard key for a style would take away Quark's F2 Cut Key; instead, you should assign Ctrl-F2 as the keyboard equivalent keys for your style.

Based On reads No Style unless you are editing or duplicating a style that uses the based-on option, described later in this chapter. You can enter or change the style name; if you choose the name of an existing style, an error message asking for a new name appears when you choose OK.

✔ **Based on** lets you begin building a group of styles by basing the group on another style. Then, if you decide to change the group, you only need to change the original base style and those changes will automatically apply to the rest of the group. For instance, if you had five body text styles created using the "Based on" option and using the same font, instead of altering all five style sheets to change your body text font, you merely edit the base style and the remaining group of styles reflects the font change.

✔ **Next Style** lets you establish linked styles. For example, you can specify that a headline style is always followed by a byline style, which is always followed by a body copy style. If you choose Next Style, here's how it works: As you type text into the QuarkXPress page, every time you enter a paragraph return after typing a byline, the style automatically changes to the body text style.

✔ **Character** calls up another dialog box where you pick text attributes such as typeface and size.

✔ **Formats** calls up another dialog box where you pick paragraph attributes such as leading and indentation.

✔ **Rules** lets you associate ruling lines with paragraphs.

✔ **Tabs** lets you define tab stops and tab types.

You can use these Edit Style Sheet dialog box features in any order and ignore ones that don't apply to the current style.

Show 'em some style

It's always a good idea to start with a good idea. In other words, before you create a style, try to develop some idea of the basic elements you want to have in your document. For example, elements in a newspaper include body text, headlines, bylines, captions, and page numbers (folios). In addition, lead text, pull-quotes, biographies, subheads, sidebar heads, bulleted lists, and other more specialized types of formatting may be necessary. Don't worry about knowing in advance all the types of formatting you need to assign styles to — it's very easy in QuarkXPress to add a new style at any time.

Start with the body text because that's the bulk of your document. You can create a style called something like Body Text, or you can modify the Normal style that QuarkXPress defines automatically for each new document and use that as your body text style.

The initial setting for Normal is left-aligned, 12-point Helvetica with automatic leading. To change any attributes of Normal, close all open documents, access the Style Sheets dialog box by selecting Edit↔Style Sheets, and edit the Normal style in the usual way, described next. These settings are saved as the new defaults for all future new documents. When creating this default Normal style, you don't need to use real text because real text is used only to gauge the effects of the style formatting. Similarly, any style sheet created without a document open becomes part of the default style sheet for all new documents.

Now, let's go ahead and create a style so that you can see just how easy it is. For our example, we imported a text file to be used in a brochure whose style has not yet been defined. When loaded, the text took on the attributes of the Normal style because we did not use style options in the original word processor. This text has five main elements: the body text, the body lead (which has a drop cap but otherwise is like the body text), the byline, the headline, and the kicker (the small headline above the headline that identifies the type of story — in this case, a commentary). Our newsletter also needs styles for captions, folios (page numbers), the publication name, and the publication date, all of which typically run at the top or bottom of each page. In addition, we need styles for subheads and sidebar heads (for simplicity, we decided that sidebar text will be the same as the body text).

What's our first step? To get the Edit Style Sheets dialog box to appear, a process described earlier in this chapter. After we called up that dialog box, we selected the Character button to open the Character Attributes dialog box, shown in Figure 8-4. Then we changed the Century Old Style, the Size to 12, and the Track Amount to –2. We left the other attributes alone because they seemed okay for body text. We clicked OK to return to the Edit Style Sheets dialog box.

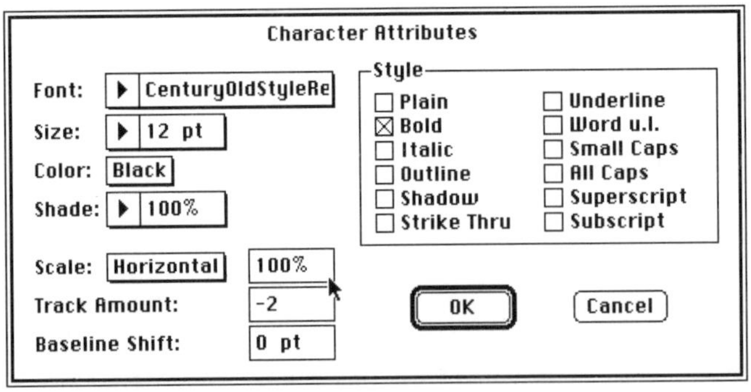

Figure 8-4:
The
Character
Attributes
dialog box.

Character Attributes

Font:	▶ CenturyOldStyleRe
Size:	▶ 12 pt
Color:	Black
Shade:	▶ 100%
Scale:	Horizontal	100%
Track Amount:	–2
Baseline Shift:	0 pt

Style
- ☐ Plain
- ☒ Bold
- ☐ Italic
- ☐ Outline
- ☐ Shadow
- ☐ Strike Thru
- ☐ Underline
- ☐ Word u.l.
- ☐ Small Caps
- ☐ All Caps
- ☐ Superscript
- ☐ Subscript

OK   Cancel

QuarkXPress dialog boxes often include pop-up menus to help you make selections faster. For example, in the Character Attributes dialog box, Font, Size, Color, and Shade all offer pop-up menus. You also can enter the value you want directly into the field. In the Font field, QuarkXPress displays the first typeface it finds that begins with the letter you type in. Entering the first letters of the typeface name enables you to jump quickly to or near a particular typeface — which is convenient if you have a long list of typefaces to scroll through. Figure 8-5 shows the pop-up menu for the Font field.

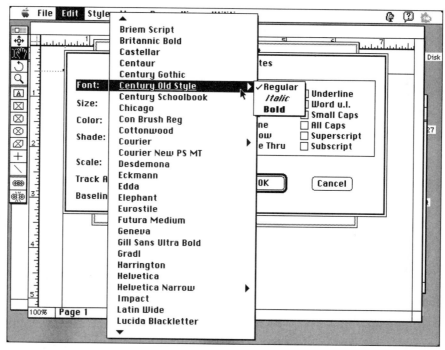

Figure 8-5:
The Font drop-down list in the Character Attributes dialog box.

Let's see, now; where were we? Ah, yes, we were in the middle of setting up a style. After selecting all the character attributes, next we opened the Paragraph Formats dialog box (see Figure 8-6) by selecting the Formats button in the Edit Style Sheet dialog box. We changed the First Line field so that the first line of each paragraph is indented 9 points. We also changed Alignment to Left and Leading to +2 points, which tells QuarkXPress to make the leading 2 points more than the point size; the default is Auto, which makes leading 120 percent of the point size.

Figure 8-6:
In the
Paragraph
Formats
dialog box,
you set style
specifications
that affect
how
paragraphs
in a certain
style appear
in the
document.

We then chose OK to leave the Paragraph Formats dialog box, OK to leave the Edit Style Sheets dialog box, and Save to save all our changes to the Normal style. Figure 8-7 shows this sequence of two of these dialog boxes.

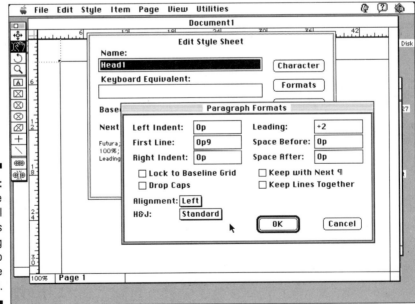

Figure 8-7:
You use
several
dialog boxes
within dialog
boxes to
save style
attributes.

Making Styles Happen

When you count them up, you really have three possible ways to apply a style, and you can see two of the ways in Figure 8-8:

- ✔ **Option 1:** Use the Style⇨Style Sheet menu option.

- ✔ **Option 2:** Use the Style Sheets palette, shown on the right side of the figure (View⇨Show Style Sheets). This option is our favorite way to apply styles in most cases.

- ✔ **Option 3:** Use the keyboard shortcut, if you defined one in the Edit Style Sheet dialog box. (In this example, we did not invoke a shortcut key). While this option is the fastest method, use it only for very commonly used styles because you need to remember the keyboard shortcuts that you assigned.

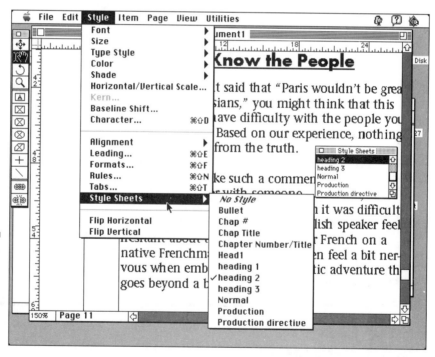

Figure 8-8:
QuarkXPress
offers
several
ways to
apply styles.

If you aren't convinced yet that style sheets can save you a great deal of time, we suggest you take a few minutes and give them a try. Most publishers find style sheets to be terrific time-savers, and we think you will, too.

Give me a little space

In publishing, the spaces between characters and words are every bit as important as the characters and words themselves. It pays to understand spaces—both the normal, everyday kind, as well as the special ones — in order to make the most of QuarkXPress. As you become more familiar with the program, you may find times when the normal spaces won't do. In these cases, you may want to impose one or more specific kinds of spacing provided by QuarkXPress:

Nonbreaking space: Ensures that a line does not wrap between two words if you do not want it to. To get a nonbreaking space, press ⌘-spacebar (Windows: press Ctrl-spacebar).

En space: Press Option-spacebar (Windows: Ctrl-Shift-6) to get this space, which is typically used in numbered lists after the period following the numeral. An en space makes a number more visible because the number is separated more from the following text than words in the text are separated from each other. En spaces also are used before single-digit numerals when a numbered list includes both single- and double-digit numerals. (In most typefaces, a numeral occupies the width of an en space. So putting an en space before numerals 1 through 9 aligns them with the 0 in the number 10.) A variation of the en space is the nonbreaking en space, accessed by pressing ⌘-Option-spacebar (Windows: press Ctrl-Alt-Shift-6).

Punctuation space: A punctuation space is the width of a period or comma. Some people call a punctuation space a thin space; regardless of its name, it is generally half the width of an en space. To get a punctuation space, press Shift-spacebar. Typically, you use this kind of space to ensure alignment of numerals when some numbers have commas and others don't—as in 1,911 and 439. To align the last three digits of both numbers, you place an en space and a punctuation space before 439. A variation is the nonbreaking punctuation space, which you access by pressing ⌘-Shift-spacebar (Windows: Ctrl-Shift-spacebar).

Flexible space: A flexible space (Mac: Option-Shift-spacebar; Windows: Ctrl-Shift-5) is a space you define as a certain percentage of an en space. If you define a flexible space as twice the width (200 percent) of an en space, you create an em space. You define the flex space width in the Typographic Preferences dialog box, which you access via Edit⇨Preferences⇨Typographic. Specify the width in percentages from 0 to 400, proceeding in increments of 0.1. For the nonbreaking variant of the flex space, press ⌘-Option-Shift-spacebar (Windows: Ctrl-Alt-Shift-5).

Changing Styles

Decisions, decisions. Just when you think you've created a great style, you decide to make some little changes to it so that it can be even better. You know, add half a point to the size of your headline, make your byline italic, change the leading on your body copy, that kind of change. Again, it's an easy thing to change a style.

To makes changes to styles, simply open the Style Sheets dialog box and select Edit. You then can change attributes as you want. You also can use this approach to create new styles that are based on current ones.

Based-on styles

When you create styles for a document, you'll probably want several similar styles, perhaps with some styles even being variations of others. For example, you might want both a body text style *and* a style for bulleted lists that is based on the body text style.

No problem: QuarkXPress uses a technique called *based-on formatting* in its styles. You can tell QuarkXPress to base the Bulleted Text style on the Body Text style (in which you defined typeface, point size, leading, justification, hyphenation, indentation, tabs, and other attributes). You then modify the Bulleted Text style to accommodate bullets — by changing the indentation, for example. The great thing about based-on formatting is that, later, if you decide to change the typeface in Body Text, the typeface automatically changes in Bulleted Text and in all other styles that you created or edited based on Body Text — saving you a great deal of work in maintaining consistent styles.

Figure 8-9 shows the Edit Style Sheets dialog box for a style named Head1.

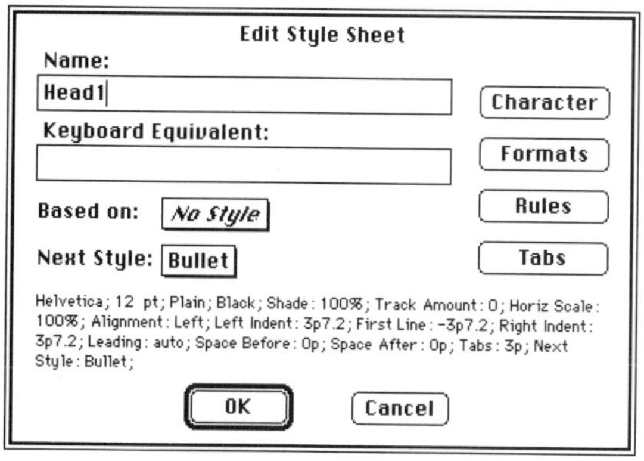

Figure 8-9: The style description lists differences between the Head 1 style and the No Style style on which it is based.

Edit Style Sheet

Name:

`Head1`

Keyboard Equivalent:

Based on: *No Style*

Next Style: `Bullet`

Helvetica; 12 pt; Plain; Black; Shade: 100%; Track Amount: 0; Horiz Scale: 100%; Alignment: Left; Left Indent: 3p7.2; First Line: -3p7.2; Right Indent: 3p7.2; Leading: auto; Space Before: 0p; Space After: 0p; Tabs: 3p; Next Style: Bullet;

Character
Formats
Rules
Tabs

OK   Cancel

Duplicating styles

Another nifty way to change an existing style or create a new one is to duplicate an existing style and then edit the attributes in that duplicate. Or you can edit an existing style and give it a new name. Duplicating a style is similar to creating a based-on style, except that the new style is not automatically updated if the style it is duplicated from is modified — unless the style you duplicated or edited is based on another style.

Importing Styles

Sometimes you'll find yourself in a situation where you already have style sheets in one QuarkXPress document that are *just right* for what you need in another one. Have no fear — there's no need to start the process all over again. All you need to do is copy styles from one document to another.

Copying styles between documents

You copy styles between documents by selecting the Append button in the Style Sheets dialog box. When you select Append, you open the Append Style Sheets dialog box (see Figure 8-10). This dialog box is similar to the dialog box for opening a QuarkXPress document. You can change drives and directories as needed to select the QuarkXPress document that has the style sheet you want.

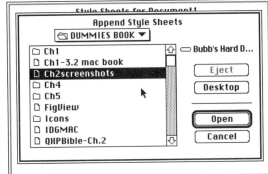

Figure 8-10: The Append Style Sheets dialog box.

When you select a document and choose OK, QuarkXPress copies all of its styles into your current document. But note that you can't pick and choose individual styles to import; if you append style sheets from another document, you get all of them. But be careful: If a style in the current document has the same name as a style you are importing, QuarkXPress preserves the *current* document's style and ignores the style in the other document — all without telling you.

Importing styles from a word processor

Some people create text right inside the text boxes of a QuarkXPress document. Others prefer to use a separate word processing program for drafting the text and only later import the text into QuarkXPress. Either way works fine, and both methods let you take advantage of style sheets.

QuarkXPress lets you import styles created in most of the popular word processors. To make the process of importing text files that include style sheets, we suggest that you check the Include Style Sheets box — at the bottom of the Get Text box — as shown in Figure 8-11.

Figure 8-11:
Check the
Include
Style Sheets
option when
you import a
word-
processor
document
that has
style sheets
associated
with it.

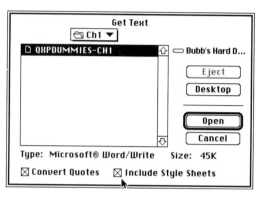

You also want to use the Include Style Sheets option if you are importing text saved in the XPress Tags format (described in an Appendix of the QuarkXPress documentation). Although the purpose of the XPress Tags format is to embed style tags and other formatting information in your text, you still must remind QuarkXPress to read those tags during import. Otherwise, QuarkXPress imports your text as an ASCII file, and all the embedded tags are treated as regular text and are not acted upon.

Figure 8-12 shows a list of styles that we imported from a Microsoft Word document.

If you check the Include Style Sheets check box for formats that have no style sheets, QuarkXPress ignores the setting. Thus, if you typically import style sheets with your text, it's good to get into the habit of always checking this box; checking the box does not cause any problems when importing other text formats.

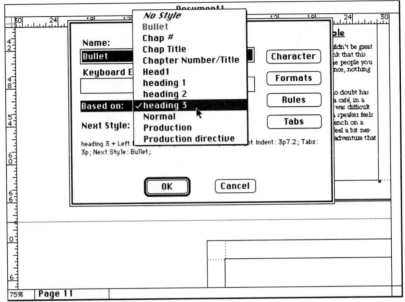

Figure 8-12:
Use the
Based On
option to
cause an
imported
word
processor
style to take
on the
attributes
of a
QuarkXPress
style sheet.

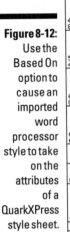

Avoiding style conflicts

The names of imported style tags are listed in the Style Sheets palette and can be edited like any other style. If the imported style sheet has a style tag that uses a name already in use by the QuarkXPress document, Quark renames the imported style tag. The new name takes the form of the old name plus an asterisk (*).

This renaming feature ensures that you don't lose any formatting. But what if you want to use an existing QuarkXPress style tag on text that uses a word processor's style tag that is formatted differently? Consider this example:

When you import your Word text with the Include Style Sheets box checked, QuarkXPress renames the Word style to Normal* because QuarkXPress has its own Normal style defined. But your goal is to have the text that was tagged Normal in Word take on the attributes of the QuarkXPress tag called Normal. You can just delete the Normal* style in the Style Sheet dialog box and tell QuarkXPress to substitute Normal.

It's nice to be able to resolve style conflicts so easily, and this capability is just one more reason to use style sheets.

As you can tell, we are style sheet fans to the core. Style sheets are a cool invention. They save you time. And saving time saves you money. And we all know that saving money is a good thing.

Chapter 9
Working with Special Characters

*B*efore desktop publishing, you could always tell homegrown publications from the professional kind by the difference in typography. Homegrown publications were typed and either dittoed, mimeographed, or photocopied, but professional publications were typeset. Anyone could spot the difference: in a homegrown publication, you saw -- as a dash, while in a professional publication you saw the — character; an apostrophe or single quote was ' in a homegrown publication, while in a professional publication it was ' or '. And, of course, a homegrown publication used "as the double quote character, while a professional publication used " or ". Professional publications also had accents on letters (at least sometimes), different styles of characters, a whole slew of symbols (at least sometimes), and even characters of different sizes.

Then came desktop publishing. Soon anyone with a Mac or PC had the same characters. The only problem was that most people didn't know how to use the characters. All sorts of keyboard commands showed these characters, but who could remember them all? So you kept seeing — and 'and " in documents that looked professional; you could tell that the documents had come off of someone's LaserWriter because of those telltale typewriter characters.

But soon QuarkXPress made working with special characters simpler. Quark would automatically convert the typewriter dashes and quotes into typographic dashes and quotes — but only when you imported text. It took until version 3.3 in 1994 for Quark to add the ability to generate those quotation characters as you typed text — unfortunately, you still have to type in dashes the hard way. Still, automating the quotes goes a long way, and now it's nearly impossible to tell by the characters alone whether a publication is professional or homegrown.

Typographic Characters

Your otherwise-humble authors are typographic snobs, so we think everyone should use the curly quotes and the long-line dash instead of the typewriter symbols. Why? Because professional typographers always use them, and they've become synonymous with professionalism. And besides, they're so easy to use now that there's no excuse not to use them.

Quotes and dashes

One of the first things you should do in QuarkXPress is set it up to automatically type in the professional characters for you. Here's how: Go to the Applications Preferences menu (Edit⇨Preferences⇨Application, or ⌘-Option-Shift-Y). You get the dialog box shown in Figure 9-1. You can ignore most of the dialog box for now; only the options in the lower left corner affect typography. Make sure that the Smart Quotes option is checked: Smart Quotes converts quotes as you type (sorry, it won't do dashes). If you're not publishing in English, you can select a different set of quote characters through the Quotes pop-up menu shown in the Figure 9-1.

For many preferences, to make them affect all QuarkXPress documents, you have to make sure no document is open before changing the preferences. Otherwise, the preferences apply only to that document. But any preferences set via the Application Preferences dialog box affect all documents, whether or not a document happened to be open when you set those preferences. Here's a case where you can lower your guard.

You also should ensure that QuarkXPress converts the quotes and, yes, dashes in text files that you import. When you import (File⇨Get Text, or ⌘-E), make sure that the Convert Quotes box is checked. So you don't forget to keep checking that box each time you import, QuarkXPress leaves it checked for all future imports, until, of course, you uncheck it. Figure 9-2 shows how the dialog box should look when you take this precaution.

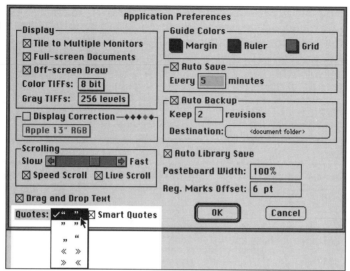

Figure 9-1:
The Application Preferences dialog box lets you set up automatic conversion of keyboard quotes into the typographically correct equivalents.

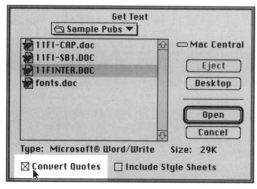

Figure 9-2:
When importing text, make sure that the Convert Quotes box is checked to automatically convert keyboard dashes and quotes.

The Mac has many built-in shortcuts for special characters and symbols, and QuarkXPress adds some of its own. Windows also supports many symbols, although it uses special codes for most, rather than keyboard shortcuts. So, when you refer to the shortcut tables throughout this chapter (including Table 9-1), keep the following three conditions in mind: (1) Not all keyboard shortcuts are available in all programs. (This is truer in Windows than on the Mac since Windows programs generally have less consistency among themselves than

Mac programs.) (2) Not all symbols are supported in all fonts; for symbols listed as *not supported,* you may be able to find a symbol or pi font that includes the symbol (as used here, *not supported* means that the symbol is not available in standard fonts). (3) To use the Windows codes, hold the Alt key and enter the four-digit numeral code from the numeric keypad, not from the numbers on the keyboard (above the letters). (The Mac does not use an equivalent numeric system; instead, all characters are accessible through some shortcut combination.)

Table 9-1	Shortcuts for Quotes and Dashes	
Character	*Mac shortcut*	*Windows shortcut*
Open double quote (")*	Option-Shift-[	Shift+Alt+[*or* Alt+0147
Close double quote (")*	Option-Shift-]	Shift+Alt+] *or* Alt+0148
Open French double quote («)*	Option-\	Ctrl+Alt+[
Close French double quote (»)*	Option-Shift-\	Ctrl+Alt+]
Open single quote (')*	Option-[	Alt+[*or* Ctrl+Alt+9
Close single quote (')*	Option-]	Alt+] *or* Ctrl+Alt+0
Breaking em dash*	Option-Shift-hyphen	Ctrl+Shift+= *or* Alt+0151
Nonbreaking en dash	Option-hyphen	Ctrl+= *or* Alt+0150
Nonbreaking em dash	⌘-Option-=	Ctrl+Shift+Alt+=

* Automatically generated if the Smart Quotes option is selected in the Application Preferences dialog box (Edit⌐Preferences⌐Application). Typing an apostrophe creates an open or closed single quote as appropriate, and typing a keyboard quote (") creates an open or closed double quote as appropriate. For double quotes, you can choose the quotation style to match those used in several European languages; you set the quotation style in the Application Preferences dialog box.

Ligatures

After you set up your Application Preferences dialog box to enable smart quotes, the very next thing to do is go to the Typographic Preferences dialog box (Edit⇨Preferences⇨Typographic, or ⌘-Option-Y). Here, you set up the treatment of ligatures. Figure 9-3 shows the appropriate dialog box.

The Typographic Preferences dialog box is different in Windows than on the Mac because Windows does not support ligatures. To say that another way: there are no ligature options in Windows QuarkXPress's dialog box.

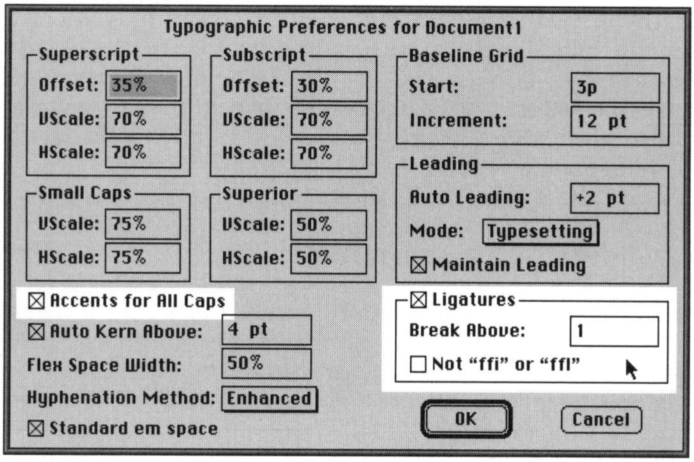

Figure 9-3:
Check the
Ligatures
box in the
Typographic
Preferences
dialog box
to enable
ligatures
(available
on the
Mac only).

```
┌─────────────────────────────────────────────────────────┐
│         Typographic Preferences for Document1            │
│ ┌─Superscript─┐ ┌─Subscript──┐ ┌─Baseline Grid────────┐  │
│  Offset: [35%]   Offset: [30%]  Start:        [3p   ]    │
│  UScale: [70%]   UScale: [70%]  Increment:    [12 pt]    │
│  HScale: [70%]   HScale: [70%] └──────────────────────┘  │
│ └─────────────┘ └────────────┐ ┌─Leading──────────────┐  │
│ ┌─Small Caps──┐ ┌─Superior───┐  Auto Leading:  [+2 pt]   │
│  UScale: [75%]   UScale: [50%]  Mode:  [Typesetting]     │
│  HScale: [75%]   HScale: [50%]  ⊠ Maintain Leading       │
│ └─────────────┘ └────────────┘ └──────────────────────┘  │
│ ⊠ Accents for All Caps        ┌─⊠ Ligatures──────────┐   │
│ ⊠ Auto Kern Above: [4 pt]      Break Above:  [1    ]    │
│ Flex Space Width:  [50%]       ☐ Not "ffi" or "ffl"   ▶ │
│ Hyphenation Method: [Enhanced]└──────────────────────┘   │
│ ⊠ Standard em space              ( OK )    ( Cancel )    │
└─────────────────────────────────────────────────────────┘
```

Ligatures are special forms of characters that are linked together. In many books, you find the combination of *f* and *i* typeset not as fi but as fi. Such a combination gets away from having the dot on the *i* getting in the way of the top curve or the bar of the *f*. There's also an fl ligature, an ffi ligature, and a ffl ligature. Figure 9-4 shows some ligatures up close. Other ligatures than these occur in some fonts, but QuarkXPress automatically handles only these four; for others (assuming that the font supports other ligatures) you have to enter the ligature code manually (a process we describe later in this chapter). In any case, text with ligatures looks better than text that doesn't, so use the option, even if you're still not sure what a ligature is. (Why do they look better? One reason is the same reason true dashes and quotation marks do — they're a sign of professionalism. The other reason is that they prevent awkward overlapping or near-overlapping of letter parts, particularly the dot in an *i* and the hook in an *f* — instead, they provide a smooth merger of the two characters.)

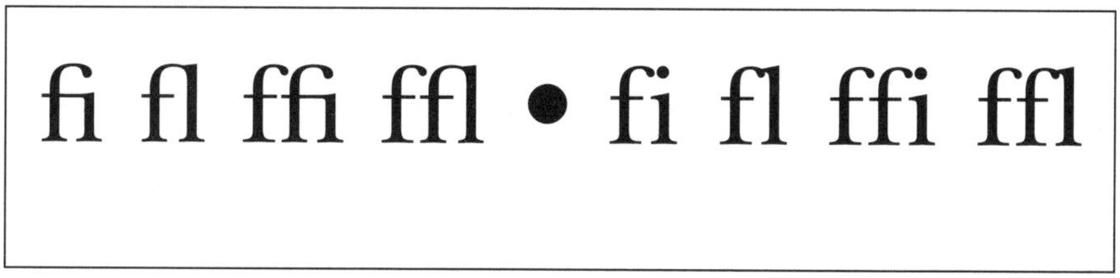

Figure 9-4:
Ligatures up
close (at
left) and the
regular
version of
the
characters
(at right).

fi fl ffi ffl • fi fl ffi ffl

If you use ligatures, you may find that sometimes the combined characters appear as a ligature and sometimes they don't. Ligatures vary because of QuarkXPress's spacing computations. Ligatures make sense if characters are close together because that's when pieces of the characters might overlap (which is the problem that ligatures were designed to solve). But, when text is spaced more widely, the characters won't overprint; in such a case, there's no reason to combine them. In fact, if you did combine them, you'd have a weird appearance (well, actually, your document would have a weird appearance) because most letters would have space between them *except for* those that are combined into ligatures. QuarkXPress automatically figures out when the characters should be combined into ligatures and when they should not, so don't worry about it. In fact, QuarkXPress is so smart that if you did a search for the word *first* and the *fi* was a ligature in your test, QuarkXPress would find the fi ligature even though you entered *fi* in the Find dialog box.

If you use the codes to insert the actual ligature character fi or fl (as shown in Table 9-2), you won't be able to search for words using those ligatures unless you also use the ligature code in your search text. When you use these codes, you actually put in the ligature character; when QuarkXPress generates the ligatures for you, it keeps the actual letters in your document but substitutes for them both on screen and when printing the ligature characters. Note that these coded ligature characters may appear in your Find dialog box as a square. That's okay: QuarkXPress will still search for the actual character. Also note that using codes to generate ligatures, rather than QuarkXPress's automatic ligature feature, will also cause the spelling checker to flag words with the coded-in ligatures as suspect words. The lesson: don't code in ligatures. It's not worth the hassle.

Table 9-2	Shortcuts for Ligatures*	
Character	*Mac Shortcut*	*Windows Shortcut*
fi	Option-Shift-5	*not supported*
fl	Option-Shift-6	*not supported*

*Automatically generated if the Ligatures box is checked in the Typographic Preferences dialog box (Edit⇨Preferences⇨Typographic).

Accented and Foreign Characters

You don't have to use accents for words like *café* that came to English from another language. *Cafe* is quite acceptable. But adding the accent to the *e* gives the word a bit more sophistication (plus it helps people pronounce it *ka-fay* rather than *kayfe*!). Of course, if your publication is international, you'll want to use the international characters and accents.

The first thing to decide is how you want to treat accents on capital letters. If you use accents, you always use them on lowercase letters, but for uppercase it's an option — so long as you are consistent and either always use the accents on capitalized letters or never use them within the same publication. QuarkXPress has an option that lets you make consistent decisions on accents a breeze.

In the Typographic Preferences dialog box (Edit⇨Preferences⇨Typographic, or Option-⌘-Y), there's an option called Accents for All Caps. (Figure 9-3 shows this dialog box for Mac QuarkXPress; Figure 9-5 shows it for Windows QuarkXPress.) If that option is checked, all accented letters will keep their accent when capitalized. If that option is not checked, the accent will be removed when the letters are capitalized and reinstated when the letters are lowercased. Having this option means that you can always add the accents as you type and then have QuarkXPress take care of handling the uppercase letters. By unchecking the Accents for All Caps box, you don't have to look out for the accents on letters that switch from lowercase to uppercase, or vice versa.

Figure 9-5:
The Typographic Preferences dialog box lets you control whether accents are displayed for capitalized letters. This figure shows the Windows dialog box; the Mac dialog box appears in Figure 9-3.

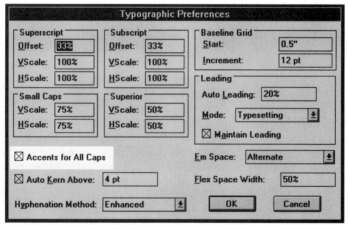

So how do you get the accents in the first place? Table 9-1 shows the various codes. Pretty daunting, you say? Relax. It's not as bad as it looks. Just follow this advice to reduce the effort needed to produce accented letters for the most common letters.

The process for accessing accents and foreign characters on Windows differs significantly from the similar process on the Mac. That's why we cover the procedures for the two platforms separately here.

Foreign characters on the Mac

For the five most common accent marks — the grave `, the acute ´, the circumflex ^, the tilde ~, and the umlaut (or trema) ¨ — you can have the Mac automatically generate the accented character by first entering the code for the accent you want and then the letter you want it applied to. Table 9-3 shows those codes: Option-` for grave, Option-E for acute, Option-I for circumflex, Option-N for tilde, and Option-U for umlaut (or trema). Thus, Option-E followed by an *o* results in *ó*. If you type a combination and get two characters (rather than an accented character), you've just discovered that the font you're using doesn't support that particular accented letter.

For some characters, you have to enter a specific code. For example, there's no accent code to generate the cedilla in *ç*, so you have to enter the code Option-C to get it. Table 9-3 shows these characters as well.

A few specific visual options help you as well. You can use the Key Caps software that comes with the Mac (it's in the Apple menu or, if you removed it or never installed it, on the Tidbits disk of your system disks, in the Apple Items folder; in System 7.5, look for it in the Custom install option list). Another option is to use the freeware control panel PopChar, available on popular on-line services. Both options show you keyboard layouts and let you select the characters you want; they also display the shortcuts for the characters. We prefer PopChar because it can be set to pop up when you click an upper corner of your screen and because it shows all available characters on one screen; Key Caps makes you hold the Option, ⌘, and other keys to see what's available for keyboard combinations using them. Figures 9-6 and 9-7 show the Key Caps and PopChar utilities.

When you're creating your text, you also can use the special-symbol features that are built into your favorite word processor. Whether you use Microsoft Word 6.0 or 5.x (via Insert⇨Symbol) or WordPerfect 3.x (via Insert⇨Symbols), both have an option to insert special characters from a PopChar-like list. Figure 9-8 shows the two dialog boxes. Also, Word 6.0 lets you assign your own shortcuts for symbols and foreign characters (for use within Word only).

QuarkXPress cannot read the latest versions of Word (6.0) and WordPerfect (3.1). If you use those programs, you need to save your files in a previous format: 5.1 for Word and 2.1 for WordPerfect. Quark does plan to have filters for these versions available (for downloading from on-line services) in early 1995.

Finally, if the foreign character you want simply is not available in your font, you may need to buy a version of the font that has the characters you want. Generally, you'll find Cyrillic, Greek, and other character sets for popular fonts like Times and Helvetica; in a pinch, you can use one of these characters with a similar font like Palatino or Univers. But if you use decorative or other less-universal fonts, you may not be able to get a version with the special characters you need. To get foreign-character fonts, try the font makers listed in Chapter 2. And keep in mind that the Symbol font that comes with the Mac includes most Greek letters.

Figure 9-6:
The Key Caps utility lets you select special characters, including accents, for use in your document.

Figure 9-7:
The free PopChar utility is easier to use than Key Caps. It displays all available characters simultaneously.

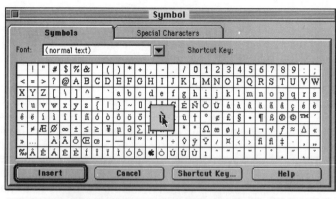

Figure 9-8:
The special-character
dialog boxes
in Word 6.0
(top) and
WordPerfect
3.1 (bottom).

Foreign characters in Windows

For the six most common accent marks — the grave ` , the acute ´ , the circum-flex ^, the tilde ˜ , the cedilla ˛ and the umlaut (or trema) ¨ — you can have Windows automatically generate the accented character by first entering a character that invokes the accent you want and then the letter you want it applied to. Table 9-3 shows those characters: ` for grave, ' for acute and cedilla, ^ for circumflex, ~ for tilde, and " for umlaut (or trema). Thus, ' followed by an *o* results in *ó*. If you type a combination and get two characters, rather than an accented character, it means the font you're using doesn't support that particular accented letter.

For Windows to generate these accented characters, you need to set it to use the US-International keyboard. You do that in the Windows Control Panel, in which you click the International icon, as shown in Figure 9-9. (The Control Panel usually resides in the Main program group, unless it was moved else-where.) That opens up the International dialog box also shown in the figure. Here, you change the Keyboard Layout option from US to US-International. But *don't* change the Language setting from English (American) to English (Interna-tional) to match the new layout. Leave it at English (American). QuarkXPress checks to see what language your operating system is using, and if it detects a mismatch — such as running the American English version of QuarkXPress on a

French Canadian or International English Windows system — then QuarkXPress won't run. (You get an error while loading QuarkXPress that makes it appear as if there's a problem loading the fonts. The problem's actually the mismatch in languages.)

Sometimes when you've set Windows to use the U.S.-International keyboard layout you'll get frustrated. You'll be typing along, minding your own business — and all of a sudden you get an accented character instead of the quoted text you wanted; for example, you type *"A man* but get *Ä man* instead. What to do? Get into the habit of typing a space after the `, ", and ' characters. Allowing for that extra measly space prevents unintended, spontaneous accents. Why? Because typing a space after those specific characters — or, for that matter, after the ^ and ~, too — tells Windows to type those characters rather than prepare for the possibility of adding an accent if the next character is accentable.

For some foreign characters, you have to enter a specific code. For example, there's no accent code to generate the hacek in š, so you have to enter the code Alt+0154 (using the numerals on the numeric keypad, not the numerals above the letter keys) to get hacek. In some cases, you'll use keyboard shortcuts to get these foreign characters, such as Ctrl+Shift+Alt+Z to get the Æ diphthong character. Table 9-3 shows these codes and shortcuts. You also can use these shortcuts if you're not using the US-International keyboard layout. Note that some programs may use the shortcuts for something else, in which case you can't use them to generate the foreign character.

What do you do in those cases? Read on.

A few visual options can help you as well. You can use the Character Map software that comes with Windows (it will be in the Accessories group unless someone moved it; if you removed it or never installed it, run the Windows setup and select it for installation). We move Character Map to our Startup group so that it's always available at the bottom of the Windows screen as a minimized icon. Or, if we've maximized QuarkXPress to fill the entire screen, we move Character Map via the Task List (Ctrl+Esc). Figure 9-10 shows Character Map. Notice how it magnifies the character that your pointer is currently on? It also displays the code for the selected character and lets you select and copy characters to the Windows Clipboard so that you can paste them into your text. You can even change fonts if the character you want is available in a different font than your text uses. (A choice of fonts comes in very handy when inserting foreign characters, like Greek or Cyrillic, not available in standard fonts.) We change fonts all the time and suspect that you will, too.

If you close Character Map, you have to relaunch it from the Accessories or Startup group (or whatever group you've put it in). There's really no easy way to prevent this, so try to get in the habit of minimizing.

When you're creating your text, you also can use the special-symbol features that are built into your favorite word processor. Whether you use Microsoft Word 6 (via Insert⇨Symbol) or WordPerfect 6 (via Insert⇨Character, or Shift+F11), both have an option to insert special characters from a Character Map-like list. (Lotus Ami Pro 3 has no equivalent feature, except to insert bullets.) Figure 9-11 shows the two dialog boxes. Word lets you assign your own shortcuts for symbols and foreign characters (for use within Word only); WordPerfect ships with TrueType fonts in several character sets (including Greek, Cyrillic, Japanese, Hebrew, Arabic, mathematical, and phonetic).

QuarkXPress cannot read the latest versions of Word and WordPerfect (6.0 for both), so you'll have to save your files in a previous format: 2.0 for Word and 5.1 for WordPerfect. Quark plans to release filters to import these versions in early 1995.

Finally, if the foreign character you want simply is not available in your font, you may need to buy a version of the font that has the characters you want. Generally, you'll find Cyrillic, Greek, and other character sets for popular fonts like Times and Helvetica; in a pinch, you can use one of these characters with a similar font like Palatino or Univers. But if you use decorative or other less-universal fonts, you may not be able to get a version with the special characters you need. To get foreign-character fonts, try the font makers listed in Chapter 2. And keep in mind that the Symbol font that comes with Windows includes most Greek letters.

Figure 9-9:
By changing your keyboard layout to US-International — but leaving your language at English (American) — you can have Windows automatically create accented characters.

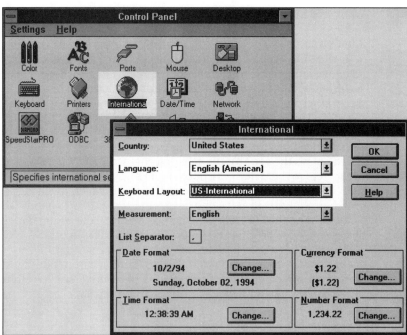

Figure 9-10:
The Character Map utility lets you select special characters, including accented ones, for use in your document.

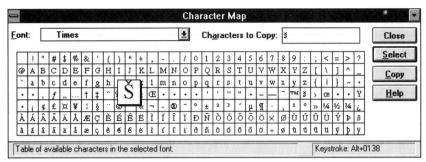

Figure 9-11:
The special-character dialog boxes in Word 6.0 (top) and WordPerfect 6.0 (bottom).

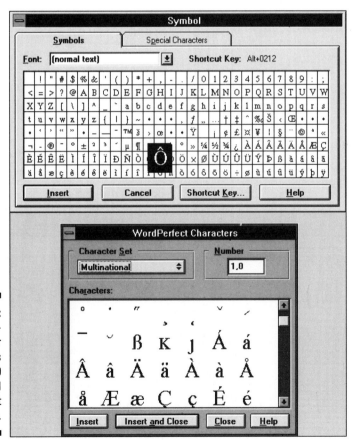

Table 9-3   Shortcuts for Accents and Foreign Characters

Character	Mac shortcut	Windows shortcut
acute (´)*	Option-E *letter*	' *letter*
cedilla (̧)*	*see Ç and ç*	' *letter*
circumflex (ˆ)*	Option-I *letter*	^ *letter*
grave (`)*	Option-` *letter*	' *letter*
tilde (˜)*	Option-N *letter*	~ *letter*
trema (¨)*	Option-U *letter*	" *letter*
umlaut (¨)*	Option-U *letter*	" *letter*
Á	Option-E A	' A *or* Ctrl+Shift+Alt+A
á	Option-E a	' a *or* Ctrl+Alt+A
À	Option-` A	' A *or* Alt+0192
à	Option-` a	' a *or* Alt+0224
Ä	Option-U A	" A *or* Ctrl+Shift+Alt+Q
ä	Option-U a	" a *or* Ctrl+Alt+Q
Ã	Option-N A	~ A *or* Alt+0195
ã	Option-N a	~ a *or* Alt+0227
Â	Option-I A	^ A *or* Alt+0194
â	Option-I a	^ a *or* Alt+0226
Å	Option-Shift-A	Ctrl+Shift+Alt+W
å	Option-A	Ctrl+Alt+W
Æ	Option-Shift-'	Ctrl+Shift+Alt+Z
æ	Option-'	Ctrl+Alt+Z
Ç	Option-Shift-C	' C *or* Ctrl+Shift+Alt+,
ç	Option-C	' c *or* Ctrl+Alt+,
Ð	*not supported*	Ctrl+Shift+Alt+D
ð	*not supported*	Ctrl+Alt+D
É	Option-E E	` E *or* Ctrl+Shift+Alt+E
é	Option-E e	` e *or* Ctrl+Alt+E
È	Option-` E	` E *or* Alt+0200
è	Option-` e	` e *or* Alt+0232

Character	Mac shortcut	Windows shortcut
Ë	Option-U E	" E or Alt+0203
ë	Option-U e	" e or Alt+0235
Ê	Option-I E	^ E or Alt+0202
ê	Option-I e	^ e or Alt+0234
Í	Option-E I	' I or Ctrl+Shift+Alt+I
í	Option-E i	' i or Ctrl+Alt+I
Ì	Option-` I	' I or Alt+0204
ì	Option-` i	' i or Alt+0236
Ï	Option-U I	" I or Alt+0207
ï	Option-U i	" I or Alt+0239
Î	Option-I I	^ I or Alt+0206
î	Option-I i	^ I or Alt+0238
Ñ	Option-N N	~ N or Ctrl+Shift+Alt+N
ñ	Option-N n	~ n or Ctrl+Alt+N
Ó	Option-E O	' O or Ctrl+Shift+Alt+O
ó	Option-E o	' o or Ctrl+Alt+O
Ò	Option-` O	` O or Alt+0210
ò	Option-` o	` o or Alt+0242
Ö	Option-U O	" O or Ctrl+Shift+Alt+P
ö	Option-U o	" o or Ctrl+Alt+P
Õ	Option-N O	~ O or Alt+0213
õ	Option-N o	~ o or Alt+0245
Ô	Option-I O	^ O or Alt+0212
ô	Option-I o	^ o or Alt+0244
Ø	Option-Shift-O	Ctrl+Shift+Alt+L
ø	Option-O	Ctrl+Alt+L
Œ	Option-Shift-Q	Alt+0140
œ	Option-Q	Alt+0156
þ	*not supported*	Ctrl+Shift+Alt+T
Þ	*not supported*	Ctrl+Alt+T

(continued)

(continued)

Character	Mac shortcut	Windows shortcut
Š	*not supported*	Alt+0138
š	*not supported*	Alt+0154
Ú	Option-E U	' U *or* Ctrl+Shift+Alt+U
ú	Option-E u	' u *or* Ctrl+Alt+U
Ù	Option-` U	` U *or* Alt+0217
ù	Option-` u	` u *or* Alt+0249
Ü	Option-U U	" U *or* Ctrl+Shift+Alt+Y
ü	Option-U u	" u *or* Ctrl+Alt+Y
Û	Option-I U	^ U *or* Alt+0219
û	Option-I u	^ u *or* Alt+0251
Ý	*not supported*	' Y *or* Alt+0221
ý	*not supported*	' y *or* Alt+0253
Ÿ	Option-U Y	*not supported*
ÿ	Option-U y	*not supported*
Spanish open exclamation (¡)	Option-1	Ctrl+Alt+1
Spanish open question (¿)	Option-Shift-/	Ctrl+Alt+/
French open double quote («)	**Option-\	Ctrl+Alt+[
French close double quote (»)	**Option-Shift-\	Ctrl+Alt+]

*On the Mac, enter the shortcut for the accent and then type the letter to be accented (for example, to get é, type Option-E and then the letter *e*. In Windows, if the keyboard layout is set to US-International (via the International icon in the Windows Control Panel), you can enter the accent signifier and then type the letter (for example, type ' and then the letter *e* to get è).

**Automatically generated if the Smart Quotes option is selected in the Application Preferences dialog box (Edit⇨Preferences⇨Application) and the French quotes are selected in the Quote pop-up list, also in the Application Preferences dialog box.

Special Punctuation

"What's the deal with punctuation?" you may ask. "That's what grammar books are for." True enough, but there are some tricks you can use to access special punctuation, much as you learned earlier for two types of punctuation for which QuarkXPress can automate the substitution of typographic versions: quotes and dashes. The other punctuation you might need can't be automated — QuarkXPress won't substitute, for example, an ellipsis (…) when you type three periods (...). Besides, you may not even know how to access these characters because they're not on your computer. This section will show you how to get those characters. Table 9-4 shows the shortcuts to get them into your document.

The many bullets (all nonlethal)

A bullet is a form of punctuation, to start an element in a list. On a typewriter, you use an asterisk (*) to indicate a bullet. But in desktop publishing (and in modern word processing), you have the real thing: the character that typographers call an en bullet (•). There are tons of symbols you can use as a bullet. For now, though, just make sure that you don't use an asterisk when you can use a bullet — it would be too tacky for words.

There are *many* more bullets than the en bullet that we all know and love. First off, bullets don't even have to be round. They could be any shape — squares, stars, arrows, triangles. They can be hollow or solid. They can be a small version of a corporate logo. They could be some other symbol — anything that clearly demarcates that the start of a new item has begun. Take a look at the symbol characters in Table 9-5, and also look at what symbols come with the Symbol and Zapf Dingbats fonts on most computers; while you're at it, check out the Wingdings fonts that ships with Windows and with the Mac version of Microsoft's Word 6.0 and Office 4.2 software. Figure 9-12 shows some example bullets.

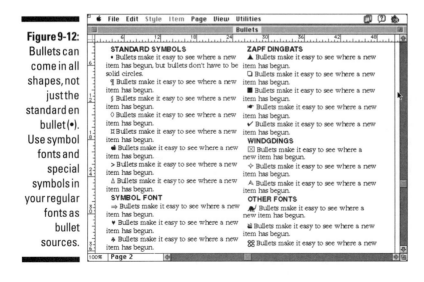

Figure 9-12: Bullets can come in all shapes, not just the standard en bullet (•). Use symbol fonts and special symbols in your regular fonts as bullet sources.

Ellipses

On a typewriter, you use three periods — some people put spaces around them, others don't — to indicate an ellipsis, the character (…) that indicates that some text is missing, particularly in quoted material. It's also used to indicate that a speaker trailed off when talking. The nice thing about using the actual ellipsis character is this: as text moves within a column, there's no chance that some of the periods will appear at the end of a line and the rest at the beginning of the next. Of course, you could get around that design *faux pas* by typing the three periods with no spaces, which would make QuarkXPress see them as a single "word." But, if you do that, then the spacing within the ellipsis could be too tight or too loose because it would be stretched or compressed like the other words on the line by QuarkXPress's justification feature. If the ellipsis is the ellipsis character, then the space between its constituent dots can't change and the ellipsis will always look like, well, an ellipsis.

If you just don't like the look of three consecutive periods *or* a font's ellipses character, you have a third option: use nonbreaking spaces between the periods.

Hyphens

Normally, a hyphen's a hyphen, right? Not always. If you are hyphenating two words to a third, such as in *"Star Trek*–like," the proper typographic style, according to the World Typography Police, is to use an en dash instead of a hyphen (compare *"Star Trek*–like" to *"Star Trek*-like"). But if you use a regular hyphen, it's still no crime. There are also variants of the hyphen, which Chapter 11 describes in more detail. These variants control the positioning of the hyphen; to a reader, a hyphen looks like a hyphen and an en dash looks like an en dash.

Spaces

A space is one of those characters you take for granted. So many people who get into desktop publishing wonder what all the fuss is about concerning different kinds of spaces. Like hyphens, the basic reasons for the different types is to affect positioning (we cover spaces in detail in Chapter 8). What you need to know here is that there are several fixed-size spaces that are really handy when trying to align numbers in a table. An en space is the width of most numerals, and a punctuation space (also called a thin space) is the width of a comma or period. (In some popular fonts, like New Century Schoolbook, use an en space for punctuation as well as for numerals. And in a few decorative fonts, the numerals and punctuation don't correspond to any of the fixed spaces' widths.) So, if you were trying to decimal-align *10,000* and *50.12* against the left margin, you'd put three en spaces and a punctuation space in front of *50.12*. Figure 9-13 shows the results.

Another type of fixed space is called the flexible space, or *flex space* for short. It's a user-defined space (via the Flex Space Width field in the Typographic Preferences dialog box, which you access via Edit⇨Preferences⇨Typographic or Option-⌘-Y). You enter its value in terms of the percentage of an en space. To get a punctuation (thin) space, you'd enter 50%; to get an em space, you'd enter 200%. Or you can create your own type of space and enter another value from 1% to 400%.

Unfortunately, you can't use these fixed spaces when right-aligning text. Say that you're trying to decimal-align *10,000* and *50.12* against the right margin. Based on the preceding example, you'd expect to put a punctuation space and two en spaces after the *10,000* before right-justifying the two numbers. But that won't work. QuarkXPress ignores spaces at the end of a line when it right-aligns (it does see them when centering, though). To get Quark to space correctly (rather than just space out) when you right-align, you have to use the tab feature in QuarkXPress instead, as Chapter 8 explains.

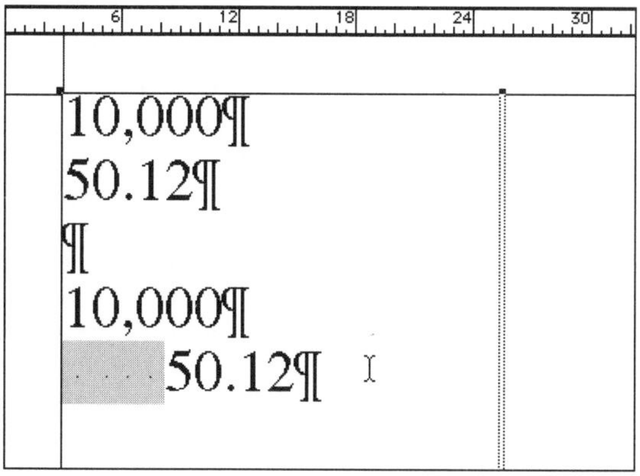

Figure 9-13:
By using en spaces and punctuation spaces, you can easily align numbers.

10,000¶
50.12¶

¶

10,000¶
    50.12¶

Table 9-4	Shortcuts for Other Punctuation	
Character	*Mac shortcut*	*Windows shortcut*
Ellipsis (…)	Option-;	Ctrl+Alt+period *or* Alt+0133
En bullet (•)	Option-8	Shift+Alt+8 *or* Alt+0149
Nonbreaking hyphen	⌘-=	Ctrl+Shift+hyphen
Discretionary (soft) hyphen	⌘-hyphen	Ctrl+hyphen
Nonbreaking en dash (long hyphen)	Option-hyphen	Ctrl+= *or* Alt+0150
Nonbreaking space	⌘-space	Ctrl+space
Breaking en space	Option-space	Ctrl+Shift+6
Nonbreaking en space	⌘-Option-space	Ctrl+Shift+Alt+6
Breaking punctuation space	Shift-space	Shift+space
Nonbreaking punctuation space	⌘-Shift-space	Ctrl+Shift+space
Breaking flexible space	Option-Shift-space	Ctrl+Shift+5
Nonbreaking flexible space	⌘-Option-space	Ctrl+Shift+Alt+5

Working with Symbols

It's amazing how many special characters there are. You get more than 100 with each regular font, and there are scores if not hundreds of fonts (called symbol or pi fonts) that contain nothing but symbols. Some people use symbols all the time; others rarely. Your own use of symbols will depend on the kind of text you work with. Table 9-5 shows the shortcuts for the symbols that most Mac and Windows fonts offer. For symbol and pi fonts, you have to use the documentation that came with the font or a keyboard-character program (like the Mac's Key Caps utility, the free PopChar shareware program for Macs, or the Windows Character Map utility) to see what's available. The section "Accented and Foreign Characters" earlier in this chapter covers these programs in more detail.

Table 9-5	Shortcuts for Symbols	
Character	*Mac shortcut*	*Windows shortcut*
Legal		
Copyright (©)	Option-G	Shift+Alt+C *or* Ctrl+Alt+C
Registered trademark (®)	Option-R	Shift+Alt+R *or* Ctrl+Alt+R
Trademark (™)	Option-2	Shift+Alt+2 *or* Alt+0153
Paragraph (¶)	Option-7	Shift+Alt+7 *or* Ctrl+Alt+;
Section (§)	Option-6	Shift+Alt+6 *or* Ctrl+Shift+Alt+S
Dagger (†)	Option-T	Shift+Alt+T *or* Alt+0134
Double dagger (‡)	Option-Shift-T	Alt+0135
Currency		
Cent (¢)	Option-4	Ctrl+/ c *or* Ctrl+Shift+Alt+C
Pound sterling (£)	Option-3	Shift+Ctrl+Alt+4
Yen (¥)	Option-Y	Ctrl+Alt+hyphen
Measurement		
Foot (')	Control-'	Ctrl+'
Inch (")	Shift-Control-"	Ctrl+Alt+"
Mathematics		
One-half fraction ($\frac{1}{2}$)	*not supported*	Ctrl+Alt+6
One-quarter fraction ($\frac{1}{4}$)	*not supported*	Ctrl+Alt+7
Three-quarters fraction ($\frac{3}{4}$)	*not supported*	Ctrl+Alt+8
Infinity (∞)	Option-5	*not supported*
Multiplication (x)	*not supported*	Ctrl+Alt+=
Division (÷)	Option-/	Ctrl+Shift+Alt+=
Root (√)	Option-V	*not supported*
Greater than or equal (≥)	Option->	*not supported*
Less than or equal (≤)	Option-<	*not supported*
Inequality (≠)	Option-=	*not supported*
Rough equivalence (≈)	Option-X-	*not supported*
Plus or minus (±)	Option-Shift-=	Alt+0177

(continued)

(continued)

Character	Mac shortcut	Windows shortcut
Mathematics		
Logical not (ÿ)	Option-L	Ctrl+Alt+\
Per mil (‰)	Option-Shift-R	Alt+-0137
Degree (°)	Option-Shift-8	Ctrl+Shift+Alt+;
Function (ƒ)	Option-F	Alt+0131
Integral (∫)	Option-B	*not supported*
Variation (∂)	Option-D	*not supported*
Greek beta (ß)	Option-S	Ctrl+Alt+S
Greek mu (µ)	Option-M	Ctrl+Alt+M
Greek Pi (∏)	Option-Shift-P	*not supported*
Greek pi (π)	Option-P	*not supported*
Greek Sigma (∑)	Option-W	*not supported*
Greek Omega (Ω)	Option-Z	*not supported*
Miscellaneous		
Apple logo ()	Option-Shift-K	*not supported*
Checkmark (✓)	Ctrl+R	*not supported*
En bullet (•)	Option-8	Shift+Alt+8 *or* Alt+0149
Light (◻)	Option-Shift-2	Ctrl+Alt+4
Open diamond (◊)	Option-Shift-V	*not supported*

Getting Attention with Drop Caps

One of the hallmarks of professional publishing is the use of drop caps — those large capital letters that often start a story's introduction and conclusion. You simply can't do them on a typewriter, and not too easily in a word processor, either. QuarkXPress makes it easy to create drop caps — all sorts of them, in fact.

Figure 9-14 shows a variety of drop caps, with the standard three-line version at left. At right are, from top to bottom, the use of a different font, the use of a symbol dropped in two lines, a three-line-deep letter dropped in two lines, the use of a different font with a drop shadow (a shadow that is offset slightly below and to the side of the letter), and a raised cap.

Why Dingbats are smart

When you hear "dingbat," you may think of Edith Bunker, of Archie Bunker, Meathead, and *All in the Family* fame. But, in publishing, a dingbat is no dummy. A dingbat is a symbol used to end a story or serve as a graphical embellishment for a certain type of text. It's sort of like a bullet, one that can be used at the beginning of each byline, for example, at the beginning of a continued line, or at the end of the text so that you know a story is over. A dingbat is a visual marker. And, as with bullets, you have a whole host of choices available to you. Take a look at the symbols in Figure 9-12 and in Table 9-5 for some ideas for dingbats. Many people use a square (hollow or solid), but you can be more creative than that. Maybe you can use a version of your company or publication logo. Or you even could use a stylized letter: *Macworld*, for example, uses a stylized *M*.

When you use dingbats, remember that you have choices in how you use them. For dingbats that end a story, you usually have the dingbat follow the last text, with an en space or em space separating them (see Table 9-4). If your text is justified against both margins, it's common to have the dingbat flush right in the last line of the story. To make it flush right, you set up a tab stop that's equal to the width of your column. So if your column is 2 $\frac{1}{2}$ inches wide, you would set up a right-aligned tab at 2 $\frac{1}{2}$ inches. (Chapter 8 covers how to set up tabs.) A shortcut is to use Option-tab on the Mac or Shift+tab in Windows, which sets up a right-aligned tab at the right edge of the column. The following figure shows some examples of dingbats: the first example uses the right-aligned approach; the rest use an en space between the text and the dingbat.

You would use the same techniques to place, say, a square before the text *Continued on page 14* or to place, say, a hollow square before a byline.

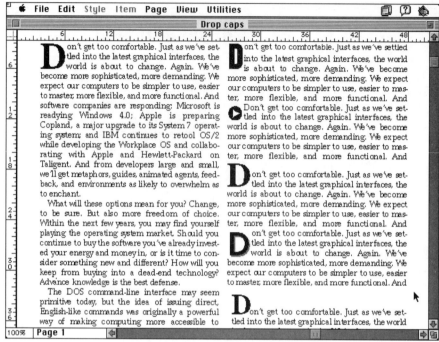

To create a standard drop cap in QuarkXPress, use the Paragraph Formats dialog box (via the Formats button in the Style Sheets dialog box or via the Style⇨Formats menu option). Check the Drop Caps option, tell QuarkXPress via the Character Count field how many characters are to be made into drop caps (usually it's just one, but you could have more, such as for a numbered list), and how many lines deep the cap should be set into the paragraph (via the Line Count field). Click OK and watch the drop cap appear. That's it! Figure 9-15 shows the dialog box.

Well, almost. One variation we think you should almost always make is to change the font of the drop cap to at least the bold version of the paragraph's font. To do this, select the drop cap and change its font via the Measurements palette, the Style menu, or a keyboard shortcut. We did this in the drop cap at the left in Figure 9-14.

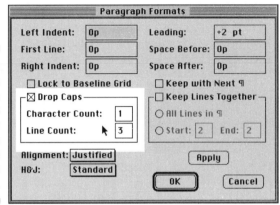

If you use a drop cap repeatedly, you should define a style sheet for it. (Chapter 8 covers the creation of style sheets.) But if you've already done the formatting and don't want to redo the effort to create the drop cap in the style sheet, just select the paragraph before you enter the Style Sheets dialog box and click the New button. QuarkXPress then copies the paragraph formats of the selected paragraph into that new style. Note that any local character formatting, such as tracking values or font changes to the drop cap, won't be picked up as part of the style sheet since styles don't include such nonglobal paragraph information.

Now to see what sleights of hand (or at least of the mouse finger) created the other variants in Figure 9-14:

- For the first variant in the right column — the use of a different font — you change the font the same way you would for any font: via the Measurements palette or the Style menu.

- For the second variant — the use of a symbol dropped in two lines — you just set the Line Count in the Paragraph Formats dialog box to 2 and then change the font to a symbol font. Then type in the character that will invoke the symbol you want (use the Key Caps or PopChar programs for the Mac or Character Map in Windows, as described earlier, to do this easily).

✔ For the third variant — the use of a three-line drop cap in a two-line drop — the technique gets a little tricky, so pay close attention: First, you set the Line Count to 2. Then highlight the drop cap character and use the Measurements palette to change the size. Notice in Figure 9-16 how the size pop-up in the palette is grayed out and a percentage has appeared instead of the point size. Instead, the size reads 150% — that's the value we changed the default of 100% to to change the two-line-deep size into a three-line-deep size. How did we get 150%? The original drop cap was 100%, so each line was 50%. To add a third line, we added another 50% — and, together with the original 100%, that makes 150%.

✔ For the fourth variant — the drop cap with a drop shadow — we changed the font as described for the first variant and also clicked the shadow button on the Measurements palette. We also could have used the Style menu to apply this attribute. The point we want to make with this fourth variant is that you can mix font changes with other character attributes.

✔ For the last variant — the raised cap — the process is radically different. First off, you don't use the Paragraph Formats dialog box at all. You don't have a drop cap, so you don't use the Drop Caps feature. Instead, you highlight the paragraph's first character and change its size to something bigger (a rule of thumb is to multiply the leading for your paragraph by the number of lines high you want it to be). But when you do this, you'll probably mess up the line spacing. The raised cap may overprint the text above (that's easily fixed: add blank lines or set a Space Before value in the Paragraph Formats dialog box). And the text below the drop cap may be moved *way* below the cap — which is *not* what you want. The reason the text moves so far below is that QuarkXPress is probably set to a leading of Auto or to an additive leading (like +2); you can see what the leading is in the Measurements palette. In Figure 9-17, it's 14 point — not Auto, not +2. The leading in the figure is an absolute value to prevent the weird spacing of text below it. By telling QuarkXPress exactly what leading to use (14 points here), you don't let QuarkXPress apply the wrong leading. (QuarkXPress can apply the wrong leading if you use automatic or additive leading because Quark bases the leading on the size of the largest character in the line in order to avoid overprinting text. But, in this case, you don't want the leading based on the largest character since that character is the drop cap, which breaks the normal spacing. Instead, you want it based on the regular text.)

You can also use an anchored text box or picture box (with a picture!) as a drop cap. See Chapter 7 for details.

Figure 9-16:
To have the drop cap larger (or smaller) than the number of lines it is set in, use the Measurements palette to change the size.

rating with Apple and Hewlett-Packard on Taligent. And from developers large and small, we'll get metaphors, guides, animated agents, feedback, and environments as likely to overwhelm as to enchant.

What will these options mean for you? Change, to be sure. But also more freedom of choice. Within the next few years, you may find yourself playing the operating system market. Should you continue to buy the software you've already invested your energy and money in, or is it time to consider something new and different? How will you keep from buying into a dead-end technology? Advance knowledge is the best defense.

The DOS primitive to English-like commands was originally a powerful way of making computing more accessible to

ter, more flexible, and more functional. And

Don't get too comfortable. Just as we've settled into the latest graphical interfaces, the world is about to change. Again. We've become more sophisticated, more demanding. We expect our computers to be simpler to use, easier to master, more flexible, and more functional. And

Don't get too comfortable. Just as we've settled into the latest graphical interfaces, the world is about to change. Again. We've become more sophisticated, more demanding. We expect our computers to be simpler to use, easier to master, more flexible, and more functional. And

X: 3p   W: 45p   △ 0°   +2 pt   New Baskerville   150%
Y: 3p   H: 34p9   Cols: 2   ◇ 0   P B I O S ⊕ U Y K K

on't get too comfortable. Just as we've settled into the latest graphical interfaces, the world

Figure 9-17:
The leading for the raised cap is set to 14 points.

...tinue to buy the software you've already invest-ed your energy and money in, or is it time to con-sider something new and different? How will you keep from ... Advance knowledge is the best defense.

The DOS command-line interface may seem primitive today, but the idea of issuing direct, English-like commands was originally a powerful way of making computing more accessible to

...tled into the latest graphical interfaces, the world is about to change. Again. We've become more sophisticated, more demanding. We

X: 3p   W: 45p   △ 0°   14 pt   New Baskerville   42 pt
Y: 3p   H: 34p9   Cols: 2   ◇ 0   P B I O S ⊕ U Y K K

Don't get too comfortable. Just as we've settled into the latest graphical interfaces, the world

Well, we're done with a lot of information on all sorts of special characters. There's a lot to absorb here, so you may want to take a break and let it all settle in.

Chapter 10

Text Editing Techniques

In This Chapter

▶ Inserting and deleting text

▶ Finding and replacing text and text attributes

▶ Setting tabs

▶ Using leader characters in tabs

▶ Getting copy to fit

*L*isten, there's no need to pull your hair out trying to make the text in your QuarkXPress document perfect the first time. (Not to mention that, if you're like some of us, you need to keep every hair you've got!) Because you have the luxury of having a hefty set of text-editing tools at your disposal, why not simply throw your thoughts onto a page and then fix 'em up later? That's what we do, and that's what you'll be able to do, too.

As we mention in Chapter 5, you can enter text into a QuarkXPress document in one of two ways: by using the built-in word processor to type the text right into a QuarkXPress document, or by creating the text in a separate word processing program and then importing the text into QuarkXPress. Even if you do use a separate word processor and edit the text in that application, you will still need to do some editing inside QuarkXPress.

For example, imagine that you are using your word processing application to create the copy for a brochure on courses that teach people about traveling to Indonesia. You prepare the text and then import it into a three-column QuarkXPress document. When the text arrives in QuarkXPress, you notice that you have a widow, the last line of a paragraph that appears — all by itself — at the top of the third column.

If you didn't have built-in tools within QuarkXPress, you'd be in a pickle. But, because QuarkXPress has editing tools that can easily handle most basic tasks such as adding or deleting text, you can fix your problem. You can also, if you'd like, use some of the program's more sophisticated tools, such as those that let you *track* text (adjust the space between selected characters or words) or change a paragraph's *leading* (increase or decrease the space between lines of text).

If you want to add or delete text, first position your text cursor (which appears if you are using the Content tool) at the spot where you want to make changes and click the mouse button. You then can start typing or deleting text.

To delete a block of text, do the following:

1. **Position the text cursor at one end of the text block.**

2. **Press and hold the mouse button as you drag the cursor to the other end of the text box.**

3. **Release the mouse button.**

   The selected text is highlighted.

4. **Press the delete key.**

   The highlighted text is deleted.

Like other programs, QuarkXPress lets you replace text by selecting it and typing in new text or pasting in text from the Clipboard (Edit⇨Paste, or ⌘-V). The new text that takes the place of the old can be from another part of your document, from another QuarkXPress document, or from another program. The new text can be a copy of text (Edit⇨Copy, or ⌘-C), or it can be text cut from another document (Edit⇨Cut, or ⌘-X).

Computers treat *cut* text and *deleted* text differently. Cut text is taken away from your document but is stored temporarily until you cut some other text or quit. Deleted text is not stored anywhere. (You delete text by using the Delete or the Backspace key.) The only way to recover deleted text is via Edit⇨Undo Typing.

You move text by cutting it from one location and pasting it into another. You duplicate text by copying it at one location and pasting it into another.

QuarkXPress also includes *drag and drop editing,* in which you drag text from one place and drop it into another. To use drag and drop editing, select the text you want to move, hold the mouse button down as you drag the selection to the new location, and then release the button.

Replacing Text

One of the most-used text editing features is replacing a word or a chunk of text with another word or chunk of text. Sometimes you want to replace just one instance of a word or phrase; other times, you want to replace a word or phrase every time it occurs in the document.

For example, imagine that you are working on the brochure for courses that teach people about traveling to Indonesia. You decide that you need to change each instance of the word "Bali" to "Indonesia." What's the best way to do this?

Actually, you have a couple of choices. You can go back to your original word-processor document, make the changes there, and then reimport the text into your QuarkXPress document. (We don't like this method simply because it involves too many steps!) Or you can use QuarkXPress's built-in replace function, which you access through the Find/Change dialog box, shown in Figure 10-1.

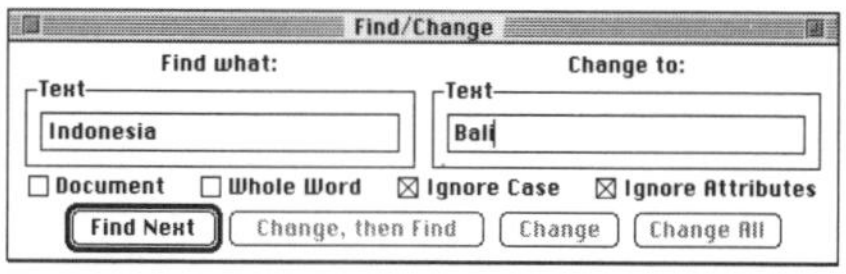

Figure 10-1:
The Find/
Change
dialog box.

As you can see, we told QuarkXPress to find "Indonesia" and replace it with "Bali."

To replace text throughout the current story, which is defined as the text in the currently selected text box and all the text boxes linked to it, use the Find/Change dialog box (Edit➪Find/Change, or ⌘-F). You also can replace text throughout the entire current document.

As you can see, the QuarkXPress replace function works like the standard search and replace tool found in most word processing programs. You can search for whole words or for words whose capitalization matches the words or characters you type in the Find What field.

The Find/Change dialog box lets you choose whether QuarkXPress should look for a whole word. (If the Whole Word box is unchecked, the program finds the string wherever is appears.) You can also have the program search and replace a word — regardless of its capitalization — by selecting Ignore Case. If the Document box is checked, the replace affects all stories and text in your document. The other buttons, such as Find Next, work as they do in word processing programs.

Changing text attributes

The Find/Change dialog box has another function that is incredibly cool. You can find and replace text attributes, typefaces, and sizes. These capabilities can be useful if, for example, you want to change all instances of 10-point Helvetica to 12-point Stone Serif.

To access these options, uncheck Ignore Attributes in the Find/Change dialog box. When Ignore Attributes is deselected, the dialog box expands and offers you attribute replacement options, as Figure 10-2 shows.

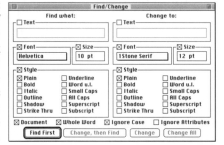

Figure 10-2:
The Find/
Change
dialog box
lets you find
and replace
text that has
specific
typeface
attributes.

In the example shown in Figure 10-2, we are replacing any text set in 10-point Helvetica with 12-point Stone Serif text.

You can select specific text, typeface, and styles for both the search and replace functions by checking the Text, Font, Size, and Style check boxes in the Find what and Change to columns of the dialog box.

If you want to use an attribute, check an attribute box in the Style section of the dialog box. Remove the check mark if you don't want to use an attribute (such as bold) in your search and replace. Make the box gray to tell QuarkXPress to retain the attributes set. (Clicking a box once unchecks it if it is checked and checks it if it is unchecked. Clicking a box twice makes it gray, retaining the attributes.)

If you leave Text unchecked in the Find What column, you replace attributes only. You may do this to change all underlined text to word-underlined text, all bold text to small cap text, all News Gothic bold text to News Gothic bold italic, or all 8-point text to 8.5-point text.

Removing carriage returns

It's not uncommon for QuarkXPress users to receive text files for typesetting that have several extra carriage returns entered between paragraphs. The Find/Change feature in QuarkXPress gives you an easy way to remove these unwanted carriage returns.

You can use Find/Change to find and delete extra carriage returns, but you can't do it by simply typing in a carriage return in the Find/Change dialog box field because pressing the Return key activates the Find button. Instead, you need to use the symbol for a new paragraph, \p.

Enter two consecutive return symbols, \p\p, in the Find what field and then enter one return symbol, \p, in the Change to field. Figure 10-3 shows what the Find/Change dialog box should look like when you are about to begin removing unwanted carriage returns, which are also referred to as *hard returns*.

Figure 10-3:
Removing
extra
carriage
returns.

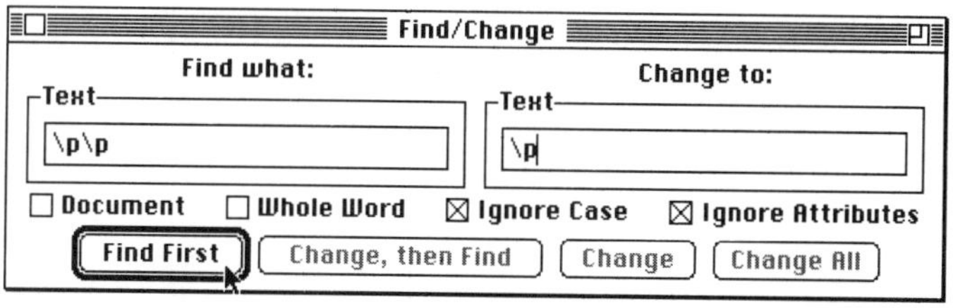

If the text you are working with has multiple carriage returns between paragraphs, you may need to repeat this Find/Change procedure multiple times.

What do you do if there's a hard return at the end of each line of text, in addition to the extra hard returns between paragraphs? If you simply delete all the hard returns by using a Find/Change procedure similar to the one shown in Figure 10-3 (where you would search for \p and replace it with nothing), you would lose all paragraph breaks. So you need to follow a two-step procedure.

First, search for paragaph breaks that are marked by two hard returns, \p\p, and replace the paragraph breaks with another character that is not used in the document, such as # (the pound sign). Then search for all the hard returns and replace them with nothing (enter \p in the Find what field and leave the Change to field blank).

After you have deleted the hard returns, you need to reinsert the paragraph breaks. To do this, enter the character you used to replace the paragraph breaks (# in our example) in the Find what field, and enter \p in the Change to field and perform Find/Change again.

Setting Tabs

Tabs are useful when you want to line up text into columns to create lists, tables, and other columnar data. QuarkXPress provides six paragraph tab options: Left, Center, Right, Decimal, Comma, and Align on. You can place up to 20 tabs in a paragraph, and you can use any printing character to fill the space between tabs. Tabs can be tricky, and it takes some practice to know how to use them effectively.

If you've ever used a typewriter, you are familiar with typewriter tabs, which are left-aligned only: you press the tab key and that moves the carriage to a new left margin. But QuarkXPress offers a wide variety of tabs, which are available through the Paragraph Tabs dialog box. Each type of tab has its own mark on the tab ruler, which appears when you are setting tabs. Figure 10-4 shows the Paragraph Tabs dialog box.

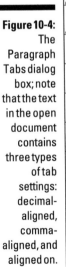

Figure 10-4: The Paragraph Tabs dialog box; note that the text in the open document contains three types of tab settings: decimal-aligned, comma-aligned, and aligned on.

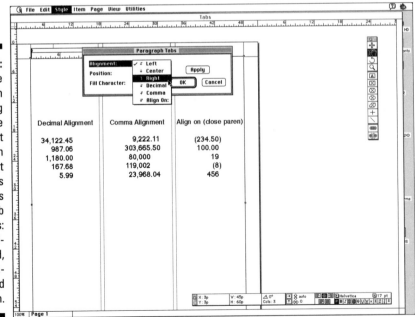

Decimal Alignment	Comma Alignment	Align on (close paren)
34,122.45	9,222.11	(234.50)
987.06	303,665.50	100.00
1,180.00	80,000	19
167.68	119,002	(8)
5.99	23,968.04	456

In Figure 10-4, the columns of copy in the open document have been set with three different tab settings:

- **Decimal** (shown in the left column): Numbers with a decimal (.) that are typed in after the tab will align on the period, or decimal. This is useful if you have columns of numbers that include decimal places.

- **Comma** (shown in the center column): Numbers with a comma (,) that are typed in after the tab will align on the comma. This tab setting is handy if you have some date with decimal places, such as 31.001, and some without, such as 2,339.

- **Align on** (shown in the right column): With this option, you select which character you want the text to align on. In our example in Figure 10-4, we aligned a column of numbers with the closing parenthesis.

Three additional tab settings, which are not shown in Figure 10-4, include:

- **Left:** Text typed after the tab will align to the tab as if the tab were a left margin. This is, by far, the most popular tab setting.

- **Center:** Text typed in will be centered, with the tab stop serving as the center of the text.

- **Right:** Text types in after the tab; it aligns to the tab as if the tab were a right margin. The right tab setting is often used with tables of numbers because it lines up the numbers with all of their rightmost digits in a row.

The default for tabs is one left tab every half inch. If you want to apply different tab settings that you can use throughout the document, choose Edit➪Style Sheets➪Tabs. If you are working on a specific paragraph or want to override a style for one paragraph, choose Style➪Tabs to access the Paragraph Tabs dialog box.

Specifying your own tabs

After you have accessed the Paragraph Tabs dialog box, here's how you set your own tabs:

1. Select the Alignment you want (Left, Center, Right, Decimal, Comma, Align On) from the Alignment option.

2. Either type in the numeric position for the tab in the Position box, or move your mouse to the tab ruler and click the mouse button to set the position of the tab.

You can also specify tabs for a selected paragraph or range of paragraphs by choosing Style⇨Formats and clicking on the ruler displayed above the box or column.

As we mentioned earlier, tabs are simple to set in QuarkXPress, but the process can be tricky if you've never done it before. We recommend that you take a few minutes to practice setting some tabs so that you will be comfortable with the process.

Using leader characters in tabs

A leader character, also known as a *tab leader*, is a series of characters that runs from text to text within tabular material. An example of a tab leader is the series of dots (periods) that you sometimes see between a Table-of-Contents entry and its corresponding page number. A tab leader's purpose is to guide the reader's eye, especially across a wide distance on a page.

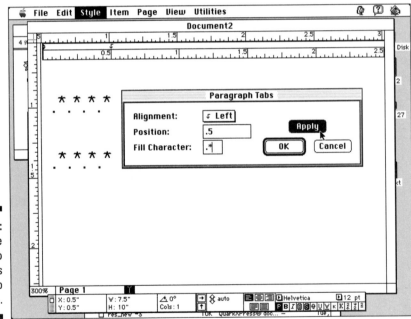

Figure 10-5:
You can use one or two characters to fill a tab space.

QuarkXPress calls a tab leader a *fill character*. To define a leader, enter up to two characters in the Fill Character text box, which you find in the Paragraph Tabs dialog box. If you enter two characters, they will alternate to fill the space between the defined tab stop and the place where you pressed the tab key. In Figure 10-5, we've used a period and an asterisk as the two fill characters. Note that, in Figure 10-5, we've left the Paragraph Tabs dialog box open so that you can see the entries we made. The resulting tab leaders can be seen at the left of the Paragraph Tabs dialog box.

Getting Copy to Fit

Sometimes it feels like you're trying to squeeze 20 pounds of lemons into a five-pound bag. *Copy fitting* is just what it sounds like: the process of fitting text into the layout. If your original, unmodified text fits the layout the first time through, consider it a stroke of luck because that's not what usually happens.

Copy fitting, when it's done well, can make your document look very professional. It can also save you money. For example, imagine that you have the budget to produce an eight-page document. You flow your text in and find that you have eight-and-a-quarter pages to deal with. By doing a good job of copy fitting, you can make the text fit into eight pages and save yourself the expense and hassle of adding an additional signature to your booklet. (A *signature* is a printed sheet, after it has been folded. Signatures, which consist of four pages, got their name because originally the person doing the folding had to initial his or her work.)

You'll find that there are a number of ways to make copy fit onto a page or within a column. Sometimes you can use just one method, and sometimes you have to use a combination of methods to make text fit in the available space.

It is most common to have more text than space. Because of that, the following tips assume the goal is to shorten text. But you can use the same procedures in reverse to expand text. Note that we give these tips in order of preference; use the last tips only if you can't make text fit using the first few.

- ✔ **Edit text** to remove extra lines. Watch for lines at the end of a paragraph that have only a few characters. Getting rid of a few characters somewhere else in the paragraph may eliminate these short lines, reducing the amount of page space needed while keeping the amount of text removed to a minimum.

- ✔ **Track text** so that it occupies less space and especially so that short lines are eliminated.

✔ **Tighten the leading** by a half or quarter point. Because this is such a small change, the average reader won't notice it; it may even save you a few lines per column, which can add up quickly.

✔ **Reduce the point size** by a half point. This action saves more space than is first apparent, because it allows you to place a few more lines on the page and put a bit more text in each line. Change point size in the style sheet or select text and use the type size controls in the Measurements palette.

✔ **Reduce the horizontal scale** of text to a slightly smaller percentage (perhaps 95 percent) to squeeze more text in each line.

✔ **Vary the size of columns** by setting slightly narrower column gutters or slightly wider margins.

Try applying these copy-fitting techniques globally to avoid a patchwork appearance. You can, however, change the tracking on individual lines; if you limit tracking changes to no more than 20 units, the changes won't be very noticeable.

Chapter 11
Devil in the Details

• •

In This Chapter

▶ How to use the spelling checker

▶ How to add new words to the spelling dictionary

▶ How to control hyphenation

▶ How to add new words to the hyphenation dictionary

▶ How to control character and word spacing

▶ How to change kerning and tracking (and what they mean)

• •

*P*robably everyone's least favorite part of publishing is the proofreading and attention to the small text details. In practically every magazine you read, there's a typo. No matter how many people look at a story, it's amazing that errors still get through. Unfortunately, there's no magic cure for these errors, but you can substantially reduce them. Old-fashioned proofreading by a fresh pair of eyes — not the author's, not the editor's, and not the layout artist's — is the first and best line of defense. A close second are the exacting typographic settings over hyphenation and justification; these settings catch errors of both grammar and ease of reading. And, although technically not a mistake, poor spacing and justification also can lead the reader to misread text — and a "reado" is as bad as a typo because it causes a problem for the reader.

But buck up. It's not all doom and gloom. Follow the advice in this chapter, and you'll minimize — and maybe on a good week even eliminate — errors.

How to Win the Spelling Bee

Many people dread spelling, and that's why word processors and publishing programs come with spelling checkers. But there's a catch: spelling checkers work by being based on lists of words. Sure, spelling dictionaries sometimes contain 500,000-odd words (QuarkXPress's has a "mere" 120,000), but industry-specific terms like *PowerPC* or people's names rarely show up in these dictionaries. So you can't completely automate spell-checking. Sorry, but you will need to have a dictionary somewhere around for referral.

TIP

The two best dictionaries are Merriam-Webster's *Third International*, the publishing standard, and Houghton Mifflin's *American Heritage*, which specializes in explaining word origins and usage notes. Webster's *Ninth Collegiate* is a smaller version of the *Third International* and is a fine reference for editors' and writers' desks; usually, your proofreader will have the *Third International*.

Although you can't automate spell-checking, you can make it a part of your routine. You should spell-check your text in the word processor before laying it out in QuarkXPress. You also should spell-check it again in QuarkXPress after you've finished your layout but before you print it out. You'd be surprised how much text gets added or changed in layout, after the stories are officially "done."

QuarkXPress provides an internal spelling checker, accessed via the Utilities menu, as Figure 11-1 shows. The menu option is Check Spelling, which has three submenus: Word, Story, and Document. You can jump directly to these options via the ⌘-L shortcut for Word, ⌘-Option-L for Story, and ⌘-Option-Shift-L for Document. Chances are that you'll use the Story and Document options the most — the ones with the hardest-to-remember shortcuts. (A story is all text in the current text box and in all text boxes linked to that text box. It's usually the contents of an imported text file.)

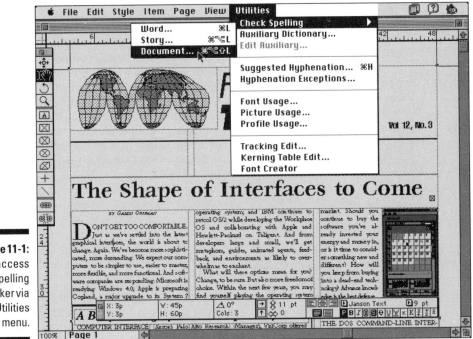

Figure 11-1: You access the spelling checker via the Utilities menu.

Windows QuarkXPress uses different shortcuts for the three spelling options: Ctrl+W for Word, Ctrl+Alt+W for Story, and Ctrl+Shift+Alt+W for Document.

To get the Story or Word options accessible, you have to have the Content tool active and the text pointer on a piece of text. You don't have to select a word to spell-check a word; just have the text pointer somewhere on the word. If you have multiple words selected and you use the Word spell-checking option, QuarkXPress will spell-check only the first word in the series. You can't spell-check a highlighted range of words.

Running the spelling checker

If you are spell-checking the entire document or the current story, you'll get the dialog box shown in Figure 11-2. You click OK to continue, which will display the dialog box shown in Figure 11-3. If you are spell-checking just a word, you go directly to the dialog box in Figure 11-4, which is a more compact version of the dialog box in Figure 11-3. These two dialog boxes differ in several ways:

✔ The Check Word dialog box has no capability to move on (via the Skip button) to the next suspect word (an option that wouldn't make sense for one-word spell-checking), as the Check Story or Check Document dialog boxes do.

✔ The Check Word dialog box automatically looks for possible correct words to replace the suspect word with; the other dialog boxes require that you click the Lookup button to get a list of possible replacements. If one of those words is the correct one, just click it and then click Replace, or just double-click the word in the list.

✔ In the Check Word dialog box, you can't enter a corrected word yourself; you click Cancel and type in the new word yourself. In the other dialog boxes, you can enter a replacement word, rather than accept a suggestion in the replacement list, because there may be several instances of the word and QuarkXPress will replace them all for you in one fell swoop.

✔ The Check Word dialog box has no Keep button, which lets you add words to your personal dictionary (explained a little later in this section).

What you can do in all three dialog boxes is select a new word and click the Replace button to have QuarkXPress make the replacement. If the word appears several times, QuarkXPress will tell you how many times it is used and replace all instances when you click Replace.

Figure 11-2:
QuarkXPress
first reports
on how
many words
it checked
and how
many it
didn't
recognize.

Word Count

Total: 5672
Unique: 1610
Suspect: 108

[OK]

Figure 11-3:
QuarkXPress
shows you
each
suspect
word in turn.

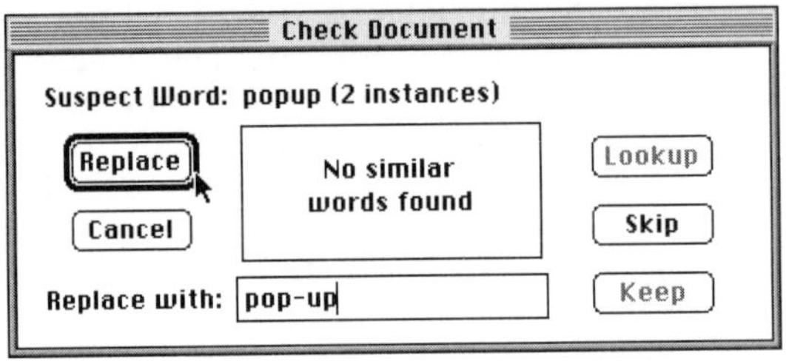

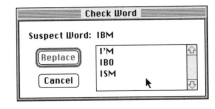

Check Document

Suspect Word: popup (2 instances)

[Replace]   [Lookup]

No similar
words found

[Cancel]   [Skip]

Replace with: pop-up   [Keep]

Figure 11-4:
When you
spell-check
a single
word, you
go directly
into this
limited
version of
the dialog
box in
Figure 11-3.

Check Word

Suspect Word: IBM

[Replace]   I'M
              IBO
[Cancel]   ISM

You may have noticed that the spelling-checker has no OK button or close box. To leave the spelling-checker, you must click Cancel or go through all the suspect words. If you click Cancel, will any changes made up to that point, either words you replaced or words you added to your spelling exception dictionary, be retained? Yes. That's counterintuitive to what the Cancel button usually does, but here it's really an OK button. Go figure.

Setting up your personal dictionaries

If you've experimented with QuarkXPress's spelling checker, you probably noticed that the Keep button stays gray. So what's it there for? For the Keep button to become active, you need to set up an auxiliary dictionary, a personal dictionary of words that QuarkXPress's own dictionary (the file XPress Dictionary on the Mac and the file XPRESS.DCT in Windows) doesn't know about.

To set up an auxiliary dictionary, use Utilities⇨Auxiliary Dictionary. The result is the dialog box shown in Figure 11-5. Any existing dictionaries in the current folder will be displayed. You can select one of them, move to a different directory to select a different dictionary, or click the New button to create a new auxiliary dictionary.

In the case of Figure 11-5, we had set up an auxiliary dictionary for the current document previously, so the name of that dictionary is displayed in the Current Auxiliary Dictionary field.

Figure 11-5:
You create or switch to a different auxiliary spelling dictionary via the Auxiliary Dictionary dialog box.

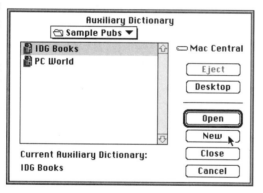

As is true for other global preferences, QuarkXPress works differently if no document is open than if one is. If you create or change auxiliary dictionaries when no document is open, QuarkXPress will use that auxiliary dictionary for all future documents (until you change the dictionary again). If a document is open, the auxiliary dictionary is created or changed specifically for that document.

The Windows QuarkXPress Auxiliary Dictionary dialog box looks a little different than its Mac counterpart because it follows the Windows conventions for an Open or Save dialog box. But it has all the same features and buttons. The only substantive difference is that what Mac QuarkXPress labels as the New button is called the Create button in Windows QuarkXPress. There's another thing about Windows auxiliary dictionaries you should know about: although the main dictionary (XPRESS.DCT) uses the extension .DCT, the auxiliary dictionaries use the extension .QDT (such as COMPUTER.QDT).

After you create the auxiliary dictionary, you have to add words to it. Oh, you don't have to — you could just add words as you find them in the spelling checker by clicking the Keep button as you come across a word like *PowerPC* that QuarkXPress doesn't know about but is correct. Or, if you know some of these words already, you can use Utilities⇨Edit Auxiliary to invoke the dialog box shown in Figure 11-6. You also can use this dialog box to remove incorrect words (maybe someone was too fast on the trigger and clicked Keep by accident).

Notice as you add words that spelling does not matter. If you enter *PowerPC*, it will display as *powerpc*. The use of only lowercase ensures that the word won't be flagged as incorrect if it were typed in all caps. Or, for a word like *uninstall,* which is not in QuarkXPress's own dictionary file, this use of only lowercase ensures that the word isn't flagged if the first letter is capitalized at, for example, the beginning of a sentence or in a title — *uninstall, Uninstall*, and *UNINSTALL* are all considered to be the same by QuarkXPress's spelling checker, which just keeps the form *uninstall* in its dictionary file.

But this lowercase-only approach means that you can't set QuarkXPress to flag incorrectly capitalized words (for example, many people write *MacWorld* even though the correct capitalization is *Macworld*). Your word processor probably has case-sensitive (which means it looks at the capitalization of words, not just at the sequence of letters in them) spell-checking, but QuarkXPress does not. That's another reason to do a spell-check in your word processor before importing the text into QuarkXPress.

You cannot use accented characters or symbols in an auxiliary dictionary. Fortunately, there are spelling XTensions that handle words in other languages that use accents. See Chapter 22 for information on where to get XTensions.

Be sure to click the Save button after making changes to your auxiliary dictionary. Otherwise, the changes won't be saved.

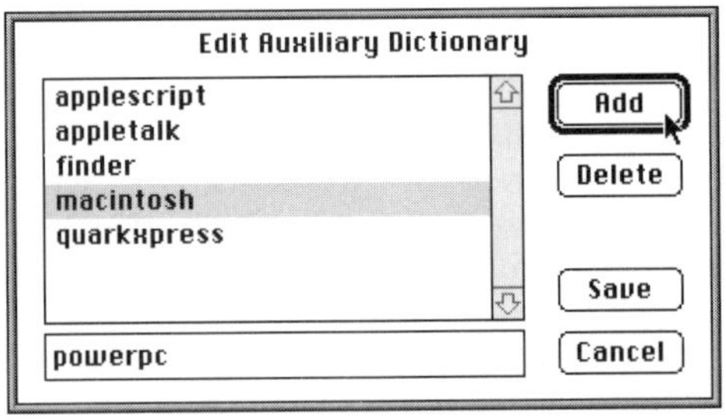

Figure 11-6:
The Edit
Auxiliary
Dictionary
dialog box
does what
its title says.

Edit Auxiliary Dictionary

applescript
appletalk
finder
macintosh
quarkxpress

powerpc

Add
Delete
Save
Cancel

Because auxiliary dictionaries are just files, you can share them over a network, which is a great way to maintain spelling consistency among several users. You also can have different dictionaries for different projects (if your work involved very different types of audiences). But one thing you can't do is share dictionaries between Windows and Macintosh users. The two dictionary formats are not compatible, and there is no way to translate one into the other's format.

By maintaining an up-to-date spelling dictionary and spell-checking at key points in the editing and layout process, you can greatly reduce typographical mistakes. Some typos (for example, words that are spelled correctly but are actually the wrong word), won't be caught this way, so you'll still need a person to proofread. But at least the obvious mistakes already will have been caught by the time a proofreader sees your text.

How to Hyphenate the Right Way

Hyphenation is even harder for many people than spelling. Where do you break a word? Between two consonants? After a syllable? There really are rules you can follow, but the English language is so full of exceptions that it's hardly worth learning the rules unless you are a copy editor. (Why so many exceptions? English takes words from tons of other languages, which forces the hyphenation to depend on other languages' rules sometimes. Besides, we still have to contend with all of ye olde Englishe words, too, and their rules are often different than those for modern English. Face it: if English were a dog, it would be a mutt, not a thoroughbred.)

As it does for spell-checking, QuarkXPress offers automatic hyphenation. In fact, the hyphenation is so good that you'll rarely need to add words to its exception dictionary — although you can if you want. Before you do that, though, let's see how to specify hyphenation.

Creating hyphenation sets

Any ink-stained newspaperman can tell you what an H&J set is. But ink-stained newspapermen are a vanishing breed (today, they're journalists, they're not just men, and they use computers instead of inky typewriters and typesetting machines), and you probably don't have one in close proximity. An H&J set is newspaper lingo for a hyphenation and justification set — the specifications for how words are divided across lines and how the text in each line is spaced. We'll cover the spacing features later in this chapter.

To set up hyphenation settings, you use Edit⇔H&Js, or ⌘-Option-H. Both methods bring up the H&Js dialog box, shown in Figure 11-7. When you first open this dialog box, you see just one listing in the H&J list: Standard. Edit this listing first so you can set up the hyphenation settings you want as the default for your text styles. Once you've edited Standard to your liking, you can create additional H&J sets for other needs. For example, you'll likely want an H&J set called No Hyphen for text (like headlines and bylines) that should have no hyphenation.

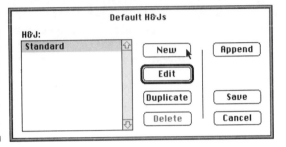

Figure 11-7:
The H&Js
dialog box
is your
gateway to
hyphenation
controls.

As is true for other global preferences, QuarkXPress works differently if no document is open than if one is. If you create or change H&J sets when no document is open, QuarkXPress will use that H&J set for all future documents (until you change the dictionary again). If a document is open, the H&J set is created or changed just for that document. You can tell whether the H&Js are being edited globally for all new documents or locally for the currently opened one: if the the dialog box says Default H&Js, you're changing the global settings; if it says H&Js for *document name*, you're changing the settings locally for whatever *document name*'s real name is (the real name will display in the title, not *document name*).

To edit an existing H&J set, select its name from the list and double-click it, or click it once and click the Edit button. To create an H&J set, click the New button. Either way, you get the Edit Hyphenation & Justification dialog box shown in Figure 11-8. The fields at the left are the ones that affect hyphenation.

Take a close look at the values in Figure 11-8; compare them to the values in your copy of QuarkXPress. Our values differ from yours because we've edited the Standard settings in our copy of QuarkXPress to work best in multicolumn layouts like newsletters, newspapers, and magazines. Let's go through the settings one by one:

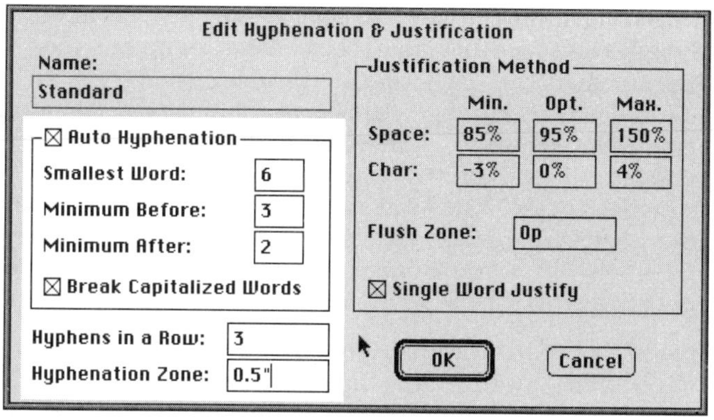

Figure 11-8:
The Edit
Hyphenation
&
Justification
dialog box
contains
hyphenation
controls at
its left side.

✔ **Name:** If you clicked New, enter the name for the H&J set here. (H&J sets are named, just as style sheets are.) If you clicked Edit to edit the Standard H&J set, you won't be able to edit the name.

✔ **Auto Hyphenation:** If this box is checked, hyphenation is turned on for any style sheet that uses this H&J set. If it is unchecked, hyphenation is turned off for any style sheet that uses this H&J set.

✔ **Smallest Word:** This field tells QuarkXPress to ignore words with fewer characters than that field's value. The default is 6, so any word of five or fewer characters won't be hyphenated. The default value of 6 is a good one because few words of 6 or fewer letters can't fit on a line with other text or look good if they are split across two lines, so there's little reason to change this default value. (One possible reason for changing it: a case where you have wide columns — say, 6 inches or more — in which case there's plenty of room for words; in this case a value of 8 would be fine.)

✔ **Minimum Before:** This field tells QuarkXPress how many characters in the word must precede a hyphen. Thus, if you leave the value set to the default of 3, QuarkXPress will not hyphenate the word *Rolodex* as *Ro-lodex*, even though that's a legal hyphenation for the word. The first place that QuarkXPress would hyphenate would be after the *l*, but that's an incorrect hyphenation point, so QuarkXPress would insert the hyphen after *Rolo*.

✔ **Minimum After:** This field is like Minimum Before, except that it tells QuarkXPress the minimum number of characters in a word that must follow the hyphen. The default is 2, although many people change that to 3 so QuarkXPress won't hyphenate verbs before the *-ed*, as in *edit-ed*. Many publishers think that looks tacky. It's a personal choice.

✔ **Hyphens in a Row:** The default is Unlimited, which means that theoretically every line could end in a hyphen. Having too many end-of-line hyphens in a row makes the text hard to read because it's hard to keep track of what line to move on to next. We suggest 3 as a good setting, although 2 and 4 are fine, too. The smaller the number, the greater the chance that QuarkXPress will have trouble spacing text in a line; a line that could really use a hyphen would be prohibited from having one just because it happened to come after that maximum number of consecutive hyphenated lines. (Let's try that again in a more specific example: If you set Hyphens in a Row to 2 and a particular paragraph turns out to have two hyphens in a row somewhere, and the third line could really use a hyphen to avoid awkward spacing, QuarkXPress will be prevented from hyphenating that third line.)

Sometimes, because of your Hyphens in a Row setting, you'll face just such peculiarly awkward spacing — the kind caused by reaching the maximum number of consecutive hyphens in the lines immediately before where a hyphen would really help. When you confront such a mishap, don't despair — and *don't* change the settings in your H&J set. Just type a regular hyphen followed by a space. (If you try to use the soft hyphen character — ⌘-hyphen — to create a break on that third line, QuarkXPress won't add the hyphen since the soft hyphens respect the Hyphens in a Row setting.) But add a regular hyphen and space only when everything else in the layout is finished — if your text were to reflow, you might find a hyphen and space in the middle of a word in the middle of a line. Oops! This cheat lets you get around the H&J limitations without changing a standard that works most of the time. And, if you're unsure where to hyphenate a word (and there's no dictionary handy), just click on the word and use Utilities⇨Suggested Hyphenation, or ⌘-H, to have QuarkXPress show you where hyphens may be added. (These suggestions follow any settings in the current H&J set you have for Smallest Word, Minimum Before, and Minimum After.)

✔ **Break Capitalized Words:** This box does just what it says. Some typographers frown on hyphenating proper names, like *Macworld* or *Alexander.* It's a silly prohibition, so make sure this box is checked. Better a broken name than awkward spacing around it.

✔ **Hyphenation Zone:** For text that is left-aligned, right-aligned, or centered, this box tells QuarkXPress how far from the outside margin to look for opportunities to hyphenate. Hyphenation Zone helps you prevent awkward gaps — something that looks like a kid's smile with no front top teeth — because a word happened to hyphenate halfway into the line. Set the zone to at least 10 percent of the column width (15 percent is better), but to no less than 0.2 inches. Thus, for a 1.5-inch-wide line, a good setting would be 0.225 inches (though you can round that to 0.2 or 0.25); that's 1.5 (inches) ×0.15 (percent). For justified or force-justified text, this setting has no effect, though, because all the text is aligned to both the left and right margins, which means that the text has no possible gaps for you to worry about.

TIP

When you click the New button, the new H&J set will take the attributes of the Standard H&J set, so it's best to edit Standard to your liking before creating new sets. That way, attributes that you'll have in several sets (such as having Auto Hyphenation and Break Capitalized Words checked) are automatically copied into the new sets. If you want to duplicate an H&J set and then make slight modifications to it (perhaps two sets are identical except for the Hyphenation Zone settings), select one of the sets in the H&J dialog box and click the Duplicate button; then modify (and rename) that duplicate set.

Figure 11-9 shows the effects of different hyphenation settings. We've used really skinny columns because thin columns emphasize the differences between hyphenation settings. The wider the columns, the less noticeable the differences are because there's more text for QuarkXPress to play around in while adjusting spacing.

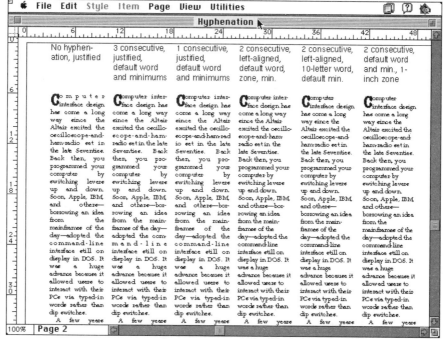

Figure 11-9:
The effects of different hyphenation settings.

Click OK when you're done creating or modifying an H&J set (or click Cancel if you want to abort those settings). Now you're back in the H&Js dialog box, from which you can create or edit other sets. When you're done, be sure to click Save to save all the work you've done — if you click Cancel, it's toast.

If you created H&J sets in another document, you can import those sets into the current QuarkXPress document by this mini-procedure: click the Append button (it really should be named Import — Append makes it sound like it will copy the current H&J set to another set, not *from* it) and then navigate the dialog box to find the document you're importing from. But remember that *all* H&J sets in that document will be imported into your current document. There's just one exception: if both documents have H&J sets with the same name, importing sets into the current document will not affect its H&J set. For example, say the current document has H&J sets Standard and No Hyphen, while the other document has the H&J sets Standard and Masthead. When you import H&J sets from the other document, Masthead will be copied into the current document but Standard won't be copied, and the current document's Standard H&J set will remain unaffected.

If you want to copy H&J sets from another document and make them the default for all future documents, make sure that no document is open in your copy of QuarkXPress and then import H&J sets from that other document. This is a great way to copy standards from a client to your system, or from a master document to a new employee's copy of QuarkXPress.

After you've set up your H&J sets — most documents will have just two: Standard and No Hyphen — edit your style sheets so that each style uses the appropriate H&J set. Headlines, bylines, and other categories of display type usually are not hyphenated, while body text, bios, captions, and sidebars usually *are* hyphenated. (Chapter 8 explains how to edit style sheets.) You also can apply an H&J set to a selected paragraph (or several selected paragraphs) by using the Paragraph Formats dialog box — Style⇨Formats, or ⌘-Shift-F — and changing the H&J field's value to the H&J set you want to apply.

Personalized hyphenation

As you can do for the spelling dictionaries, you can create your own personal hyphenation dictionaries, in which you tell QuarkXPress how to hyphenate words it doesn't know about. You also can use personalized hyphenation to change the default hyphenation for words that are hyphenated differently based on their pronunciation (such as the verb *pro-ject* and the noun *proj-ect*) or sometimes on what dictionary they appear in (such as *service*, which can be hyphenated as *ser-vice* or *serv-ice*, depending on which dictionary you consult).

To add your own hyphenation, use Utilities➪Hyphenation Exceptions. You get the dialog box shown in Figure 11-10. (Looks a lot like the dialog box for spelling exceptions, doesn't it?) Just enter the word whose hyphenation you want to personalize, include hyphens where it's OK for QuarkXPress to hyphenate the word, and click Add. (If you want to prevent a word from being hyphenated, enter it with no hyphens.) To delete a word, select it from the list and click Delete. When you're all done, click Save; clicking Cancel wipes out any changes you made.

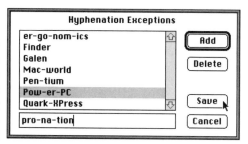

Figure 11-10:
The
Hyphenation
Exceptions
dialog box.

Unlike most QuarkXPress preferences, hyphenation exceptions are made for all documents opened by that copy of QuarkXPress, not just for the documents that are opened when you add words to (or delete words from) the exception dictionary. Thus, if you have several people working together and you trade files, make sure that everyone has the same hyphenation dictionary so that text doesn't reflow based on differences in each copy of QuarkXPress. To standardize dictionaries, copy the file XPress Preferences (on the Mac) or XPRESS.PRF (in Windows) to the QuarkXPress folder. But note that doing so replaces all local preferences — such as default colors, styles, guide settings, or anything else that's set with no document open — with the ones in the preferences file you copied from. Although that's a great way to ensure consistency, it does create problems for preferences that are matters of individual taste, such as the color of margin guides or whether rulers are displayed or not.

How to Prevent Reados

The other half of the H&J set — the J, or justification — controls the spacing of text. It's easy to overlook this aspect of typography and just go with the defaults. But you don't want to do that. How you set your spacing has a subtle but important effect on readability. QuarkXPress assumes that you're doing single-column, wide documents, which is fine for reports and price lists. But, for multicolumn documents, the default settings can result in spacing that leaves awkward gaps between words and can make the space between characters in words open enough that you might not be sure whether the characters make one word or two.

Default spacing

Take a look at Figure 11-11. It's the Edit Hyphenation & Justification dialog box described in the preceding section (Edit⇨H&Js⇨Edit). As in the previous section, we've changed QuarkXPress's defaults to what we believe are better settings. The results are that the characters in a word are closer together and that no unsightly gaps remain between words. Experiment with the values, but, before you do that, read on to find out what those values mean.

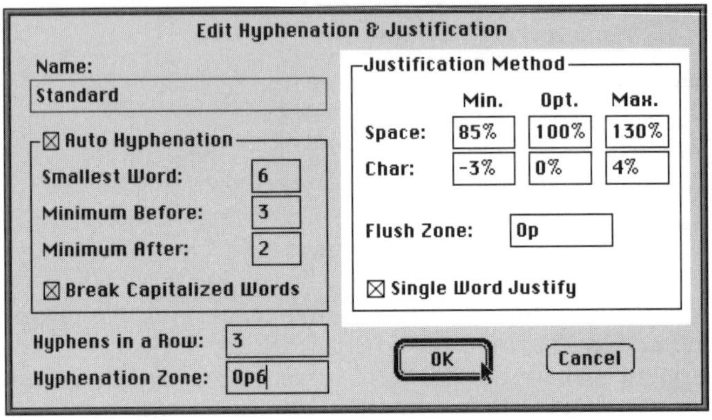

Figure 11-11:
The justification half of the Edit Hyphenation & Justification dialog box, with the authors' preferred settings.

All settings for justification are in the section of the dialog box labeled Justification Method. At the top are six fields that determine how your text is spaced between characters and words; spacing of text between characters and words is called letter spacing and word spacing, respectively. The first row determines the space between words; the second row controls the space between characters within a word. Generally, you want tighter space within a word than between words so that words look unified and the space between them is easily discernible. The three columns determine the rules by which QuarkXPress spaces characters and words.

The spacing columns may not make sense at first because they behave differently depending on how the text is aligned. If text is left-aligned, right-aligned, or centered, QuarkXPress always uses the Opt. (optimum, or target) values. If the text is justified or force-justified, QuarkXPress tries to meet the Opt. values; if it can't meet those values, though, it will use a value in the range between the Min. (minimum) and Max. (maximum) values. And if that doesn't work, then it will use a value greater than the Max. value. QuarkXPress *never* uses less than the Min. settings.

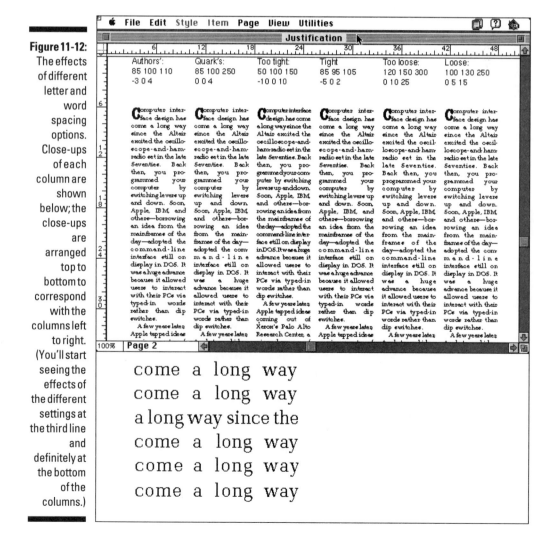

Because of how QuarkXPress applies spacing, it's best to set the Opt. values to 100% for words and 0% for characters. Those particular Opt. values tell QuarkXPress to use the defaults from the font's internal spacing specifications. (Presumably, the font's designers picked those specs for a good reason.)

For the Min. settings, we prefer 85% for words and –3% for characters. That prevents words and letters from getting too close, but it also helps balance any spaced-out text with slightly cramped text, keeping the overall average closer to the Opt. values. For Max., we allow a greater difference from Opt. than we do from Min., since the human eye can handle extra space better than it can too little space. Figure 11-12 shows several examples of different spacing settings.

Figure 11-12:
The effects of different letter and word spacing options. Close-ups of each column are shown below; the close-ups are arranged top to bottom to correspond with the columns left to right. (You'll start seeing the effects of the different settings at the third line and definitely at the bottom of the columns.)

Local space controls: tracking and kerning

But wait, there's more! You can override these spacing settings for selected text or even with a style sheet. But, pray, why would you do this? Consider these scenarios:

✔ Perhaps some text is too spacey, or you know that if some text were just a little closer together, you'd get the text to rewrap and take one line less. Here's where you would use QuarkXPress's tracking feature to tighten (or loosen) the space among characters in a selected block of text.

✔ Or maybe your Standard H&J set's justification settings work fine for your body text but not for your headlines. Rather than create a new H&J set for headlines, you just adjust the tracking settings in your Headlines style sheet to compensate for the difference.

✔ Or maybe only a few characters don't quite mesh. Here and there, a couple of letters in a word seem to be too close or two far apart. Just use QuarkXPress's kerning feature to adjust the space between those two characters.

Tracking and kerning are pretty much the same thing — ways to adjust the spacing between characters. So what's the difference? The scope of the adjustments they make. *Kerning* adjusts spacing between just two characters, while *tracking* adjusts spacing between all characters selected. QuarkXPress uses the same menus for these two features because they really are just variations of the same feature. Thus, you see Style⇨Kern if your text pointer happens to be between two characters, but you see Style⇨Track if you select several characters. Similarly, the horizontal arrows on the Measurements palette adjust kerning if the pointer is between two characters, and they adjust tracking when several characters are selected.

Figure 11-13 shows text that has been kerned and tracked, along with the Measurements palette settings and the Kern Amount and Track Amount dialog boxes for that same text (you get these dialog boxes via Style⇨Kern and Style⇨Track). These dialog boxes and multiple Measurements palettes won't appear simultaneously — we combined them into one illustration so that you could see the effects of the two operations and see the different ways for achieving them. Figure 11-14 shows where you set tracking in the Character Formats dialog box, either for a specific paragraph (via Style⇨Character, or ⌘-Shift-D) or in a style sheet (via Edit⇨Style Sheets⇨Edit⇨Character).

It's best to use the keyboard shortcuts or the Measurements palette to adjust tracking and kerning since you can see the effects of your changes as you make them, rather than make the longer effort of opening a dialog box, entering a value, closing the dialog box, seeing the result, reopening the dialog box to further adjust the spacing, and so on. Use ⌘-Shift-] to increase spacing in $1/20$th em increments and ⌘-Shift-Option-] in $1/200$th em increments. To decrease spacing, use ⌘-Shift-[and Ctrl+Alt+Shift+[.

Figure 11-13:
You can access kerning and tracking via the Style menu (which results in the dialog boxes) or via the Measurements palette, as this composite image shows.

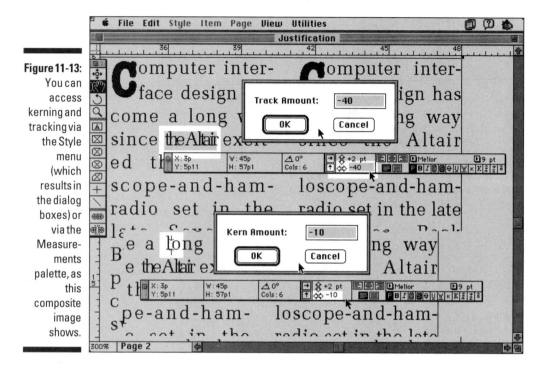

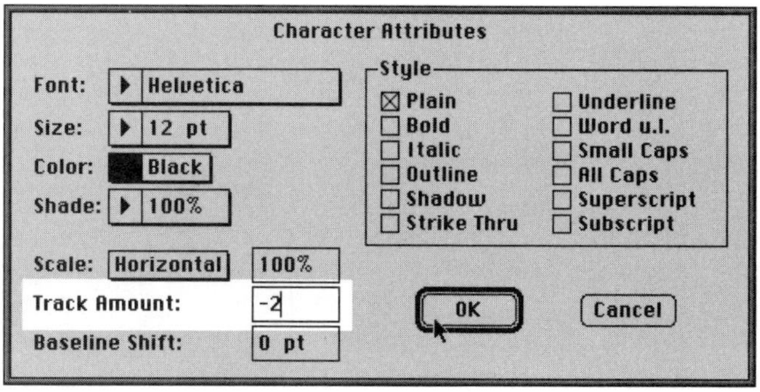

Figure 11-14:
You also can set tracking via the Character Formats dialog box, either for selected text or for an entire paragraph within a style sheet.

The values QuarkXPress uses for tracking and kerning are not percentages, as they are for the H&J sets' spacing options. Instead, for tracking and kerning QuarkXPress uses a unit of measurement called (of all things) a *unit* — a handy little length that measures all of $1/200$ths of an em space. An em space is as wide as a font is high; thus, an em space for 9-point type is 9 points wide. That means that a unit is $9/200$ths of a point for 9-point type, $8/200$ths (or $1/50$th) of a point for 8-point type, and so on. As you can see, then, a unit really is another way to express a percentage: 0.05% (that's the decimal way to represent $1/200$th). That's a pretty small value. So, in the Measurements palette, QuarkXPress jumps in 10-unit increments when you click the left and right arrows to adjust tracking or kerning. You of course can select your own precise values by entering in a number. A positive number adds space; a negative number removes it.

Part IV
The Picasso Factor

"YEAH, MY PEOPLE ARE STILL GETTING HEADACHES — DANG THESE VDT SCREENS!"

In this part ...

*P*ublishing would be no fun if it was just about text, even with all those fonts to choose from. Fortunately, publishing is as much about graphics as it is text, and we all know it's the graphics that grab people's attention. You notice the look before anything else, right? The four chapters in this part will explain how to achieve that special graphics look, whether it be a special effect or the use of color. Prepare to be dazzled as you learn to dazzle your readers.

Chapter 12

Frame It!

*P*icture this: it's a hot, sultry July day and you are walking up to the counter at your favorite ice cream store, money in hand. You ask the clerk to list the ice cream flavors available today, and he answers, "Vanilla, vanilla, and vanilla." You answer him with a plaintive cry, "Is that all? Don't you have strawberry, or chocolate, or mocha safari delight?" Disappointed when he answers in the negative, you put the dollar back into your pocket and sulk all the way home.

Sometimes plain old vanilla is just not enough. And sometimes, when you are working on a document, plain old text and picture boxes aren't enough, either. One way to spice up a dull text or picture box is to add a frame — a decorative border placed inside or outside the box — to it. And new users like frames because they are easy to understand and easy to use.

Introducing Frames

The capability to frame text and picture boxes is, quite honestly, a minor event when it comes to desktop design. Professional designers usually steer clear of frames or use very simple ones, such as single lines that have the thickness of a hairline (a quarter point, in publishing measure). But, for many of us, there are those times when we feel that we really need to put a border around a page or box. If so, frames are a very handy feature to have in a publishing program.

When would you want to use a frame? One obvious time is if you are called upon to create a certificate commemorating a special event or a job well done. Figure 12-1 shows a typical certificate with one of the built-in QuarkXPress frame designs applied to it.

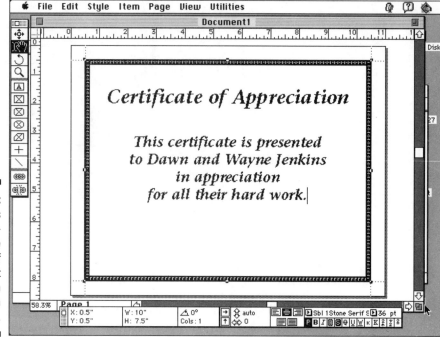

Figure 12-1:
Certificates
of appre-
ciation are
one type of
document
that you can
make with
frames.

You get the picture. Frames go around boxes and make the boxes look fancy. Now we'll tell you how you can control exactly where around the box the frame should go.

Is it an "inny" or an "outy"?

Inny or outy? No, we're not talking belly buttons here, and we could care less what your belly button looks like. (We like you either way!) What we're referring to is whether the frame you want to apply to a text or picture box appears inside or outside the borders of the box itself.

Look closely at the frame around the box shown in Figure 12-2. If you look carefully, you'll see that the box's sizing handles — those little squares at the outer edge of the text or picture box that you use to change the size of the box — are on the outside of the box, and the frame is on the inside of the box.

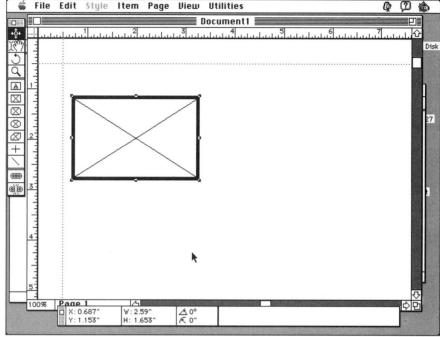

Figure 12-2:
Frames can be inside or outside a text or picture box. In this example, the frame is inside the box.

When it comes right down to it, does it really matter if the frame is inside or outside the text or picture box? Probably not. It depends on what else is happening on the same page where the frame appears. For example, if you are putting a framed box onto a page that is already pretty much full of text and graphics, you may want to have the frame inside the box so that it is less likely to "bump" into other items on the page.

You control whether frames appear inside or outside of boxes by making a selection in General Preferences (Edit⇨Preferences⇨General). As you can see in Figure 12-3, the General Preferences dialog box has a Framing pop-up menu, from which you can select framing that occurs inside or outside text or picture boxes.

Suppose you have created a document with several framed boxes, all of which have the framing on the outside because — hey, this is logical! — framing has been set to Outside (in the General Preferences dialog box). Now, what do you think happens when you change the General Preferences dialog box (Edit⇨Preferences⇨General) so that Framing is set to Inside? Well, all previously created framed boxes keep their frames on the outside, and all new framed boxes you create have the frames on the inside. In other words, a changed Framing preference is not retroactive to other frames in the document.

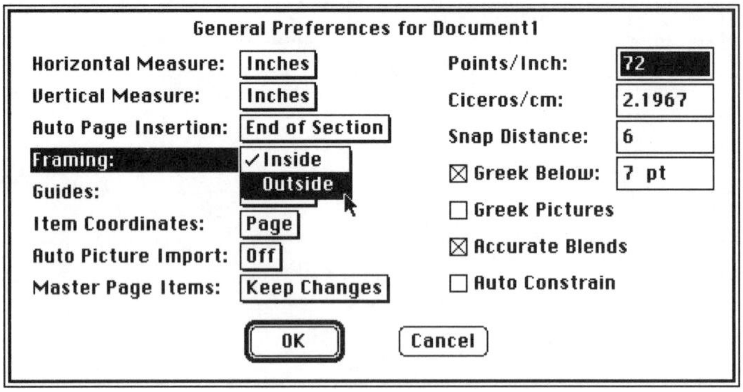

Figure 12-3:
Use General
Preferences
to
determine
whether
frames
appear
inside or
outside the
boxes to
which they
are applied.

General Preferences for Document1

Horizontal Measure:	Inches	Points/Inch:	72
Vertical Measure:	Inches	Ciceros/cm:	2.1967
Auto Page Insertion:	End of Section	Snap Distance:	6
Framing:	✓ Inside / Outside	☒ Greek Below:	7 pt
Guides:		☐ Greek Pictures	
Item Coordinates:	Page		
Auto Picture Import:	Off	☒ Accurate Blends	
Master Page Items:	Keep Changes	☐ Auto Constrain	

[OK]   [Cancel]

Specifying frames

If you are going to use frames, it's nice to know that you have some say in how the frames look. In fact, QuarkXPress lets you specify several characteristics about a frame. To do so, you access the Frame Specifications dialog box (Item⇨Frame).

Probably the most important fact about the Frame Specifications dialog box, which is shown in Figure 12-4, is that this box lets you select from all of the default frame styles that came with the program. In addition, it lets you choose from those that you may have created using the Frame Editor (a separate utility that comes with the Mac version of QuarkXPress; we explain how to use it later in this chapter).

How can you tell how the frame will look? Well, it's easy, since the Frame Specifications dialog box shows you a sample. Look at Figure 12-4. As you can see, we have selected the ornate frame that is third in the part of the scroll list that is visible. Note also that the frame appears around the name of the dialog box, giving you a quick preview of how the frame will look. If we decide that we don't care for that particular frame style, we simply make a different selection. We then get a chance to preview our new selection by watching it appear around the title of the dialog box, "Frame Specifications."

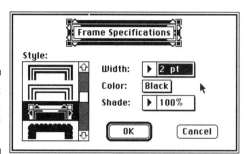

Figure 12-4:
The Frame
Specifications
dialog box.

QuarkXPress actually has two kinds of frames: bitmap frames and mathematical frames. Bitmap frames can go only on rectangular boxes; you create bitmap frames with the Frame Editor utility, which we tell you about later in this chapter. Mathematically defined frames can be placed on boxes of any shape.

Using the Frame Editor

Separate but related. No, we're not talking about your ex, and we're also not talking about your in-laws. We're talking about the Frame Editor, which is actually a mini-program that is separate from QuarkXPress but comes with the Mac and Power Mac versions of the program.

QuarkXPress for Windows, Macintosh, and Power Macintosh is, for the most part, one application that is consistently applied on these different platforms. True, there are some minor differences because of the variations among the various operating systems, but a vast majority of the program's functions work the same on any platform. A few features, though, might exist on one platform and not the others. Framing is supported by all three platforms, but the Windows version does not include a separate Frame Editor.

To get to the Frame Editor, you exit QuarkXPress and then open the Frame Editor application. When you open the Frame Editor, the first screen displayed resembles the one shown in Figure 12-5 and contains a scrolling list for Style Selection.

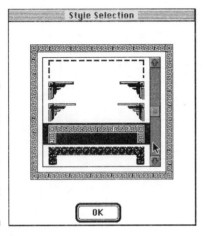

Figure 12-5:
The first
thing you do
when you
open the
Frame Editor
is select
a style.

You may decide that you don't want to use one of the existing frame styles that you see in the Style Selection box. That's okay, because the real purpose of the Frame Editor is to let you create your own frame style.

Once you have the Frame Editor open and the Style Selection window is displayed (as in Figure 12-5), here are the steps to follow to create a new frame style:

1. **Choose File⇨New Style.**

2. **Enter a width value in the dialog box and click OK.**

   An Enter new size dialog box appears, asking you to enter the width (also sometimes called the *weight*) you want the frame to be.

3. **In the Element Selection window (shown in Figure 12-6), select (by clicking the mouse button over it) the corner or side you want to create.**

   The next screen you see is the window called Element Selection, as shown in Figure 12-6. (Note that, by using the Frame Editor, you need to create both the sides and corners of the frames that you are developing.) In our example in Figure 12-6, we have selected the top left corner of the frame.

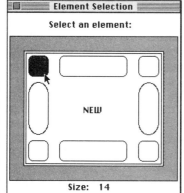

Figure 12-6:
The Element
Selection
window of
the Frame
Editor.

4. **When a dialog box appears, enter the values you want for Height and Width of the frame element you are creating and then click OK.**

5. **When you see the Frame Edit window, in the left area of that window, click on the screen to create or delete individual pixels.**

The Frame Edit window lets you create, one pixel at a time, the frame element. The element you are creating appears — in a magnified size to make it easy to edit pixels — in the scroll window at the left of the Frame Edit window. Figure 12-7 shows a Frame Edit window, where we are editing the lower middle element of a frame.

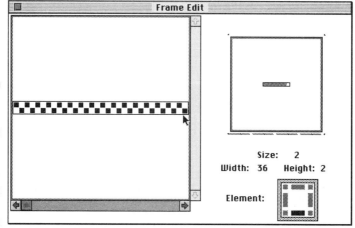

Figure 12-7:
In the
Frame Edit
window, you
can design
a frame one
pixel at
a time.

In Figure 12-7, notice that the Element box at the lower right of the window shows you which frame element you are currently creating. In our example, we are creating a checkerboard pattern. We do this simply by clicking pixels on and off in the left side of the Frame Edit window. Design your frame element in the same manner.

6. **Repeat Steps 3, 4, and 5 for each frame element.**

   Note that you need to create at least one corner element and one side element; you then can copy the elements. (Copy elements by choosing Element⇨Copy Element, clicking on the element you want to copy, and specifying where you are copying the element to.) Also note that you cannot copy a corner into a side element or a side element into a corner.

7. **Click on the Close box to close the Element Selection window.**

8. **Click Yes in the dialog box to save the changes you just made.**

9. **Close the Size Selection window.**

   The frame that you just created is now displayed in the Style Selection menu.

10. **To return to QuarkXPress, quit the Frame Editor and open QuarkXPress.**

Chapter 13

Warped Images

A picture is worth a thousand words. Now that's a statement of monumental importance. It's a stale saying, but we can all agree that there's some truth in it. Sometimes words just can't say what pictures can.

And isn't it nice to know that you don't have to settle for reality when it comes to pictures? With QuarkXPress, you can slant, rotate, warp, and tweak pictures to your heart's content. In this chapter, we show you some easy ways to pummel your pictures into shape.

Two Ways to Warp

Although you can warp an image in a number of ways, the two most common are using the Picture Box Specifications dialog box and using the Measurements palette. Both ways work just fine, and choosing the better of the two is really a matter of finding which works better for you.

The Picture Box Specifications dialog box

You can make changes to a picture contained in an active picture box by using the Picture Box Specifications dialog box, shown in Figure 13-1. To display the dialog box, select the picture box to make it active and then choose Item➪Modify.

```
                    Picture Box Specifications

   Origin Across:  [ 1.25" ]      Scale Across:   [ 120% ]
   Origin Down:    [ 0.5" ]       Scale Down:     [ 120% ]
   Width:          [ 6.344" ]     Offset Across:  [ -0.095" ]
   Height:         [ 4.723" ]     Offset Down:    [ 0" ]
   Box Angle:      [ 0° ]         Picture Angle:  [ 0° ]
   Box Skew:       [ 0° ]         Picture Skew:   [ 0° ]
   Corner Radius:  [ 0" ]       ┌─Background──────────
   ☐ Suppress Picture Printout    Color:  [ White ]
   ☐ Suppress Printout            Shade:  [▶] [ 100% ]

            [    OK    ]   [ Cancel ]
```

Figure 13-1:
The Picture
Box Speci-
fications
dialog box.

We won't go into too much detail, but we will give you a general idea about all the things you can do to a picture using the Picture Box Specifications dialog box.

The Origin Across, Origin Down, Width, and Height fields control the position and size of the picture box. In Figure 13-1, the origin (the upper-left corner of the picture box) is 1.25" from the left and 0.5" from the top of the page. The picture box width is 6.344", while the height is 4.723". (We didn't really need to make the width and height three decimal places long; we made them so long just to illustrate that you can specify these values in units as small as .001 in any measurement system.)

Entering a value in the Box Angle field rotates the picture box around the center of the box. Box angle values range from –360 to 360 degrees, in increments as small as .001 degrees. Box Skew slants the sides of the box.

Entering a value in the Corner Radius field changes the shape of a picture box's corners. This field contains the word *radius* because invisible circles exist in the corners of boxes drawn in QuarkXPress. These circles are located within the bounds of the box corners and touch the two sides of the box next to them. The radius is the size of the circle used to form rounded edges to the box. When you first create a rectangular picture box, its corner radius values are 0 (zero). You can enter a measurement value from 0 to 2 inches (0 to 12 picas) in .001 increments of any measurement system.

Two of our favorite features in the Picture Box Specifications dialog box are Scale Across and Scale Down. When you first fill a picture box with a picture (by choosing File⇨Get Picture), QuarkXPress places the picture in the text box at its full size — that is, at 100 percent scale. But the picture may easily be larger or smaller than you would like. No problem. You can change its size by entering new values in the Scale Across and Scale Down fields. In our example, we entered a value of 120 percent in each field, which made the picture 20 percent bigger than it was when we imported it.

The Offset Across and Offset Down fields let you adjust the placement of the picture within the box; in Figure 13-1, we set the Offset Across value to –0.095", which moves the picture box contents to the right by 0.095".

The Picture Angle field is useful if you want to change the angle of a picture without changing the angle of the picture box itself. Actually, when you enter a value in the Picture Angle field, you cause the picture to rotate — around its center — within the box.

The Picture Skew field lets you *skew,* or slant, a picture within its box. You can enter values from –75 to 75 degrees, in increments as small as .001 degrees. If you enter a positive value, the picture skews to the right; if you enter a negative value, the picture skews to the left.

Suppress Picture Printout and Suppress Printout are options that speed document printing — something you may want to consider when you print proofs or rough copies. If you select Suppress Picture Printout, the frames or backgrounds of picture boxes print, but the contents of the picture boxes do not. Selecting Suppress Printout takes this option one step further. It prevents picture box frames, backgrounds, and contents from printing. To choose either option, check the box next to the option label.

The Background Color field lets you add color to the background of a picture box and control the depth (*saturation*) of the color. To add color to the background of an active picture box or to change an existing background color, select a color from the Color list box in the Picture Box Specifications dialog box or use the Colors palette (if it's not visible, use View⇨Show Colors to make it appear). See Chapter 14 for more information on applying colors and creating custom colors.

After you select the background color that you want to apply to the picture box (and you've selected a color other than None or White), you can specify the saturation level of the color. Select a predefined shade (0 to 100 percent) in the Shade list box or enter a custom shade value (in increments as small as 0.1 percent) in the Shade field. There's a pop-up list for shade increments in the Colors palette as well (at the top right), in which you can use your own values or choose from the existing ones.

The Measurements palette

As you make changes to values in the Picture Box Specifications dialog box, you might notice that the Measurements palette also changes to reflect the new values. You can bypass the Picture Box Specifications dialog box for any function displayed in the Measurements palette by entering the appropriate values in the palette itself.

To use the Measurements palette to modify the contents of a picture box, you must first make the picture box active. (If the box is active, its sizing handles are visible around the edge of the box.) You also must display the Measurements palette. (To display the palette, choose View⇨Show Measurements.)

The Measurements palette appears at the bottom of the screen in Figure 13-2. You can make several changes to the picture box through the Measurements palette, which is the simplest way to manipulate picture boxes and their contents.

Figure 13-2:
The
Measure-
ments
palette for
pictures.

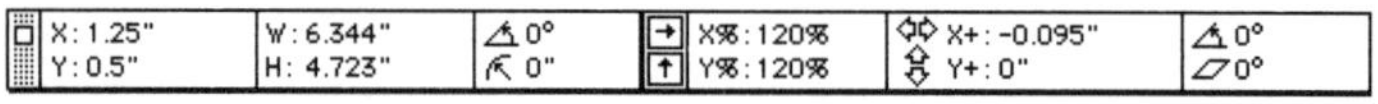

X: 1.25"	W: 6.344"	◿ 0°	→ X%: 120%	✥ X+: −0.095"	◿ 0°
Y: 0.5"	H: 4.723"	◹ 0"	↑ Y%: 120%	↕ Y+: 0"	◿ 0°

Enter new values in the X and Y fields to change the distance of the picture box border from the page edge.

The W and H fields control the width and height of the picture box. In Figure 13-2, the current dimensions are 6.344" by 4.723". Those exacting coordinates indicate that the picture box was drawn by hand; if we had sized the box via the Measurements palette, we would have rounded off the coordinates to something like 6.3" by 4.7".

◿ The Rotation field (shown at left) rotates the picture box. Because the box in Figure 13-2 is not rotated, the value in the field is 0 (zero) degrees.

The Corner Radius field (shown at left) changes the shape of the picture box corners.

The settings in the X% and Y% fields in Figure 13-2 are percents. Changing the percent values in the X% and Y% fields reduces or enlarges the picture in the picture box. To keep the proportions of the picture the same, enter the same value in the X field that you enter in the Y field.

Entering any value except zero in the Rotation field (shown at left) located at the right side of the palette rotates the picture *within* the picture box. (The Rotation field on the left side of the palette rotates the entire picture box.) The current value for the picture box in Figure 13-2 is zero, which means the box is not rotated. Likewise, the value for the image is zero, so it is also not rotated.

Entering any value except zero in the Slant field (shown at left) slants the contents of the picture box. In Figure 13-2, the picture-box contents are not slanted.

Clicking either of the Horizontal or Vertical Shift handles (shown at left) moves an image within the picture box. Each click moves the image in 0.1 increments (0.1 inches, 0p1, and so on). To move the image in coarser increments, choose the Content tool, move the pointer to the image (the grabber icon will appear), hold the mouse down, and reposition the image within the picture box. You also can enter values for the image to be shifted within the picture box.

The Flip Horizontal and Flip Vertical icons (shown at left) flip the image along the X and Y axes, respectively. The arrow's direction changes in the icon to let you know whether a picture has been flipped. You also can use the Flip Horizontal and Flip Vertical items in the Style menu.

Figure 13-3 shows the effect of rotating the *contents* of the picture box by 30 degrees; you can see that we entered a value of 30 in the rotation field at the right of the Measurements palette.

Figure 13-4 shows the same picture, but this time the entire box, including its contents, have been rotated by 10 degrees. Here, you can see that we entered a value of 10 in the Rotation field on the left of the Measurements palette.

After you use the Measurements palette to make changes to the picture box, press Return or click the mouse to apply the changes.

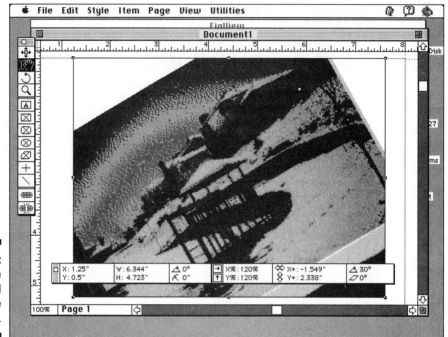

Figure 13-3:
A picture
rotated
within the
picture box.

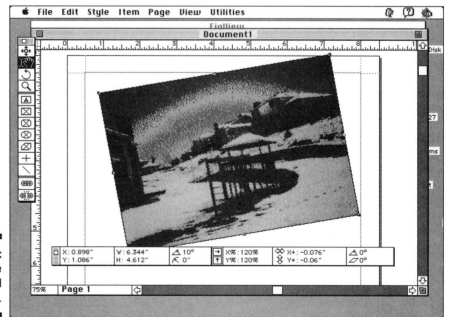

Figure 13-4:
A picture
box rotated
ten degrees.

Using Line-Screen Controls

Most people never worry about line screens (in fact, many desktop publishers don't know what they are), but they can have a major effect on how your bitmap images print.

To understand how line screens work, think of a screen door. The places between the wires of the screen door let light through; the wires on the screen keep light out. Line screens split an image into a series of spots.

In traditional printing, a line screen is an acetate mask covered with a grid of spots. Printers use line screens to convert a continuous-tone image — like a photograph — into the series of spots, called a *halftone*, that is required to reproduce such an image on a printing press. Take a magnifying glass to a photo — either color or black-and-white — in a newspaper or magazine, and you'll see the spots that the photo is made of. These spots are usually dots, but they can be any of several shapes.

When making a halftone in the traditional way, a line-screen mask is placed on top of a piece of photographic paper (such as Kodak's RC paper, used for decades in traditional photography). The continuous-tone original is then illuminated in a camera so that the image is projected through the mask onto the photographic paper. The photographic paper is exposed only where the mask is transparent (in the grid holes, or spots), producing the spots that make up the image to be printed. The size of each spot depends on how much light passes through, which in turn depends on how dark or light each area of the original image is. Think of a window screen through which you spray water: the stronger the spray, the bigger the spots behind the screen's holes.

The spots that make up the image are arranged in a series of lines, usually at a 45-degree angle (this angle helps the eye blend the individual spots to simulate a continuous tone). The number of lines per inch (the *halftone frequency*) determines the maximum dot size as well as the coarseness (*halftone density*) of the image (thus the term *line screen*). The spots in the mask need not be circular — they can be ellipses, squares, lines, or more esoteric shapes like stars. These shapes are called *screen elements*. Circular dots are the most common type because they result in the least distortion of the image.

When you use line screens, you need to know a little bit about lpi and dpi. Lines per inch (lpi) and dots per inch (dpi) are not related because the spots in a line screen are variable-sized, while dots in a laser printer are fixed-sized. *Lines per inch* specifies the grid through which an image is filtered, not the size of the spots that make it up. *Dots per inch* specifies the number of ink dots per inch produced by the laser printer; typically, these dots are the same size. A 100-lpi image with variable-sized dots will therefore look finer than a 100-dpi image.

Depending on the size of the line-screen spot, several of a printer's fixed-sized dots may be required to simulate one line-screen spot. For this reason, a printer's or image-setter's lpi number is far less than its dpi number. For example, a 300-dpi laser printer can achieve about 60-lpi resolution; a 1270-dpi image setter can achieve about 120-lpi resolution; a 2540-dpi image setter about 200-lpi resolution. Resolutions of less than 100 lpi are considered coarse, and resolutions of more than 120 lpi are considered fine.

But there's more to choosing an lpi setting then knowing your output device's top resolution. An often-overlooked issue is the type of paper the material is printed on. Smoother paper (such as *glossy-coated* or *super-calendared*) can handle finer halftone spots because the paper's coating (its *finish*) minimizes ink bleeding. Standard office paper, such as the kind used in photocopiers and laser printers, is rougher and has some bleed (meaning that ink diffuses easily through the paper) that is usually noticeable only if you write on it with markers. Newsprint is very rough and has a heavy bleed. Typically, newspaper images are printed at 85 to 90 lpi; newsletter images on standard office paper print at 100 to 110 lpi; magazine images are printed at 120 to 150 lpi; calendars and coffee-table art books are printed at 150 to 200 lpi.

Other factors affecting lpi include the type of printing press and the type of ink used. Your printer representative should advise you on preferred settings.

Effects of line screens

Seeing is believing when it comes to special graphics effects, so you'll want to experiment with line-screen settings before printing your document. In most cases, you should use Normal Screen, which is the default for all imported images. The default line-screen frequency for Normal Screen is set in the File menu's Page Setup dialog box through the Halftone Screen option. The default screen angle is 45 degrees, and the default screen element is a dot; you can change neither of these defaults.

But when you want to do something special, you can. As a rule, most people using line-screen effects prefer coarser halftone frequencies to make the image coarser but bolder. They usually also change the screen element to a line or other shape to alter the image's character. In acknowledgment of this tendency, QuarkXPress predefines three line-screen settings that you can apply directly from the Style menu:

Line screens can only be applied to black-and-white bitmap pictures, or to TIFF/RIFF line art or grayscale pictures.

✓ **Normal Screen:** This setting uses the defaults defined via File⇨Printer Setup.

✓ **60-lpi Line Screen/0°:** This setting creates a 60-line-per-inch (lpi) halftone frequency, using lines aligned at 0 degrees (horizontal) as the screen element.

✓ **30-lpi Line Screen/45°:** This setting creates a 30-lpi halftone frequency using lines aligned at 45 degrees as the screen element.

✓ **20-lpi Dot Screen/45°:** This setting creates a 20-lpi halftone frequency using dots aligned at 45 degrees.

If you've already applied one of the line-screen settings to an image, a check mark appears to the left of the appropriate icon.

The last option available from the Style menu is Other Screen, which lets you define any combination of frequency, element, and angle you want. Selecting this option opens the Picture Screening Specifications dialog box, shown in Figure 13-5.

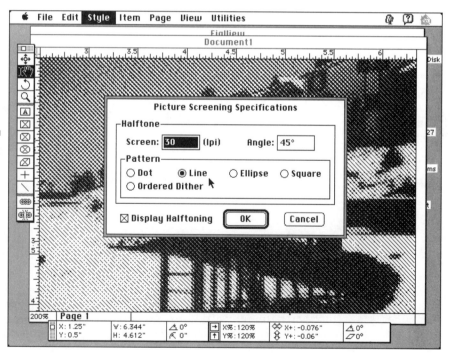

Figure 13-5: The Picture Screening Specifications dialog box; behind it is a view of an image set at 30 lpi with a dot-screen element at 45 degrees.

To see the effects of different line-screen elements, compare Figures 13-5 through 13-8. All are set at 30 lpi, and all are viewed at 200 percent in order to magnify the differences between the screen elements. Figure 13-6 shows the effects of using dots as the screen element. Figure 13-7 shows a line screen with ellipses as the screen element. In Figure 13-8, squares are used as the screen element. In all four figures, the screen elements are arranged at a 45-degree angle.

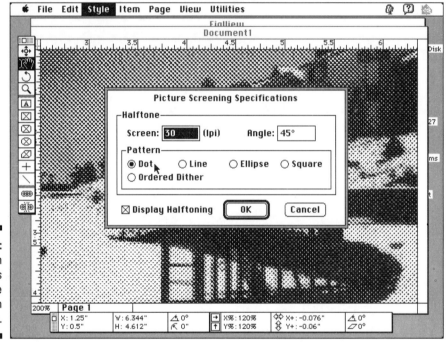

Figure 13-6: A screen that uses dots as the screen element.

Dithering

Dithering is an effect that replaces gray levels with a varying pattern of black and white. This pattern does not attempt to simulate grays; instead, it merely tries to retain some distinction between shades in an image when the image is output to a printer that does not have fine enough resolution to reproduce grays (through the fine grid of dots used in screening to reproduce each gray shade). In other words, dithering uses coarse patterns of dots and lines to represent the basic details in a gray-scale image. A set of mathematical equations determines how the dithered pattern appears for each image. The basic technique is to replace dark shades with all black, medium shades with alternating black and white dots or lines, and light shades with a sparse pattern of dots or lines.

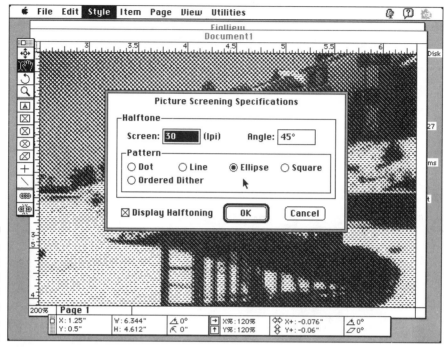

Figure 13-7:
A screen that uses ellipses as the screen element.

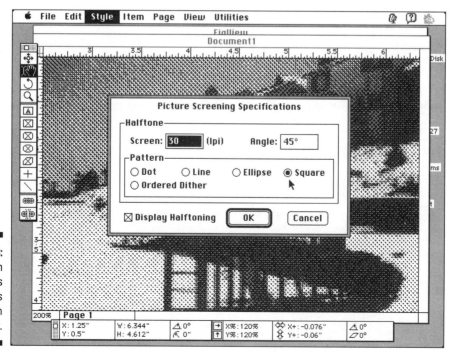

Figure 13-8:
A screen that uses squares as the screen element.

QuarkXPress uses an equation called *ordered dithering*, which you select by choosing Ordered Dither in the Picture Screening Specifications dialog box. Figure 13-9 shows the dialog box and an image to which ordered dithering is applied. We've placed the normal image (using the default settings for screen frequency and elements) at the left; the dithered version is at right. To apply other dithering equations, you must dither the image in a paint or graphics program that supports dithering before importing the image into QuarkXPress.

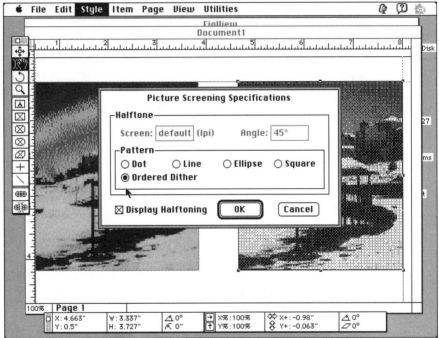

Figure 13-9:
The Ordered Dither option converts gray-scale images (left) into coarse, patterned, black-and-white images (right) for output to low-resolution printers.

Scaling a picture

Sometimes you might want to warp a picture by making it narrower or wider than it was originally, changing its X and Y axes in the process. This process is also known as *changing the picture's aspect ratio*.

For example, let's say that you have a really neat photo of your favorite climbing rocks. You want to fit the photo into a narrow space, but you don't want to lose any parts of the picture. Let's also say that you don't mind if your picture gets a bit warped (hey, some people would call this *artistic*) in the process.

Figure 13-10 shows what we are talking about. The picture in the box at the left is scaled at 100% on both its X and Y axes. The picture on the right is warped in terms of its aspect ratio. The picture on the right is 50% scale on the X axis and 100% on the Y axis. You can achieve this effect by making changes in the Measurements palette or the Picture Box Specifications dialog box.

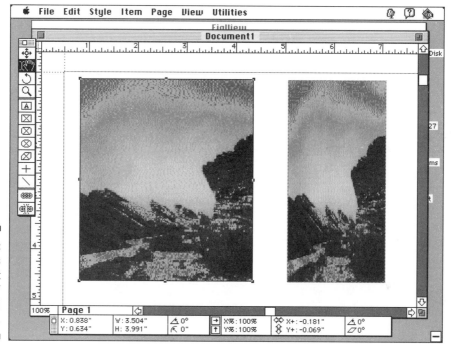

Figure 13-10: The effects of different X and Y axes applied to a picture.

Chapter 14
Color for the Masses

*Y*ou see in color. You dream in color. Color is everywhere, a natural part of the human experience. But you probably have a black-and-white ink jet or laser printer that can manage grays but not color. Your computer shows colors — maybe as many as 16.7 million of them. (Do you ever wonder if every color has a name, and who gets to name them? No? Oh well, never mind.) QuarkXPress shows colors, too. In fact, QuarkXPress lets you print in color — if you have a color printer, of course.

Color is tricky. It's everywhere, so we take it for granted. We don't usually spend a lot of time thinking about color theory or color physics. (And we won't spend a lot of time doing so here, either.) In the wonderful world of computers, color is becoming more common. You can get good-quality color ink jet printers for $500 to $600, and they're great for limited run output (a few dozen copies or for use in a color copier). You can also buy more expensive color printers (for $7000 to $20,000) using technologies with intimidating names like dye sublimation and thermal wax. These printers are for professional publishers doing color proofing of works, such as magazines and catalogs, that will be reproduced at a commercial printing plant. Or you can have your work printed by a commercial printer that does color work — in which case, your "lowly" gray-scale laser printer is merely a proofing device for your text and image placement.

It's the professional color publishers at which QuarkXPress's color tools are really aimed. (IDG Books' *Macworld QuarkXPress 3.2/3.3 Bible* delves into professional color in detail.) But that doesn't mean you can't benefit from color as well. After all, who can resist using color, especially if you have one of those inexpensive color ink jets?

Color Boot Camp

Prepare to see all sorts of acronyms when you explore color. It's like the military—capital letters and confusion everywhere.

RGB vs. CMYK

As far as desktop publishing is concerned, color comes in two basic types, RGB and CMYK. Computer displays use RGB, while printers use CMYK. Because the color types differ, you never receive an exact match between what you see on-screen and what your printed output looks like. In fact, sometimes you never even receive a close match. (Fortunately, QuarkXPress can warn you about such mismatches, as we explain later.)

These type of color schemes—RGB, CMYK, and others—are called *color models*—the model is the physics behind the colors. For example, RGB stands for *red, green, blue*, which are the three colors of light that a monitor or TV uses to create all colors. When you play with finger paints or crayons, mixing colors together probably gives you dark grays and browns. As a kid, you probably played with prisms (some adults still do, although they call them crystals or gems). Prisms split white light into its constituent colors. White light goes in one side of the prism, and out the other side comes a rainbow. Well, that's what happens with a monitor or TV: red, green, and blue combine to form white. Green and red combine to produce yellow. Red and green light have different frequencies, and as they merge, they change to the frequency of yellow light. These colors are known technically as *subtractive colors*. You can think of a monitor as a prism in reverse. Figure 14-1 shows how subtractive colors combine.

Keep in mind that the colors shown in the figure are the basic ones. For example, where green and red combine to make yellow, the actual color could be yellow-green (more mustardy) or orange (more flamelike), depending on the proportion of each light. You can get a better feel for this process by looking at the color wheel to the right of the drawing in Figure 14-1 that shows the intersections of the three colors of light.

CMYK stands for *cyan, magenta, yellow, and black.* (The *K* in CMYK represents the *k* in black. Publishers don't use *B* because it usually indicates blue.) Cyan is like an electric sky blue, the color of some ice mints, mouth washes, and sapphires. Magenta is a darker hot pink, the one favored in punk haircuts, spandex cycling shorts, and highlighter markers. By mixing the colors in the CMYK combination, you can simulate most colors that the human eye can discern.

Unlike RGB, CMYK does not combine colored light to create colors. Instead, it reflects light off ink and combines the reflections to form colors. For example, a yellow ink actually absorbs all other colors, so only yellow is reflected to your eye. Like crayons, adding these colors together on paper causes the colors to become darker (because more colors of light are absorbed), so adding all four makes a supersolid black. These colors are known as *additive colors.* Figure 14-2 shows how additive colors combine. At right is a cube that represents how the cyan, magenta, and yellow colors combine; black is added through a slider and has the effect of lightening or darkening the colors in the cube.

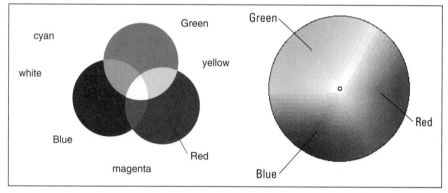

Figure 14-1: Even in gray, you can see that in the RGB color model, colored light combines differently than ...

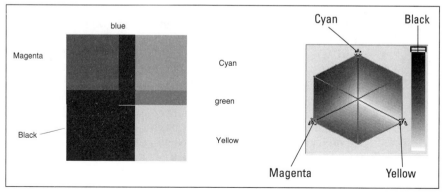

Figure 14-2: ... the reflections of light of ink in the CMYK color model.

There's a variant of CMYK called CMY (no black). Cheaper printers (such as the sub-$400 ink jets) often use CMY, creating black with a combination of cyan, magenta, and yellow. The problem is that this black is actually a muddy dark gray and doesn't look very good, especially in fine details and shadows. Therefore, commercial printers use CMYK.

Because the color that you see on the printed page is based on how light is filtered through and reflects off ink, the type and quality of ink determines the color you see. That's why a flesh tone in a magazine looks better than a flesh tone in a newspaper, or why a green on an expensive dye-sublimation printer looks better than a green on an inexpensive ink jet printer.

Spot colors vs. process colors

Commercial color printing presses, as well as most office color printers (such as ink jet), use CMYK — RGB just isn't a factor. In publishing lingo, CMYK colors are known as *process colors*. But there are other special inks available to create colors that are impossible to make by mixing various amounts of cyan, magenta, yellow, and black. For example, pastels, metallics, neons, and frosted colors can't be accurately produced in CMYK. In a photo, CMYK may be okay — because there's so much color, the human eye adjusts for the few that are off. But if you're creating a drawing or using a tint, you'll either have to settle for the closest color you can get (like a mustardy orange for gold or a light gray for silver), or you'll have to use a special ink. These special inks are called *spot colors* because they are usually used on just part of a page (a spot).

If you've worked with artists or publishers, you've probably heard the word *Pantone* or the acronym *PMS,* both of which are shorthand for the *Pantone Matching System,* the most popular set of spot-color inks. Pantone color sets include one for uncoated (rough) paper and another for coated (glossy) paper. QuarkXPress can work with these colors, along with other colors such as Trumatch, Focoltone, DIC (Dainippon Ink & Chemical), and Toyo.

You can use both process and spot colors in a document. But — and it's an important one — if you use a spot color and print it to a printer that supports only CMYK, the spot color is translated to the nearest CMYK combination. It's automatic; there's nothing you can do about it. Therefore, you really can only use spot colors if you're printing on a commercial printing press, where you supply a separate negative for each color used (one for each of the CMYK process colors and one for each spot color). Of course, if you're only using black and one or two spot colors (maybe for just a logo and some tints behind text boxes) and no other color (no color photos or drawings), you don't have to have the CMYK negatives created. If you are using both process and spot colors, keep in mind that most commercial printers can't handle more than six colors on a page, and even having six may not be possible on small-run jobs or at small printing plants.

Just to make things a little weirder, the Trumatch system is based on CMYK, so any Trumatch color can be faithfully converted (*color-separated*, in publishing lingo) into process colors. (That's why they call it Trumatch.) With Trumatch, you can thus use a premixed CMYK color for spot colors (that's cheaper than CMYK if you print fewer than four colors total, including black). And if you end up using more than three colors, you can just have QuarkXPress convert all the Trumatch spot colors to CMYK combinations during output and know that you'll get an accurate rendition. The folks at Pantone realized they had to respond, so they created a color model called Pantone Process, which is basically just the Pantone colors that have faithful CMYK equivalents. QuarkXPress includes the Pantone Process model as well.

To see an example of colors that don't match their equivalent CMYK combinations, take a look at Figure 14-3. You see the standard green that QuarkXPress includes as a default in all documents. (Don't worry yet about where this dialog box is or what it does; you'll get to it soon.) But we've changed its color model from the RGB model that QuarkXPress used to create it to the CMYK color model. You can see the two color swatches next to the words New and Old. New is the green converted to CMYK; Old is the original green. (QuarkXPress shows you the effects of a conversion so you can cancel, adjust the color yourself, or pick a different color.)

See how even in gray-scale reproduction they don't match? Notice also the triangle with an exclamation point next to Old? That's QuarkXPress's warning that the original color won't print correctly *if* you have the EfiColor XTension that came with QuarkXPress installed. How does it know? Because it checks to see what kind of printer you're set up for and figures out what color model that printer uses (remember that most printers use CMYK). Then it checks the color model in which that color was created and performs an internal conversion to see if the converted color matches the original color. If not, it displays the warning icon. This process happens as soon as you open the Edit Color dialog box or change a color's model. On some machines, it may take a few seconds for the icon to appear, so don't hot-rod through this dialog box.

Figure 14-4 shows the same dialog box with the same green in its original color model (RGB). Now, the New and Old swatches both have the warning icon. But how do you know what colors fall within the printer's capabilities? Take a look at the right side of the dialog box. See the outline that looks sort of like a hand with a finger extended? That's the boundary of what RGB colors will print on a CMYK printer. Anything inside will print correctly; anything outside will have to be converted to an approximation. The shape and scope of that boundary change based on the color models you're starting from and printing to and on the intensity of the color. The slider bar at the far right is like a dimmer switch; the brighter an RGB color, the less chance there is that CMYK can print it correctly. If there is no boundary, that means any color displayed will print accurately.

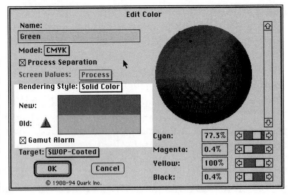

Figure 14-3: The same green is different in the RGB and CMYK color models.

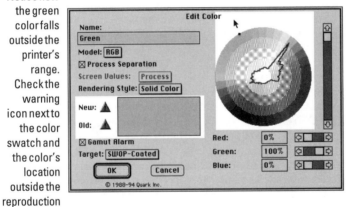

Figure 14-4: Notice how the green color falls outside the printer's range. Check the warning icon next to the color swatch and the color's location outside the reproduction boundary.

Now look for the arrow pointer on screen. Below it, you see a black square — that's the green color's position in the color model. If you hold the mouse down and move it through the color wheel, you see the New swatch's color change. Release the mouse and that square appears at the new color's location on the color wheel.

For some reason, you can't move the mouse pointer through the color wheel if you are defining colors in the CMYK model; you have to enter the cyan, magenta, yellow, and black values in the fields at the lower right or use their sliders.

Creating Color

OK, OK. Enough with the theory — on to using colors. First, you have to create the color you want to use. There are three ways:

~ Define the colors within QuarkXPress itself

~ Import the colors defined in another QuarkXPress document

~ Import the colors defined in an EPS file

No matter how you define them, the available colors display in the Colors palette. If that palette's not available, you can display it via View➪Show Colors. Figure 14-5 shows the default Colors palette.

Figure 14-5:
The Colors palette shows available colors.

Defining colors in QuarkXPress

To define, alter, or remove colors, use the Colors dialog box. To get there, use Edit➪Colors. The dialog box in Figure 14-6 appears. The options relevant to basic color use are New (to create a new color); Edit (to change an existing color); Duplicate (to copy an existing color, such as to have one color as both a process color and a spot color); Delete (to remove unwanted colors); and Append (to import colors from other QuarkXPress documents). Don't worry about Edit➪Trap; it changes how colors print when they are side by side. Only skilled and knowledgeable color publishers should change QuarkXPress's defaults.

You may note that the Edit and Delete buttons are sometimes grayed out. That's because some basic colors cannot be altered: cyan, magenta, yellow, black, and white.

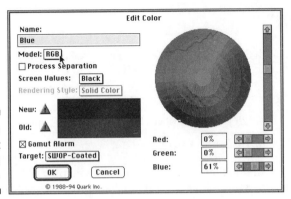

Figure 14-6:
The Edit
Color dialog
box.

Another color called Registration, which looks like black but isn't, can be
altered but not deleted. Registration can serve two purposes. One is for elements that you want on all your negatives, such as crop marks or file names. If
you define Registration to be 100 percent of cyan, magenta, yellow, and black,
anything in the Registration color will print on all those negatives. Alternatively,
you can use Registration to create a rich black — something that looks like
outer space or licorice, not flat like a Magic marker. To create a rich black (also
known as *superblack*), use 100 percent black and either 100 percent magenta or
100 percent yellow. The combination of black and either of these colors makes
the black richer and more appealing when printed.

Whether you click New or Edit, the dialog box shown in Figure 14-6 appears.
Look familiar? It's the one you saw earlier in this chapter, in Figures 14-3
and 14-4. Here's how you should use the dialog box to edit or create a color:

1. **Change your color model to CMYK or, if you're using spot color, to the
   spot color model (Pantone, Trumatch, etc.) you want to use by opening
   the Model pop-up list, shown in Figure 14-7.**

   (Figure 14-8 shows the swatches that appear for Pantone — these
   swatches appear for the Pantone, Trumatch, DIC, and Toyo colors, instead
   of the color wheel shown in Figure 14-6.) While you can create colors in the
   RGB or HSB (hue, saturation, and brightness) models (HSB is a variant of
   RGB), few printers can accurately reproduce them, so why bother? You
   should only use these models when creating colors for a computer-
   generated slide show.

Figure 14-7:
The pop-up
menus for
changing
color
models (top)
and printer
types
(bottom).

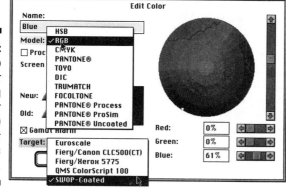

Figure 14-8:
Spot colors
are shown
as
swatches,
not via a
color wheel.
A line
through a
swatch
means the
color will
not print
accurately
on the
target
printer.

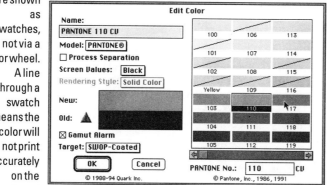

2. Check the Process Separation box if you are using a commercial printer and will be producing CMYK negatives.

Leave it unchecked if you are using spot colors (in which you want the printer to use a special ink for that color rather than a CMYK mix) or if you are printing to a non-CMYK ink jet, dye sublimation, or other color printer device.

3. **Make sure the Gamut Alarm box is checked (if the EfiColor XTension is installed; see the sidebar "All about EfiColor" in this chapter) so that you'll be told of colors your printer can't print.**

(EfiColor gives QuarkXPress its capability to detect unprintable colors.) For Pantone, DIC, and Focoltone, you see a diagonal line through a swatch to indicate that the color is outside the printer's color boundary. Otherwise, you see a boundary in the color wheel. (Colors inside the boundary will print accurately. If all the colors can be faithfully printed, no boundaries will display in the color wheel.) In either case, you'll also receive the warning icon next to the New color swatch.

4. **To tell QuarkXPress what printer to use, select from the list at the Target menu (also shown in Figure 14-7).**

If these options don't display, you need to install the EfiColor add-on

5. **Change the color to the one you want, either by using the color wheel or swatches to select a new color, or by changing the value in the Cyan, Magenta, Yellow, and Black fields (or by using their sliders).**

Make sure the color you pick falls within the printable color range.

6. **Give the color a new name if you're creating a color or modifying a duplicate.**

If you're changing a color (whether its color model or its hue), you can change the name of the color to better reflect the model or the hue. For example, you could rename the RGB color Green to Process Green if you convert the original green to CMYK, and if you change Dusky Rose to look like fuchsia, you may also change the name to Fuchsia.

7. **Click OK.**

8. **Make other changes to your colors, and click Save when done.**

Your Colors palette reflects the new colors.

For some reason, you can't move the mouse pointer through the color wheel if you are defining colors in the CMYK model; you'll have to enter the cyan, magenta, yellow, and black values in the fields at lower right or use their sliders.

To change the default colors for all future new documents, launch QuarkXPress but don't open any documents. Then change colors as described in the preceding steps. This process changes the defaults. If a document is open, the color changes affect that document only.

If you have the same color in different color models (such as Pantone 145 as a process color and as a spot color), make sure the color names reflect this difference. For example, you may have colors named Pantone 145 Spot and

Pantone 145 Process. Therefore, you have to choose the right color for accurate reproduction based on whether you plan to print the color as a CMYK color separation or with a special ink.

Importing colors

You can import colors defined in other QuarkXPress document or in an EPS file. Doing so saves work and could save errors defining a color differently in QuarkXPress than in, say, Adobe Illustrator.

To import a color from a QuarkXPress document, use the Append button in the Colors dialog box (Edit⇨Colors). The dialog box shown in Figure 14-9 appears. QuarkXPress imports any colors from the selected QuarkXPress document, *except* colors with the same names as colors in your current document. For example, say that your current document and the one from which you're importing both have a color named Puce. QuarkXPress will display this alert message: "A color named Puce already exists but is defined differently." You'll have the choice of renaming the imported Puce (that's the default option) or of using the existing color (which prevents the import of that other document's Puce).

Figure 14-9:
The Append
Colors
dialog box
lets you
import
colors from
other
QuarkXPress
documents.

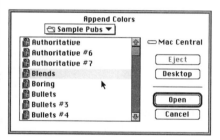

It's clear why you may need to import a color defined in another QuarkXPress document, but why would you need to import a color defined in an EPS file? There are two reasons. One, you may have a color for a logo or other image that you want to use in your QuarkXPress document. Two, perhaps the color in the EPS file is defined as a spot color, but you want to print it as a process color. By having the color definition imported into QuarkXPress, you can then edit that color in QuarkXPress to be a process color. Importing the color definition is automatic when you import the EPS file via File⇨Get Picture — as long as EfiColor is active. Your Colors dialog box will be updated to reflect the imported colors as soon as the image has been imported. Pretty easy, huh?

Actually there's a third reason: if EPS colors didn't import into QuarkXPress, QuarkXPress wouldn't be able to color-separate them easily. (It's possible to color-separate an EPS file's unimported colors: you'd have to know which colors are in your EPS file and define colors with the same names in QuarkXPress. That's a lot of work, and you might miss one or two. Before version 3.3 of QuarkXPress, this torturous process is what you had to do to color-separate colors in EPS files, and why most artists converted all colors in their EPS files to CMYK before importing into QuarkXPress — QuarkXPress automatically defines those four colors.)

All about EfiColor

EfiColor is an XTension, which is an add-on program for QuarkXPress. EfiColor comes with QuarkXPress 3.2 or later. You have to make sure you install it when you install QuarkXPress. If you forgot to do so, you can reinstall EfiColor from your QuarkXPress installation disks; see Chapter 19 for more details on installation.

EfiColor calibrates colors created both inside and outside QuarkXPress with the printer you're using. It adjusts the colors as necessary to print as accurately as possible; this process is called *color matching* in the color publishing business.

EfiColor Preferences for Document3 ◆◆◆◆◆
☒ Use EfiColor
┌ Color Printer Corrections ─────────────
☒ Convert Pictures
┌ Convert QuarkXPress Colors ───────────
☒ CMYK Colors   ☒ Named Colors
☒ RGB/HSB Colors

┌ Default Profiles ─────────────────
RGB/HSB Colors: [EFI Calibrated RGB]
CMYK Colors: [SWOP-Coated]
© 1991–94, Electronics for Imaging, Inc.

[OK]   [Cancel]

You know that EfiColor is active because it changes several of your dialog boxes. In the Edit Colors dialog box, the Gamut Alarm and Target options aren't grayed out. In Get Picture, you see a field labeled EfiColor Profile and another labeled Rendering Type. In the Edit⇨Preferences menu, you see a submenu called EfiColor, in which you set up EfiColor. Take a look at the EfiColor Preferences dialog box, shown in the following figure.

If you plan on doing commercial color printing, make sure that the Use EfiColor option is checked. There's no reason not to use EfiColor for commercial printing because it makes sure that QuarkXPress outputs colors as faithfully as

possible to any printer. (If you're just printing to an ink jet printer or other desktop color printer, you don't need to have EfiColor installed, as these printers can't take great advantage of EfiColor's capabilities. What's the advantage to not installing it? Well, EfiColor takes a great deal of memory — a couple megabytes — and it can slow QuarkXPress down. So if you're not taking advantage of EfiColor, why waste your computer's resources?)

Then check all the boxes in the Convert QuarkXPress Colors section of the dialog box. This action ensures that all colors used will be adjusted if needed by EfiColor. (A *named color,* by the way, is a spot color.)

Finally, set the default profiles. QuarkXPress comes with a set of profiles that tell EfiColor how to deal with different types of input and output. The first option, RGB/HSB Colors, enables you to select the source for your RGB images. The default is EFI Calibrated RGB. You can change this to a particular monitor or scanner type if all or most of your RGB images come from a particular device. Otherwise, leave this at EFI Calibrated RGB. The second option, CMYK Colors, tells EfiColor what kind of printer you have. Again, stick with the default (SWOP-Coated, which is designed for use in commercial printing presses for catalogs and magazines) unless one of the other options matches your target printer.

You can buy EfiColor profiles from Electronics for Imaging (EFI), at 415-286-8600, but don't bother unless you're doing large-scale printing. For ex-ample, if you're producing a newspaper with QuarkXPress and need a SWOP-Uncoated pro-file, it's worth the several hundred dollars to get the profile. But if you're printing to, say, a Canon ink jet, don't waste the money; the printer can't print the fine gradations of color that the EfiColor profile allows.

When you import an RGB picture, you can tell QuarkXPress to use a different profile other than the default by changing the EfiColor Profile pop-up menu option. Note that this option has a dash if there is no need for a profile (for example, for a gray-scale image, or for a CMYK EPS or CMYK TIFF file). You can also change an image's pro-file after it's imported into QuarkXPress by se-lecting the image with the Content tool and using Style⇨Profile.

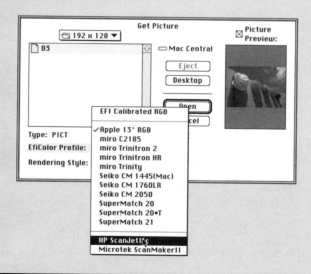

Applying Color

Now the fun part. You have your colors; now use them! You can apply colors to any of the following:

- ✔ A picture or text box background or frame
- ✔ Text in a text box
- ✔ A gray-scale TIFF image
- ✔ A black-and-white TIFF, PICT, PCX, BMP, or other image
- ✔ A line

The easiest way to apply colors is via the Colors palette. Figure 14-10 shows the palette. Notice the three icons at the top. From left to right, they are frame, contents, and background. You click the icon that's appropriate for what you want to color (use the content icon for text or for gray-scale and black-and-white images) and then click the color you want to apply. Simple! (The palette changes when a line is selected, as is also shown in the figure.)

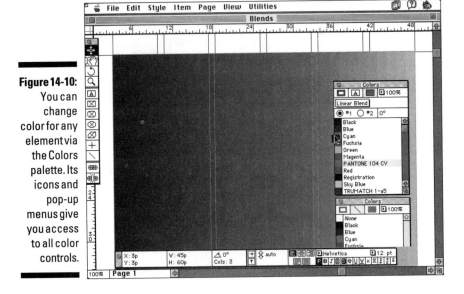

Figure 14-10:
You can change color for any element via the Colors palette. Its icons and pop-up menus give you access to all color controls.

If you want to apply a shade of a color, first apply the color and then enter a new shade value where you see the percentage at the upper-right corner of the Colors palette. You can click the triangle to the left of the current percentage (usually 100%) and receive a pop-up menu, or you can highlight the current percentage and type in a new number.

If you click a color square on the Colors palette and hold the mouse down, you can drag a color onto an object. Note that with this action, QuarkXPress assumes that you want to change the object's background color, no matter what icon is selected in the Colors palette. You can see this drag-and-drop color feature in Figure 14-10 (look for the mouse pointer "holding" the color square over a picture box).

The most interesting effect is the use of blends for a text box or picture box's background color. You see a *blend* — a gradation of color from one side to the other — in Figure 14-10. QuarkXPress lets you create several types of blends, as Figure 14-11 shows. To create a blend, select a box, click the background icon in the Colors palette, and then select a blend type from the pop-up list that appears beneath the top left icons. Note the two radio buttons, #1 and #2, as well as a field for entering the blend's angle in degrees. First click the #1 button and then select a color. Then select the #2 button and select a different color. QuarkXPress blends from color #1 to color #2. Change the angle to change the direction of the blend (see Figure 14-11).

You can use white as a the second color when creating a blend. That produces a fade-away effect.

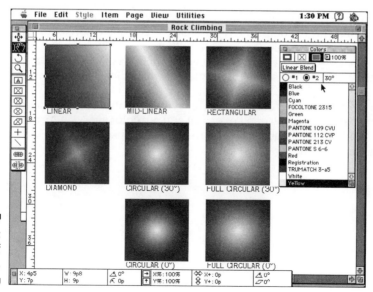

Figure 14-11: Types of blends.

When you apply a blend background, the selected item appears to have a solid background, equivalent to the color selected for the #1 radio button. Don't panic. As soon as you click something else, the blend appears. In fact, we had to cheat in Figure 14-10 to show the blend and the Colors palette; we used Adobe Photoshop to superimpose the palette over the picture box's blended background.

About the only things you can't do from the Colors palette are. . . . Well, actually, you can do everything you need. You can use the Style menu (with the Content tool selected) and its Color and Shade options to change a box's background or a line's color. You can also use the Picture Box (or Text Box) Specifications dialog box (Item⇨Modify) to change a box's background and the Frame Specifications dialog box (Item⇨Frame) to change a box's frame color. But these procedures are not as straightforward as using the Colors palette. In fact, the only reason not to use the Colors palette is that you happen to be using these other menus or dialog boxes when you need to change color.

Not obvious to most users, another thing you can do from the Colors palette is edit colors. How do you do that? Hold the ⌘ key when clicking a color and you'll jump directly to the Edit Color dialog box. What a timesaver!

When editing a color, you can rename it. But if you want to replace all, say, blues with reds, there's no specific find and replace function to do so, as there is for text attributes. But have no fear, because there is a make-shift way to do a find and replace of colors in QuarkXPress. First, use Edit⇨Colors to get a list of current colors in your QuarkXPress document. Select the color that you want to change and then click the Delete button. You'll be asked what you want to replace that color with for objects using the deleted color. That's how you can find and replace colors. Of course, following these steps deletes the original color from the document. If you want to keep that color definition but still replace it in your document with a different color, use the Duplicate button first to make a copy of the color that you want to change. Then go ahead and delete the original color so you can replace it with a different one.

Hey! Now you're a color expert, and you're ready to color your document. Just make sure that you don't overdo it and put color everywhere or use clashing colors. Remember: a good effect is one that is used sparingly so that it's noticed, not obnoxious.

Chapter 15
Text as Art

- -

In This Chapter

▶ Skewing, rotating, and flipping text

▶ Creating shadows and outlines

▶ Embossing text

▶ Expanding and compressing text

- -

*T*hanks to the miracle of computer science, the once mighty barriers between text and art have fallen. Today, you can stretch, squash, and otherwise distort text as if it were taffy. These capabilities open the way for innovative, creative use of text as art, as well as some really hellish looking materials. But no one reading this book would ever do something like that!

You have to know, of course, when to use artistic effects; knowing only how to create the effects is just not enough. You'll get to the how to use part after the how to create part.

Special Type Effects in QuarkXPress

Figure 15-1 shows what you can do in QuarkXPress. All the variants of the standard Times text were accomplished with QuarkXPress's features. For italics or boldface, you may use the Style menu to make changes to the selected text. For fancier effects such as rotating or skewing (slanting) text, you may actually change the text box that contains the text. Of course, you can combine these effects. This section describes how we made Figure 15-1 look like it does (from top to bottom).

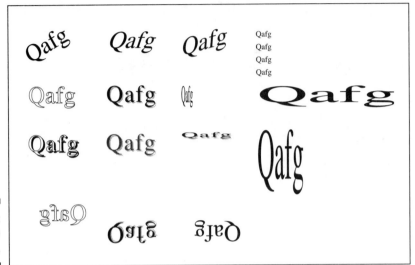

Figure 15-1:
Various type
effects.

To edit the contents of a text box, you need to use the Content tool. For some effects, such as rotation, that affect the text box itself (as well as its contents), you can use either the Item tool or the Content tool.

Row 1:

- ✔ We rotated the text box 30 degrees, via the Measurements palette or via the Text Box Specifications dialog box (Item⇨Modify).

- ✔ We skewed the text box 20 degrees via the Text Box Specifications dialog box.

- ✔ We rotated the text box 15 degrees and skewed it 20 degrees.

- ✔ We changed the text box's vertical alignment to Justified in the Type pop-up menu in the Text Box Specifications dialog box. This feature spaces out all paragraphs in the text box so that they are spaced evenly the full depth of the text box, as long as that spacing does not exceed the Inter ¶ Max value in the dialog box.

Row 2:

- ✔ We used the outline type attribute in the Measurements palette (you could use Style⇨Type Style instead).

- ✔ We used the shadow type attribute, also in the Measurements palette (and via Style⇨Type Style).

✔ We compressed the text horizontally to 30 percent with Style⇨Horizontal/ Vertical Scale.

✔ We expanded the text horizontally to 300 percent.

An easy way to change the scaling of text is to hold the ⌘ key (Ctrl in Windows) when resizing a text box. This action makes the text resize the same way as the box. Here's how it works: Click and hold the mouse button on a text-box handle until the item in the box flashes once. Then start dragging the text-box handle in the direction you want to scale the text. This lets you see the effects of the resizing as they happen, so you can see when the new scale is what you want it to be.

Row 3:

✔ We used both the shadow and outline attributes.

✔ We used the shadow attribute and changed the text's shade to 60 percent, via Style⇨Shade.

 You can also change color via StyleÍColor or the Colors palette with the palette's Color content tool (shown at left) selected.

✔ We compressed the text vertically to 30 percent.

✔ We expanded the text vertically to 300 percent.

Horizontal and vertical scaling work basically the same way. Because it seems to be human nature to start at the vertical size desired and then scale to make the text skinnier or fatter, most people scale text horizontally. Therefore, the default in the dialog box is Horizontal. Of course, that may be because for years, even in the old days before desktop publishing, that's just how the tools worked.

Row 4:

✔ We applied the outline attribute to the text and flipped it horizontally (via the Measurements palette or Style⇨Flip Horizontal).

Flipping affects the entire contents of the text box, so you may expect that you need to use the Item tool. Well, actually, you're supposed to use the Content tool for this one. Even though you could argue that flipping affects the entire box (in which case, you would use the Item tool), QuarkXPress thinks that flipping only affects the contents of the box (and not the box itself). So Content tool it is.

✔ We applied the shadow attribute and flipped the text vertically (via the Measurements palette or Style⇨Flip Vertical).

✔ We flipped the text both horizontally and vertically.

We count 11 effects here. That's a lot to use, and they can give you some very interesting designs when used in combination with each other (see Figure 15-2).

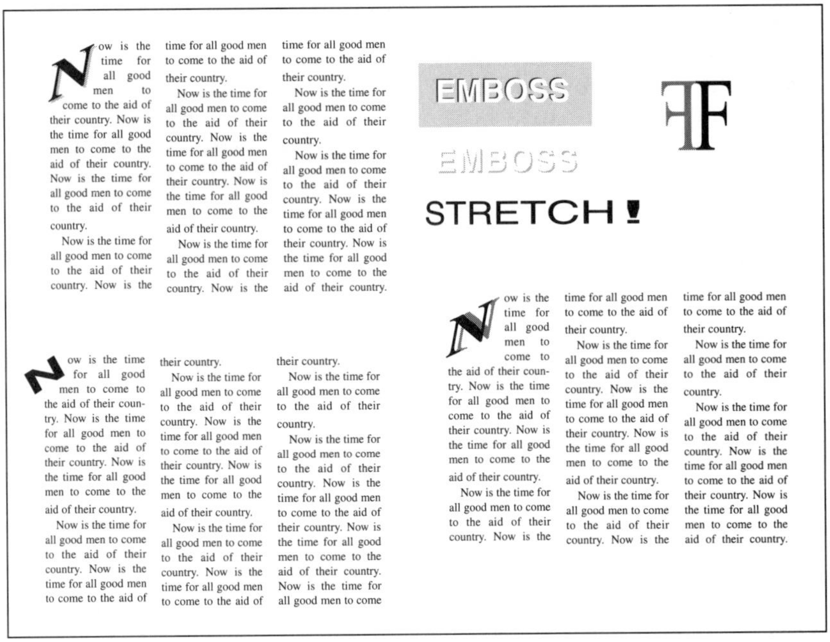

Figure 15-2:
Examples of
type-
distortion
effects you
can do in
QuarkXPress

Custom drop caps

As you can see, several examples in Figure 15-2 show rotated drop caps (large letters inset into a paragraph; see Chapter 9 for more details on QuarkXPress's drop-cap feature). All the drop caps are in their own text boxes — you can't rotate drop caps created through QuarkXPress's standard drop-cap feature. Here's how we created the drop caps:

- ✔ The one at bottom left is rotated 30 degrees; the font is different than the body copy and expanded 200 percent, so the letter covers the full diagonal of the text that it cuts across.

- ✔ The drop cap at upper left is a little trickier. It uses a combination of skewing (15 percent) and rotation (25 degrees), and the text is the bold italic shadowed variant of the body copy font. The result of these combinations has the slanted strokes of the *N* actually run almost vertically.

✔ The other drop cap, at bottom right, is a modified version of the other shadowed drop cap. To get its shadow, we couldn't use the shadow type attribute. Instead, we have two text boxes that are slightly offset, both of which are set so that runaround is off (which causes the horizontal rather than diagonal shadow effect you see in Figure 15-2). Figure 15-3 shows the two text boxes for the shadowed drop cap, while Figure 15-4 shows the runaround turned off, via Item⇨Runaround. Finally, there's a regular text box with no text in it, under the drop cap to provide the square runaround. We used Item⇨Send to Back to send that empty text box back; then we sent the three-column text box to the back, which put it behind the empty text box. The rotated and skewed text boxes containing the drop cap and its shadow weren't sent anywhere, so they remain on top of the other two boxes.

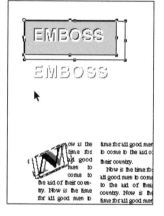

Figure 15-3: Creating embossed text (top) and drop shadows (bottom) by super-imposing text boxes.

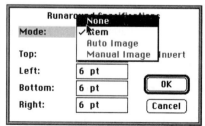

Figure 15-4: The Run-around Specifications dialog box.

Although this multiple-text-box approach to building shadows can take some effort, it lets you create exactly the type of shadow you want, down to the color and shade and the exact distance from the letter. QuarkXPress's shadow feature cannot be customized; you receive just what QuarkXPress is preprogrammed to do.

When you're done creating your shadow, don't forget to group (Item⇨Group, or ⌘-G) the text boxes that form it, so one of them doesn't get accidentally moved later.

Embossed text

You'll also notice in Figure 15-2 two examples of text that appear to be embossed (at the upper right). The top example was created via multiple text boxes, like the drop cap below it. In fact, in Figure 15-3, you can see those text boxes. The one below that was created by combining two type attributes: shadow and changing the color to white. It just so happens that this particular combination is attractive. If you wanted a more dimensional look, or different colors or shadow angle, like the top embossing, you have to use that time-consuming multiple-box technique.

Other effects

The other two effects seen in Figure 15-2 are fairly simple to create:

✔ The *Stretch!* text uses the horizontal scaling feature to make each subsequent letter scaled more: 110 percent for the *T*, 120 percent for the *R*, and so on. The *!* was scaled 200 percent to make it really wide to, er, emphasize the point.

✔ The reverse *F* is in a separate text box than the regular *F* next to it. The idea was to make the *F* a symbol, almost like in a coat of arms. We also made the flipped *F* gray to help make the regular *F* more readable. You can use this effect as a drop cap or as a logo.

Another neat effect in some circumstances is to have text follow a curve or other path. You should use an art program like Adobe Illustrator to do this, since it has built-in features to make the work simple. But if you have only an occasional need for this effect, you can achieve it in QuarkXPress — if you're willing to put in the effort. Here's how: Use a picture box (oval, rectangle, polygon, or several of these overlapping) to create the shape whose border you want the text to follow. Then create a text box for each letter that will follow this path. Enter the letters in each text box. Now drag the text boxes to the point on the path they belong to, and then rotate the text box so the letter matches the path's orientation at that spot. When you're done, delete the picture box(es), group the text boxes, and lock them into place. Figure 15-5 shows this effect used to make text follow a semicircle.

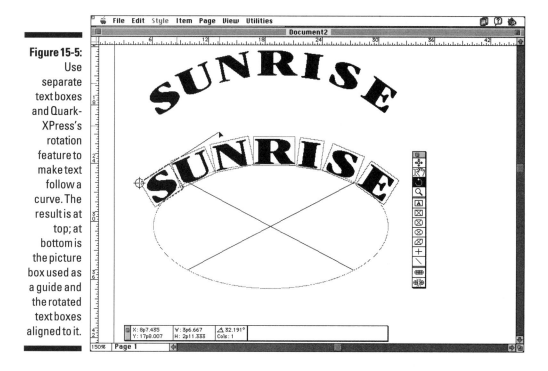

Figure 15-5:
Use separate text boxes and Quark-XPress's rotation feature to make text follow a curve. The result is at top; at bottom is the picture box used as a guide and the rotated text boxes aligned to it.

Tips for Using Text as Art

It may seem obvious, but it's not to a lot of people: Use special effects sparingly. And don't mix dissimilar effects, such as putting skewed text, compressed text that is not skewed, and embossed text all on the same page. Unless you're creating a sheet of examples, as in Figures 15-1 and 15-2, all you'll do is make the reader notice the dissimilarities and wonder just what you were thinking.

It's best if special text effects are designed to work with other graphical elements. For example, if there are several items that are slanted, have them slant the same amount, whether they're text or lines.

Pay attention to spacing. If text looks a lot like a graphic, give it more space than you would if it looked like just a weird part of the text. A good rule of thumb is to put minimal space around warped text if that text is meant to be read with other text. For example, drop caps should not be so removed from the rest of the paragraph so that the reader doesn't realize they *are* drop caps. Conversely, don't position a graphic that happens to be made of a symbol, such as in a logo, so close to similar text that people try to read it as part of the text. Obviously, the more different the warped text looks from the regular text, the easier it will be for the reader to know that the text is different, and you won't have to worry so much about spacing.

Save the radical-effects work for an art program. For example, if you routinely want to make text look stretched, or follow a curve, or have patterns, don't fool around in QuarkXPress trying to approximate these effects. Get FreeHand or Illustrator (or whatever) and use it.

That's it! You've come to the end of the special effects. Congratulations — this is the most difficult stuff because it requires an active imagination, an understanding of the tools in QuarkXPress to turn that imagination into reality, and patience in applying these tools. Have fun experimenting!

Part V
The Big, Bad World Out There

Bob, the laser printer repairman, finds an idle moment that costs him his sideburns.

TECHNICALLY, YOU SHOULD BE ABLE TO LIGHT YOUR CIGARETTE ON THIS THING PRETTY EASY.

In this part ...

Almost everyone involved with publishing—whether it's a magazine, newsletter, or business catalog—has to work with other people: writers, editors, printers, artists, and so on. The three chapters in this part show you how to navigate the treacherous waters of collaboration, from getting your printouts out to dealing with those mystical service bureaus that turn your disk files into the negatives that make the final printed page possible.

Chapter 16

Preparing for the Printed Page

· ·

In This Chapter

▶ How to set up printers on the Mac and in Windows

▶ Working on a network

▶ Why you want a PostScript printer

▶ Switching among printers

▶ How to send fonts to printer memory

· ·

Printing is easy — you just use File⇨Print. Right? Well, maybe on a good day. But there's more to printing than just printing. QuarkXPress and the Mac (and Windows) give you control over printing — control that you'll want to have.

This chapter covers the basics of printer setup — because it can be a little tricky — before the next chapter covers QuarkXPress's printing controls. If you already have the Mac or Windows set up for printing, go directly to the next chapter.

Although printing is built into your computer's operating system, the printing capabilities you want may not be. Or the printing services may not be optimized for the best output quality or print speed. These printing services are critical to getting your programs — QuarkXPress included — to print at their best. So read on to fine-tune your printing. It's like giving your car a tune-up: a little regular checking and maintenance can keep the engine humming, the gas consumption down, and the speed high.

Because the Mac's and Windows' setups are so different from each other, we've divided the setup coverage based on platform. If you're working in a cross platform, you have to read both sections (sorry!). For detailed help on general Mac setup, read David Pogue's and Joseph Schorr's *Macworld Mac and Power Mac Secrets* and Andy Rathbone's *Windows 3.1 For Dummies*, both from IDG Books Worldwide.

Macintosh Setup

Plug a printer into your Mac, and it's ready to go, right? Nope. Even though the Mac is plug-and-play, you still have to tell it what kind of printer you have. If you work in an office that has an information services staff to set up computers, chances are they'll set up your printer for you. But read on anyway; by knowing how the setup works, you may be able solve problems that come up later.

Types of printers

Your printer is probably a PostScript printer. PostScript is a language from Adobe Systems that computers use to give instructions to printers. PostScript is the best printer language around on computers, and it's become the standard for publishers and artists.

Most Apple printers are PostScript. Most Mac printers that aren't PostScript are QuickDraw. QuickDraw is the Mac's own language for printing and drawing what's on the screen. It's good enough for on-screen display, but not as good as PostScript for printing. If you use a PostScript printer, the program and the Mac translate between the Mac's QuickDraw for on-screen display and the printer's PostScript for printing to paper. You don't need to worry about this — it's automatic. Just remember that this process is one reason that what you see on screen is a bit coarser and less exact than what prints.

The Mac system software comes with the necessary software (called a driver) to translate QuickDraw to PostScript; it's a file called LaserWriter or PSPrinter that resides in the Extensions folder in the System Folder. The latest versions are LaserWriter 8 and PSPrinter 8. These come with System 7.5 but are not automatically installed. For other versions of System 7, you have to download the driver from an on-line service, get it from Apple (408-996-1010), or get it from a program that includes the driver (most of Adobe's CD-based programs include the driver). Just make sure that you have version 8.1.1 or later. (In the Finder, select the icon for the driver, press ⌘-I, and make sure the second line of the dialog box reads *LaserWriter 8 (or PSPrinter 8) Software v1.1* or uses a number greater than 1.1.) Earlier versions are buggy and may cause system crashes or incorrect printing.

Another type of printer is one designed for a PC. The two most common types are those that use either the Hewlett-Packard PCL or Epson languages. You usually come across these only if you work in a company that has Macs and PCs connected on the same network. These printers require special drivers that tell the Mac how to translate between QuickDraw and PCL or Epson; if you don't have such software, you can get it from GDT Softworks (604-291-9121), whose PowerPrint driver software regularly gets high marks.

Because QuarkXPress can take full advantage of PostScript printers' advanced functions such as blends, detailed grays, kerning, and sophisticated graphics, you should use a PostScript printer. If you use EPS graphics, you have to use a PostScript printer to get decent output. A PostScript laser printer can cost as little as $900 for a personal one, as little as $1600 for a mid-volume shared departmental printer, about $2500 for a high-speed multi-tray, multiuser printer, and as much as $20,000 for a color one. A QuickDraw printer can cost much less — just a few hundred dollars — but you should avoid it for any work but rudimentary proofing (printing versions to see a mockup or "sketch").

For several years, you could find programs such as Color Age's Freedom of the Press that let you print PostScript to a non-PostScript printer. Basically, these programs translate PostScript language into the printer's language, letting you have the high quality of PostScript on an inexpensive printer. At least in theory. Sometimes they work, sometimes they don't. They could survive their problems because PostScript printers used to be very expensive. Prices are way down, so there's less need for an alternative. Anyway, Color Age has discontinued its Freedom of the Press products, and the other ones available have not been well regarded by magazines like *Macworld*. If you happen across a copy of Freedom of the Press and have a QuickDraw printer, go ahead and try it out. But don't invest a lot or think it will replace a PostScript printer — it's really just a stopgap. (For some color Apple Stylewriter QuickDraw printers, you can use GDT Softworks' new StyleScript, which includes the real PostScript, not an iffy clone.)

Plugging in

When you install a printer, you usually plug it into the Mac's printer port. Sometimes, though, you plug it into the Mac's modem port. The Mac doesn't care — both are serial ports (called GeoPorts on the newest Macs) that are designed to connect to printers and modems. You can put a modem (including a network) or printer on either port. Apple labels them with specific icons to make new users know where to plug in components.

If your office uses a network, you probably have printers connected to the network and not directly to your Mac. Of course, you can have a network with no printers, or you can have a network that has some printers on the network and other printers hooked up to an individual Mac. With the Mac, you can have printers simultaneously connected directly to the Mac and a network. For example, the head honcho probably has his very own printer (which no one else can use) connected to his Mac (to print out those secret plans he works on all day with the door closed) and the ability to use the network printer.

Of course, keep in mind that Macs have only two serial ports. If you have a LocalTalk network (which connects to Macs via a serial port — most people connect it to the printer port, although there's no law that requires it), a modem, and a printer you want to attach directly to your Mac, you have to decide which of the three devices you want to attach to those two connectors. As you may expect, some savvy engineer figured out how to let you connect three devices to those two ports. Axion's Axion Switch (408-522-1900) lets you plug up to three devices into one serial port, although you can't use two devices simultaneously. Therefore, you can have the network on one port and the local printer and modem on the other port. Just don't try to print to the local printer when you're on-line. If you're using a Ethernet network, you don't have to worry because the network connects to the Mac via its own port, not via a serial port.

Why are we telling you all this? Because if you work in an office with a network, you may have access to more printers than you think. It's common for an office to have several laser printers, usually placed near clusters of people, for general use, perhaps one color printer for everyone to use, and one printer that contains stationery paper. Always select the printer you want and then print to it.

If you're using Ethernet or another network, sometimes the network can get disconnected, making the network printers disappear from the Chooser. Use the Apple menu to select the Control Panels folder. In the Control Panels window, select the Network icon. You see a window with icons for each network — LocalTalk, EtherTalk, and perhaps others such as Remote Only or MacTCP. Click the icon for the one that you should be connected to (chances are, something reset the Mac to the default of LocalTalk). Then you should see the printers again in the Chooser.

Setting up the printer

After you plug the printer into your Mac (or added a printer to the network), you can tell your Mac how to deal with the printer. Go to the Apple menu and select Chooser. The Chooser is a program that comes with the Mac that lets you choose printers and servers.

In Figure 16-1, you see the Chooser for one of our Macs, with the LaserWriter 8 icon selected. Note the other printer icons, such as LQ ImageWriter in the window at the left. Also note the icon for a fax modem, which is just another printer as far as the Mac is concerned. If you had different types of printers connected to your Mac or your Mac network, you can switch among printer types by clicking a new icon.

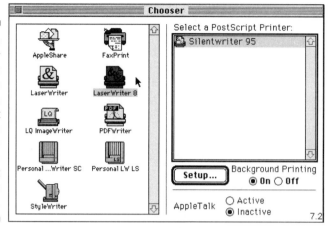

Figure 16-1:
The Chooser
lets you
change
printer types
and select
from
available
printers. You
can also set
up printers
here.

In the figure, the only PostScript printer connected to that Mac is displayed in the right window. Remember: the printer must be turned on and connected for its name to appear. If multiple printers are available, they appear on the right. Remember that the Mac only shows the printers that work with the selected driver. If we had selected the LQ ImageWriter driver, no printers names would appear because we don't have any ImageWriter printers.

Make sure that Active is selected so that all the printers on your network are accessible. Figure 16-2 shows how our printer options grow when we turn on AppleTalk. Note that whether you use LocalTalk or Ethernet as your network, you want AppleTalk turned on. You also need AppleTalk turned on to connect to file servers.

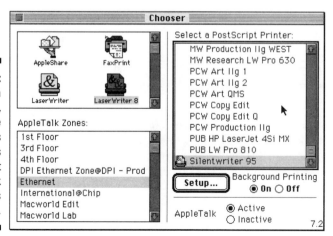

Figure 16-2:
On a
network,
make sure
AppleTalk is
selected as
Active to get
all network
printers
displayed.

The Mac system software installs a whole truckload of printer drivers, which you just don't need. Go to the Extensions folder in the System Folder and drag any unneeded drivers to the Trash. To know the names, first look at the driver icons' names in the Chooser; the driver files have the same name as the icons. If a driver is missing (maybe it was accidentally deleted or you bought a printer that uses a driver type that you removed earlier), check the Printing disk that came with your system software. (With System 7.5, run the installation program and select just the drivers you want to install. Unlike previous versions, System 7.5 doesn't let you just copy them directly from the installation disks.) The popular Apple drivers and the PostScript (LaserWriter) drivers are on that disk. Just drag them into the Extensions folder, and they're ready to be used. You have to quit the Chooser after copying the files, and sometimes — if the icons don't appear in the Chooser — you may need to restart your Mac. For other (non-PostScript) printers, you should have received a disk with your printer. If not, call the printer company and ask them to send you a disk or get the company's BBS number so that you can download the driver yourself.

Setting up the Chooser

Here's how you set up the printing capabilities for your printer on the Mac.

1. **After you select the printer name for the first time, click the Setup button.** You get a dialog box like the one in Figure 16-3. You can click Fewer Choices to reduce the number of choices and More Choices to increase them (after you reduce the number of choices). You'll keep coming back to this dialog box for each of the following steps.

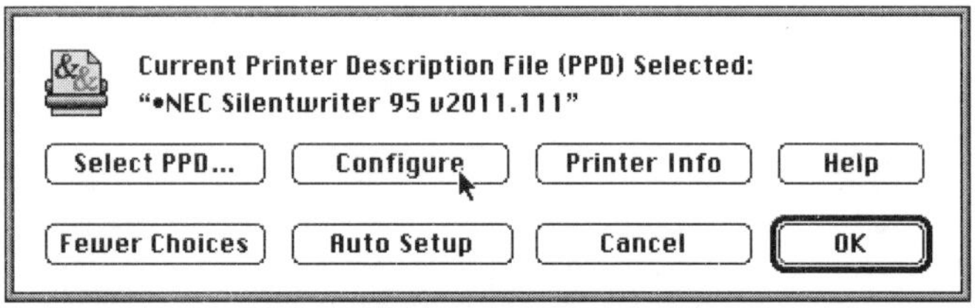

Figure 16-3:
The choices available in setting up a printer.

Current Printer Description File (PPD) Selected:
"•NEC Silentwriter 95 v2011.111"

| Select PPD... | Configure | Printer Info | Help |

| Fewer Choices | Auto Setup | Cancel | OK |

2. **If you have a PostScript printer, click the Select PPD button.** The dialog box in Figure 16-4 appears. When you install QuarkXPress or other programs, you are probably asked what kind of printer you have. If you answer, the program copies a PPD file — a PostScript Printer Description — to the Mac. Sometimes, your printer comes with a disk that includes a PPD file. A PPD stores information about a printer — whether it has multiple paper trays, its resolution, how much memory it has, and so on — so that

you can take advantage of that printer's specific abilities. Scroll through the list of PPD files and pick the one that most closely matches your printer. (Often, the version numbers may not match.) If none comes close, contact your printer manufacturer or check the printer manual to see what PPD file they recommend. In the meantime, click Use Generic.

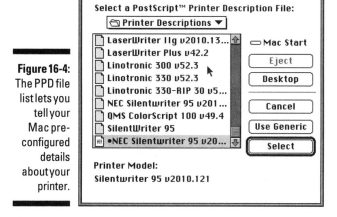

Figure 16-4:
The PPD file list lets you tell your Mac pre-configured details about your printer.

3. **With the correct PPD file selected, click the Configure button.** Now you can set up specific printer information, such as the amount of printer RAM and which trays are installed. Figure 16-5 shows the Configuration dialog box for one of our printers.

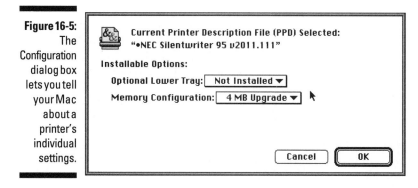

Figure 16-5:
The Configuration dialog box lets you tell your Mac about a printer's individual settings.

4. **You can check printer settings by clicking the Printer Info button.** (See Figure 16-6 for the Printer Info dialog box.). You may need to click Update Info the first time you select a printer. This information can ensure that you've selected the best PPD file or correctly set up options such as the amount of printer RAM.

Figure 16-6: The Printer Info dialog box lets you verify information about a printer's setup and capabilities.

Current Printer Description File (PPD) Selected:
"•NEC Silentwriter 95 v2011.111"

Printer Information:

PostScript™ Level: 2
PostScript™ Version: 2010.121
Resolution: 300 dpi
Fax Support: No
Total Memory Installed: 4 MB
Total Memory Available: 2.2 MB

Update Info   OK

Background printing

In the Chooser (look again at Figure 16-1), there's an option for Background Printing. You should click On. Doing so lets your Mac process your printing while you're doing something else. Otherwise, you can't do anything else until the file prints. In QuarkXPress, where you may have complex layouts with lots of text and graphics, that can be tens of minutes.

Turning background printing on activates the Mac's *print spooler,* which is computer lingo for a holding bin. With the spooler activated, the Mac actually prints to your hard disk instead of directly to your printer, which allows you to continue working. When you pause, such as between mouse movements or keystrokes (or just when you're thinking), the Mac sends pieces of the print instructions saved to disk on to the printer. This process is known as *spooling*.

As you print several documents, the Mac places each print file in that spool and processes them one by one. You can see what's in the spool by looking at the PrintMonitor. In the Applications menu (the one at the far right, which you select by holding the mouse on the icon that represents the Finder or whatever program is currently in use), PrintMonitor appears after you start printing. Select PrintMonitor to get the window shown in Figure 16-7. (When you click Set Print Time, the window to the bottom of the screen appears; use this window to reschedule a print job.) You can delete print jobs, reorder them (just drag a print job to a new order in the spool), or pause them.

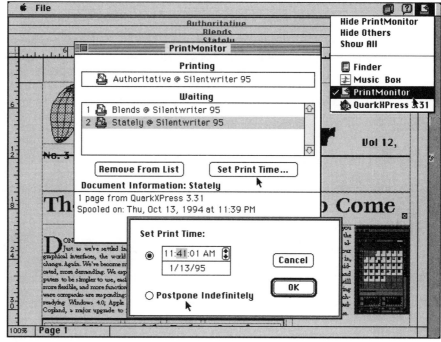

Figure 16-7:
The
PrintMonitor
lets you see
what print
jobs are
pending.
You can
also
reschedule,
reorder,
delete, and
pause print
jobs.

Switching printers

To change printers, go to the Chooser and click the printer name that you want.
You may first need to click the printer icon in the left window if the new printer
you want to use is of a different type. For example, you may normally use a
QuickDraw printer such as an Apple Personal LaserWriter SC for proofing and
then a color PostScript printer such as a QMS ColorScript 100 for your final
output. If so, you have to click the Personal LaserWriter SC driver (it appears in
the Chooser as Personal . . . Writer SC to save space) and then the printer name
to activate the QuickDraw proofing printer. To change to the QMS ColorScript,
you have to click the LaserWriter or LaserWriter 8 driver and then the printer
name to activate it.

Note that most programs ask you to go to Page Setup dialog box in the File
menu of any active program so that the program knows the printer has
changed. You can frequently get away with skipping this step. But if you have
unusual printing problems, go to the Page Setup dialog box, click OK, and try
printing again.

Sending fonts to the printer

Your printer probably came with some fonts installed in its built-in memory — fonts such as Helvetica, Helvetica Narrow, New Century Schoolbook, Bookman, Courier, Palatino, Avant Garde, Times, Symbol, Zapf Chancery, and Zapf Dingbats, all of which comprise the 11 fonts of PostScript 35 (no, not a criminal gang) that PostScript printers have had for years. (Each of the first eight fonts has four variants — regular, italic, bold, and bold italic. If you do the math, that comes to 35.)

Except for these fonts, your computer has to send the printer a copy of any font your QuarkXPress document uses. That can take a lot of time because QuarkXPress must resend the font information for each and every page. It takes only a few fonts to have average print times of 6 minutes (rather than 40 seconds).

What can you do? If you're using a PostScript printer and you're using PostScript, TrueType, or Apple's own fonts (like Chicago and New York), you can send those fonts into your printer's memory. When you send fonts into your printer's memory, they sit there ready to be used when you need them.

To send fonts to your printer's memory, you use a utility that resides on your Mac's system disks. The utility, called the LaserWriter Font Utility, is in the Apple Utilities folder of the Tidbits disk. (Apple never has been good at coming up with sexy names for anything except its Macs.) You can run it from the Tidbits disk or copy it to your hard disk and run it from there. In System 7.5, it's called the LaserWriter Utility; you must use the installation program to install it. You can't just run or copy it from a floppy disk. When installing, choose Custom Install from the pop-up menu at the upper-left corner of the initial installer screen, click the right-pointing triangle next to the Printing option to get a list of printing options, and check the LaserWriter Utility box. Then click the Install button.

When you use this utility, use File⇨Download Fonts to select the fonts you want to send to the printer. Then click the Add button to receive a dialog box that lets you move to the folder that contains the fonts (typically, the Fonts folder in the System Folder). Select a font and click Add. Select another font and click Add. Keep doing this until all the fonts you want have been added. Then click Done. When you're finished, a dialog box like the one shown in Figure 16-8 appears. Click the Download button, and off the fonts go to the printer's memory. It may take a few minutes, so be patient.

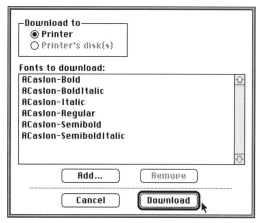

Figure 16-8:
If you use
Apple's
PostScript
font-
downloading
utility, click
Download to
send fonts
to your
printer's
memory.

This Apple utility has a serious limitation: in versions of System 7 before 7.5, it works only with the LaserWriter driver. If you are using the LaserWriter 8 driver, it doesn't work. If you use LaserWriter 8, you can switch temporarily to LaserWriter to send fonts to the printer and then switch back to LaserWriter 8 for actual printing. Or you can use a different utility. Adobe Systems bundles a utility called Downloader with several of its programs and with many fonts. It works similarly to the Apple utility, but it's not limited to just the LaserWriter driver — but the Adobe utility works only with PostScript fonts, not with the Mac's system fonts.

When you turn off a printer, the fonts are removed from memory, which means that you have to reload the fonts if you want use them again. Some printers have hard disks or cartridges to store fonts that stay active even when you turn your printer's power off. You can remove fonts from your printer's memory only by turning the printer off. If you load too many fonts into your printer's memory, you leave insufficient room to process your documents. (The rule of thumb says to save 1.5MB to 2MB of memory for the document.)

Sending fonts to the printer's memory is called *downloading* fonts, even though the technically accurate term would be *uploading*. To upload is to send to; to download is to receive from. However, many people use the terms interchangeably, and practically every program and manual uses the incorrect *download* to describe the action of sending fonts to a printer.

Windows Setup

Printing in Windows requires about the same effort as printing with a Mac. With Windows, you must be careful that you set the printer up correctly. After the setup, printing is usually a piece of cake.

Types of printers

While PostScript printing is the standard among desktop publishers, who tend to hail from the land of Mac, in the PC universe, it's PCL — Hewlett-Packard's Printer Control Language — that rules. However, the best art software, the best publishing software, and some even argue, the best fonts are based on PostScript. Therefore, we recommend that you at least get a PostScript printer for your final output. If your documents will ultimately be printed at a commercial printer or service bureau on a Linotronic or other imagesetter, you'll be using PostScript because it's the language those printers speak. If you use EPS graphics, you have to use a PostScript printer to get a decent output.

A PostScript laser printer can cost as little as $900 for a personal one, as little as $1600 for a mid-volume, shared departmental printer, about $2500 for a high-speed, multi-tray, multiuser printer, and as much as $20,000 for a color one. A PCL printer can cost much less — just a few hundred dollars — but you should avoid it for anything but rudimentary proofing work. Most PostScript printers support both PostScript and PCL, and many PCL printers support the use of a PostScript card that adds the PostScript language.

Other types of printers also exist, such as those that support the Epson language. Don't use anything but PCL or PostScript for serious Windows work. If you're working with graphics and fonts, you should use PostScript.

But don't panic if the printer at your desk is a LaserJet IIID or something else that uses PCL. Even if you use a non-PostScript printer as your daily printer, you can still print your final output to a PostScript printer or have your service bureau do it. QuarkXPress doesn't care whether your printer uses PCL or PostScript. (Well, not when you're creating documents. Printing can be another story, especially when it comes to color, which we'll tell you about later.)

Whether you use PostScript or PCL (or both), make sure that you have the latest drivers. Microsoft updates these regularly and posts the latest on its forums on CompuServe (GO MKSB and GO MICROSOFT) and on its own BBS (206-936-6735 in the U.S. and 905-507-3022 in Canada). The Windows system software comes with the necessary software (called a driver) to translate Windows' own display format (called GDI, or Graphical Device Interface) to

PostScript or PCL. For PostScript, the file is called PSCRIPT.DRV; for PCL, it's called HPPCL5MS.DRV or HPPCL5A.DRV. Both reside in the \WINDOWS\SYSTEM directory.

When this book went to press, the latest version was 3.58 for PostScript; for PCL, it depends on the type of printer and version of PCL that it uses. If you are using the latest version of Windows or Windows for Workgroups and have the UNIDRV.DLL file in the \WINDOWS\SYSTEM directory, you should be fine. If you bought a PCL printer after November 1993, use any driver that came with the printer. If your printer is older than that, use the driver for Windows or Windows for Workgroups 3.11; they're dated November 1, 1993.

You can tell which version you have by going to the Windows Control Panel and double-clicking the Printers icon. If you have more than one printer installed, select the printer you want to check. Then click the Setup button. In the new dialog box, click the About button. A dialog box showing the driver version should appear. (Figure 16-9 shows this sequence of dialog boxes.)

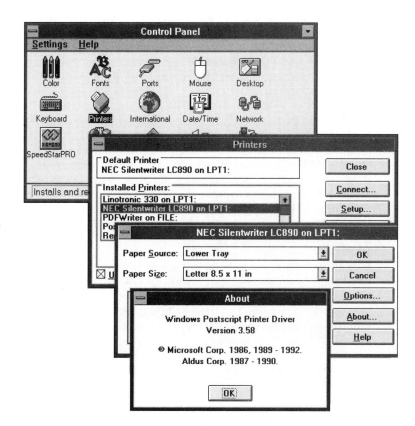

Figure 16-9:
The dialog boxes you go through to check the printer driver's version via the Printers control panel.

Plugging in

Physically, all that you have to do is plug the printer into a parallel port. But which parallel port? Many PCs have two — LPT1 and LPT2. Some PCs even have an LPT3. It doesn't really matter which, as long as you tell Windows which it is. Most people plug the printer into the LPT1 port because all PCs come with one. Many PCs come with both LPT1 and LPT2 ports. It's difficult to know which port is which, because PC makers are absolutely terrible about labeling them. Of course, it doesn't help that you can reprogram the ports so that LPT1 is LPT2! The easiest thing to do is plug the printer cable into the port on the back of your PC that it fits into. (The other ports on the back of a PC — the COM1 and COM2 ports for modems and mice and the VGA port for the monitor — are usually a different size and have pins sticking out of them, rather than holes in them like a parallel port has.)

If your office uses a network, you probably have printers connected to the network and not directly to your PC. Of course, you can have a network with no printers, or you can have a network that has some printers on the network and other printers hooked up to individual PCs. Windows lets you have printers simultaneously connected directly to the PC and a network. For example, the head honcho probably has her very own printer (which no one else can use) connected to her PC to print out those secret plans she works on all day with the door closed. In addition, she can probably print to any printer connected to the network.

You can't tell that network printers are hooked up to the network, though. Network printers are listed as being connected to LPT1, LPT2, or LPT3, even though they're not physically connected to them. These LPT things are used as placeholders in Windows. Windows and DOS were written before networks existed and when all printers connected directly to a physical port. When networks started being widely used, it was easier for Microsoft to fool DOS and Windows into believing that a printer was directly attached to a physical port rather than add the capability to have names (like LPT1 — maybe NET1??) for network connections.

Why are we telling you all this? Because if you work in an office with a network, you may have access to more printers than you think. Any printer that you have access to you can set up each from your PC. (Remember that the setup tells your PC how to deal with the printers; it doesn't change the printers themselves or affect how other network users interact with them.) It's common, for example, for there to be several laser printers in an office, usually placed near clusters of people for general use, perhaps one color printer for everyone to use, and one printer that contains stationery paper. Always select the printer you want and then print to it.

Sometimes the network can get disconnected, in which case the network printers disappear from the list of printers in the Printers control panel and in your Windows programs. If you have this problem, go to the Control Panel icon and double-click it; then double-click the Printers icon. Click the Connect button to get a list of all printers connected, including network connections. Note that any printer you set up is listed, even if it's not currently plugged in.

You can assign several printers to the same port and then change which one is plugged in when you need. Sometimes, you assign the same printer to the same port with different setups, such as when you have a printer that supports both PCL and PostScript and want to be able to switch between the languages. Ditto for network printers. You may have 10 network printers all assigned to LPT3; the networking software keeps track of where the actual printers are on the network. Windows and DOS don't care that all of them seem to be connected to the same physical port.

Networked printers have a printer name instead of a *local port*. (A local port is a physical port on your PC.) If a network printer is missing from this list of printers, click the Network button and enter the network path. See Figure 16-10 for the dialog boxes used in this process. You probably have other software on your PC that lets you create those paths (and thus save you the work of manually entering the paths). Figure 16-11 shows one such program, the PhoneNet software from Farallon used for LocalTalk Mac and PC networks. In this program, the list of connected network printers is shown in the window at the upper-right corner; use the Connect button to make the printer available to your PC. At the bottom of the screen, you can see that this printer has already been connected. Use the Disconnect button if you want to remove it from the list of printers that you have access to.

Setting up the printer

After you physically connect your printer to the PC or to the network, you need to tell Windows how to deal with the printer. First, go to the Control Panel window by double-clicking the Control Panel icon. (The icon is usually in the Main or Accessories program group.) Then double-click the Printers icon.

If you're adding a new printer, click the Add>> button; the dialog box shown in Figure 16-12 appears. Scroll through the list on the bottom of the screen and see if the printer you're installing is listed. Select it if it is. If it is not there, select the Install Unlisted or Updated Printer option (at the top of the printer list). Then click the Install button. You'll be prompted for a Windows or Windows for Workgroups disk, or for a disk supplied with your printer. When the installation is complete, the printer appears in the Installed Printers list at the top of the Printers dialog box.

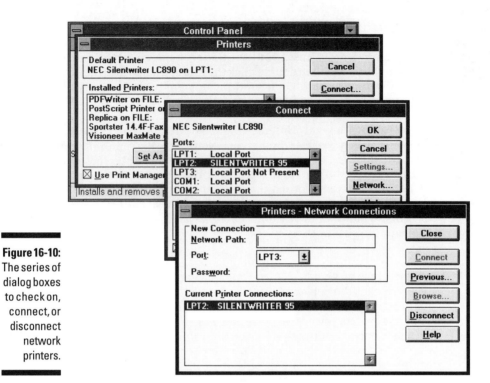

Figure 16-10:
The series of dialog boxes to check on, connect, or disconnect network printers.

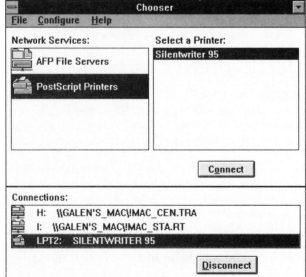

Figure 16-11:
Each type of network has its own software for controlling printer access; this screen shows the software for Farallon's PhoneNet networking for LocalTalk networks.

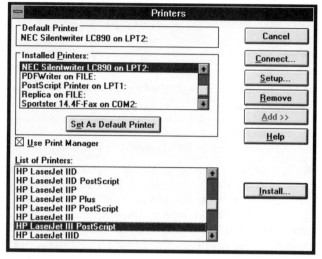

Figure 16-12:
The Printers
dialog box is
where you
install and
set up new
printers.

Notice that Windows probably assigned the printer to LPT1. If you installed an Apple LaserWriter II NT, the list of printers now includes *Apple LaserWriter II NT on LPT1*.

If you want the printer connected to LPT2 or some other port, click the Connect button and then scroll through the list of ports. Select the new one and then click OK. Unless your PC is an older model, make sure the Fast Printing Direct to Port box is checked. You can tell if your PC is too old and thus too slow to handle this option by checking the option. If there's a problem using this option, you encounter printing errors, such as incomplete printing of some pages.

Now you're ready to tell Windows about your printer's preferences, which is how you maximize its capabilities and performance.

Setting up PostScript printer preferences

Because PostScript is such a full-function printing language, there are many options to set up. But relax — the result is worth the effort.

1. **Click the Set as Default Printer button if you want the new printer to be the one that your programs print to by default.** (If you have only one printer installed, this action happens automatically.) Some programs have a print icon in a button bar that lets you skip the Print dialog box. If you use a shortcut icon, the program prints to whatever printer is set as the default in the Control Panel's Printer dialog box. Note that the default printer is listed in its own box at the top of the Printers dialog box.

2. **Click the Setup button.** The dialog box shown in the upper-left corner of Figure 16-13 appears. The defaults for this dialog box should rarely be changed. (If your printer has more than one paper tray, you may want to select a tray other than the default to be the one that your printer automatically uses.)

3. **Click the Options button to get the Options dialog box at the upper-right corner of Figure 16-13.** You should rarely change anything in this dialog box. If you need to create EPS files of your pages for printing by a service bureau, click the Encapsulated PostScript File option. You rarely need to do so for QuarkXPress, because QuarkXPress has its own option for this.

4. **Click the Advanced button to get the dialog box shown in the lower-left corner of Figure 16-13.** Now the fun begins. Your setup should match that in the figure, with the exception of the settings for Memory. The settings for memory depend on your printer. Check the Clear Memory per Page box if you have only a few megabytes of printer memory and use a lot of fonts (more than six at a time). The amount of virtual memory is determined by your printer. The Windows defaults are often too small, which slows down printing time.

5. **To find the optimal setting, use the File Manager or a DOS window to go to the \WINDOWS\SYSTEM directory.** In File Manager, highlight the file names TESTPS.TXT and use File⇨Copy (or F8) to copy the file to your printer port (such as LPT1); make sure that, in the To field in the Copy dialog box, you put a colon after the printer port (such as *LPT1:*). In DOS, give the command COPY TESTPS.TXT LPT1: (substitute the correct port name for LPT1). You should receive a single sheet from your printer that has a line called Max Suggested VM (KB). Use whatever value is specified there for the Virtual Memory (KB) field in the Advanced Options dialog box.

6. **Check the Use Printer Fonts for all TrueTypes Fonts box if you want to use a TrueType font on-screen but have its PostScript equivalent print.** If you only want this to be true for certain fonts, check the Use Substitution Table box and then click the Edit Substitution Table button to get the Substitution dialog box shown in the lower-right corner of Figure 16-13. Select the TrueType font in the left window and then the PostScript equivalent in the right window. (By associating the TrueType font with Download as Soft Font, you tell Windows to send the TrueType font to the printer after first converting that font to PostScript format.)

7. **Click OK to close each dialog box.** Now your printer is set up.

Setting up PCL printer preferences

If you are using a PCL printer, follow these steps.

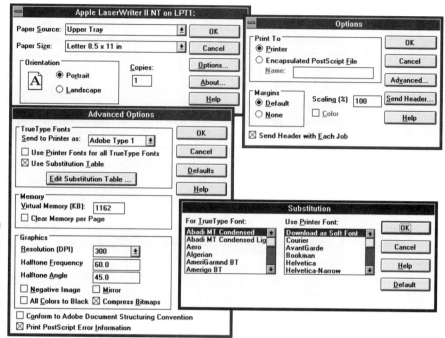

Figure 16-13:
Dialog
boxes used
to set up a
PostScript
printer.

1. **Click the Set as Default Printer button if you want the new printer to be the one that your programs print to by default.** You can see this in Figure 16-12. (If you have only one printer installed, it happens automatically.) Some programs have a print icon in a button bar that lets you skip the Print dialog box. If you use such a shortcut icon, the program prints to whatever printer is set as the default in the Control Panel's Printer dialog box. Note that the default printer is listed in its own box at the top of the Printers dialog box.

2. **Click the Setup button.** The dialog box shown in the top of Figure 16-14 appears. Use the Resolution pop-up menu to make sure the printer is set to the resolution you want; 300 dpi (dots per inch) or higher resolution is the best option for QuarkXPress and other font- and graphics-intensive programs. You may need to have 4MB or more of printer memory to print at this resolution. Make sure the Memory pop-up option is set for the correct amount of printer memory.

3. **Click the Options button.** The Options dialog box at the bottom of Figure 16-14 appears. This box should rarely be changed. One item you may change is the Dithering option. Selecting Fine ensures the best reproduction of photographs and color and gray-scale bitmaps. Selecting Line Art ensures the best reproduction of text and drawings. Experiment to see

which works best for your set of documents. *Never* select the Print TrueType as Graphics box; it slows printing down considerably unless you only a have a few characters on a page. That's so unlikely that the small amount of slowdown that would occur on such pages is not worth the hassle of changing the settings. Click OK to return to the dialog box shown at the top of Figure 16-14.

4. **If you have downloadable PCL fonts, click the Fonts button.** This action tells Windows which fonts you have available for that printer. Remember that Windows translates all TrueType fonts to PCL format, so you can use TrueType fonts with a PCL printer. And if you have Adobe Type Manager, you can print PostScript fonts on a PCL printer. In other words, don't worry too much about PCL fonts.

5. **Click OK to exit each dialog box.** Now your printer is set up.

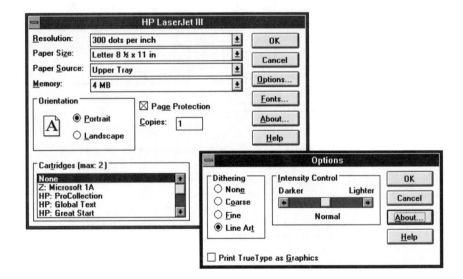

Figure 16-14:
Setting up a
PCL printer.

Background printing

You may have noticed in the Printers dialog box in Figure 16-12 the Use Print Manager option. If it's checked, Windows sends your print jobs to disk, creating what's called a *spool* file (that's a fancy name for a queue). While you're doing other work, Windows works with the printer to print the file. In a complex document with lots of images, we're talking the difference of perhaps tens of minutes — that's a great savings. Check this option when you want to save print time.

Switching Printers

You can use the Printers control panel to switch printers by setting a different printer as the default. You can also use the Print Manager (see the sidebar "Exploring the Windows Print Manager"). Or you can do it the easy way and change printers in QuarkXPress or any other Windows program.

Almost every Windows program, including QuarkXPress, has an option in the File menu named Printer Setup or Print Setup. (In QuarkXPress, you can use File⇨Printer Setup or Ctrl+Alt+P.) This menu typically lets you set attributes like the page size and orientation, as well as change the Printers control panel setup for your printer (usually via the Options button). It's also where you can change your printer. In QuarkXPress, you can easily choose a different printer by clicking the Specific Printer button and picking the printer from a list of installed printers. Figure 16-15 shows an example of a fax modem being chosen. You can also access this dialog box through the Print menu by clicking a button such as Setup (that's the name in QuarkXPress's Print dialog box). That lets you get to the right dialog box without having to close the Print dialog box; after you change the printer, QuarkXPress puts you back in the Print dialog box so that you can immediately print.

In some programs, such as Microsoft Word 6, you have to change the printer from the Print dialog box. Typically when you select a new printer, that printer becomes the default printer for all programs — in Word, you select the printer from the Printers list and then click the Set as Default Printer button. Remember that when you change printers in QuarkXPress, you affect only QuarkXPress, not other programs. Figure 16-16 shows Word's method for comparison to QuarkXPress's.

Sending fonts to the printer

One of Windows' great failings is the lack of control over font handling for printing. Unlike the Mac, you can't easily send a font to the printer's memory, which speeds up print time. Adobe's PostScript fonts come with a DOS utility that loads fonts into the printer's memory. (It's called PSDOWN.EXE and usually resides in the \PSFONTS directory.) Some printers come with similar DOS utilities; NEC Technologies provides one, for example. For Windows, Ares Software's FontMinder font-management utility (415-578-9090) is the only one we know of that lets you load fonts into printer memory — we couldn't even find any shareware utilities that do this task.

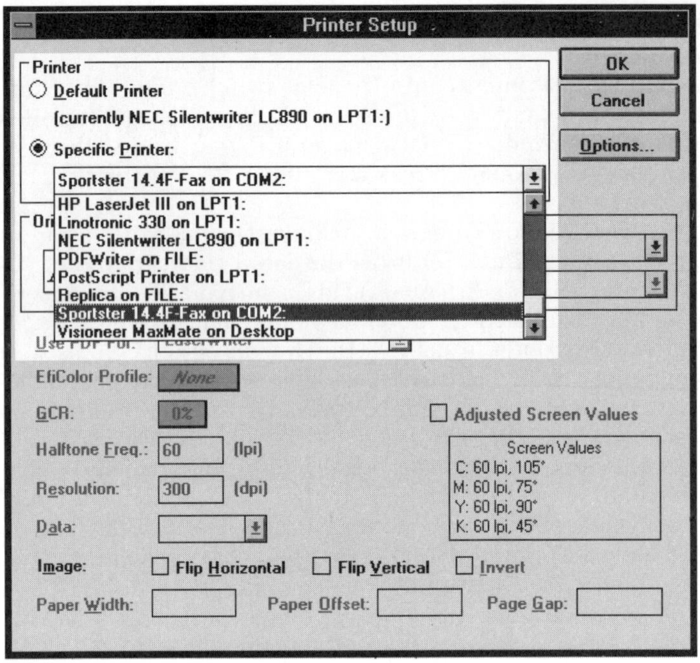

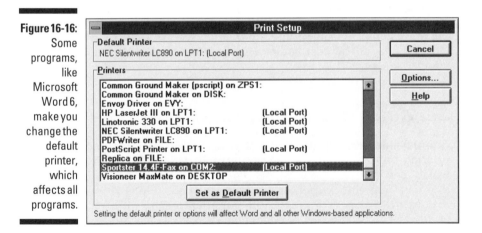

Figure 16-15:
Changing printers for specific document is easy in QuarkXPress.

Figure 16-16:
Some programs, like Microsoft Word 6, make you change the default printer, which affects all programs.

When you use a DOS utility to send fonts to a printer, you have to tell Windows that the fonts are loaded in the printer's memory. Otherwise, Windows sends the font any way that it can to the printers. Telling Windows which fonts are in the printer is easy but dangerous. You have to edit the WIN.INI file that contains most Windows setup information. Figure 16-17 shows the part of the file that determines font loading. Notice how the font information is repeated for each font. Also note the file extension .PFB, which instructs Windows to send the font to the printer when the font is used in a document. If the part of the line after the comma (,) is not there — the part highlighted in one line in Figure 16-17 — Windows assume the font is already loaded in the printer. (That's why standard fonts like Avant Garde — the ones in the SOFTFONT37 through SOFTFONT40 lines — don't have that second part in their *SOFTFONTxx=* statement, as shown in the figure.)

You must edit WIN.INI without changing it from an ASCII, text-only file, and then restart Windows to make changes in the fonts that are downloaded. That's inconvenient at best, and dangerous in many cases because someone may make another change accidentally. If you use Adobe Type Manager, you can specify that a font is *not* to be sent to the printer by *not* checking the Install as autodownload fonts for the PostScript driver check box when you install a font. However, you can't change a font's download status in ATM after a font is installed — unless you remove it and reinstall it. You can avoid all of this danger and hassle with the FontMinder software; it manages the WIN.INI for you by sending fonts to the printer's memory without requiring you to restart Windows. Figure 16-18 shows the utility.

Figure 16-17:
The lines within WIN.INI that control whether a font is sent to the printer by Windows. The highlighted part of the line must be removed to prevent Windows from loading the font to the printer.

```
softfont26=c:\psfonts\pfm\loel____.pfm,c:\psfonts\loel____.pfb
softfont27=c:\psfonts\pfm\lol_____.pfm,c:\psfonts\lol_____.pfb
softfont28=c:\psfonts\pfm\lob_____.pfm,c:\psfonts\lob_____.pfb
softfont29=c:\psfonts\pfm\lorg____.pfm,c:\psfonts\lorg____.pfb
softfont30=c:\psfonts\pfm\lobl____.pfm,c:\psfonts\lobl____.pfb
softfont31=c:\psfonts\pfm\pyrg____.pfm,c:\psfonts\pyrg____.pfb
softfont32=c:\psfonts\pfm\pym_____.pfm,c:\psfonts\pym_____.pfb
softfont33=c:\psfonts\pfm\pymi____.pfm,c:\psfonts\pymi____.pfb
softfont34=c:\psfonts\pfm\pyi_____.pfm,c:\psfonts\pyi_____.pfb
softfont35=c:\psfonts\pfm\lnoscrpt.pfm,c:\psfonts\lnoscrpt.pfb
softfont36=c:\psfonts\pfm\vrb_____.pfm,c:\psfonts\vrb_____.pfb
softfont37=c:\psfonts\pfm\agw_____.pfm
softfont38=c:\psfonts\pfm\agd_____.pfm
softfont39=c:\psfonts\pfm\agdo____.pfm
softfont40=c:\psfonts\pfm\agwo____.pfm
softfont41=c:\psfonts\pfm\bm_____.pfm,c:\psfonts\bm_____.pfb
```

Sending fonts to printer memory is called *downloading* fonts, even though the technically accurate term would be *uploading*. To upload is to send to; to download is to receive from. However, many people use the terms interchangeably, and practically every program and manual uses the incorrect *download* to describe the action of sending fonts to a printer.

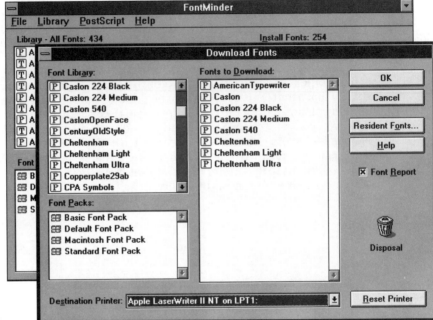

Figure 16-18:
The FontMinder 2.5 program can send fonts to the printer's memory and does not require you to mess with Windows setup files.

Chapter 17

Printing to Pages

In This Chapter

▶ Setting up the best output for your printer

▶ Using Print dialog box features

▶ Working with service bureaus

*P*hew! With Chapter 16 out of the way, you're finally done with the work of setting up your printer. This chapter covers printing with QuarkXPress. For basic printing, you can use File➪Print or ⌘-P. Of course, why stick with the basics when you can have control over some of the details?

Anatomy of a Page Setup Dialog Box

Before you print, you should set up the basic parameters that QuarkXPress uses to determine the output quality for your document. You do this via File➪Page Setup or ⌘-Option-P. Figure 17-1 shows the LaserWriter Page Setup dialog box.

In Windows, the menu name and dialog box are slightly different. Use the File➪Printer Setup command; the dialog box shown in Figure 17-2 appears. Some of the names of options differ.

Here's what you need to know about the Page Setup dialog box:

These options remain set from document to document, so you don't need to change them each time you print unless you have changed printers or need to change the settings to match your document's particular characteristics. Note that options that aren't relevant for a particular printer or document are grayed out.

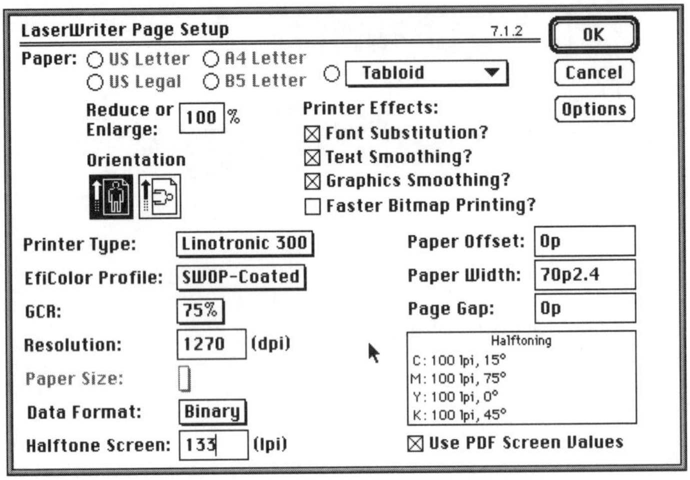

Figure 17-1:
The Mac
LaserWriter
Page Setup
dialog box.

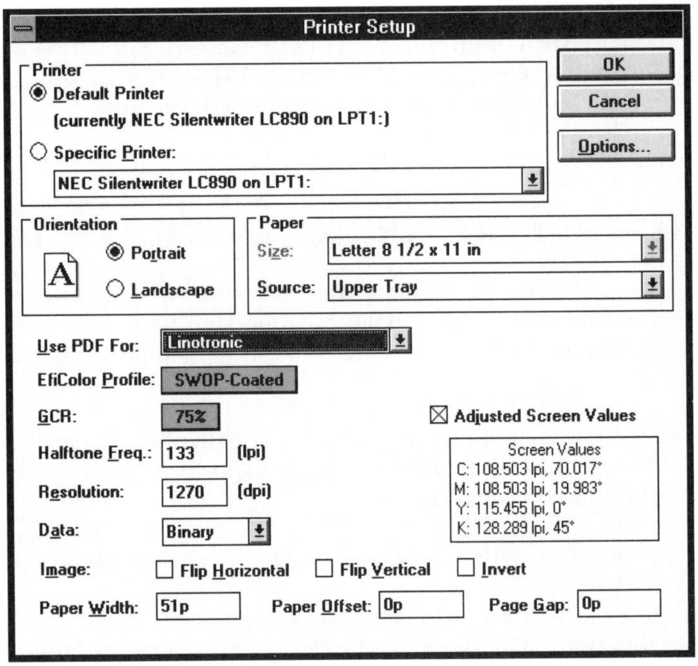

Figure 17-2:
The
Windows
Printer
Setup dialog
box.

✔ The Paper Size should be at least as large as the document size you select in File⇨Document Setup. You may want a larger paper size (assuming your printer supports it) to leave room for crop marks and other page information. If you're printing to an imagesetter, the size is not adjustable; the driver for your imagesetter (like a Linotronic) determines the size of the paper.

✔ The Orientation should also match the settings in File⇨Document Setup. If your document is a portrait document (taller than wide), make sure that you select Portrait; if your document is a landscape document (wider than tall), make sure that you select Landscape. The icons show the orientation.

✔ The Printer Type (in Windows, Use PDF For) should match that of the output printer. The list of types is based on the PDF (PostScript Description Files) installed in your computer. These get installed from your printer's driver disks. Programs such as QuarkXPress also come with PDFs for common printers. (You generally install PDFs after you are asked to pick a printer from a list during the program installation.) If you don't have a PDF that matches your printer, pick the closest one you can. In the worst case, pick an Apple LaserWriter of roughly the same age (for example, a LaserWriter for a printer four years or older, a IIg or IIf for a printer a couple years old, a LaserWriter 810 for a recent 600 dpi printer, and so on). The PDF determines a whole range of quality settings, such as top resolution. Pick from these options as described in the following five items.

✔ If you're printing in color and using the EfiColor XTension, pick an EfiColor Profile. Use SWOP-Coated if you're printing to a commercial printer (such as a magazine or catalog). If no profile matches your printer, call Electronics for Imaging and see if they have one available for sale; their numbers are 415-286-8503 and 800-285-4565.

✔ Leave GCR at its default unless your commercial printer or service bureau tells you otherwise. GCR stands for *gray component replacement,* which is the process by which grays in a color image are converted from mixtures of yellow, cyan, and magenta to shades of black. The use of black to achieve grays results in a sharper image than the use of a mix of other colors.

✔ Resolution should be set to match your printer's best resolution; typically, the resolution sets automatically when you change the printer type. For imagesetters, use 1270 dpi for black-and-white and gray-scale output and 2540 dpi for color output unless your commercial printing press or service bureau tells you otherwise.

✔ Data Format (in Windows, D<u>a</u>ta) should be set at Binary unless you encounter printing problems (such as pages that process endlessly or process for a while and then stop). Then try ASCII or, on a PC only, PC Binary. Binary makes the files smaller and speeds transfer of data to the printer. However, in some cases it makes the actual print time longer, which is why a service bureau or commercial printing press may sometimes ask you to change the option.

✔ Halftone Screen (in Windows, Halftone <u>F</u>req.) should usually be left at the printer's default. For an imagesetter, pick 133 or 150 for color work output at 2540 dpi resolution and 120 or 133 for gray-scale and black-and-white work output at 1270 or higher dpi resolution. If you're printing in color and your printer type matches your actual printer, check the Use PDF Screen Values box (in Windows, Adjusted Screen Values); this option uses optimized settings for your printer based on information in the printer's driver and PDF file. (This option only comes into play if you're printing in color.)

✔ Several options — Paper Offset, Paper Width, Flip Horizontal, Flip Vertical, and Invert Image (<u>I</u>nvert in Windows) — designed for printing to an imagesetter should be changed or checked only if requested by your commercial printing press or service bureau. If you're printing to an imagesetter, you should specify a Page Gap of 2 or 3 picas ($^1/_4$ to $^1/_2$ an inch). Doing so gives sufficient room for crop marks between pages and for the service bureau to cut apart the pages. (Imagesetters print pages on rolls of film or paper, like some fax machines.) The Flip Horizontal, Flip Image, and Invert Image options are available from the Mac's Page Setup dialog box only after you click the Options button to open the LaserWriter Options dialog box.

Typical Setups

Typically, you set up your printer as follows:

✔ When printing to a laser printer, set the Orientation at Portrait, the Paper at Letter, the Printer Type to match your target printer, Halftone Screen at 60 lpi (for 300-dpi printers) or 80 lpi (for 600-dpi printers), and Data Format as Binary.

✔ When printing to a color printer such as an ink jet or dye-sublimation, set the Orientation at Portrait, the Paper at Letter, the Printer Type to match your target printer, Halftone Screen at 60 lpi (for 300-dpi printers) or 80 lpi (for 600-dpi printers), EfiColor Profile to match your target printer or set to None, GCR at 75%, Data Format as Binary, and Use PDF Screen Values checked.

✔ When printing to an imagesetter at your site for color separations, set the Orientation at Portrait, the Printer Type to match your target printer, the Resolution at 2540 dpi, Halftone Screen at 133 or 150 lpi, EfiColor Profile to match your target printer or set to None, GCR at 75%, the Data Format as Binary, Use PDF Screen Values checked, and the Page Gap at 3p.

✔ When printing to an imagesetter for black-and-white or gray-scale output, set the Orientation at Portrait, the Printer Type to match your target printer, the Resolution at 1270 dpi, Halftone Screen at 120 or 133 lpi, the Data Format as Binary, and the Page Gap at 3p.

Anatomy of a Print Dialog Box

The QuarkXPress Print dialog box (shown in Figure 17-3) is your last destination in the journey to paper. It's fairly simple to use, so here goes. The following items describe the features that are not always so obvious. We don't waste your time telling you such things as how to enter the number of copies you want printed in the Copies field — you already know how to do these things.

```
LaserWriter  "Silentwriter 95"                      7.1.2    [ Print  ]
Copies: [1]          Pages: ◉ All  ○ From: [    ] To: [    ]  [ Cancel ]
Cover Page:    ◉ No ○ First Page ○ Last Page
Paper Source: ◉ Paper Cassette ○ Manual Feed
Print:         ○ Black & White   ◉ Color/Grayscale
Destination:   ◉ Printer         ○ PostScript® File
Page Sequence: [All]          □ Collate      □ Back to Front
Output:        [Normal]       □ Spreads      □ Thumbnails
Tiling:        [Off]    ▸  Overlap: [18p]
Separation:    [Off]       Plate:  [All Plates]
Registration:  [Off]       OPI:    [Include Images]
Options:       □ Calibrated Output   ☒ Print Colors as Grays
               □ Include Blank Pages
```

Figure 17-3:
The Print
dialog box.

The Windows dialog box for printing is essentially the same as the Mac version; the only significant differences are that (1) the Cover Page option in Windows uses a pop-up list rather than buttons to select the option; (2) there is a Setup button to jump you to the Printer Setup dialog box in Windows; (3) there is no Paper Source option in the Windows Print dialog box (you use the Printer Setup dialog box instead); (4) the options Black & White and Color/Grayscale are replaced with a check box called Print Colors as Grays. To print to file (for use if you're using a service bureau to output your pages and you don't want to send the original files for fear a setting might accidentally be changed), use the Setup button to go to the Printer Setup dialog box and then use the Options button to go to the Options dialog box. Change the Print To setting to Encapsulated PostScript File.

✔ Here's a tip that will save you some guesswork in the Pages portion of the dialog box: If you want to print from a certain page through the last page of your document but you can't remember what the last page number is, just type *end* in the To field.

✔ The Page Sequence pop-up list lets you tell QuarkXPress to print all pages in the sequence (All, or the range specified in From and To in the Pages section of the dialog box), all even pages, or all odd pages.

✔ Output lets you set the quality level. The default is Normal. The other two options are Low Resolution (which substitutes the coarser screen preview for images) and Rough (which prevents images from printing). Use these two options when you want a quick proofing copy and don't care for top-notch graphics.

✔ Tiling lets you print large documents on smaller sheets of paper. For example, you may have a large calendar that you want to print out, but your laser printer or imagesetter doesn't accept paper large enough to print the calendar. If you change Tiling to Automatic, QuarkXPress prints out the page in sections — like a quilt — that you then assemble to create the final version. QuarkXPress leaves enough overlap between the sections so that you can properly align the sections. (Use the Overlap field to determine the overlap.) The Manual option requires that you set the section breaks.

✔ The Spreads box tells QuarkXPress to print facing pages on a continuous sheet paper (assuming your printer supports it). If your printer supports 11×17 paper, for example, and your pages are $8^1/_2 \times 11$, you may want to use this option. But if you're outputting pages for duplication at a copy shop or commercial printing press, check with them before using this option.

✔ The Thumbnails box tells QuarkXPress to print your pages in reduced versions, eight to a sheet. Use this feature if you want to quickly proof layouts without taking lots of room.

✔ The Include Blank Pages option tells QuarkXPress to print blank pages. To save paper, leave this option unchecked. (Unfortunately, the default for QuarkXPress is to have it checked, so be sure to turn it off.) But you may want to print blank pages so that, for example, a photocopier printing two-sided copies has placeholder sheets to keep the page sequence correct.

✔ The Separation options (On or Off) tell QuarkXPress whether to make color separations — a separate sheet for each color in a document. You want to do color separations when you're outputting to an imagesetter for color reproduction on a commercial printing press. When this option is set to On, you can decide which colors (called *plates*) are printed via the Plate option. Your choices are All Plates or a specific color. All colors defined in the document display in the pop-up list. Process (CMYK) colors don't have separate plates because, by definition, a process color is broken up into cyan, magenta, yellow, and black components. Generally speaking, you should have only cyan, magenta, yellow, and black listed. If there are other colors, they should be colors that you are printing on a separate plate (such as a neon or metallic or Pantone) because there is no accurate way to reproduce them via CMYK printing. If other colors are listed, leave the Print dialog box and delete or redefine the other colors as process colors. (Chapter 14 shows you how.)

✔ The Registration options tell QuarkXPress to print crop marks (the marks that indicate the live image area of a page) and other information (such as the file name and, for color separations, the color ink to be used for a particular negative). It's up to your service bureau or commercial printing press as to whether they prefer Centered or Off Center registration marks. Note that preferences for the offset amounts are set via Edit⇨Preferences⇨Application.

✔ The OPI options are used for service bureaus and commercial printing presses that do image scanning for you, send you a placeholder version for layout, and keep the high-resolution version for the final printing. Leave these options at the default of Include Images unless your service bureau or commercial printing press tells you otherwise.

✔ Check Calibrated Output if you're not using EfiColor. If EfiColor is loaded, it takes over the Calibrated Output function and is grayed out. Calibrated Output adjusts the colors in your document for the best possible reproduction on your printer. EfiColor has better calibration techniques, so we encourage you to have it active (see Chapter 14).

✔ Check Color/Grayscale when printing to a color printer or when you want to print grays (including colors printed as shades of gray) on a black-and-white printer, such as a laser printer. In Windows, use the Printers control panel function instead. You can access this control panel from QuarkXPress's Print dialog box or by going to the Printers icon in the Windows Control Panel. Either way, use Setup⇨Options⇨Advanced to get the Advanced Options dialog box. Check the All Colors to Black box to force colors and grays to print as black and white. Fortunately, printing in color or gray scale is the default for Windows, so you need only change this option if you want to force all colors and grays to black and white.

Note that the Print Colors as Grays is a separate option; it converts colors to shades of gray when printing to a non-color printer. If you have Color/Grayscale checked but not Print Colors as Grays, any color images are converted to black-and-white, and grays print as grays. If you have both options checked, both colored and gray items print as shades of gray.

Typical Setups

Typically, you set up your printing as follows:

✔ When printing to a laser printer, check Color/Grayscale, Printer as the Destination, All as the Page Sequence, Normal as the Output, Off for the Separation, and Print Colors as Grays. Uncheck Include Blank Pages.

✔ When printing to a color printer, such as an ink jet or dye-sublimation, check Color/Grayscale, Printer as the Destination, All as the Page Sequence, Normal as the Output, and Off for the Separation. Uncheck Print Colors as Grays and Include Blank Pages.

✔ When printing to an imagesetter at your site for color separations, check Color/Grayscale, Printer as the Destination, All as the Page Sequence, Normal as the Output, On for the Separation, Centered or Off Center as the Registration, All Plates as the Plates, and uncheck Print Colors as Grays and Include Blank Pages.

✔ When printing to an imagesetter for black-and-white or gray-scale output, set the same options as for color output *except* turn Separation Off.

Tips for printing to file

When printing to file on the Mac, follow the settings in the Typical Settings section in this chapter, as appropriate for the printer the file will ultimately be printed to. But also set up the print-to-file settings in the dialog box (shown in the following figure) that will display when you click Save (the Print button changes to Save when you select the PostScript® File option for Destination).

Make sure you select PostScript Job as the Format option. It's also best to select Binary, rather than ASCII, because it saves disk space. Check Level 2 Only only if you're certain that the printer the file will be output to is compatible with the new version of PostScript (the one that is supported by LaswerWriter 8) — check Level 1 Compatible if you're not sure. (Level 2 printers can accept Level 1-format PostScript files.)

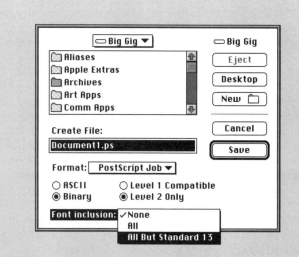

Finally, select an option from the Font Inclusion pop-up list. If all fonts in your document are in the printer's memory, select None. If no fonts are, select All. You should select All But Standard 13 only if you're using a printer that has Courier (normal, bold, italic, and bold italic), Helvetica (normal, bold, italic, and bold italic), Times (normal, bold, italic, and bold italic), and Symbol in built-in memory — that means almost every PostScript laser printer and most imagesetters.

Windows does not let you set most of these controls over print-to-file output. Whether fonts are downloaded is determined by the settings for printer in WIN.INI, as explained in Chapter 16. Windows does not yet support PostScript Level 2, so all output uses the Level 1 format. You *can* set whether the file prints in ASCII or binary via the Print dialog box's D<u>a</u>ta option.

Working with Service Bureaus

Many QuarkXPress users end up sending their work to service bureaus (including the in-house production departments at a commercial printing press) to print the final copies. After all, QuarkXPress is the publishing tool of choice for professional publishers, and it's the professional publishers who tend to print color magazines, high-volume newsletters, crisp brochures, and other materials that need a professional printer, not just a photocopier.

Working with a service bureau can be a trying experience, particularly if you don't understand what the service bureau needs. Basically, a service bureau needs whatever the document has in it or takes advantage of. Here's a check list to go over before sending your QuarkXPress files to a service bureau:

✔ Who prints the files? If you give the service bureau your QuarkXPress files, the service bureau can make any adjustments needed for optimal printing or solve unexpected problems with, for example, images or colors. But it could possibly make a mistake by changing something it shouldn't. By printing the file yourself, you can avoid this potential problem. When you print the file yourself, you're responsible for the final output; a service bureau can't edit your PostScript print file. In addition to being uneditable, these files can be huge (even larger than the document and associated files they're based on — tens of megabytes). In most cases, the service bureau should print from your files, but you should mark on hard copy all colors, ruling lines, images, and fonts in order to give the service bureau something to check against. You also should insist on color-match prints (called by several trade names, such as Matchprints and Fujichromes) for color pages and bluelines for black-and-white or spot-color pages. *Color-match prints* and *bluelines* are copies of your publication made from the negatives in which you can see your publication before the mass printing begins. Expect to pay about $135 per color-match print page and $20 per blueprint page.

✔ Does the service bureau use the same version of QuarkXPress that you use? If you use QuarkXPress Version 3.3 and your service bureau has version 3.2, the service bureau can't open your files. If you have 3.2 and the service bureau has 3.3, you can't read the files the service bureau gives back to you if they save the files after making changes. When a version changes, check to ensure that you and your service bureau are in synch. Note that for minor upgrades, such as QuarkXPress 3.31, compatibility problems rarely occur.

✔ Do you and the service bureau use the same XTensions? If you use EfiColor, make sure your service bureau does, too. Ditto for anything else that affects the printed appearance, such as import filters for unusual graphics formats. You may even want to give your service bureau a copy of all your XTensions in order ensure that nothing is missing. Note that you don't need to worry about XTensions that don't affect the actual content; items that display information on graphics or bypass various warnings don't change the appearance of your document when loaded into a system that doesn't have them.

✔ Does the service bureau use the same fonts that you use? If you're not sure whether your service bureau has the same fonts that you do, send copies of yours. Note that most service bureaus can't use TrueType fonts, so check first before sending them. (You can convert TrueType fonts to PostScript format with Ares Software's FontMonger or Altsys Corp.'s Fontographer, as described in Chapter 2.) Don't forget to tell the service bureau all the fonts your document uses.

✔ Does the service bureau have the right colors? If you're doing four-color process (CMYK) output, have you made all colors process colors? Do you have some colors that are spot colors, and are they defined as such? Have you deleted any color plates your document doesn't use? Don't forget to tell the service bureau what colors should print. (Use the Collect for Output feature, described later in this chapter, to get a list of these items.)

✔ Does the service bureau have the same EfiColor profiles that you have? Don't forget to copy the EfiColor profiles used in your document as well. Chances are that the service bureau has the basic ones, such as SWOP-Coated and EFI Calibrated RGB. If you have special profiles that you purchased from Electronics for Imaging, make sure you share those with your service bureau.

Most service bureaus are Mac-based; they probably don't know what to do with your QuarkXPress for Windows files, even though Mac QuarkXPress can read them. You can probably get them over the hump of loading your files (see Chapter 20 for specific details), but there are two gotchas that may mean you need to convert to Mac QuarkXPress yourself, use the print-to-PostScript-file option, or find a Windows-savvy service bureau. First, most XTensions are not available for Windows, and some Windows XTensions have no Mac equivalents. Therefore, if you depend on such XTensions, you need to use a Windows-savvy service bureau or forgo the XTensions. Second, while PostScript fonts exist on both Mac and Windows, you can't give a Mac-based service bureau your Windows PostScript fonts. You have to translate them to Mac format with FontMonger or Fontographer. Beware of using "almost the same" fonts across platforms: even if they look alike, subtle differences in spacing can cause text to flow differently, perhaps even leading to a story flowing longer than originally planned and thus having some lines cut off.

Fortunately, this list of questions is manageable. You don't have to worry about certain things. QuarkXPress keeps all tracking, kerning, and hyphenation information with the document, and your service bureau knows to click the Keep Document Settings button when it loads your file into its copy of QuarkXPress and is asked whether to preserve your settings.

QuarkXPress also provides a tool to help you gather all the components of a document. It's called Collect for Output, and you can access it from the File menu. The resulting dialog box is shown in Figure 17-4. You can collect the document and its components into any folder or directory, and even create a new folder or directory to store the materials.

What's in a Collect for Output folder? A copy of the QuarkXPress document itself, plus all linked graphics are in the folder, as is a text file that is the name of the QuarkXPress document plus the word *report*. (In Windows, the name of the text file is the same as the document's file name, except the extension is .RPT.)

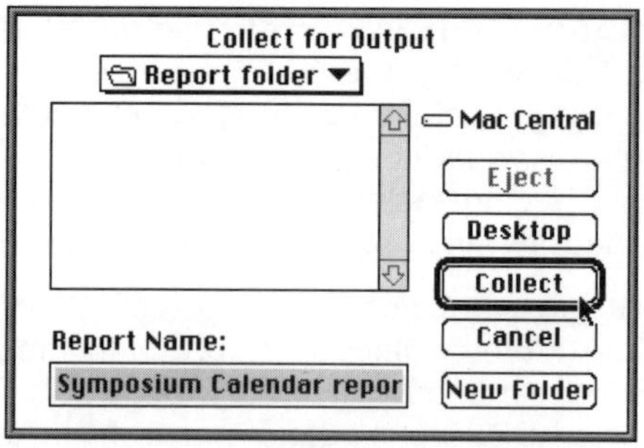

Collect for Output

📁 Report folder ▼

⊂⊐ Mac Central

Eject

Desktop

Collect

Cancel

New Folder

Report Name:

Symposium Calendar repor

Figure 17-4:
The Collect
for Output
dialog box.

This report contains a whole treasure trove of information about your QuarkXPress document. We suggest you send the report to your service bureau or load it in to a word processor or QuarkXPress and print out a copy for inclusion. Figure 17-5 shows part of a report that includes a list of all XTensions used (and distinguishes between those required for opening the document from those used in the document); a list of all fonts used (including those in graphics — unfortunately, it lists a graphic each time it is used, not just once), a list of all styles used; a list of all EfiColor profiles used; a list of all H&J sets used, a list of all colors used (including a list of all color plates used); a list of trapping settings used; and information about the types, sizes, rotation, skew, positions, and scaling of all graphics.

QuarkXPress can tell you which XTensions are required to open a document. But don't assume that an XTension used in a document but not listed as required in the Collect for Output report is therefore optional. Take the JPEG filter XTension: you can open a document that has JPEG images even if the filter is not present. But you won't be able to print those JPEG images.

QuarkXPress also comes with a template called Output Request (it's in your QuarkXPress folder; on Windows, it's called COLL4OUT.QXT) that makes a great cover sheet for print jobs sent to a service bureau (see Figure 17-6.) At the bottom of the form is an empty text box in which you can import the report created by Collect for Output and create a unified cover sheet with all the details your service bureau — and you — would ever want to know about your document. Remember that you can modify this QuarkXPress document's layout to match your or your service bureau's preferences. And also remember to check the Include Style Sheets box when you use File⇨Get Text to import the Collect for Output report into the Output Request template.

```
┌──────────────────────────────── Document1 ────────────────────────────────┐
│         6|      12|       18|       24|       30|       36|      42|     48| │
│    8⌐    3.31r2 Macintosh format                                             │
│     │Total Pages: 1                                                          │
│     │Page Width: 33"                                                         │
│     │Page Height: 20.75"                                                     │
│     │Required XTensions:                                                     │
│    2⌐      None                                                              │
│    4│Active XTensions:                                                       │
│     │    EfiColorXTension;  Frontier™ Menu Sharing 2.0;   Kern/Track Editor;  Cool Blends; JPEG │
│     │Import;    MacWrite® 5.0/II;  Multiple Master Utilities (3.2);   Microsoft® Word 4.0; │
│     │Microsoft® Works 2.0;    PCX Import XT;   PhotoCD XTension; WordPerfect® 2.0.2; │
│    3⌐WriteNow® 3.0 Import;   WriteNow® 2.0;   XPress Tags               │
│    0│                                                                        │
│     │DOCUMENT FONTS                                                          │
│     │External Name    Internal Name     PS Filename                         │
│     │ «Plain»XB Futura ExtraBold    XB Futura ExtraBold      FuturExtBol     │
│    3⌐ «Bold+Italic»XB Futura ExtraBold     XB Futura ExtraBold     FuturExtBolObl │
│    6│ «Plain»Futura      FuturaFutur                                         │
│     │ «Italic»Futura     FuturaFuturObl                                      │
│     │ «Bold+Italic»FuturaFutura.FuturHeaObl                                  │
│     │ «Plain»Caslon 224 Book  Caslon 224 Book    CasloTwoTweFouBoo          │
│    4⌐admin.eps    No fonts used.                                             │
│    2│casedsgn.eps      No fonts used.                                        │
│     │marrsym.eps No fonts used.                                              │
│     │mktsym.eps  No fonts used.                                              │
│     │admin.eps    No fonts used.                                            │
│    4⌐casedsgn.eps      No fonts used.                                        │
│    8│marrsym.eps No fonts used.                                              │
│     │mktsym.eps  No fonts used.                                              │
│     │admin.eps    No fonts used.                                            │
│     │casedsgn.eps      No fonts used                                         │
│ 100% │ Page 1                                                                │
└─────────────────────────────────────────────────────────────────────────────┘
```

Figure 17-5:
Part of the report QuarkXPress generates via the Collect for Output feature.

Technically speaking, it's illegal for you to copy programs (including XTensions), fonts, and images you don't own or license from others and give them to other people. Practically speaking, though, you have no choice. To ensure compatibility, you and your service bureau need to have the same tools and sources. To stay within the spirit of the law (if not the letter), make sure that your service bureau understands that the programs, fonts, and images you copy for them are to be used only in connection with printing your documents.

The best advice for working with a service bureau is to ensure a high degree of communication. Talk with your service bureau to see what it needs from you. And make it clear to the service bureau what you need. Your service bureau's is to help you get the best output you can while still making a living wage. Your job is to minimize your headaches and the service bureau's headaches to ensure affordable, cheerful, professional, and timely service.

ELECTRONIC OUTPUT REQUEST

CLIENT INFORMATION
Contact Person: _____
Company: _____
Address: _____
City, ST, Zip: _____
Office Phone: _____
Home Phone: _____

DELIVERY INFORMATION
__ Deliver   __ Hold For Pickup   __ Call When Complete
Delivery Address: _____
City, ST, Zip: _____

TURNAROUND INFORMATION
__ Normal   __ Rush   __ Emergency

FONT INFORMATION
__ Adobe/Linotype   __ Font Company   __ Agfa Compugraphic
__ Bitstream   __ Monotype   __ _____

COPYRIGHT INFORMATION
All that appears on the enclosed medium (including, but not limited to, floppy disk, modem transmission, removable media) is unencumbered by copyrights. We, the customer, have full rights to reproduce the supplied content.
Signature: _____
Date: _____

OUTPUT MEDIA (CHECK ALL THAT APPLY)
__ Film   __ RC Paper   __ Color Proof
__ Laser Print   __ Color Slides   __ _____
__ Negative   -or-   __ Positive
__ Emulsion Down -or-   __ Emulsion Up

OUTPUT SPECIFICATION
__ Output All Pages
__ Output The Following Specified Pages...
  From: _____   To: _____

CROP MARKS
__ Yes   __ No

RESOLUTION/DPI
__ 1200/1270   __ 2400/2540   __ 3000+

SCREEN RULING/LPI
__ 65   __ 85   __ 120
__ 133   __ 150   __ _____

COLOR SEPARATION PLATES
__ Cyan   __ Magenta   __ Yellow   __ Black
__ _____   __ _____   __ _____   __ _____

COLOR PROOF SPECIFICATION
__ Proof All Pages
__ Proof The Following Specified Pages...
  From: _____   To: _____

LASER PROOF PROVIDED WITH JOB?
__ Yes   __ No

OTHER INFORMATION
Type information about the job here.

DOCUMENT
Source Pathname: Mac Central:IDG Books:QXP 3.3 Dummies:Sample Pubs:brochure:Symposium Calendar
Destination Pathname: Mac Central:IDG Books:QXP 3.3 Dummies:Sample Pubs:brochure:Report folder:
Last modified: 7:17 PM; 10/16/94
Document Size: 272K
Most recently saved version: 3.31r2 Macintosh format
Document has been saved by the following versions of QuarkXPress:
    3.00
    3.10r0
    3.10G1
    3.31r2 Macintosh format
Total Pages: 1
Page Width: 33"
Page Height: 20.75"

Figure 17-6:
The first page of a service-bureau cover sheet that is included with QuarkXPress. Note that you can import your Collect for Output report into the text box at the bottom of the form.

The 5th Wave   By Rich Tennant

Chapter 18

Working with Other People

*S*ome things are nice to do alone. Running around the track at your local high school, riding a bicycle, making a wood carving, eating a sandwich, flossing your teeth — all are examples of things you usually can manage to do all by your little old lonesome. Notice that we didn't put *publishing* on this list.

For almost everyone we know, publishing isn't a solo activity. The typical publisher or designer using QuarkXPress isn't likely to be doing everything alone. One (or more) of the group made up of writers, editors, artists, photographers, layout and production professionals, art directors, and managers ends up getting involved in producing a publication. Before a document is finished, it may end up being touched by several additional people, including copy editors and reviewers. No, publishing is definitely not a career you should pursue if you want to avoid working with others.

It's also common for more than one writer or designer to work on a document; sometimes the work is even shared by several of each. Each of these people uses a computer, and these computers may not always be similar. For example, one writer could be working on a Macintosh, while another writer is working on a Windows machine, while the designer is using a Power Macintosh. Sharing files becomes an issue, as does the way fonts behave. Often a network links these multiple computers together. A file server on the network lets team members share electronic files. But such an appearance of compatibility is just fiction: the reality is that many of the applications and systems used by workgroups to create publications aren't completely compatible.

Now for the good news: Quark has done a really good job at making QuarkXPress compatible across platforms. And another bright spot: many smart people have gone before us in this quest to make things work well in a publishing workgroup, and we now pass some of this accumulated insight on to you.

Being on a Team

Collaborating with others to produce publications requires a good deal of common sense. This means that, for example, you want to make sure that common elements needed by members of a team are located where they are easy to get to. It also means that standards — the ways in which things are done — need to be established, communicated among those who need to know about them, and followed.

Here are a couple of key points to keep in mind when publishing in a workgroup:

- ✔ Whether or not you use a network, keep a master set of disks; even with a network, keeping a master set is a good backing-up idea.

- ✔ Copy elements from the master disks into a folder (Mac) or directory (Windows) on each person's computer. Update these folders or directories each time a standard element changes on the master disks.

- ✔ If you do use a network, create a folder (Mac) or directory (Windows) to hold all standard elements, and place the folder or directory on a network drive that all members of the group can access.

- ✔ Update the folder or directory of standard elements each time one of these elements changes.

Working in a Mixed Mac/Windows Environment

QuarkXPress is a fully cross-platform application. In case you're wondering what exactly that means, it's simple: QuarkXPress performs pretty much the same whether you use a Macintosh, a Power Macintosh, or Windows. Many users benefit from this cross-platform compatibility. The beneficiaries include corporate users whose various divisions have standardized on different platforms, service bureaus whose clients use a wide variety of machines, and independent publishers or layout artists who deal with multiple clients.

Cross-platform successes

If your workgroup is a mixed Mac/Windows environment, you'll be happy to know that QuarkXPress is functionally the same — with only a few very minor differences — on all platforms. Some elements transfer easily from a Mac to Windows, or vice versa. With some limits, which we've noted in the following list, you can transfer many elements across platforms (Mac to Windows or Windows to Mac):

✔ Graphics not supported by the platform version are replaced during printing with their PICT preview images. However, the graphics links are retained (which means that the graphic "remembers" what kind of picture it really is, even when it disguises itself as a PICT preview image); if you move the document back to the platform it was originated on, the original graphic will be available for printing.

✔ Some PICT previews from the Mac and some Windows metafile previews on Windows will not translate correctly when transferred. To generate a new preview, you need to reimport the graphic or update the link to it.

✔ Although the Windows version of QuarkXPress does not save preview images for the Open dialog box, such previews created on the Mac are retained when you transfer the document back and forth.

✔ Styles are retained and may be imported across platforms.

✔ H&J sets are retained and may be imported across platforms.

✔ Hyphenation exceptions are retained.

✔ Kerning data may be imported to Windows from the Mac, but we don't recommend this procedure because the font characteristics are different enough on each platform that you should customize kerning on each separately.

✔ Document preferences are retained, but the XPress Preferences file (Mac) and XPRESS.PRF (Windows) cannot transfer across platforms.

✔ Color definitions not supported on one platform are translated to their CMYK equivalents. Keep in mind, though, that you can import colors ("append" them in the Edit Colors dialog box, which you access by choosing Edit➪Colors) from one platform to another if you don't want the colors to change to CMYK equivalents.

✔ If you want to move a document that has made use of XTensions across platforms, the receiving platform needs to have the equivalent XTension or the document may not open.

Items that don't transfer across platforms

As you can see, a whole bunch of stuff transfers well across platforms. A few elements, though, do not transfer:

✔ Libraries

✔ Auxiliary dictionaries

✔ Flipped graphics — they won't print or display correctly when moved from Mac to Windows. When transferred back to the Mac, all graphic settings for such pictures (such as flipping and sizing) are lost.

✔ Custom frames created by the Frame Editor on the Mac — they don't import into Windows version 3.1.

Platform differences

They *are* different computers, so it shouldn't surprise you to find out about some basic differences between Windows and Macintosh.

File name differences

One of the first differences between Macintosh and Windows that you'll notice is how files are named. Macintosh files follow these rules:

✔ Names can be as long as 31 characters.

✔ Any character — except for the colon (:) — is allowed in the file name.

✔ Uppercase letters are considered to be different from lowercase letters, so a file named as "MISC" is a separate file from one named "misc" or "Misc."

Windows files follow these rules:

✔ Names are limited to eight characters.

✔ Names can have an extension of up to three characters; a period separates the file name from its extension (for example: MISC.TXT). Often, the program used to create the file adds the 3-character extension.

✔ Any character is allowed in the file name, except for punctuation characters: pipes (|), colons (:), semicolons (;), periods (.), commas (,), asterisks (*), equal signs (=), plus signs (+), brackets ([and]), less-than and greater-than symbols (< and >), question marks (?), and slashes and backslashes (/ and \).

✔ Uppercase and lowercase letters are considered the same, so a file name of "MISC" is the same as "Misc" or "misc." This quirk is important to know because, if you have a file named "MISC" and you create or copy a file named "misc," the "MISC" file will be overwritten.

Because these differences exist, if you work in a mixed Macintosh/Windows environment, you definitely want to consider establishing some file-naming standards to make transfers go smoothly. For example, you might want to ask Macintosh users to follow Windows file-naming rules so that, when files are transferred back and forth, they don't need to be renamed. Using transferrable names is particularly important because, within the QuarkXPress document itself, the original names are still used; when QuarkXPress tries to open these files, it will look for them by their original names.

Don't forget the file extensions used in QuarkXPress: QXD for documents and QXT for templates. Other Quark extensions are QXL for libraries, QDT for auxiliary dictionaries, and KRN for kerning tables, but neither of the two versions can read these files from the other platform.

Typical extensions for cross-platform graphics are TIF for TIFF, EPS for Encapsulated PostScript, AI for Adobe Illustrator, and PCT for PICT. Windows file formats that are not supported on the Mac include PCX, BMP, RLE, MAC, PNT, GIF, CGM, WMF, PLT, CT, and DRW.

Font differences

Major typeface vendors, such as Adobe Systems and Bitstream, offer their typefaces for both Macintosh and Windows users. However, these typefaces are not always the same on both platforms. Differences occur in three areas:

✔ The internal font name is not quite the same for the Mac and Windows versions of a typeface. The discrepancy causes an alert box to appear on your screen; the alert lists the fonts used in the document that are not on your Mac or PC. The solution is to replace all instances of the unrecognized font name with the font name that is correct for the platform you are using. You can make such replacements with the Font Usage dialog box or with the Find/Replace dialog box. For example, the Mac might identify a font as Times Roman, but on a PC, it's TimesRoman (no space between the words).

✔ Sometimes, even when typefaces *do* have the same internal names, other information about the font (tracking, kerning, and so on) may differ between the two platforms, causing text to reflow. Because such reflow can negatively affect your documents, it's a good idea to get into the habit of checking the ends of all your stories to make sure that the text did not get longer or shorter when you brought the document over from another platform.

✔ Symbols often do not translate properly; the character maps for symbol fonts vary on Macintosh and Windows platforms, even when the fonts were created by the same manufacturer. To solve the problem of improper translation of symbols, carefully proofread any documents that you may have brought over from other platforms — and then watch for symbols that are incorrect. You can use the Find/Change dialog box to replace the incorrect symbols.

To minimize font problems, consider using a program like Altsys's Fontographer (214-680-2060) or Ares Software's FontMonger (415-578-9090) to translate your TrueType and PostScript files from Mac to Windows format or vice versa. Using such a program will ensure that the internal font names, symbols, and other information are the same on both platforms.

Standardizing Preferences

Every now and then you learn a simple trick that makes life easier. For example, you learn to roll your car windows up when you park your car for the night after the weatherman has mentioned the possibility of rain. Or you keep a can of soup in your office desk drawer for those days when you are too busy to go out for lunch.

A *really* important (and relatively simple) trick that will save you lots of frustration when publishing in a workgroup is setting common settings and preferences. Members of your workgroup can access some standard elements from a common folder or directory because QuarkXPress can import certain elements that are stored outside QuarkXPress documents. These standard elements include graphics files, libraries, kerning tables, and spelling dictionaries.

Keep in mind that other elements exist within documents and templates and cannot be saved in separate files. These elements include edited tracking tables, style sheets, hyphenation-exception dictionaries, H&J sets, color definitions, Master Pages, and picture-contrast specifications. Style sheets, H&J sets, and color definitions can be imported from one document to another, and it's fairly easy to copy Master Page elements from one document to another. The following sections explain what you can standardize on.

If you define preferences (via Edit⇨Preferences) when no document is open, those preferences become the default preferences that are applied to any new document. If you get into the habit of keeping your XPress Preferences current with your latest preferences, you then can apply those new preferences to previously created documents by clicking Use XPress Preferences in the Nonmatching Preferences alert.

The Nonmatching Preferences alert, shown in Figure 18-1, appears when you open a document that was created with preferences that are different from the current settings. If you are working in a workgroup, assign someone in the workgroup the responsibility of giving a copy of the latest preference settings to every member of the team. That way, you won't need to worry about things such as documents reflowing when they are opened on various machines in the workgroup.

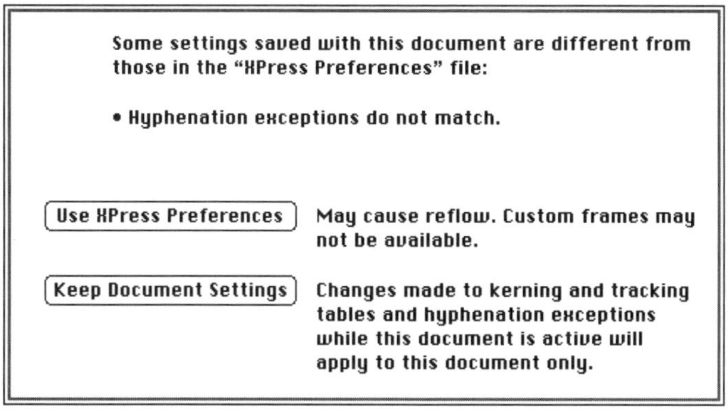

Figure 18-1:
You can
apply master
preference
settings to
existing
documents
by clicking
Use XPress
Preferences
in this alert.

Some settings saved with this document are different from those in the "XPress Preferences" file:

• Hyphenation exceptions do not match.

[Use XPress Preferences]   May cause reflow. Custom frames may not be available.

[Keep Document Settings]   Changes made to kerning and tracking tables and hyphenation exceptions while this document is active will apply to this document only.

Kerning Tables

Changes to kerning tables are part of a document's preferences if they are made when the document is open. If you make kerning table changes when no document is open, they become the new kerning preferences. You also can import and export kerning tables from one document to another.

After you have changed the kerning values for a particular typeface, you can export the new values as a text file that can be imported into other documents. Figure 18-2 shows the Kerning Values dialog box that you access by choosing Utilities⇨Kerning Table Edit. As you can see, an Export button sits at the bottom right of the dialog box. When you click on this button, you create a kerning file. Figure 18-3 shows the dialog box you see when importing previously created kerning files.

By periodically exporting kerning tables and then importing them into QuarkXPress when no documents are open, you can update the global preferences set in XPress Preferences so that all future documents use these new kerning values.

Figure 18-2:
The Export button lets you create a kerning file for exchange among documents.

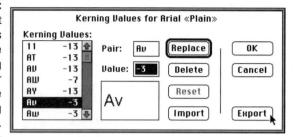

Figure 18-3:
The dialog box for importing kerning files. In this example, we are importing the kerning files for the Arial Plain typeface.

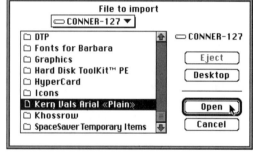

Color Definitions

In a workgroup, it can be very useful to keep color definitions consistent among documents. For example, your company may have specific corporate-identity colors that need to be used as a second color in all documents.

You can import colors created in other documents by clicking the Append button in the Colors dialog box (Edit⇨Colors), as shown in Figure 18-4. After you click the Append button, a dialog box will appear so that you can search for the file with the color definitions you want. All colors that are defined in the other document, but not in the current document, will be imported.

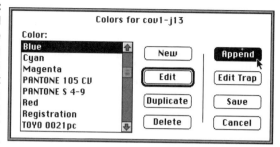

Figure 18-4:
The Append
button in the
Colors dialog
box lets you
import
colors
defined in
another
document.

Dictionaries

To add words to the built-in spelling dictionary, you need to either create an Auxiliary Dictionary (Utilities⇨Auxiliary Dictionary) or open an existing Auxiliary Dictionary. Figure 18-5 shows the Auxiliary Dictionary dialog box. Any number of documents can use the same dictionary.

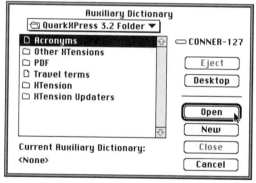

Figure 18-5:
You can
create or
open
Auxiliary
spelling
dictionaries
using the
Auxiliary
Dictionaries
dialog box.

Graphics and Text Files

The simplest method of ensuring that the latest versions of your workgroup's standardized graphics and text are used is to keep them all in one folder or directory, either on each computer or on a network drive. This method works well as long as these elements are updated in the central folder or directory. Keeping everyone's work in one place does carry one drawback, though: it does not ensure that graphics and text are updated in QuarkXPress documents if the elements are changed after they were first placed into the documents.

We suggest that you gather the members of your workgroup together and decide how to keep standard files current. You might want to consider using a QuarkXPress library to hold common text and graphics.

QuarkXPress libraries are a great aid in keeping documents consistent. Because libraries are stored in their own files, you can put them in common folders or directories. You can even access them across a network.

Templates

As your workgroup builds documents, you'll likely develop templates that you'll want to use and use again. QuarkXPress can save a document as a template. The only difference between a document and a template is that you use Save As, rather than Save, to save a template. (If you used Save, you would overwrite the template, making it unavailable for use in creating new documents.)

Even with templates, you will need to be able to transfer basic layout elements from one document to another. QuarkXPress lets you import ("Append") styles and related items.

Styles

The Style Sheets dialog box (Edit⇨Style Sheets) lets you import styles from other QuarkXPress documents and templates. In Figure 18-6, you can see that we have positioned the pointer at the Append button; this is the button you would click to import styles.

Figure 18-6:
You can import styles from other QuarkXPress documents by clicking the Append button in the Style Sheets dialog box.

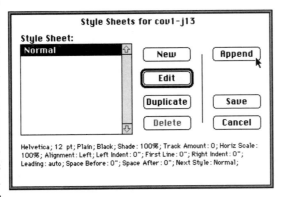

By importing styles with no document open, you copy all new styles into your global defaults, which means that they become part of your default preferences. This technique is a handy way of bringing new styles into your default settings without affecting existing styles.

H&J Sets

You import H&J sets in a manner much like the way you import styles: just click on the Append button in the H&Js dialog box (Edit⇨H&Js), as shown in Figure 18-7. If an H&J set that you are importing has the same name as an H&J set in your current document, you see a warning and you also get a chance to save the imported styles in the current document or in the general preferences.

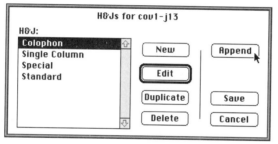

Figure 18-7: The Append button in the H&Js dialog box lets you import H&J sets from other documents.

If you import the H&J sets when no document is open, you will copy all new H&J sets into your global defaults. This is a handy way of bringing new H&J sets into your default settings without affecting existing H&J sets.

Master Pages

You can move Master Pages from one document to another by first copying the master page items into a Quark library. Here are the steps to follow when copying Master Pages across documents:

1. **Open a library (File⇨Open⇨Library) or create a library (File⇨New⇨Library).**

2. **Open the document with the Master Page that you want to copy and display that Master Page (Page⇨Display).**

You might want to change the view to Fit in Window (⌘-O) so that you can see the entire page.

3. **Select the Item tool and then select all items (Edit⇨Select All).**

4. **Drag (or copy and paste) the items into the open library and release the mouse button.**

   Every element on the Master Page will appear in its own library box (see the bottom library box in the library shown in Figure 18-8).

5. **Open the document that you want to copy the Master Page into.**

6. **Insert a new, blank Master Page into the second document.**

7. **Drag (or copy and paste) the library item containing the first document's Master Page elements into the new Master Page (this Master Page is at the bottom of Figure 18-8).**

8. **Rename the new Master Page so that you can remember it.**

   That's it!

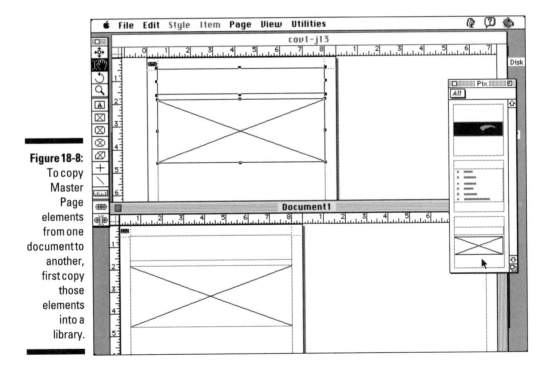

Figure 18-8:
To copy Master Page elements from one document to another, first copy those elements into a library.

Part VI
Guru in Training

The 5th Wave   **By Rich Tennant**

5th Wave Power Tip: To increase application speed, punch the Command Key over and over and over as rapidly as possible. The computer will sense your impatience and move your data along quicker than if you just sat and waited. Hint: This also works on elevator buttons and cross walk signals.

In this part ...

You're about ready to graduate from novice to expert, and the chapters in this part will give you the extra credits you need to graduate with honors. QuarkXPress is aimed at publishing experts, even though it can be used by almost anyone. After you've learned about these techniques, you'll find yourself the local guru — the expert that your colleagues come to with questions. Enjoy the fame and attention!

Chapter 19
Installing QuarkXPress

· ·

In This Chapter

▶ What to do before installing QuarkXPress

▶ How to install QuarkXPress for Macintosh, Power Macintosh, or Windows

▶ How to install multiple copies

· ·

*T*he documentation that comes with your QuarkXPress package contains detailed information on how to install QuarkXPress. But we tell you how to do it here, too, just in case you've misplaced your documentation or have had a problem with your computer that requires you to install the program again.

Before You Install

Whenever you install or upgrade any computer software, you can do a few things to make sure that the installation goes smoothly. This rule applies to installing QuarkXPress, too. Getting ready to install QuarkXPress involves temporarily turning off background programs that could possibly interfere with the Installer or Upgrader. It's possible for the installation or upgrade to be successful without disabling background programs, but you could end up getting an error message later when you try to open QuarkXPress.

Before installing QuarkXPress for Macintosh or Power Macintosh

Before you begin to install QuarkXPress on a Macintosh or Power Macintosh, disable all control panels (CDEVs), non-Systems extensions (INITs), and virus detection software. If you are using a version of System 7, hold down the Shift key while you restart the computer; this action disables System extensions and control panels. If you are using a version of System 6, move any CDEVs and INITs that you can do without outside of the System Folder and restart the computer.

The Quark disks you are using should be virus-free: Quark thoroughly tests the disks for viruses before they ship the disks. But, if it'll make you feel more comfortable about the installation, you can check the Quark application disks for viruses first and then you can disable your virus protection software before you install the program.

Before installing QuarkXPress for Windows

Before you install QuarkXPress on a Windows machine, you need to disable programs that might be running in the background. These programs are found in your StartUp group (in the Windows Program Manager), CONFIG.SYS file, and AUTOEXEC.BAT file.

Changes to StartUp

Applications that are present in the StartUp window load every time Windows starts up. Disable these startup programs either by moving the StartUp group to another group or by giving the "StartUp" group a different name.

Also, temporarily disable the Windows Screen Saver via Control Panel⇨Desktop⇨Screen Saver Name drop-down list⇨(None).

Restart Windows to make sure that all these changes have taken effect.

Changes to CONFIG.SYS and AUTOEXEC.BAT

Before you make any changes to your computer's CONFIG.SYS and AUTOEXEC.BAT files, make copies of them.

Put a REM out statement ("REM") in any phrases that are not required when starting up your computer. Here is a list of items that we recommend you temporarily disable: device drivers, CD-ROM and multimedia drivers, terminal emulation software, network software, screen savers, disk imaging utilities, TSRs, UNDELETE, and DOSSHELL.

✔ Do not "rem out" CONFIG.SYS statements that contain the following words: HIMEM.SYS, DOS, FILES, SMARTDRV, STACKS, or COMMAND.COM.

✔ Likewise, do not "rem out" AUTOEXEC.BAT statements that contain @ECHO, COMMAND.COM, PROMPT, SMARTDRV, SHARE, PATH, SET TEMP, DOSKEY, IFX, NETX, OCI, IPX/SPX, or LOGIN.

After you have made these changes to the CONFIG.SYS and AUTOEXEC.BAT files, save the modified versions of these files and restart your computer.

If you need additional information about modifying your CONFIG.SYS and AUTOEXEC.BAT files, consult your Microsoft Windows documentation. Or, if you have one, ask your friendly System Administrator to help you.

Installing QuarkXPress

In a perfect world, software would install itself. You'd buy the package of QuarkXPress, place it next to your computer, peel off the shrink wrap, and walk to the nearest park to feed the pigeons. Everything else would be automatic; you'd return to your computer a few hours later to find the software loaded and ready to go.

Okay, so it's not a perfect world. But installing QuarkXPress, while not a walk in the park, is pretty easy — especially when you follow the instructions.

What happens when, after you install QuarkXPress, you realize that you've forgotten to install a word processing filter that you need? No problem. On the Mac, simply drag-copy the filter into your QuarkXPress folder or directory. On Windows, rerun the QuarkXPress install program, uncheck the box next to QuarkXPress (since it's already installed), and check the boxes next to the filters that you need.

Installing QuarkXPress for Macintosh

Follow these steps to install QuarkXPress on a Macintosh.

1. **Insert Program Disk 1 and open its icon when it appears on your screen.**

   You see the window shown in Figure 19-1.

Figure 19-1:
The window
that appears
on your
screen
when you
insert
Program
Disk 1.

2. Double-click on the QuarkXPress Installer icon to begin the installation.

You'll see the alert shown in Figure 19-2, which lets you know that you are going to be asked where to place QuarkXPress and its associated files.

3. Continue to follow the instructions that appear on your screen.

You can choose which XTensions and word processing filters to install simply by placing a check in the box next to the appropriate item. QuarkXPress copies all selected XTensions and filters into a folder named XTension, which is created during the installation. QuarkXPress also creates a folder named PDF, which stores the Printer Description Files that you will be using.

4. A message appears, letting you know that installation was successful.

Restart your Macintosh before using QuarkXPress. Oh, by the way, don't forget to turn the CDEVs, INITs, and virus detection software back on.

Installing QuarkXPress for Power Macintosh

Installing QuarkXPress on a Power Macintosh is similar to installing it on a Macintosh, with some variations based on the fact that the software comes on CDs. Follow these steps to install QuarkXPress on a Power Macintosh.

1. **Be sure that you have disabled CDEVs, INITs, and virus protection software (except for the ones that allow you to use your CD-ROM drive).**

2. **Insert the CD into your CD-ROM drive and insert the Installer diskette into your disk drive.**

3. **Double-click on the QuarkXPress Installer icon and follow the instructions that appear on your screen.**

   You can choose which XTensions and word processing filters to install simply by placing a check in the box next to the item. QuarkXPress copies all selected XTensions and filters into a folder named XTension, which is created during the installation. QuarkXPress also creates a folder named PDF, which stores the Printer Description Files that you will be using. The Installer program also installs the AppleScript Lib file in your computer's System Folder; this file is required for QuarkXPress for Power Macintosh to run.

4. **A message appears, letting you know that installation was successful.**

   Restart your Macintosh before using QuarkXPress and turn the CDEVs, INITs, and virus detection software back on.

Installing QuarkXPress for Windows

Follow these steps to install QuarkXPress for Windows.

1. **Follow the instructions given in the "Before Installing QuarkXPress for Windows" section earlier in this chapter.**

2. **Launch Windows and then insert Program Disk 1 into your computer's floppy drive.**

3. **In the Program Manager, choose Run from the File menu; then enter A:\Install or B:\Install, depending on which drive Program Disk 1 is in, and follow the instructions on the screen.**

4. **In the dialog box shown in Figure 19-3, click the Customize button if you want to select some, but not all, of the XTensions and filers.**

QuarkXPress copies all selected XTensions and filters into a subdirectory named XTension, which is created during the installation. QuarkXPress also creates a subdirectory named PDF, which stores the Printer Description Files that you will be using.

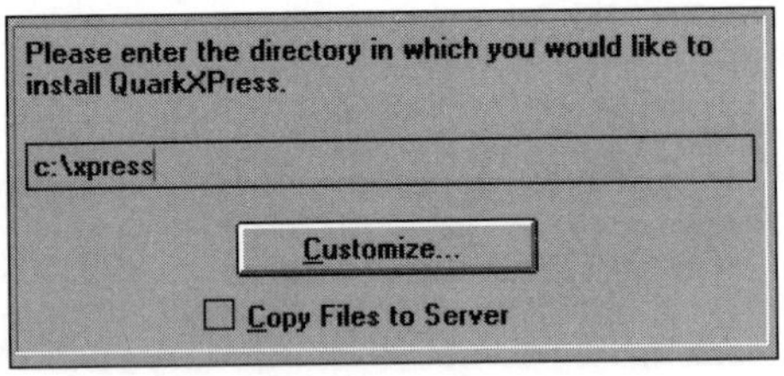

Figure 19-3:
You can
choose to
customize
the list of
XTensions
and filters
that are
installed.

> Please enter the directory in which you would like to
> install QuarkXPress.
>
> `c:\xpress`
>
> [Customize...]
>
> ☐ Copy Files to Server

Installing Multiple Copies of QuarkXPress

Some users may need to install several individual copies of QuarkXPress. This
section discusses some steps that you can take to make the process of installing multiple copies go more smoothly.

Installing multiple copies of QuarkXPress for the Mac and Power Mac

If you are installing several individual copies of QuarkXPress, you'll save time
by using the Copy Registration feature of the QuarkXPress Installer. Copy
Registration enables you to copy the User Registration File information from the
first installation and use it in subsequent installations.

Before you copy the User Registration File information, though, you need to
completely install one copy of QuarkXPress. The version of the User Registration File that you want to install must match the version of the Installer (for
example, you cannot use a 3.1 User Registration File with a 3.3 Installer).

Have the User Registration Disk from the first installation on hand. You will
need it to use Copy Registration. (You will need the registration disks from
every copy.) Then follow these steps:

1. **Insert Program Disk 1 and double-click the QuarkXPress Installer.**

2. **Click the Copy Registration button.**

   The "Select the User Registration File to use" dialog box will be displayed.

3. **Click Eject to eject Program Disk 1.**

4. **Insert the User Registration Disk from the completed installation and select the User Registration File on that disk.**

5. **Click Open.**

6. **The Installer will retrieve the User Information File information and eject the disk.**

7. **Insert Program Disk 1 again when prompted and complete the registration.**

   The registration dialog boxes will display information entered during the previous installation.

8. **When registration is complete, click Install; Program Disk 1 will be ejected.**

9. **Insert the blank User Registration Disk from the new QuarkXPress package you are installing.**

   The User Registration File containing the new serial number and machine configuration will be placed on the disk and the disk ejected.

10. **Insert Program Disk 1 and proceed with the installation.**

11. **Write your name and address on the User Registration Disk and mail it to Quark using the prepaid envelope included in the QuarkXPress package.**

Installing multiple copies of QuarkXPress for Windows

QuarkXPress for Windows lets you install multiple copies in a similar fashion. The Copy Registration feature of the QuarkXPress Installer lets you copy the User Registration File information from the first installation and use it in subsequent installations. You do need the User Registration Disk from the first installation to use Copy Registration.

Completely install one copy of QuarkXPress before using the Copy Registration feature. The version of the User Registration File must match the version of the Installer (for example, you cannot use a 3.1 User Registration File with a 3.3 Installer).

To install QuarkXPress using the Copy Registration button, follow these steps:

1. **Insert Program Disk 1 and double-click the QuarkXPress Installer (INSTALL.EXE).**

2. **Click the Copy Registration button.**

3. **Insert the User Registration Disk from the first installation when prompted.**

4. **Click OK.**

   The Installer will retrieve the User Information File information.

5. **Complete the registration screens.**

   The registration screens display information entered during the previous installation.

6. **When you're prompted to do so, insert the blank User Registration Disk from the new QuarkXPress package you are installing.**

   The reginfo.dat file containing the new serial number and machine configuration will be placed on the disk.

7. **Insert Program Disk 1 when prompted and proceed with the installation.**

8. **Write your name and address on the User Registration Disk; then, using the prepaid envelope provided, mail the User Registration Disk to Quark, Inc.**

Chapter 20

Details for Windows Users

● ●

In This Chapter

▶ How Windows and the Mac differ

▶ How Windows QuarkXPress differs from the Mac version

● ●

*F*ace it: the Mac is the platform of choice for desktop publishing. But Windows has been making inroads in the last couple of years, and top programs like QuarkXPress are now available in Windows versions that have almost all the same features as their Mac counterparts. The few differences between the two Quark programs are almost always due to differences between the Mac and Windows. Whether you're a cross-platform user who needs to understand the discrepancies between the two versions or a Windows user looking for advice specific to your needs, read on.

But Windows users should read the rest of the book, too: throughout the book, Windows icons (like that handy little gizmo to the left of this paragraph) point out things that are different for Windows QuarkXPress. Otherwise, you can assume that what is described for the Mac is true for you, too. Another great reference that goes into more detail (once you graduate from your Quark novitiate) is our very own *QuarkXPress for Windows Designer Handbook,* also published by IDG Books Worldwide. However, it is current only through Version 3.1 for Windows and won't cover some of the newest features, such as EfiColor, polygon text boxes, automatic file backup, smart quotes, and drag-and-drop text editing. But do note that we cover those features in *this* book!

Both Windows-only and cross-platform users should make a point to read Part V, which deals with how to work with others. The chapters there focus on the kinds of Windows-versus-Mac issues that you'll likely come across in working with outsiders. Our *Macworld QuarkXPress 3.2/3.3 Bible* (also from IDG Books) covers cross-platform issues, as well as all QuarkXPress features, in greater detail. Take a look at that book, too, after you get comfortable with QuarkXPress.

Where Mac and Windows Differ

Before we get to the differences between the Mac and Windows versions of QuarkXPress itself, it's helpful to know about some differences between the Mac and Windows. Why look at such basic stuff in a book on QuarkXPress? Because the underlying platform differences affect operations everywhere— including QuarkXPress.

Keyboard

PC and Mac keyboards may look alike, but actually they differ in two major ways.

First off, some of the control keys are different, at least in their appearance and names. The Mac has a key that looks like a butterfly (⌘); it's called the Command key, and it's basically the same as a PC's Ctrl key. There's also a key labeled Option; it's basically the same as the PC's Alt. Some Mac keyboards have a key labeled Ctrl — it's *not* the same as the Command key or the PC's Ctrl key. Throughout this book, Windows users, unless instructed otherwise, should substitute Ctrl for ⌘ and Alt for Option for all keyboard sequences.

The other significant difference is in how you delete. PCs use a key labeled Del or Delete to delete text to the right of the cursor (the thing that Mac folks call the pointer) and a Backspace key to delete text to the left of the cursor (this key is a holdover from typewriters). Some Mac keyboards have a Del key, but many don't. On a Mac, the Backspace key is called Delete. Where a PC user would hit Del, you use Shift-Delete on a Mac. That can feel weird — QuarkXPress for Mac won't let you use the Del intstead of Shift-Delete to delete a range of text — even on keyboards that have the Del key. Instead, you can use Del only for one character at a time.

You'll probably notice all those underlines in your Windows menus and dialog box options. Those underlines mean you can access a function by holding the Alt key and pressing the underlined letter. So, even if there's a shortcut assigned to a specific function, you always have the option of using the underlined-letter sequence. For example, Ctrl+P is the shortcut to print in QuarkXPress — but you also can use Alt+F Alt+P, which opens the File menu and then the Print dialog box.

We use the command underlines in text only when we're talking about Windows-specific actions. Otherwise, we leave them out, and our descriptions apply to both the Mac and Windows versions.

You may have noticed that this book uses hyphens to connect keys for a Mac sequence but a + to show key-connections for a Windows sequence. What gives? Nothing more than different styles on each platform. In the context of keyboard shortcuts, a - and a + are the same thing. Of course, to a mathematician, they're not at all the same — but that's a different story.

Files and directories

Everyone knows that the PC has a dumb naming structure: names of eight letters followed by a period and then up to three more letters. On a Mac, when you name a file you can type up to 31 characters, including spaces and punctuation, except for a colon (:). On a PC, that three-letter suffix, called an extension, identifies the file type. For QuarkXPress, the extension is .QXD; similarly, .QXT designates a QuarkXPress template, .QXL a QuarkXPress library, .QDT a spelling dictionary, and .XXT a QuarkXTension add-on program. On a Mac, you just look for the icons. See Table 20-1 for comparisons.

On a PC, a *directory* contains files; on a Mac, a *folder* does. Except for the difference in names, the two file containers are the same. Their similarity becomes clear as you use Windows: it calls directories folders, too. But don't confuse the Program Manager's *groups* with folders. A group is a collection of shortcuts (called aliases on a Mac) to programs and files — the structure of files and programs in the File Manager is the real structure. On a Mac, you don't find two views of your system, but just the Finder, which is basically the same as the Windows File Manager.

Environment controls

On a Mac, there's a folder called Control Panels (it's also available via the Apple menu) that contains mini-programs to change system settings, like colors, network options, and mouse tracking. In Windows, most of these mini-programs are stored in a program called Control Panel.

The Control Panel programs and other mini-programs let you manage basic operations in Windows. We'll cover the three most important to a QuarkXPress user: printing, multitasking (switching between active programs), and fonts.

Printing

You set up your printers in the Windows Control Panel, but you also can switch printers by using the Printer Setup dialog box in your programs. (Sometimes this Printer Setup dialog box has its own entry in the File menu; sometimes it's an option in the Print dialog box. How you access the dialog box depends on the design of the program you're using. In QuarkXPress, the Printer Setup dialog box is available both ways.) On a Mac, you have to use a program called the Chooser to switch printers — a real pain. The new System 7.5 lets you change printers from within your program, but only if you have System 7.5 and its QuickDraw GX option installed. Considering that this option takes about 4MB of RAM and offers a host of sophisticated features that practically no programs take advantage of, chances are good that you don't have it installed, even if you run System 7.5. Figure 20-1 shows the different setups for the print features. Similar features with different names are identified by giving each equivalent feature the same letter.

Figure 20-1:
The Mac and Windows handle printing differently, so the printing controls used by the two versions of QuarkXPress are arranged differently. The letters indicate features that have different names on the platforms but do the same thing.

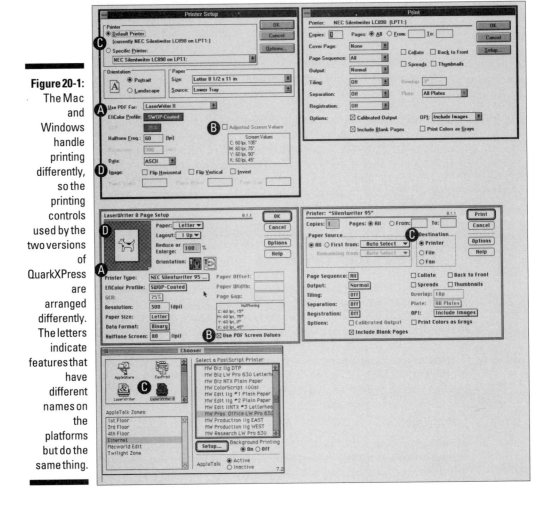

Multitasking

If you're using QuarkXPress, you probably have a pretty good system — an 040-based Mac or Power Mac, or a 486-based or Pentium-based PC. After all, publishing demands solid resources. And you probably have more than one program loaded in memory at a time. The fancy name for this is *multitasking* (back in System 6 days, the Mac called it MultiFinder).

On the Mac, all active programs are available for switching to and from via that pull-down menu at the far right of the menu bar — the Application menu, although practically no one knows its name. The currently active program's icon appears in the upper left corner; if you select it, a menu of all active programs pops down. In Windows, all active programs are available through the Task Manager, which you select by entering Ctrl+Esc. If you minimize a program — that is, if you click the down-pointing triangle at the upper right of the program's menu — its icon also appears at the bottom of the Windows desktop. You can double-click that icon (if it isn't obscured by another window) to make it active, or you can use the Task Manager.

Note that in Windows, you can cycle among open programs by pressing Alt+Tab.

Fonts

Both Macs and Windows PCs support TrueType and PostScript Type 1 fonts (usually through Adobe Type Manager), but fonts are slightly different on the two platforms. In some cases the names differ only slightly, such as Helvetica Compressed on the Mac and HelveticaCompressed in Windows. In most cases, Windows fonts have some characters — like $1/4$ and ± — that Mac fonts usually don't. At the same time, though, Mac fonts have some characters — such as Σ, ✓, ✍, and fi — that Windows fonts usually don't (even if they do have the same name).

It's also possible that fonts with the same name will have different spacing and even character widths. This situation usually occurs with older fonts created when an Iron Wall stood between Mac and PC — back in the olden days of the 80s when developers didn't worry about cross-platform users.

You can translate fonts from Mac format to Windows format, or vice versa, with programs like Ares Software's FontMonger and Altsys Corp.'s Fontographer, which are available for both Windows and the Mac. Our experience shows that Fontographer is a more stable product — its translated fonts invariably work, while FontMonger's fonts sometimes work and sometimes don't. We also recommend that you do your translation on the Mac; because the Mac's internal file format is weird compared to the PC's, Mac font files created on a PC don't always survive the translation process. Font files are more susceptible to this than data files (like QuarkXPress, graphics, or text files) because, on the Mac, a font is a bit like a program and so it has resource information that can easily get corrupted when stored on a PC. We're not saying that you *can't* create Mac fonts on Windows, just that we've had better luck creating them on the Mac. You also can use these programs to translate PostScript to TrueType or vice versa.

Table 20-1	Mac and Windows Equivalents	
Item	*Windows*	*Macintosh*
Keys		
	Ctrl	⌘ (Command)
	Alt	Option
	no equivalent	Control
	Del	Del
	Delete	Backspace
	right mouse button	Option-mouse button (or ⌘-mouse or Control-mouse button in some programs)
close window	Ctrl+F4	⌘-W
exit program	Alt+F4	⌘-Q
Files		
Document	.QXD	
Template	.QXT	
Library	.QXL	
XTensions	.XXT	

Not Quite Clones

Even considering the differences between Windows and the Mac, QuarkXPress has some other differences that have less to do with platform differences than, well, just differences in what Quark decided to do on each version. The list is not huge, but it will look bigger than it is because of the illustrations that show the differences.

View controls

To change your view percentage on a Mac, you use Control-V — remember, this is not the Mac's ⌘ key or the PC's Ctrl key — to quickly highlight the view-percentage field (at the bottom left corner of the QuarkXPress screen) so that you can enter a new zoom amount. There is no equivalent on the PC, probably because there is no Control key or equivalent on a PC.

Quark's Mac and Windows versions differ in a couple of ways in their Application Preferences dialog boxes (⌘-Shift-Option-Y or Ctrl+Alt+Shift+Y), as Figure 20-2 shows.

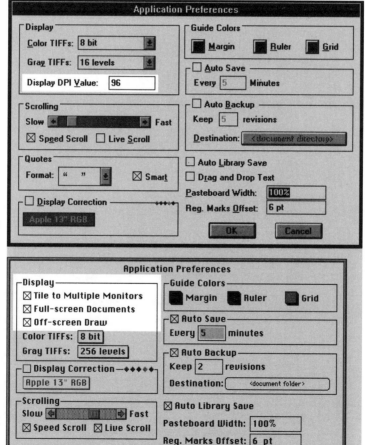

Figure 20-2:
Differences in Windows (top) and Mac (bottom) video support result in a few different options in the Applications Preferences dialog box.

One way is that Windows QuarkXPress offers an option for Display DPI Value. This option is in essence a zoom control that stays in place for all QuarkXPress documents until you change it again; if you make the number larger, QuarkXPress shows a more magnified image.

Another way is that Windows video supports multiple resolutions — you probably know that you can change your desktop from, say, 640 by 480 pixels to 800 by 600 or 1024 by 768. Such a change makes everything smaller but increases the size of the working area. Until 1994, Macs couldn't work this trick easily, and today switching resolutions on a Mac still requires a PC-style monitor, so QuarkXPress doesn't offer this capability for the Mac. The Mac offers several controls to handle the display of documents across multiple monitors. Since Windows doesn't support tiled monitors, there is no equivalent in Windows QuarkXPress.

The most obvious difference between Windows and the Mac is the View menu. First, they're in different locations, as you can see from Figure 20-3.

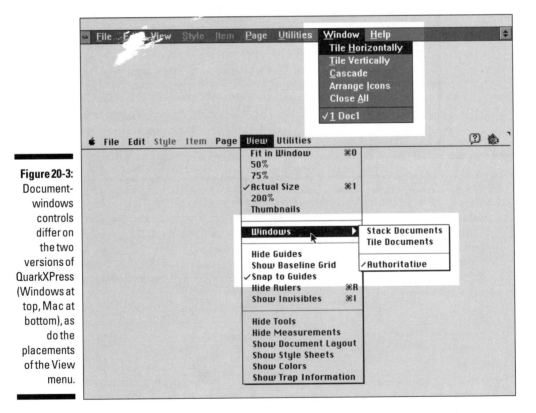

Figure 20-3: Document-windows controls differ on the two versions of QuarkXPress (Windows at top, Mac at bottom), as do the placements of the View menu.

Second, the controls over how document windows display are in different places, as Figure 20-3 shows. Both versions of QuarkXPress support tiled views — the automatic arrangement of multiple open QuarkXPress layouts. But the Windows version supports several arrangements — tile horizontally (left to right), tile vertically (top to bottom), cascade (overlapping stacks), and iconized — while the Mac version supports only vertical tiling and cascading (stacking). Finally, Windows QuarkXPress also has a menu command to close all the document windows; on the Mac, you can use the keyboard shortcut ⌘-Option-W (for which there is no Windows equivalent).

Typography

Because Windows doesn't support ligatures — letters that are merged together, such as *fi* and *fl* — Windows QuarkXPress doesn't offer the ligature controls in the Typographic Preferences dialog box (⌘-Option-Y or Ctrl+Alt+Y) that the Mac version does. Figure 20-4 shows the different dialog boxes. If you want to use ligatures in Windows, you need to use a typeface that has them as symbols. Note that if you use ligatures on the Mac and bring the QuarkXPress document into Windows QuarkXPress, the ligatures will be replaced by the standard letter combinations, and they'll be translated back into ligatures when loaded into Mac QuarkXPress. It's unlikely — but possible in some rare circumstances — that this ligature replacement could affect the text flow as the file is transferred back and forth.

Mac QuarkXPress comes with a utility called Font Creator that, if you install it, lets you create new variants of typefaces — as long as they are PostScript Type 1 Multiple Master typefaces. Windows QuarkXPress has no such utility, but Adobe Type Manager 3.0 (a must-have font-scaler for anyone doing publishing) does, so you can use it to get the same result. Figure 20-5 shows Mac QuarkXPress's multiple-master editing facility and Windows Adobe Type Manager 3.0's. Note that there are other programs that let you create variants of fonts, such as Ares Software's Font Chameleon, which is available in Mac and Windows versions.

As must-have as Adobe Type Manager is, the 3.0 version is a memory and resource hog. It's so greedy that it won't work on many systems — even with 16MB of memory — that have a network or other DOS-based device drivers installed (in AUTOEXEC.BAT and CONFIG.SYS). That means you may not be able to use the program. In that case, you can use the earlier 2.5 or 2.6 version, but they don't support multiple-master editing.

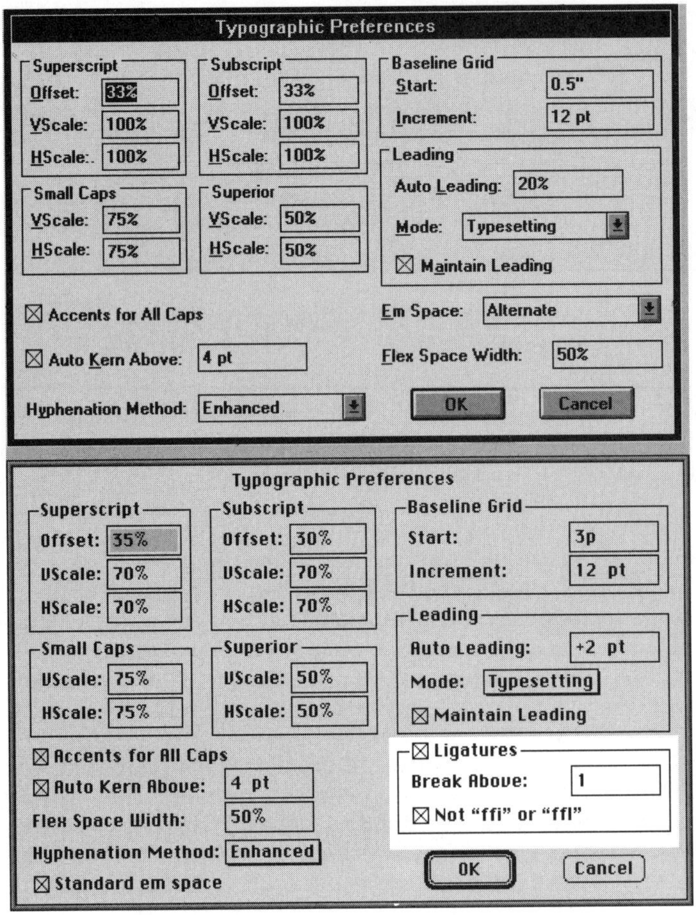

Figure 20-4: Windows QuarkXPress (top) offers no ligature controls because Windows does not support ligatures. The Mac does (bottom).

Font names on the Mac and Windows can differ, so even if you have the same fonts installed on both systems, you may get a message saying that a font is missing when you open a document. You get the opportunity, if you select the List Fonts button, to tell QuarkXPress immediately which font to use instead. Or you can use the Utilities⇨Font Usage option to open the Font Usage dialog box, which lets you do the same thing at any time.

Linked objects

Both versions of QuarkXPress support *hot links* to objects in other programs. On the Mac, the method is called Publish and Subscribe; on Windows, it's called Object Linking and Embedding (OLE for short). In both cases, the theory is that

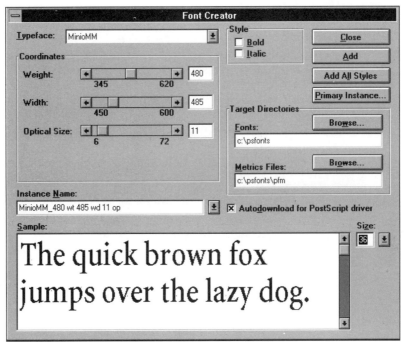

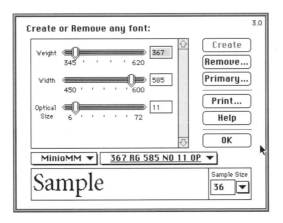

Figure 20-5:
Mac
QuarkXPress
comes with
a utility to
create new
variants of
Multiple
Master fonts
within
QuarkXPress
(bottom). In
Windows,
you need to
use a
separate
program like
Adobe Type
Manager 3.0
(top).

you can have your layout retrieve the latest version of a chart or other graphic as soon as the graphic is changed in the original program. In practice, using hot links requires significant trade-offs, too: you can't link text this way unless you want it converted into an image; if both programs aren't loaded, the object won't get updated automatically; you need a great deal of memory to use this feature; and you can't use most of QuarkXPress's image controls on these images. We recommend that you don't worry too much about them.

But, if you do use hot links, take a look at Figures 20-6 and 20-7. Figure 20-6 shows the differences in menu options. On Windows, you get two sets of choices. The first set is Paste Special and Paste Link, which you can use if you've created an OLE object in another program by selecting it and copying it to the Windows clipboard (just using Ctrl+C or Ctrl+X will do that). Whether it's an embedded objected (Paste Special) or a linked object (Paste Link) depends on the application that created it. The second set is just Insert Object. You use Insert Object to launch a program that you want to create the OLE object in. (Figure 20-7 shows the Paste Special and Insert Object dialog boxes.)

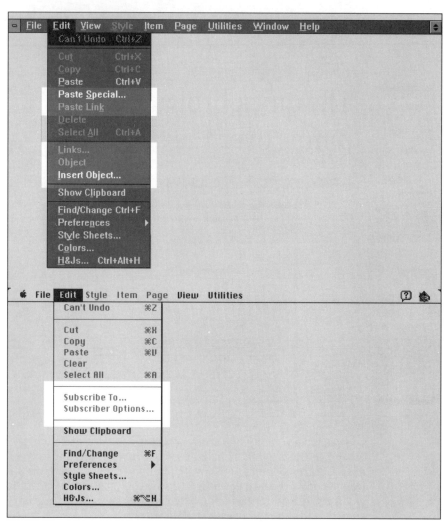

Figure 20-6:
Because of different hot-link technologies, the Windows (top) and Mac (bottom) versions of QuarkXPress have different menu options for linked file import.

Then there're the Links and Object options, which let you update and edit an OLE object, respectively, whether it was brought into QuarkXPress via Paste Link, Paste Special, or Insert Object. On the Mac, you have Subscribe To and Subscriber Options to import and update, respectively, a hot-linked object. The Mac's Subscriber options are basically the same as the Windows Links and Object options.

Figure 20-7:
Two options for creating hot links in Windows: by pasting in a link created on the Windows clipboard by another program (top), or by deciding what kind of object you want linked in and then launching a program that can create it (bottom).

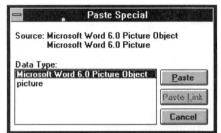
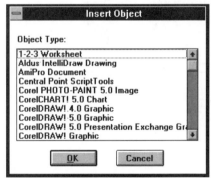

Item manipulation

When you create objects in QuarkXPress — lines, picture boxes, and text boxes — they are automatically layered so that the most recently created or pasted one is on top of the previous one. Sometimes you'll want to change their stacking order so that a particular box overprints another. Both versions of QuarkXPress offer controls to move objects, but Windows QuarkXPress offers finer controls. In both versions, you can send an object to the front or the back via controls in the Item menu (see Figure 20-8). But in Windows QuarkXPress, you also can move an object one layer at a time, via the Bring Forward and Send Backward options in the Item menu. (To get these options in the Mac version of QuarkXPress, you have to hold the Option key before selecting the Item menu.)

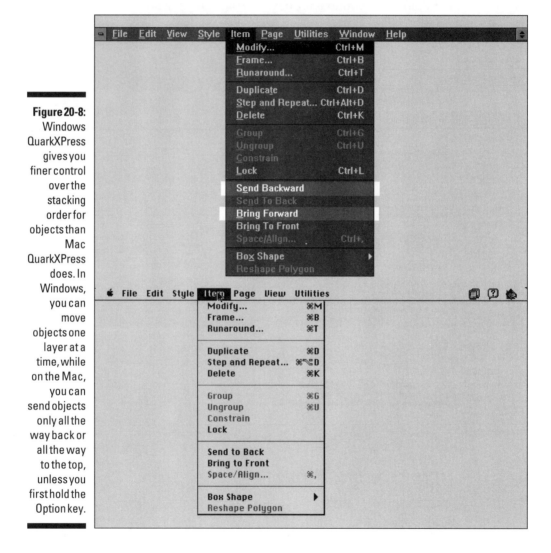

Figure 20-8:
Windows QuarkXPress gives you finer control over the stacking order for objects than Mac QuarkXPress does. In Windows, you can move objects one layer at a time, while on the Mac, you can send objects only all the way back or all the way to the top, unless you first hold the Option key.

Mac QuarkXPress comes with a utility called Frame Editor that lets you create custom frames for use with your text and picture boxes. (Figure 20-9 shows this utility's opening dialog box.) Windows QuarkXPress can use these frames — it imports them directly from the QuarkXPress document, so don't worry about transferring a special file over — but it can't create its own because there is no Windows version of Frame Editor.

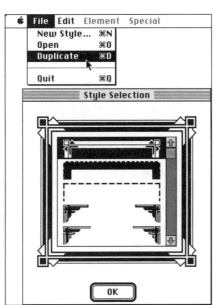

EPS pages

Through the Save Page as EPS dialog box (⌘-Shift-Option-S or Ctrl+Alt+Shift+S), you can export a page of your layout as an EPS file. There's a slight difference in the dialog box between the Mac and Windows versions, as Figure 20-10 shows. The Mac version has options for Mac and PC files, and the Windows version has no such options. The option for Mac or PC format refers to the preview header — the bitmap embedded in the EPS file that programs like QuarkXPress use to display the EPS image on screen (the actual PostScript code in the file is what's used for printing). The Mac and Windows use different formats for the preview header — the Mac uses PICT and Windows uses TIFF. On Mac QuarkXPress, you can decide which preview QuarkXPress will use; but, on the PC, you have no choice but to have a TIFF preview or no preview at all.

Interestingly, the Mac has no option that lets you choose not to have a preview. Because every Mac program that handled EPS files expects a PICT file, there was never a reason for Quark's developers to offer an option to disable the preview. However, there's really no reason to disable the preview in Windows QuarkXPress — the worst that will happen for 99 percent of the programs out there is that you'll get a gray box or a big *X* on screen when you import the EPS file, but it will print correctly. The same might happen if you load a Mac file into a Windows program.

Figure 20-10:
Windows
QuarkXPress
(top) lets
you choose
whether
there's a
preview
header for
QuarkXPress-
generated
files, while
the Mac
version
(bottom) lets
you choose
between
Mac-style
(PICT) and
PC-style
(TIFF)
previews.

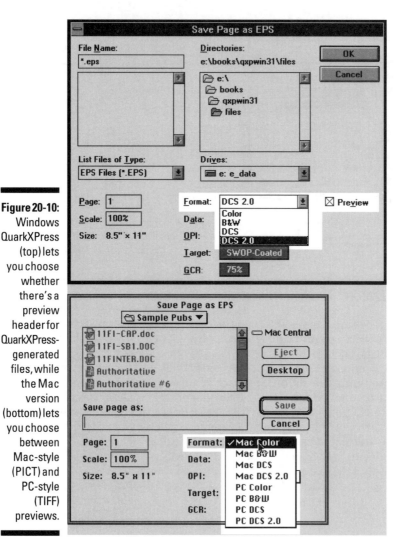

Chapter 21

QuarkXPress on Steroids

· ·

In This Chapter

▶ Making QuarkXPress run as fast as possible

▶ Understanding native and non-native Power Macintosh software

▶ Simplifying design with QuarkPrint and Printer Calibration XTensions

▶ Looking at the free fonts

▶ Sampling the QuarkLibraries

▶ Reviewing the demo XTensions and image-database software

· ·

*E*veryone knows that the Power Macintoshes are the ultimate speed demons, challenging the Pentium PCs that Windows users salivate over. QuarkXPress is available in a version for the Power Mac that takes advantage of the Power Mac's high speed to offer better performance for your layout work. The Power Mac version also includes a bunch of goodies — fonts, demo XTensions, and libraries — that you'll want to explore.

Because of all the goodies that Quark includes with its Power Mac version of QuarkXPress, they had to distribute it via a CD — all that stuff won't fit on floppies, at least not in a software box that a computer store will carry, which means you need a CD-ROM drive in your Mac. Fortunately, practically every Power Mac includes one, and most Quadras do, too. If your Mac doesn't have one, you'll find that CD-ROM drives are now cheap — just a few hundred dollars for a double-speed model, which is all you need for installing software from. Quark is not alone in using CDs. Adobe Systems, for example, now ships "deluxe" versions of its Photoshop and Illustrator programs on CDs; these deluxe versions include clip art and fonts similar to Quark's.

You can tell you're running QuarkXPress for Power Mac because you'll get the startup screen shown in Figure 21-1 when you launch QuarkXPress. If you missed seeing the screen when you launched (maybe you were on the phone or talking to a colleague), you can verify that the Power Mac version is running by using Apple menu⇨About QuarkXPress. If you see the Power Mac startup screen, you're OK.

When you run the Power Mac version of QuarkXPress, you find that functions related to image import, screen resizing, font changes, find and replace, and using the Thumbnail view are noticeably faster than they are on a Quadra or Centris. But operations related to using the disk, such as opening and saving a layout, will occur at about the same speed because the speed of the hard drive determines most of the performance for such functions. (Image import, which you'd rightfully assume involved the disk drive, is sped up for most images on a Power Mac. Why? Because the creation of the on-screen image preview is sped up under a Power Mac, even if the actual reading in of the image data is not.)

What You Need to Outpace Your Friends

We all love speed — fast cars, fast skates, fast bikes, fast skateboards, fast money, and certainly fast computers. The contest for speed is so intense that it seems that your Mac (or PC) gets obsolete a mere few months after you bought it. That's not true, of course; after only a few months, your computer is just as good as it ever was. It's just that you know there's now something a little better — which means you're no longer king of the Ego Hill.

Picking a Power Mac upgrade

Relax. Fast is good, but you can get a great deal of mileage from almost any Mac you already have. Sure, if your Mac is more than three years old, you should consider upgrading it to a faster model or getting a new Mac. If you do choose to upgrade, chances are good that you want to move to a Power Mac. If you don't want to get a new system, though, then you want an upgrade.

For most Quadras, you can run the Power Mac version of QuarkXPress if you install Apple's Power Macintosh Upgrade Card or DayStar Digital's PowerPro card. You also can buy a Power Mac Upgrade Card from Apple (called the PowerCard in the identical version sold by DayStar) that works in the Quadra 605, Quadra 630, LC 630, Performa 600 series, LC 475, Performance 470 series, LC 575, and Performa 570 series. These upgrade cards turn your Mac into a Power Mac. To get a card, call Apple at 408-996-1010 or DayStar Digital at 404-967-2077 (or see your local Mac dealer). Apple also will let you trade in the motherboard — the part of the Mac that does all the computing work — for a Power Mac version, but only if you have certain models. You can trade in the motherboard of a Centris 610, Centris 660AV, Quadra 610, or Quadra 660AV for a Power Mac 6100/60 motherboard for about $1000. You can trade in the motherboard of a IIvi, IIvx, Performa 600, Centris 650, or Quadra 650 for a Power Mac 7100/66 motherboard for about $1500. And you can trade in a Quadra 800 or Quadra 840AV motherboard for a Power Mac 8100/80 motherboard for about $1900.

If you have an AV Mac, you can't use an upgrade card. You must replace the motherboard. You can replace it with a non-AV motherboard as described above or with an AV Power Mac motherboard. These AV motherboards cost about $300 more than their non-AV counterparts.

By running the Power Mac version on a Power Mac, you'll get the ultimate speed. Obviously, the faster the Power Mac, the faster QuarkXPress will run. But don't worry too much about spending a thousand or more extra dollars on getting the fastest Power Mac. You'll find, for example, that a Power Mac 6100/60 or 6100/66 is more than capable for doing most layouts. Only those doing very sophisticated, color-intensive layouts with tens of megabytes of images — or those who are doing other work on the same Power Mac that requires that kind of processing — should consider a Power Mac 8100/80 or 8100/110. A Power Mac 7100/66 or 7100/80 makes sense only if you need to add NuBus cards, such as for 24-bit color, 19-inch-monitor video display. (In Apple's Power Mac naming scheme, the number after the slash refers to the system's speed. For example, a Power Mac 8100/110 runs at 110 megahertz, while a Power Mac 6100/66 runs at 66 megahertz.)

If you use a Power Mac upgrade card, the speed will depend on a couple of factors: the type of card and the speed of the Mac using the card. DayStar's PowerPro cards run at a fixed speed: either 66MHz or 80MHz, with plans for a 100MHz version, too. The speeds of Apple's and DayStar's other cards depends on what Mac it is plugged into. On a Quadra 800, Quadra 650, Quadra 630, Performa 600, or LC 630, you'll get a 66MHz Power Mac. On a Centris 610, you'll get a 40MHz Power Mac. On the other systems, you'll get a 50MHz Power Mac. We suggest that you not settle for anything less than a 50MHz Power Mac, and that you seriously consider getting a 60MHz or 66MHz model.

Why regular Mac programs run slowly on a Power Mac

You can run the regular version of QuarkXPress on a Power Mac, but you can't run the Power Mac version of QuarkXPress on a regular Mac (called a 680X0 Mac — shorthand for the 68000, 68020, 68030, and 68040 processor chips used in pre-Power Macs). But the 680X0 version of QuarkXPress — or any program — runs much slower on a Power Mac than the native Power Mac version of the program does. (680X0 is pronounced *68 Kay* — the *kay* is from the letter *K*, which is substituted for the *0X0* because the 0X0 stands for thousand, and K is the metric abbreviation for thousand.)

A Power Mac runs 680X0 software more slowly than Power Mac software because the Power Mac has to translate the 680X0 language into the language of the Power Mac's PowerPC processor chip. Think of it this way: you can talk pretty fast with a friend using the same language. But think how much longer it takes to talk with someone when you're translating your native language into theirs — you're translating your English thoughts into high-school French to talk with a European tourist, for example, or a colleague is serving as an interpreter between you and a Japanese-speaking business visitor. The same thing happens when a Power Mac runs 680X0 software.

Even if you have Power Mac software, it might run more slowly than expected on a Power Mac. If the Power Mac software has to interact with 680X0 software, then that interaction will cause the Power Mac to stop to translate the 680X0 software some operations slow down. For QuarkXPress, the danger of such slowdown comes in two forms:

✔ If you run XTensions (see Chapter 22) that are 680X0 software, the Power Mac version of QuarkXPress will have to slow down any time you use a feature of that 680X0 XTension. You can tell whether an XTension is 680X0 or Power Mac-native by holding the Option key when entering Apple menu⇨About QuarkXPress. (Make sure that you hold down the Option key *before* you select the Apple menu item.) Figure 21-2 shows the resulting dialog box. At right is a list of installed XTensions. If the name is in italics, it's a 680X0 XTension, not a Power Mac XTension, and it will run slowly. You really notice the slowdown on the JPEG import filter, which relies on the portion of the processor chip that is the hardest to translate. In fact, the JPEG filter works faster on a Quadra than on a Power Mac, even though the Power Mac is a much faster machine than a Quadra.

✔ If you use Adobe Type Manager (and who doesn't these days?), make sure that you have version 3.8 or later. Previous versions are 680X0 software and therefore will slow down QuarkXPress on a Power Mac any time you use PostScript fonts.

Note that some programs (like, for example, ATM 3.8) run on both Power Macs and 680X0 Macs. Companies make such dual use possible by putting the 680X0 and Power Mac software in one file; before the program runs, it checks to see what kind of Mac it's running on and then runs only the appropriate portion. But this combination of 680X0 and Power Mac software can make the program size almost double, which is why it's usually just small programs, like ATM, that use this technique. (By the way, these two-in-one programs are called *fat binary* programs because they take more room than a 680X0-only or Power Mac-only version.)

Figure 21-2:
This dialog box lets you see which XTensions are native Power Mac and which are not (the ones in italics are not).

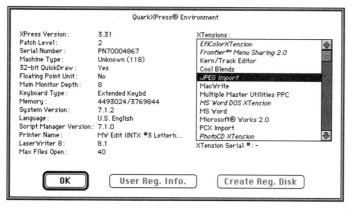

The Power Mac Extras

Functionally, the QuarkXPress 3.3 versions for Macintosh, Windows, and Power Macintosh offer the same things. That's great if you work in a multiplatform environment and want to ensure file and feature compatibility. But the Power Mac QuarkXPress CD does come with several freebies that extend its capabilities. The most important are two XTensions — plug-in programs (which we cover in Chapter 22) — that enhance QuarkXPress's printing controls. Added XTensions (QuarkPrint and Calibration) are one reason why the Power Mac version of QuarkXPress costs about $100 more than the Macintosh and Windows versions. (Basically, you get QuarkPrint thrown in for half its $200 usual price and the other stuff is free.) You can get these same features for the Macintosh version of QuarkXPress (but not for Windows).

XTensions for better printing

Printing is a key task in QuarkXPress. Often we take it for granted because we spend so much time working on our layout and content. But, without printing, no one would be able to read the documents we so painstakingly labor over. Printing in QuarkXPress is pretty straightforward (see Chapter 17 for details on QuarkXPress printing and Chapter 16 for printing setup on the Mac), but several Quark printing features could be simplified or made more powerful. Respectively, QuarkPrint and Calibration help you pull off those two improvements.

QuarkPrint

QuarkPrint makes it easier to set up printer settings, particularly if you are printing to an imagesetter. But even if you don't have an imagesetter, QuarkPrint is great to have. When you install QuarkXPress for Power Mac, QuarkPrint is automatically installed unless you deselect it from the XTensions list.

If you want to "share" your copy of QuarkPrint with friends or colleagues, you won't be able to do so if they use the 680X0 version of QuarkXPress: the QuarkPrint that comes with the Power Macintosh version of QuarkXPress is a native Power Mac XTension.

You can tell when QuarkPrint has been installed because your menus will change. Figure 21-3 shows what's different. The biggest change is in the new menu item, File⇨Print Job, which you can also access via ⌘-Shift-P. A print job is a set of instructions, which is great for setting up tasks and settings that you use repeatedly. Figure 21-4 shows the dialog box you get. Notice how you can set nonconsecutive ranges of pages, like pages 1 through 4, 7 through 9, 11, and 13. Also notice how uncluttered the dialog box is — it's more visually attractive than the standard Print dialog box. QuarkPrint also provides you the following notable features:

- The capability to select a destination: the printer or a PostScript file.
- The capability to select a specific color plate.

    This option is grayed out in the figure because Separations, which you access via the Print Setup dialog box, was not turned on in the Print Setup dialog box.

- The capability to set up page options, via the Options button, for output of both black-and-white and color negatives to an imagesetter, as Figure 21-5 shows.

    The nicest option is the capability to change the screen function — the type of element used to create the "dots" the make up an image.

✔ The capability to set up page options like the paper size and scaling (via the Page Setup button).

✔ A graphical representation of the output orientation and setup, as shown in the bottom right of Figure 21-4 and the upper left of Figure 21-5.

This feature lets you see the effects of your settings.

But the best feature of all at first seems innocuous: the Print Job pop-up menu. The default option is, well, Default. A print job is a group of printer settings that have been saved so that you can apply them to a document. For example, say that you publish a magazine. On your laser printer at the office, you print pages in gray scale, with no crop marks, at 60 lpi with separations turned off. That's so you can proof the copies. But when you print to your imagesetter, you change the lpi to 133, turn separations on, make the negatives print emulsion side down (you don't know what it means but you know you're supposed to do it), and turn crops mark on. By saving these sets of settings, you don't have to worry about forgetting to change a setting as you switch printers or types of publications — you just select the print job set you created from the Print Jobs pop-up menu. Cool!

It's easy to create a print job set — the process is like setting up a style sheet, color definition, or H&J set. Just use Edit➪Print Jobs to create and save the set.

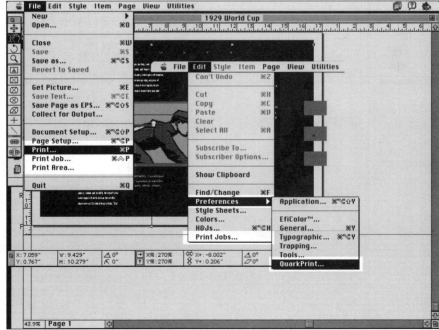

Figure 21-3:
The menu items that are added to QuarkXPress (the highlighted items) when QuarkPrint is installed.

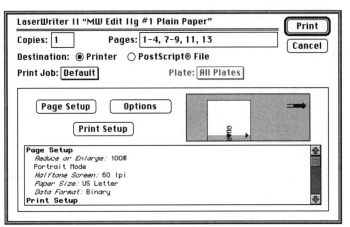

Figure 21-4:
The Print
Jobs dialog
box lets you
print non-
consecutive
pages and
use
predefined
printer
settings.

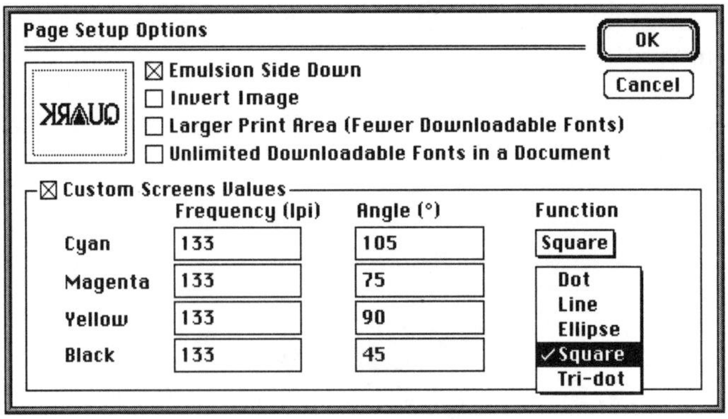

Figure 21-5:
The options
you can
set with
QuarkPrint
include the
capability to
change the
screening
element for
a print job.

QuarkPrint offers a few other features that are less useful:

✔ You can change QuarkPrint preferences via Edit⇨Preferences⇨ QuarkPrint.

Figure 21-6 shows the dialog box. It's repeated so that you can see the options in the two pop-up lists. XPress Preferences lets you bypass that annoying message that appears when you load a QuarkXPress document whose settings differ in any way from the default settings for your copy of QuarkXPress. You're asked to tell QuarkXPress whether to leave the document settings alone or to override them with QuarkXPress's current default settings. (Most people wisely choose to leave the document settings alone.) This option lets you tell QuarkXPress once and for all which option you want.

For a service bureau, this option is great because none of their customers' documents will have settings that match the service bureau's settings, and the service bureau doesn't want to accidentally override the customers' settings. So a service bureau would set this option to Keep Document Settings. However, you can always leave this option at Display Dialog, which ensures that the annoying question is asked each and every time you load a document. The other preference you can set is Picture Measurement, which is basically the origin point for picture measurements. It's something you should leave alone.

↙ You also can print selected portions of a page via File⇨Print Area.

Figure 21-7 shows the dialog box. You enter the upper-right corner of the location where you want to print from in the Origin Across and Origin Down fields and then the width and depth you want printed in the Width and Height fields. Basically, this is an easier way to do manual tiling (covered in Chapter 17).

↙ You can print or save to file any of several types of information about the current QuarkXPress document, as shown in Figure 21-8.

This Document Statistics feature is a utility aimed at service bureaus that try to figure out what's in a customer's document in order to catch any possible mistakes or missing elements before printing.

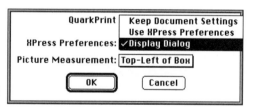

Figure 21-6:
The QuarkPrint Preferences dialog box and its two pop-up menus.

Figure 21-7:
The Print
Area dialog
box.

```
                    Print Area

    Origin Across:  [        ]    Width:  [        ]

    Origin Down:    [        ]    Height: [        ]

              [   OK   ]    [ Cancel ]
```

Figure 21-8:
The
Document
Statistics
dialog box.

```
 Utilities                                   ▣ ⑦ ▨

   Check Spelling              ▶
   Auxiliary Dictionary...
   Edit Auxiliary...

   Suggested Hyphenation...  ⌘H
   Hyphenation Exceptions...

   Font Usage...
   Picture Usage...              ┌─ Document Statistics for Document1 ─┐
   Profile Usage...              │  Destination:   ● File  ○ Printer   │
                                 │  ┌─Options────────────────────────┐ │
   Tracking Edit...              │  │ ☒ Fonts        ☒ Style Sheets  │ │
   Kerning Table Edit...         │  │ ☒ Pictures     ☒ H&Js          │ │
   Font Creator                  │  │ ☒ Color Plates ☒ Colors        │ │
   Document Statistics...        │  │ ☐ Print Jobs   ☐ Trapping      │ │
                                 │  └────────────────────────────────┘ │
                                 │       [   OK   ]    [ Cancel ]       │
                                 └──────────────────────────────────────┘
```

Printer calibration

Fewer people will find Printer Calibration useful because it is intended primarily for high-end users. Because it can benefit other users, though—for example, users very like you—we'll quickly go over it here. Note that you must install this XTension from the floppy disk that came with the CD—the version on the CD is incompatible with the Power Mac version of QuarkXPress. Someone goofed when they made the CD.

And another goofy thing: The XTension is called Calibration, but the menu item it adds to the Utilities menu is called Printer Calibration. Go figure.

Figure 21-9 shows the menu option (Utilities⇨Printer Calibration) and dialog boxes for Printer Calibration. The dialog box at the upper right lets you select your printer; then you get the dialog box at bottom, which lets you change the ink density for that printer. Basically, you're telling the printer how much ink to print based on how dark the document specifies an area to be. Normally, a printer goes easy the darker the image gets, since after about 60-percent black (or of any hue), the ink starts to smear and blend, which makes the item look even darker. But for extra-dark areas (like 90 percent), the printer adds extra ink because, at this density (or darkness), there's going to be smearing and the image will look better if the ink is more solid rather than mottled or specked where the ink didn't smear evenly. (This smearing of ink is called *gain.*) Maybe you want to hold back the ink even more. Or maybe the printer's holding back too much ink and making the dark areas appear weak. You can adjust the ink density with this XTension.

For example, a Linotronic imagesetter outputs 69 percent black (which is called 0.69 ink density) for an image that is 80-percent black. In Figure 21-9, we've changed the density for low-resolution output (at the left of the bottom dialog box) to make it lighter (0.62, which you can see at the bottom right of the dialog box). We did so by moving the point for 80 percent coverage down from its original position of 0.69 to its new position of 0.62.

Clearly, such an involved process is something that only a service bureau — whether in-house or a separate vendor — should be doing. You really have to understand the printing characteristics of your printing press to pick the right options.

Figure 21-9:
The Printer Calibration XTension lets you change how a printer prints shades in order to compensate for ink smearing on the printing press.

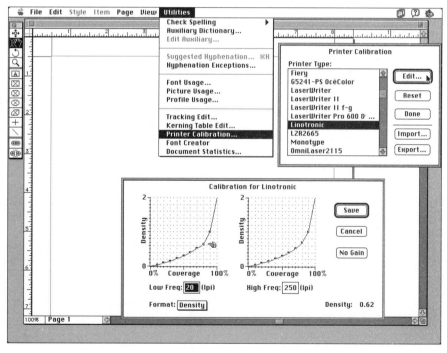

Free fonts

Everyone loves fonts. If you could afford them, you'd probably have hundreds. Thanks to the proliferation of CD-installed programs, you may get to add to your font collection without spending a great deal of money. For example, Adobe Illustrator 5.5 comes with dozens of PostScript fonts — which, if you install them, let you turn a perhaps scraggly collection of fonts into a full-blown type library. QuarkXPress for Power Mac's CD also comes with a selection of free fonts, although they're more modest than the potpourri that comes with Adobe's CD-based software. Still, QuarkXPress's collection does come from several respected type sources: Bitstream, Monotype, the Font Bureau, and Linotype-Hell. They're in the Fonts Sampler folder on the CD.

But do remember this little ray of good news: you can save the effort of copying the Linotype-Hell fonts. They're just screen fonts, so they won't print well at any size but 10 points. So don't worry about them. Instead, take a gander at the six free ones that do print at any size and on any PostScript printer.

For more information on fonts, see Chapter 2.

Ready-to-use libraries

Libraries are probably one of the most underused features of QuarkXPress because they require people to think about creating them. A library is a type of QuarkXPress document that contains images and text. You create a library via File⇨New⇨Library (Quark asks you to give the library a name and to specify where you want to save it). You get a palette on your screen that contains nothing. To put elements into the library, just select the Item tool and drag a picture box or text box to the library — that process copies the box's contents into the library (while leaving the original picture or text box's contents and location intact). When you save QuarkXPress, the library will be saved, too. You also can use copy (⌘-C) and paste (⌘-V) to place an item in the library: just select the item in the QuarkXPress document, copy it, click the library palette, and paste the item. To delete a library item, select it with the Item tool and then use ⌘-X. To use library items in your layout, select a picture or text box (as appropriate), and then either drag a library item to it (the pointer will change to a pair of glasses) or use copy and paste. It's that simple!

Go to the Application Preferences dialog box (Edit⇨Preferences⇨Application) and check the Auto Library Save box. Then, whenever you add or remove something to or from a library, the library is saved.

You even can open multiple libraries simultaneously. That way, you can organize items by topic and select from any of the topics as needed. And because libraries and layouts reside in separate files, anyone can use a library file in any layout document. As you can see, libraries are a great resource because they let you organize your commonly used materials and share them with others.

As we said, though, despite libraries' usefulness, most people don't bother to create them. But the folks at Quark did: they put 16 libraries on the QuarkXPress for Power Mac CD in a folder called QuarkLibraries. Figure 21-10 shows a sampling of the available libraries. Of course, you can add to these libraries by dragging your own elements into them. We hope that these prebuilt libraries will encourage you to build or enhance your own.

And remember — the Macintosh and Power Macintosh libraries are compatible with each other, which means that you can exchange libraries with any Mac users. Unfortunately, you can't exchange library files with Windows users; the QuarkLibrary format is different on a PC than on a Mac.

Figure 21-10: QuarkXPress for Power Mac comes with 16 libraries of images for use in any document.

Demo XTensions

The QuarkXPress for Power Mac CD comes with 38 demo XTensions that you have to copy from the folder labeled 3rd Party Demo XTensions on the CD. We won't cover the XTensions here because there are so many that you probably won't ever use; many are aimed primarily at higher-end users. But do check out Chapter 22 for more information on XTensions, and feel free to try out the demo XTensions that came on your QuarkXPress CD.

So that you can try out these demo XTensions without getting them completely for free, the folks at Quark have branded the XTensions on the CD with a nasty form of protection against unpaid free use. When you install these demo XTensions, your copy of QuarkXPress gets changed so that it saves your layouts in a format that you can't read in another copy of QuarkXPress. If you remove the XTensions, you can save again in the normal QuarkXPress format — but you still won't be able to open any documents saved when the demos were installed. Therefore, *never* use a real document when you try out one of these XTensions and *never* do any real work with them. If you experiment with a demo XTension and decide you like it, you may be tempted to start using it for real work. But, as soon as you save, that document can't be read by any copy of QuarkXPress (including your own) that does not have the demo XTension installed. Fortunately, QuarkXPress will repeatedly warn you that a demo XTension is installed and that saving a file will make it incompatible with QuarkXPress — so it's hard to accidentally save your work in a file format you won't be able to use later. Still, this is nasty stuff.

Demo image database software

The QuarkXPress CD also has two demo versions of image-database programs. This software lets you browse through images on a CD, hard disk, or network. It's a bit more convenient than using the Get Picture (File➪Get Picture, or ⌘-E) feature in QuarkXPress because, with an image database, you can see all the images at once.

The first demo image database is Canto Software's Cumulus. The demo version of Cumulus doesn't work reliably with all Power Macs, so we won't explain how to use it. Besides, it's a fairly complex piece of software, and the other demo image database is easier to use.

That other database is Imspace Systems' Kudo. The beauty of Kudo is that you select an image from a database and then you can place it into QuarkXPress. All you have to do is have QuarkXPress open with a document and a picture box selected. Then you use Image➪Place➪QuarkXPress® to place the image into that selected picture box. Pretty neat, huh?

Chapter 22
The Hows and Whys of XTensions

*N*ow we're going to ask you to put your creative mind to use.

Imagine that QuarkXPress, instead of being a page-layout program, is a prefabricated, one-room house. Your copy of the house sits on a street with a dozen other houses just like it. You breathe a sigh of relief when you find out that your next-door neighbor, a wild saxophone player who keeps you up at night with his playing, has decided to build a music room onto his house. A few weeks later, your other next-door neighbor gives birth to triplets and begins to build a second story to house all the little darlings. You, on the other hand, have a better idea for how to personalize your home: You decide to add a greenhouse room in front of the house so that you can keep your orchid collection healthy and growing in any season.

The point of this homely analogy is that, like the neighbors described above, QuarkXPress users all have different likes and needs. Just as the people in our imaginary neighborhood were unsatisfied by simply living in their identical little prefab houses, publishers and designers also would be unsatisfied if they were forced to use one flavor of QuarkXPress. It's obvious (when you think about it) that someone using the program to produce a two-color school newspaper has different needs than a designer using QuarkXPress to create process color ads for magazines.

Probably the wisest thing the people who created QuarkXPress ever did was to realize that every user of this program is unique. By maintaining a continuing dialog with their customers, Quark's developers came to understand that it would be impossible to create a single application that would meet the needs of every user. So, instead of trying to make the program all things to all people, adding a truckload of features that would inhibit the overall performance of the program, the developers created an ingenious architecture that allows QuarkXPress to be customized to suit each individual user.

Quark's architecture allows for *XTensions* to be developed. XTensions are add-on programs that target specific needs not otherwise addressed by QuarkXPress. XTensions are developed both by Quark and by hundreds of third-party XTension developers. XTensions are available for QuarkXPress for Macintosh, Power Macintosh, and Windows.

Why would you need an XTension? Let's say that you produce documents that are full of complicated tables. Rather than try to use QuarkXPress to format tables, you can simply buy an XTension that automates most of the formatting, saving you hours and hours of production time. Maybe you need to add an index to a book you've just written using QuarkXPress; because QuarkXPress does not include an indexing feature, you can buy an indexing XTension to do the job instead of having to develop the index manually. In other words, XTensions let you add to the power of QuarkXPress in a way that is customized to exactly the kind of publishing you do.

How XTensions Happen

When you install an XTension, it "merges" with QuarkXPress. If an XTension is installed, you access it directly from within QuarkXPress by simply clicking on a menu item that appears for each XTension.

We'll show you in a minute how this works. But first there are a few things you should know about XTensions. Think of them as rules of the game.

Rules about XTensions

XTensions are easy to install and easy to use, as long as you keep a few general rules in mind:

- ✔ XTensions must be installed in the XTension folder that comes with QuarkXPress; on Windows, they must be within the same subdirectory as QuarkXPress.

- ✔ XTensions take up system memory, so keep unused or infrequently used XTensions in a different folder or subdirectory. Mac users can use the Other XTensions folder that is created automatically when you install new XTensions.

✔ An installed XTension adds itself to one or more of the regular
QuarkXPress menus, or it adds its own menu(s) and/or palette(s), or a
combination of these.

✔ XTensions often have their own icon. Figure 22-1 shows you what an
XTension icon looks like.

Installing XTensions

Installing XTensions is a matter of placing the XTension in the XTension folder
or subdirectory. In Figure 22-1, you can see how the Mac screen appears when
you are installing an XTension. Here's how you do it:

1. **Insert the disk holding the XTension into the disk drive.**

2. **Open the QuarkXPress folder and locate the XTension folder.**

3. **Open the XTension disk icon by double-clicking on it.**

4. **If the XTension disk contains an installer, double-click on the installer
   icon and follow the directions on the screen; if the XTension does not
   come with an installer, drag the XTension icon onto the XTension
   folder.**

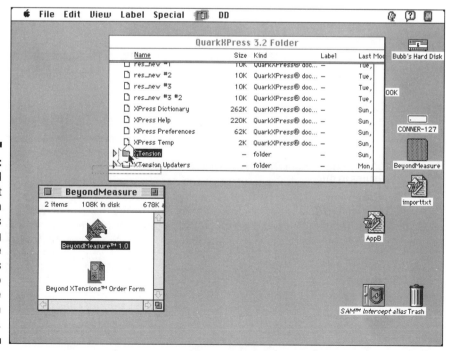

Figure 22-1:
You install
most
Macintosh
XTensions
by dragging
the
XTension's
icon onto
the
XTension
folder.

After the XTension is installed, you're ready to use it. There's no need to restart the computer. Figure 22-2 shows how the XTension we just installed, BeyondMeasure, creates a new menu item in the View menu.

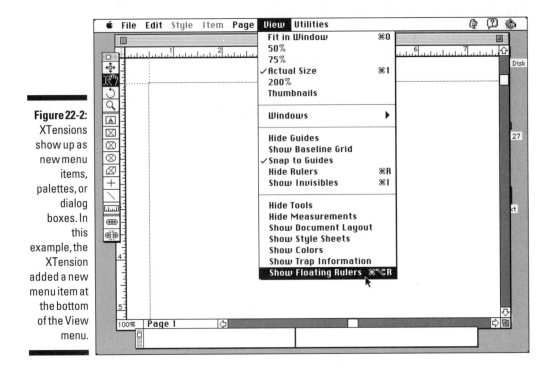

Figure 22-2:
XTensions show up as new menu items, palettes, or dialog boxes. In this example, the XTension added a new menu item at the bottom of the View menu.

Some Sample XTensions

There are *hundreds* of XTensions. We won't list them all for you here; it would be a futile effort, anyway, because new XTensions enter the market every day. If you want to get a complete list of XTensions, the best way to do it is to call XChange, an independent users and developers group that both develops its own XTensions and serves as a clearinghouse between QuarkXPress users and XTension developers. XChange membership is $99 per year in the U.S. and $149 per year in other countries. XChange members get a discount on some XTensions and a monthly demo disk. XChange can be reached at the following locations: 724 Whalers Way, Suite 101, Fort Collins, CO 80525; telephone 800-788-7557; fax 303-229-9773; CompuServe 75300,2336; AppleLink XChange.CO.

Another source of XTensions or demo versions is an on-line service, such as America Online or CompuServe, that has a desktop publishing forum. Quark also posts free XTensions on these on-line services. You'll often find other free or shareware XTensions on these services that may offer the features you need at a price that is lower than what you would pay for a more complete commercial product.

And now, a word (actually, quite a few words) about some XTensions that we think are particularly cool.

BeyondMeasure

BeyondMeasure is an XTension that is so nifty, you'll wonder how you ever managed without it. This XTension helps you position items, with precision, anywhere on a page. BeyondMeasure does this by providing floating rulers that can have their own measurement units or use those of the document.

After you've installed BeyondMeasure, it adds a Measure tool to the QuarkXPress Tool palette. Then, any time you want to measure the distance between two points in a document, just click on the Measure tool, drag the crosshair pointer to the first endpoint of the item you are measuring, and then click and drag the crosshair pointer to the second endpoint of the item you are measuring. The item's horizontal width, vertical height, total distance, and angle between the two endpoints are displayed on the screen.

Figure 22-3 shows the Measure tool that is added to the tool palette and two floating rulers that you can implement using BeyondMeasure.

You can position BeyondMeasure's floating rulers together, or separately. To move both rulers together, you press the Shift key while clicking on either ruler, and then you drag the ruler pair into position. You can also move one ruler at a time by clicking on it and dragging it into position, as you can see in Figure 22-4.

BeyondMeasure is produced by *Acrobyte*, 2501 Forest Street, Denver CO 80207; fax 303-322-3902; eWorld: Acrobyte; AppleLink: ACROBYTE; CompuServe: 72037,2474.

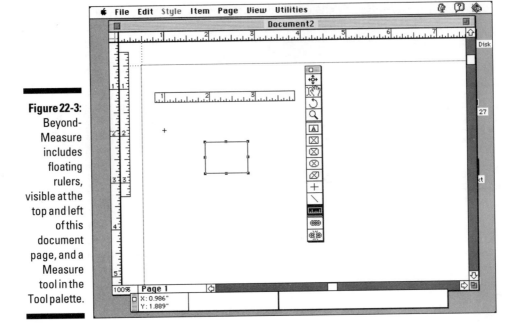

Figure 22-3:
Beyond-
Measure
includes
floating
rulers,
visible at the
top and left
of this
document
page, and a
Measure
tool in the
Tool palette.

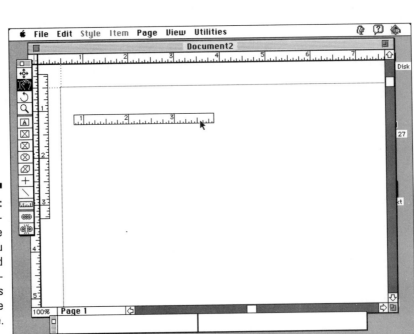

Figure 22-4:
Beyond-
Measure
lets you
click and
drag mini-
rulers
anywhere
on the page.

The KitchenSink

Some XTensions are really several XTensions bundled together. KitchenSink is one such product.

KitchenSink is an XTension that aims to make QuarkXPress easier to use. Its main feature is Command Pad, a floating palette that lets you access nearly all of the QuarkXPress dialog boxes and palettes with a click of a mouse. KitchenSink also includes some other handy items, such as Co-Pilot, a palette that lets you click once to scroll to any location in the current spread; a nudge palette for quickly nudging layout items into place; and the capability to change text boxes to picture boxes, and vice versa. These are just a few of the dozen or so productivity enhancers that come with this XTension. Figure 22-5 shows what the Command Pad looks like.

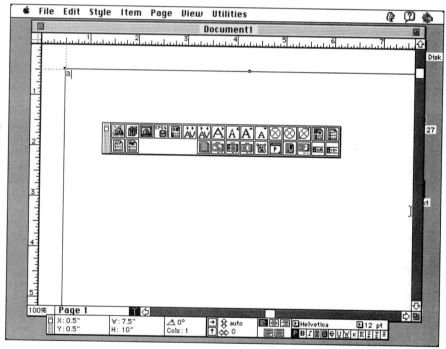

Figure 22-5: KitchenSink includes Command Pad, a floating palette that lets you access QuarkXPress features with one mouse click.

KitchenSink is produced by *a lowly apprentice production*, 2474 Manchester Avenue, Cardiff-by-the-Sea, CA 92007; telephone 619-942-1968; fax 619-942-0575; AppleLink PSCHMITT; America Online PSCHMITT.

AuxDict XT

You'd be surprised (we were) to find out just how many wonderful XTensions are either free or available as shareware at very low cost. AuxDict XT is one such XTension.

AuxDict XT is a free XTension that has been extracted from the more advanced XState and the SuperXState XTensions as a means of advertising some of the two XTensions' features. Full working demos of these XTensions are available by contacting their developer.

AuxDict XT keeps track of your last used auxiliary dictionaries and adds their names to a pop-up menu attached to the Utilities⇨Auxiliary Dictionary menu item. After this XTension is installed, you can select a dictionary from the Auxiliary Dictionary menu to make it the currently active dictionary. This is a handy XTension for those who need access to multiple auxiliary dictionaries. Figure 22-6 shows how AuxDict XT modifies the QuarkXPress Utilities menu.

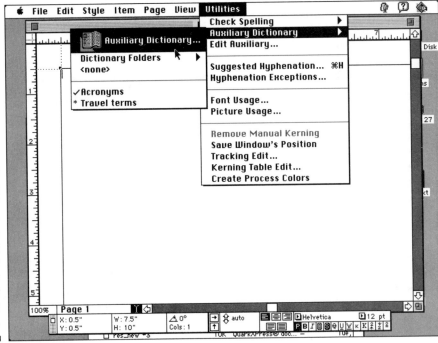

Figure 22-6:
AuxDict XT adds a pop-up menu to the Utilities⇨ Auxiliary Dictionary menu selection.

AuxDict XT is produced by *Markzware*, 3337 S. Bristol, Suite 87, Santa Ana, CA 92704; telephone 800-300-3532; fax: 714-241-3874; AppleLink: Markzware.

Create Process Colors

This XTension is distributed as shareware. You are allowed to use the XTension for free for four weeks; after that time, you need to pay a small fee to register your copy.

Create Process Colors changes all colors in a document into CMYK colors. This XTension is useful if you print QuarkXPress documents that require four-color separation. Service bureaus find this XTension to be very time-saving: it means that they can avoid problems with documents that have colors specified as both spot and process colors. Figure 22-7 shows how you access Create Process Colors.

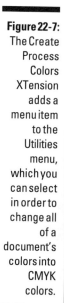

Figure 22-7:
The Create Process Colors XTension adds a menu item to the Utilities menu, which you can select in order to change all of a document's colors into CMYK colors.

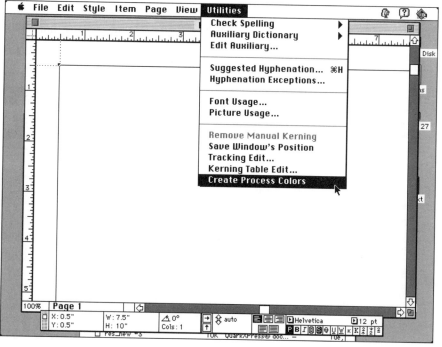

Create Process Colors is produced by *media one GmbH*, Benzstr. 28, 82178 Puchheim/Munich, Germany; telephone +49 (89) 8901310; fax +49 (89) 8913199; CompuServe 100042,2234.

Thing-a-ma-bob

As we mentioned previously, Quark also produces XTensions. Thing-a-ma-bob (don't you just *love* the name?) is one such Quark XTension.

Thing-a-ma-bob has four main features:

- ✔ A *Value Converter* palette converts values between six measurement systems.
- ✔ A *Remove Manual Kerning* feature lets you strip manual kerning from selected text.
- ✔ A *Word Space Tracking* feature lets you apply tracking to word spaces only, instead of to both characters and words.
- ✔ Our favorite, a *Make Fraction/Make Price* feature, formats fractions and prices automatically.

Let's talk about how just one of the XTension's features, Thing-a-ma-bob Make Fraction, works. First, you type the fraction like this: 13/16. Then you select the fraction that you want to convert and choose Style➪Type Style➪Make Fraction (this menu selection is created when you first install Thing-a-ma-bob). When you highlight a range of characters and select Make Fraction, only the highlighted characters are transformed.

Make Fraction is produced by *Quark Inc.*, XTensionland, 1800 Grant Street, Denver, CO 80203; telephone 303-894-8888; fax 303-894-3399.

We have shown you these sample XTensions just to give you an idea of all they can do. If you have a particular need that isn't addressed by QuarkXPress, we encourage you to see if you can find an XTension that will take care of it.

Part VII
The Part of Tens

By Rich Tennant

In this part ...

The chapters in this part are the icing on the cake. You'll learn interesting facts, discover professional advice, and generally find the jewels that no manual will ever contain. And best of all, the information comes to you in the form of top-ten lists, so you don't have to go through a lot of text to find those invaluable nuggets.

Chapter 23

More Than Ten Shortcuts

QuarkXPress has tons and tons of shortcuts. You won't memorize most, but you'll no doubt find yourself using a handful or two all the time. The following is a complete list, broken down by task.

Remember to use Ctrl for ⌘ and Alt for Option. If a Windows QuarkXPress shortcut differs from the Mac shortcut, it follows in italicized text.

Interface Controls

Changing Views

Fit in window	⌘-0 (zero)
Actual size	⌘-1 *also: right mouse click*
Thumbnails view	Control-V T Enter *Ctrl+Alt+V T Return*
Enter View Percent field	Control-V *Ctrl+Alt+V*
Temporary Page Grabber Hand tool	Option-click
Temporary Zoom tool (+)	Control *Shift+right mouse click*
Temporary Zoom tool (–)	Option-Control *Ctrl+Shift+right mouse click*
Toggle between Actual Size and Fit in Window	Option-click *right mouse click*
Toggle between 200% and Actual Size	⌘-Option-click *Ctrl+right mouse click*

Display Guides, Palettes, and Tools

Show/hide rulers	⌘-R
Show/hide invisibles	⌘-I
Show/hide guides	F7
Show/hide baseline grid	Option-F7 *Ctrl+F7*
Show/hide Tools palette	F8
Toggle between Item and Content tools	Shift-F8
Select next tool in Tools palette	⌘-tab
Select previous tool in Tools palette	⌘-Shift-tab
Show/hide Measurements palette	⌘-Option-M or F9
Show/hide Styles palette	F11
Show/hide Document Layout palette	F10 *F4*
Show/hide Colors palette	F12
Show/hide Trap Information palette	Option-F12 *Ctrl+F12*

Working with Documents

File Management

New document	⌘-N
New library	⌘-Option-N
Open	⌘-O
Close	⌘-W *also: Ctrl+F4*
Close all	⌘-Option-W *not supported*
Quit	⌘-Q *also: Alt+F4*
Save	⌘-S
Save as	⌘-Option-S

Formatting

Document setup	Option-Shift-⌘-P
Open Section dialog box	Click on page number icon
Show/hide Document Layout palette	F10 *F4*
Insert multiple pages	Option-drag Master Page icon
Apply Master Page to selected pages	Option-click Master Page icon

Navigation

Go to Page	⌘-J

Working with Items

Item Selection:

Obscured item (with Content tool)	⌘-Option-Shift-click
Visible item	click

Item Resizing

Constrain*	Shift-drag
Maintain aspect ratio	Option-Shift-drag
Scale picture	⌘-Option-Shift-drag
Decrease line size (within presets)	⌘-Shift-<
Increase line size (within presets)	⌘-Shift->
Decrease box/scale (full range)	⌘-Option-Shift-<
Increase box/scale (full range)	⌘-Option-Shift->

* constrains a box to square, an oval to circle, or a line to 0, 45, or 90 degrees

Preset line widths: 0.25 points (hairline), 1, 2, 4, 6, 8, and 12 points

Full-range line widths: 0.25 points (hairline) to 504 points in 1-point steps

Full-range picture scales: 10% to 1,000% in 5% steps (.1% increments are available through the Modify option)

Item Dragging

With Item tool active	drag
Without Item tool active	⌘-drag
Constrain horizontally or vertically	⌘-Shift-drag
Left in 1-point increment	left arrow
Left in .1-point increment	Option-left arrow
Right in 1-point increment	right arrow
Right in .1-point increment	Option-right arrow
Up in 1-point increment	up arrow

Working with Items

Item Dragging

Up in .1-point increment	Option-up arrow
Down in 1-point increment	down arrow
Down in .1-point increment	Option-down arrow

Item Controls

Enter Measurements palette	⌘-Option-M
Show/hide Measurements palette	F9
Modify selected	⌘-M or double-click with Item tool
Frame	⌘-B
Runaround	⌘-T
Step and repeat	⌘-Option-D
Space/align	⌘-,
Group	⌘-G
Ungroup	⌘-U
Duplicate	⌘-D
Clear (delete)	⌘-K
Lock/unlock	F6 *also: Ctrl+L*
Bring to front	F5
Send to back	Shift-F5
Bring forward one layer	Option-F5 *Ctrl+F5*
Send backward one layer	Option-Shift-F5 *Ctrl+Shift+F5*
Snap to guides	Shift-F7

Color Usage

Show/hide Colors palette	F12
Apply color	⌘-click on color name in Colors palette
Edit Colors dialog box	Shift-F12

Polygon Editing

Create new handle	⌘-click on segment
Delete handle	⌘-click on handle
Delete runaround polygon	⌘-Shift-click
Inhibit redraw during editing	hold the spacebar with the above shortcuts

Graphics Files

Get picture	⌘-E
Get picture at 36 dpi resolution	⌘-Shift-E *not supported*
Get picture at full monitor dpi resolution	not supported *Shift+Ctrl+E*
Picture Usage dialog box	Option-F13 *not supported*
Save page as EPS	⌘-Option-Shift-S

Graphics Sizing

Fit to box	⌘-Shift-F
Fit to box (maintain aspect ratio)	⌘-Option-Shift-F
Center in box	⌘-Shift-M

Image Effects

Negative	⌘-Shift-hyphen
Normal contrast	⌘-Shift-N
High contrast	⌘-Shift-H
Posterized	⌘-Shift-P
Other contrast	⌘-Shift-C
Other screen	⌘-Shift-S

Line Controls

Decrease size (within presets)	⌘-Shift-<
Decrease size (in 1-point increments)	⌘-Option-Shift-<
Increase size (within presets)	⌘-Shift->
Increase size (in 1-point increments)	⌘-Option-Shift->
Set width	⌘-Shift-\

Preset widths: 0.25 points (hairline), 1, 2, 4, 6, 8, and 12 points

Working with Text

Highlighting Characters

Character	1 click
Word	2 clicks
Line	3 clicks
Paragraph	4 clicks
Entire story	5 clicks

Note: You can hold the Shift key and drag the mouse to extend the current selection.

Moving through Text

Key	Unmodified	⌘	⌘-Option
left arrow	previous character	previous word	start of line (also: Home)
right arrow	next character	next word	end of line (also: End)
up arrow	previous line	previous paragraph	start of story (also: Ctrl+Home)
down arrow	next line	next paragraph	end of story (also: Ctrl+End)

Text Selection

Key	Shift	⌘-Shift	⌘-Shift-Option
left arrow	previous character	previous word	start of line (also: Shift+Home)
right arrow	next character	next word	end of line (also: Shift+End)
up arrow	previous line	previous paragraph	start of story (also: Shift+Ctrl+Home)
down arrow	next line	next paragraph	end of story (also: Shift+Ctrl+End)

Deleting, Cutting, Copying, Pasting, and Selecting

Delete next character	Shift-Delete
Delete previous character	Delete
Delete next word	⌘-Shift-Delete
Delete previous word	⌘-Delete
Cut	⌘-X or F2 *Ctrl+X or Shift+Delete*
Copy	⌘-C or F3 *Ctrl+C or Ctrl+Insert*
Paste	⌘-V or F4 *Ctrl+V or Shift+Insert*
Select all	⌘-A

Note: You can hold the Shift key and drag the mouse to extend the current selection.

Editing Text

Find/change	⌘-F
Find first	Option and click Find Next *Ctrl and click Find Next*
Check spelling for current word	⌘-L
Check spelling for current story	⌘-Option-L
Check spelling for entire document	⌘-Option-Shift-L

Text Files

Get text	⌘-E
Save text	⌘-Option-E

Text Attributes

Plain	⌘-Shift-P
Bold	⌘-Shift-B
Italic	⌘-Shift-I
Underline	⌘-Shift-U
Word underline	⌘-Shift-W
Strikethrough	⌘-Shift-/

Text Selection

Text Attributes

Outline	⌘-Shift-O
Shadow	⌘-Shift-S
All caps	⌘-Shift-K
Small caps	⌘-Shift-H
Superscript	⌘-Shift-+ *Ctrl+Shift+0*
Subscript	⌘-Shift-hyphen *Ctrl+Shift+9*
Superior	⌘-Shift-V
Character attributes	⌘-Shift-D
Enter Measurements palette at Font section	⌘-Option-Shift-M
Next font	Option-F9 *Ctrl+F9*
Previous font	Option-Shift-F9 *Ctrl+Shift+F9*
Font Usage dialog box	F13 *F2*

Paragraph Formatting

Left	⌘-Shift-L
Centered	⌘-Shift-C
Right	⌘-Shift-R
Justified	⌘-Shift-J
Forced justify	⌘-Option-Shift-J
Leading	⌘-Shift-E
Formats	⌘-Shift-F
Rules	⌘-Shift-N
Tabs	⌘-Shift-T
Remove all tabs	Option-click on tab ruler *Ctrl+click on tab ruler*
Copy formats to selected paragraphs*	Option-Shift-click
Enter Measurements palette	⌘-Option-M
Show/hide Styles palette	F11
Open Style Sheets dialog	⌘-click on style name or Shift-F11
Apply style	⌘-Shift-click on style name

*First click the paragraph with the Content tool and then use Option-Shift-click to select the style from the Styles palette.

Hyphenation and Spacing

Breaking hyphen	hyphen
Nonbreaking hyphen	⌘-= *Ctrl+Shift+hyphen*
Discretionary (soft) hyphen	⌘-hyphen
H&Js dialog box	⌘-Option-H or Option-Shift-F11 *Ctrl+Alt+H or Ctrl+Shift+F11*
Suggested Hyphenation dialog box	⌘-H
Typographic Preferences dialog box	⌘-Option-Y
Breaking space	space
Nonbreaking space	⌘-space
Breaking en space	Option-space *Ctrl+Shift+6*
Nonbreaking en space	⌘-Option-space *Ctrl+Shift+Alt+6*
Breaking flexible space	Option-Shift-space *Ctrl+Shift+5*
Nonbreaking flexible space	⌘-Option-Shift-space *Ctrl+Shift+Alt+5*
Breaking punctuation space	Shift-space
Nonbreaking punctuation space	⌘-Shift-space
Decrease kern/track 1/20 em	⌘-Shift-{
Increase kern/track 1/20 em	⌘-Shift-}
Decrease kern/track 1/200 em	⌘-Option-Shift-{
Increase kern/track 1/200 em	⌘-Option-Shift-}
Decrease leading 1 point	⌘-Shift-:
Increase leading 1 point	⌘-Shift-"
Decrease leading 1/10 point	⌘-Option-Shift-:
Increase leading 1/10 point	⌘-Option-Shift-"
Leading dialog box	⌘-Shift-E
Decrease baseline shift 1 point	⌘-Option-Shift-hyphen
Increase baseline shift 1 point	⌘-Option-Shift-+

Line and Indentation Controls

New line	Shift-Return
New paragraph	Return
Box break	Shift-keypad Enter
Column break	keypad Enter

(continued)

Line and Indentation Controls (continued)

Discretionary new line	⌘-Return
Indent here	⌘-\
Right-indent tab	Option-tab

Page Numbers

Current text box page #	⌘-3
Next text box page #	⌘-4
Previous text box page #	⌘-2

Special Symbols

Enter one Symbol font character	⌘-Shift-Q
Enter one Zapf Dingbats character	⌘-Shift-Z
Breaking em dash (—)	Option-Shift-hyphen *Ctrl+Shift+=*
Nonbreaking en dash (–)	Option-hyphen *Ctrl+=*
Nonbreaking em dash (—)	⌘-Option-= *Ctrl+Alt+Shift+=*
Open double quote (")*	Option-Shift-[
Close double quote (")*	Option-Shift-]
Open French double quote («)	Option-\ *Ctrl+Alt+[*
Close French double quote (»)	Option-Shift-\ *Ctrl+Alt+]*
Open single quote (')*	Option-[
Close single quote (')*	Option-]
Bullet (•)	Option-8 *Alt+Shift+8*
Copyright (©)	Option-G *Alt+Shift+C*
Registered trademark (®)	Option-R *Alt+Shift+R*
Trademark (™)	Option-2 *Alt+Shift+2*
Paragraph (¶)	Option-7 *Alt+Shift+7*
Section (§)	Option-6 *Alt+Shift+6*
Dagger (†)	Option-T *Alt+Shift+T*
Double dagger (‡)	Option-Shift-T *Alt+keypad 0135*
Ellipsis (…)	Option-; *Ctrl+Alt+period*
Spanish open exclamation (¡)	Option-1 *Ctrl+Alt+!*

Spanish open question (¿)	Option-Shift-/ *Ctrl+Alt+?*
Cent (¢)	Option-4 *Ctrl+/c*
Pound sterling (£)	Option-3 *Shift+Ctrl+Alt+4*
Yen (¥)	Option-Y *Ctrl+Alt+hyphen*
One-half fraction (¹/₂)	not supported *Ctrl+Alt+6*
One-quarter fraction (¹/₄)	not supported *Ctrl+Alt+7*
Three-quarters fraction (³/₄)	not supported *Ctrl+Alt+8*

*If the Smart Quotes option is selected in the Application Preferences dialog box, the appropriate double quotes are created automatically when you type the " key; the appropriate single quotes are created automatically when you type the ' key.

Text Sizing

Font Sizes dialog box	⌘-Shift-\
Decrease horizontal/vertical scale 5%	⌘-[
Increase horizontal/vertical scale 5%	⌘-]
Increase horizontal/vertical scale 1%	⌘-Option-]
Increase horizontal/vertical scale 1%	⌘-Option-]
Decrease size (within presets)	⌘-Shift-<
Increase size (within presets)	⌘-Shift->
Decrease size/scale (full range)	⌘-Option-Shift-<
Increase size/scale (full range)	⌘-Option-Shift->
Resize box and scale text	⌘-drag handle
Constrain and resize*	⌘-Shift-drag handle
Resize and scale w/ proportions**	⌘-Shift-Option-drag handle

* constrains the text box to a square

** constrains size, automatic leading, horizontal and/or vertical scaling proportionately to the dimensions of the text box

Preset text sizes: 7, 9, 10, 12, 14, 18, 24, 36, 48, 60, 72, 96, 120, 144, 168, and 192 points

Full-range text font sizes: 2 to 720 points in 1-point steps (.001-point increments are available through the Other option)

Print Commands

Page setup *Printer setup*	⌘-Option-P
Print	⌘-P

Information

Help	⌘-? or ⌘-/ or Help *F1*
About QuarkXPress Environment	Option-Apple menu⇨About QuarkXPress Environment *Ctrl+click Help⇨About QuarkXPress*

Preference Dialog Boxes

Application Preferences	Option-Shift-⌘-Y
General Preferences	⌘-Y
Typographic Preferences	⌘-Option-Y
Trapping Preferences	Option-Shift-F12

Overrides

Undo/redo	⌘-Z or F1 *Ctrl+Z or Alt+Backspace*

Inside Dialog Boxes

Apply settings	⌘-A *Alt+A*
Automatic apply settings	⌘-Option-A *Ctrl and click Auto*
OK (or other highlighted button):	Return or keypad Enter
Cancel	⌘-period *Esc*
Apply	⌘-A
Yes	⌘-Y *Y*
No	⌘-N *N*
Cut field	⌘-X
Copy field	⌘-C
Paste field	⌘-V *Ctrl+P*
Revert to original	⌘-Z *not supported*
Highlight next control	Tab
Highlight previous control	Shift-Tab

Chapter 24

The Ten Most Common Mistakes

*I*t takes time to learn how to use QuarkXPress. It takes even longer to learn how to use it right! Knowing that, we thought we'd try to save you some time (and maybe even a few tears) by pointing out some of the most common mistakes people make when they start dabbling in desktop publishing. Take a few minutes and read through them. Why? Because we *like* you, that's why.

Forgetting to Register

Let's say you just bought a brand-spanking-new copy of QuarkXPress. You peel off the shrink wrap, open the box, take a peek at the manuals, peel open the disk envelope, and install the software. Ready to rock and roll, right? Not so fast. Don't make the mistake too many users make by failing to take a few minutes to fill out the disk-based registration information and mail it back to Quark.

What are the advantages of registering your copy of QuarkXPress? Simply put, registering your product puts you in Quark's user database. Being in the database is required if you want to use the free first-90-days-after-purchase technical support privileges, purchase an extended service plan, or be eligible for product upgrades. And a word to the wise: Quark is very focused on providing service to *registered* users and is less likely to be supportive if your name and serial number are never recorded. It only takes a few minutes, and we think that it's a few minutes well spent.

Using Too Many Fonts

Avant Garde. Bellevue. Centaur Gothic. Desdemona. Fonts have cool names, don't they? Plus, it's fascinating to look at a font list and see all the many possibilities for fonts you can use in your document.

Yes, we know it's tempting to try out a great many fonts. This urge overcomes nearly everybody who first gets into desktop publishing. (The few who *don't* begin their QuarkXPress careers by liberally sprinkling fonts throughout a page are often those with traditional design or typesetting backgrounds; in other words, they already know better.) In almost every instance, try keeping the number of fonts used on a page to two. Once you start having three, four, or five fonts, the document takes on an amateurish look, quite frankly because those who are experts at page design never use several fonts together.

Putting Too Much on a Page

You've probably seen them before: pages that are filled to overflowing with *stuff*. Words, pictures, rules — you name it. The pages are filled to overflowing, to the point that you don't know where your eyes need to go.

One of the best things you'll ever learn about page design is the value of white space, or the places on the page where there's no text, no pictures, no lines — just the plain paper showing through. Pages that are crammed full of text and pictures are pages that readers avoid. Keep some space between text columns and headlines, and between items on the page and the edges of the page.

Finding white space on a page is like going to a crowded beach and finding — in the middle of the crowd — a perfectly smooth, empty spot with a gorgeous view for you on your beach blanket. It "feels" great to your eyes and makes you more likely to get the message that's being conveyed by the words and pictures on the page.

Overdoing the Design

By now, you've got the message: QuarkXPress is pretty powerful stuff. It lets you do all *kinds* of nifty things. But this does not mean that you should do all those things just because you *can*.

Nothing looks worse than a complex design created by a publishing novice. Professionals know that, as they say, less is more. In other words, yes, it's possible to rotate text, skew text and graphics, make cool blends, add multiple colors, stretch and condense type, and bleed artwork off the page. But using all these effects at once can overwhelm readers and make them miss the whole point of the message you are trying to convey.

Here's a good rule of thumb: limit special effects to a maximum of three on a two-page spread. Wait — here's an even better rule of thumb: if you are in doubt about whether to add an effect to a page, *don't*.

Not Consulting a Designer

Yes, we know it's not rocket science. But designing a document still can get fairly complicated. It's a good idea to know when it makes sense to consult a professional graphic designer.

The decision is best made by taking into consideration how the document will be used. Is it a one- or two-color newspaper for a small club or organization? Then it's probably perfectly fine for a new QuarkXPress user to tackle the job. But if the document is a full-color display ad that will run in a national magazine, leave it to the pros.

When you have a high-end document to design, professional graphic designers are worth their weight in gold. Sure, you may have to spend a few bucks to hire a talented designer, but you may save that much and more by having that person craft your document for you. These people are trained to know what works visually (and — even more important — what doesn't), how to select the right paper, how many colors are appropriate, and how to have the document printed. In short, a good graphic designer can make your pages sing, and you end up smelling like a rose.

Not Using Master Pages

Before you start working on a document, it's a good idea to have an idea about what it will look like. Will it have two columns? Will the top half of every page have a graphic? Where will the page numbers appear?

Once you have these things figured out, you really should set up Master Pages for all of the elements — such as page numbers — that will repeat in the same spot, page after page. Master Pages make things so much easier, and they are easy to create. People who don't use Master Pages are people who like to do things the hard way. And we know you're smarter than that.

Here's how to begin creating a Master Page: with a document open, choose Page⇨Display⇨Master. Anything you create on that page becomes part of the Master Page and appears on every page in the document that is based on that particular Master Page. Each document can have up to 127 pairs of Master Pages.

Not Using Smart Quotes and Dashes

Nothing, and we mean nothing, bothers a professional designer or publisher more than seeing inch marks where typesetter's quote marks should appear, or skinny little hyphens in place of em dashes (an em dash is a dash that is the same width as the current font's capital M).

Using the correct quotes and dashes is easy in QuarkXPress. In fact, you even can choose from a variety of quote formats — including some that work with foreign languages. The point is that you *want* to use typographically correct quotes and dashes because they make your document look much more professional.

You can get typographically correct quotes and dashes by making selections in the Application Preferences dialog box (Edit⇨Preferences⇨Application). You also can get the right kinds of quotes and dashes when you import text from a word processing application; just make sure that the Convert Quotes box is checked in the Get Text dialog box.

Forgetting to Check Spelling

Typos are like ants at a summer picnic: they show up all the time. You can avoid some typos if you always remember that the last thing to do any time you are about to print your document is to check spelling. Checking spelling won't catch every possible error (you'll still need to do a thorough proofread to catch them all), but using the built-in spelling checker in QuarkXPress is easy to do, and it can save you from embarrassing typos and misspellings.

Not Talking with Your Printer

Like your teachers always told you, a little bit of planning goes a long, long way. This advice is totally true with publishing a document. True, you may "wing it" once in a while, designing a document as you go, but — eventually — failure to plan will catch up with you.

If you are creating a document that will eventually be commercially printed, be sure to have a conversation with your printer early in the game. Hey, you might talk to this Jo(e) only once in a while, but your printer prints documents all day long, every day, and sometimes even on Saturdays.

The whole idea is simple: these folks know their business. A talk with your printer early on can help you plan your document, pick the right number of colors to use in it, and produce it cost-effectively. Your printer will appreciate your concern, too, and will likely invest extra effort in doing a great job for you if you show you care enough to consult with the pros early on.

Not Giving the Service Bureau All Your Files

If you've never worked with one before, you might think that the people who work at your service bureau — the place where you take or send your QuarkXPress documents so that they can be output to an image-setting device — are downright snoopy. They poke and prod, ask millions of questions, and want to know every little thing about your document. They give you the third degree, asking about every file for every graphic on every single page.

Although it may seem like it, these people are not out to pick on you. They truly do need to know about all the fonts and files necessary to output your document. And many people forget to give their service bureaus everything they need, which often results in additional costs.

Why do service bureaus need so much from you? Because they just do, that's why. Seriously, the equipment they use needs to have everything you used to create a document. For example, if your document included an EPS file that has text in it, the service bureau needs to have the font that was used in the text. If that font is not available, the EPS file prints incorrectly and the job has to be output again.

The Collect for Output feature in QuarkXPress (File⇨Collect for Output) can help. It copies all of the text and picture files necessary to produce your document into a folder. It also generates a report for your service bureau, listing the fonts used in the document, its dimensions, and trapping information.

But the Collect for Output feature can't replace your brain. You still need to think about your document. When it comes right down to it, you are ultimately the person responsible for making sure that your service bureau has everything it needs to output your document the right way, the first time.

The 5th Wave By Rich Tennant

"...AND TO ACCESS THE PROGRAMS 'HOT KEY', YOU JUST DEPRESS THESE ELEVEN KEYS SIMULTANEOUSLY. HERB OVER THERE HAS A KNACK FOR DOING THIS THAT I THINK YOU'LL ENJOY—HERB! GOT A MINUTE?"

Index

Title	Author	ISBN	Price
			11/11/94
INTERNET / COMMUNICATIONS / NETWORKING			
CompuServe For Dummies™	by Wallace Wang	1-56884-181-7	$19.95 USA/$26.95 Canada
Modems For Dummies™, 2nd Edition	by Tina Rathbone	1-56884-223-6	$19.99 USA/$26.99 Canada
Modems For Dummies™	by Tina Rathbone	1-56884-001-2	$19.95 USA/$26.95 Canada
MORE Internet For Dummies™	by John R. Levine & Margaret Levine Young	1-56884-164-7	$19.95 USA/$26.95 Canada
NetWare For Dummies™	by Ed Tittel & Deni Connor	1-56884-003-9	$19.95 USA/$26.95 Canada
Networking For Dummies™	by Doug Lowe	1-56884-079-9	$19.95 USA/$26.95 Canada
ProComm Plus 2 For Windows For Dummies™	by Wallace Wang	1-56884-219-8	$19.99 USA/$26.99 Canada
The Internet For Dummies™, 2nd Edition	by John R. Levine & Carol Baroudi	1-56884-222-8	$19.99 USA/$26.99 Canada
The Internet For Macs For Dummies™	by Charles Seiter	1-56884-184-1	$19.95 USA/$26.95 Canada
MACINTOSH			
Macs For Dummies®	by David Pogue	1-56884-173-6	$19.95 USA/$26.95 Canada
Macintosh System 7.5 For Dummies™	by Bob LeVitus	1-56884-197-3	$19.95 USA/$26.95 Canada
MORE Macs For Dummies™	by David Pogue	1-56884-087-X	$19.95 USA/$26.95 Canada
PageMaker 5 For Macs For Dummies™	by Galen Gruman	1-56884-178-7	$19.95 USA/$26.95 Canada
QuarkXPress 3.3 For Dummies™	by Galen Gruman & Barbara Assadi	1-56884-217-1	$19.99 USA/$26.99 Canada
Upgrading and Fixing Macs For Dummies™	by Kearney Rietmann & Frank Higgins	1-56884-189-2	$19.95 USA/$26.95 Canada
MULTIMEDIA			
Multimedia & CD-ROMs For Dummies™, Interactive Multimedia Value Pack	by Andy Rathbone	1-56884-225-2	$29.95 USA/$39.95 Canada
Multimedia & CD-ROMs For Dummies™	by Andy Rathbone	1-56884-089-6	$19.95 USA/$26.95 Canada
OPERATING SYSTEMS / DOS			
MORE DOS For Dummies™	by Dan Gookin	1-56884-046-2	$19.95 USA/$26.95 Canada
S.O.S. For DOS™	by Katherine Murray	1-56884-043-8	$12.95 USA/$16.95 Canada
OS/2 For Dummies™	by Andy Rathbone	1-878058-76-2	$19.95 USA/$26.95 Canada
UNIX			
UNIX For Dummies™	by John R. Levine & Margaret Levine Young	1-878058-58-4	$19.95 USA/$26.95 Canada
WINDOWS			
S.O.S. For Windows™	by Katherine Murray	1-56884-045-4	$12.95 USA/$16.95 Canada
MORE Windows 3.1 For Dummies™, 3rd Edition	by Andy Rathbone	1-56884-240-6	$19.99 USA/$26.99 Canada
PCs / HARDWARE			
Illustrated Computer Dictionary For Dummies™	by Dan Gookin, Wally Wang, & Chris Van Buren	1-56884-004-7	$12.95 USA/$16.95 Canada
Upgrading and Fixing PCs For Dummies™	by Andy Rathbone	1-56884-002-0	$19.95 USA/$26.95 Canada
PRESENTATION / AUTOCAD			
AutoCAD For Dummies™	by Bud Smith	1-56884-191-4	$19.95 USA/$26.95 Canada
PowerPoint 4 For Windows For Dummies™	by Doug Lowe	1-56884-161-2	$16.95 USA/$22.95 Canada
PROGRAMMING			
Borland C++ For Dummies™	by Michael Hyman	1-56884-162-0	$19.95 USA/$26.95 Canada
"Borland's New Language Product" For Dummies™	by Neil Rubenking	1-56884-200-7	$19.95 USA/$26.95 Canada
C For Dummies™	by Dan Gookin	1-878058-78-9	$19.95 USA/$26.95 Canada
C++ For Dummies™	by Stephen R. Davis	1-56884-163-9	$19.95 USA/$26.95 Canada
Mac Programming For Dummies™	by Dan Parks Sydow	1-56884-173-6	$19.95 USA/$26.95 Canada
QBasic Programming For Dummies™	by Douglas Hergert	1-56884-093-4	$19.95 USA/$26.95 Canada
Visual Basic "X" For Dummies™, 2nd Edition	by Wallace Wang	1-56884-230-9	$19.99 USA/$26.99 Canada
Visual Basic 3 For Dummies™	by Wallace Wang	1-56884-076-4	$19.95 USA/$26.95 Canada
SPREADSHEET			
1-2-3 For Dummies™	by Greg Harvey	1-878058-60-6	$16.95 USA/$21.95 Canada
1-2-3 For Windows 5 For Dummies™, 2nd Edition	by John Walkenbach	1-56884-216-3	$16.95 USA/$21.95 Canada
1-2-3 For Windows For Dummies™	by John Walkenbach	1-56884-052-7	$16.95 USA/$21.95 Canada
Excel 5 For Macs For Dummies™	by Greg Harvey	1-56884-186-8	$19.95 USA/$26.95 Canada
Excel For Dummies™, 2nd Edition	by Greg Harvey	1-56884-050-0	$16.95 USA/$21.95 Canada
MORE Excel 5 For Windows For Dummies™	by Greg Harvey	1-56884-207-4	$19.95 USA/$26.95 Canada
Quattro Pro 6 For Windows For Dummies™	by John Walkenbach	1-56884-174-4	$19.95 USA/$26.95 Canada
Quattro Pro For DOS For Dummies™	by John Walkenbach	1-56884-023-3	$16.95 USA/$21.95 Canada
UTILITIES / VCRs & CAMCORDERS			
Norton Utilities 8 For Dummies™	by Beth Slick	1-56884-166-3	$19.95 USA/$26.95 Canada
VCRs & Camcorders For Dummies™	by Andy Rathbone & Gordon McComb	1-56884-229-5	$14.99 USA/$20.99 Canada
WORD PROCESSING			
Ami Pro For Dummies™	by Jim Meade	1-56884-049-7	$19.95 USA/$26.95 Canada
MORE Word For Windows 6 For Dummies™	by Doug Lowe	1-56884-165-5	$19.95 USA/$26.95 Canada
MORE WordPerfect 6 For Windows For Dummies™	by Margaret Levine Young & David C. Kay	1-56884-206-6	$19.95 USA/$26.95 Canada
MORE WordPerfect 6 For DOS For Dummies™	by Wallace Wang, edited by Dan Gookin	1-56884-047-0	$19.95 USA/$26.95 Canada
S.O.S. For WordPerfect™	by Katherine Murray	1-56884-053-5	$12.95 USA/$16.95 Canada
Word 6 For Macs For Dummies™	by Dan Gookin	1-56884-190-6	$19.95 USA/$26.95 Canada
Word For Windows 6 For Dummies™	by Dan Gookin	1-56884-075-6	$16.95 USA/$21.95 Canada
Word For Windows For Dummies™	by Dan Gookin	1-878058-86-X	$16.95 USA/$21.95 Canada
WordPerfect 6 For Dummies™	by Dan Gookin	1-878058-77-0	$16.95 USA/$21.95 Canada
WordPerfect For Dummies™	by Dan Gookin	1-878058-52-5	$16.95 USA/$21.95 Canada
WordPerfect For Windows For Dummies™	by Margaret Levine Young & David C. Kay	1-56884-032-2	$16.95 USA/$21.95 Canada

Order Center: **(800) 762-2974** *(8 a.m.–6 p.m., EST, weekdays)*

IDG BOOKS

Quantity	ISBN	Title	Price	Total

Shipping & Handling Charges

	Description	First book	Each additional book	Total
Domestic	Normal	$4.50	$1.50	$
	Two Day Air	$8.50	$2.50	$
	Overnight	$18.00	$3.00	$
International	Surface	$8.00	$8.00	$
	Airmail	$16.00	$16.00	$
	DHL Air	$17.00	$17.00	$

*For large quantities call for shipping & handling charges.
**Prices are subject to change without notice.

Ship to:

Name _____

Company _____

Address _____

City/State/Zip _____

Daytime Phone _____

Payment: ☐ Check to IDG Books (US Funds Only)

☐ VISA   ☐ MasterCard   ☐ American Express

Card # _____ Expires _____

Signature _____

Subtotal _____

CA residents add
applicable sales tax _____

IN, MA, and MD
residents add
5% sales tax _____

IL residents add
6.25% sales tax _____

RI residents add
7% sales tax _____

TX residents add
8.25% sales tax _____

Shipping _____

Total _____

Please send this order form to:

IDG Books Worldwide
7260 Shadeland Station, Suite 100
Indianapolis, IN 46256

Allow up to 3 weeks for delivery.
Thank you!

❏ YES!

Please keep me informed about IDG's World of Computer Knowledge.
Send me the latest IDG Books catalog.